# Emerging Perspectives on Organizational Justice and Ethics

A Volume in
Research in Social Issues in Management

*Series Editors:*
Stephen W. Gilliland, *University of Arizona*
Dirk D. Steiner, *Université de Nice-Sophia Antipolis*
Daniel P. Skarlicki, *University of British Columbia*

## Research in Social Issues in Management

Stephen W. Gilliland, Dirk D. Steiner,
and Daniel P. Skarlicki, Series Editors

*Emerging Perspectives on Organizational Justice and Ethics* (2011)
Edited by Stephen W. Gilliland, Dirk D. Steiner, and Daniel P. Skarlicki

*Justice, Morality, and Social Responsibility* (2008)
Edited by Stephen W. Gilliland, Dirk D. Steiner, and Daniel P. Skarlicki

*Managing Social and Ethical Issues in Organizations* (2007)
Edited by Stephen W. Gilliland, Dirk D. Steiner, and Daniel P. Skarlicki

*What Motivates Fairness in Organizations* (2005)
Edited by Stephen W. Gilliland, Dirk D. Steiner,
Daniel P. Skarlicki, and Kees van den Bos

*Emerging Perspectives on Values in Organizations* (2003)
Edited by Stephen W. Gilliland, Dirk D. Steiner, and Daniel P. Skarlicki

*Emerging Perspectives on Managing Organizational Justice* (2002)
Edited by Stephen W. Gilliland, Dirk D. Steiner, and Daniel P. Skarlicki

*Theoretical and Cultural Perspectives on Organizational Justice* (2001)
Edited by Stephen W. Gilliland, Dirk D. Steiner, and Daniel P. Skarlicki

# Emerging Perspectives on Organizational Justice and Ethics

edited by

**Stephen W. Gilliland**
*University of Arizona*

**Dirk D. Steiner**
*Université de Nice-Sophia Antipolis*

and

**Daniel P. Skarlicki**
*University of British Columbia*

IAP

Information Age Publishing, Inc.
Charlotte, North Carolina • www.infoagepub.com

**Library of Congress Cataloging-in-Publication Data**

Emerging perspectives on organizational justice and ethics / edited by
Stephen W. Gilliland, Dirk D. Steiner and Daniel P. Skarlicki.
p. cm. — (Research in social issues in management)
Includes bibliographical references.
ISBN 978-1-61735-581-3 (paperback) — ISBN 978-1-61735-582-0 (hardcover) —
ISBN 978-1-61735-583-7 (ebook)
1. Organizational justice. 2. Organizational behavior—Moral and ethical
aspects. 3. Business ethics. I. Gilliland, Stephen. II. Steiner, Dirk
(Dirk Douglas) III. Skarlicki, Daniel.
HD6971.3.E452 2011
174'.4—dc23

2011031941



Printed and bound by CPI Group (UK) Ltd, Croydon, CR0 4YY

# CONTENTS

# PREFACE

**Stephen W. Gilliland, Dirk D. Steiner, and Daniel Skarlicki**

More than any other time in recent history, the public is questioning the ethics of business leaders. The financial sector is seen as being responsible for the global economic recession, and many want to blame the leaders of banks and investment firms for the downfall. Unethical behavior rather than poor decision making is the accused culprit. Business schools are also coming under scrutiny for educating the leaders that appear to be lacking in ethical awareness. Are we truly seeing a rash of unethical behavior, or are people looking for explanations and lack of leadership ethics is the simplest answer? Whether or not there is any validity to these claims is not our central concern in writing this book. Rather, we believe that new models must be developed to help us evaluate ethicality and justice in organizations. To truly understand the "zeitgeist" of questioning business ethics, our models must examine both ethical actions and the process of perceiving the ethics of others.

The field of organizational justice provides a solid theoretical foundation for grounding this discussion. Over the past 30 years, organizational justice research has grown from social psychological theories of equity and procedural justice to become one of the dominant theories of attitude formation and motivation in organizations (Greenberg & Colquitt, 2005). At the heart of organizational justice is the realization that people seek fairness in social and economic exchanges. The absence of fairness is a powerful motivator for retaliation and withdrawal. Ensuring fairness builds

*Emerging Perspectives on Organizational Justice and Ethics*
pp. vii–xii

trust, commitment, and the willingness to go above and beyond expectations in working for an organization. Whereas sometimes the motivation for fairness comes from the desire to maximize personal outcomes, desires for belonging and trust within an organization can also motivate attention to fairness. There is also a moral foundation to the desire for justice, not only when a victim feels morally violated, but also when unaffected third parties react with outrage to others' injustices.

With connections to trust and morality, the links between organizational justice and ethics have started to emerge. In recent years, organizational justice scholars have begun to apply models of justice to understanding ethical and unethical behavior in organizations. In 2008, a group of organizational justice scholars met in Lisbon, Portugal to discuss issues of organizational justice and ethics. Some of the same scholars and some different ones met again in 2010 in Orlando, Florida, to continue this discussion. The focus of both of these roundtables was on developing new ways of looking at organizational justice and ethics. Creativity and innovation in theory development were emphasized over concrete data and tightly designed studies. Authors from each of these meetings were invited to develop their thoughts into book chapters, the result being the collection of works presented in this volume.

We have organized the chapters around two related themes. The first theme is expanding models of organizational justice. After 30 years of research, a natural question is whether we have reached the useful limits in developing theories of organizational justice. The clear answer you will see after reading these chapters is no. There are many interesting and important avenues to further expand and explore the desire for justice in organizations. Each of the chapters in the first section of this book pushes our thinking about organizational justice in a new direction.

In the first chapter, Guo, Rupp, Weiss, and Trougakos suggest that the prevailing paradigm for examining organizational justice tends to be focused on organizational entities (i.e., organizations and managers) rather than on individuals and their subjective experience of events. What may seem like a slight shift in perspective is actually a profoundly different approach to theorizing. The prevailing paradigm treats individuals as variance, with the focus on relationships between attributes, perceptions, and behaviors rather than individual points in a scatter plot. In the "person-centric" model presented in this chapter, cognitive and affective reactions of individuals are based on justice judgments and narratives about specific, significant justice events. To understand justice from a person-centric perspective, we must understand the events that lead to justice perceptions.

As though responding to this call for person-centric theory, in Chapter 2, Cojuharenco, van Prooijen, and Patient consider the impact of memory on organizational justice evaluations. Building on cognitive psychology and memory research, they examine the ways in which the differential availability in memory of past experiences can lead to biases in perceptions of justice. Important implications of this research are the influences of time on justice judgments, as time can impact memories, and the malleability of both memories and justice judgments by intervening events.

Continuing in the person-centric theme, the third chapter by Barclay and Whiteside suggests that the basic focus on justice perceptions may be limiting our ability to understand individual experiences of justice. To capture the richness of individual experiences, they suggest that researchers attend to the intensity of justice experiences. In addition to reactions to events varying on a dimension of fair to unfair, reactions can also vary in intensity, which is a result of a dynamic interplay between perceptions, beliefs, and affective reactions. As the authors suggest, feeling something is unfair but not really caring is very different from feeling something is unfair and being outraged. Beyond introducing and defining justice intensity, they identify some factors that contribute to this construct and suggest methods of assessing intensity.

Chapter 4 by Goodstein, Aquino, and Skarlicki moves organizational justice research in an entirely new direction by considering the processes by which justice offenders can be reintegrated into the workplace. Typically, justice research has examined the impact of unfairness on attitudes and behavior of victims or observers. But, what happens to leaders who have treated employees unfairly? These leaders may have erred in their ways, but they can still stand to make a significant contribution to an organization and society. When and how are they forgiven? Offender reintegration is defined as the psychological willingness to maintain working relationships with individuals who have violated social and moral norms valued by an organization. This is a particularly interesting construct when one considers our current need to forgive and start trusting investment bankers and mortgage brokers again.

Moving beyond one individual forgiving another, the final chapter in this section on expanding models of organizational justice, examines the influence of organizational justice on social capital in the workplace. Social capital is a social currency that is embedded within social networks and trust relationships. In Chapter 5, James, Drown, and Burlacu suggest that social capital has reciprocal influences on organizational justice. Justice can be experienced from many levels in an organization and this can shape social capital at different levels. Social capital can also influence how justice is perceived. This chapter provides an interesting model for considering the various ways in which people interrelate and create mutually advantageous relationships for one another in organizations.

The second section of this book is concerned with the theme of applying organizational justice theories to developing models of ethical and unethical behavior in organizations. These models address both the ethicality and the perceived ethicality of actions. Research on injustice motivating retaliatory behaviors provides a template for understanding the influence of organizational justice on ethical behavior. Similarly, research on perceptions of justice helps provide an understanding of perceptions of unethical behavior. Both of these issues are explored in chapters in Part II of this book.

Chapter 6 by Gilliland and Anderson examines the construct of greed. Rather than focusing on how greed can motivate certain actions, this chapter addresses perceptions of greed and presents a model of how these perceptions are formed. Using distributive justice as the theoretical foundation, they propose that greed is perceived when someone is viewed as seeking outcomes that violate the equity, need, and equality principles of distributive justice. Attributions of responsibility are also part of this perceptual process. Of particular interest in their presentation are the fact that greed has not been studied by management scholars and the suggestion that greed may simply be a way to blame others for unfair situations.

In Chapter 7, Bell and Khoury explore another type of unethical work situation created by injustice in their examination of dehumanization at work. Dehumanization is the experience of feeling objectified by an organization and made to feel like a tool or instrument for the organization. They propose that injustice is dehumanizing and also suggest that justice can be humanizing. Organizations are discussed as the primary source of dehumanization and injustice, but Bell and Khoury also recognize that supervisors and peers can contribute to these experiences. A central suggestion with strong ethical implications is that organizational justice gets to the core of what it means to be human and social beings.

Building on themes of ethics and morality, Chapter 8 by Greenbaum, Folger, and Ford presents the concept of moral contracts. They suggest that employees may respond unfavorably to an organization's unethical actions, even if not directly impacted, because that organization has failed to uphold its moral obligations or contract with employees. Much like greed, moral contracts are a perceptual construct and exist in the minds of those holding organizations accountable. This chapter provides a theoretical model of moral contracts, contract breach, and contract violations. It is interesting to speculate whether part of the outrage with the role of financial institutions in the economic recession is a result of perceived moral contract violations.

Moving from perceptions to actions, Hamilton and Knouse examine ethical actions in organizations in Chapter 9. Building on existing models, they present an experience-focused model of ethical actions that identifies and describes the processes of producing an ethical action, from the perspective of how the individual experiences those processes. This process model draws on recent research in neuroscience and moral psychology. In a demonstration of the utility of this model, the authors apply the model to reexamine organizational justice research. More than an application, this discussion highlights important connections between ethics research and organizational justice research.

The final chapter in this volume is an invited integrative commentary by Carol Kulik. Rather than simply summarizing the nine chapters in this book, Kulik takes a step back and asks what we know and do not know about organizational justice. She presents five things that she knows for certain about organizational justice and then also questions how well we are equipped to apply organizational justice to current challenges facing organizations. The nine chapters are used to illustrate and expand upon these suggestions.

In summary, the chapters presented in this volume were conceived and developed at a time when the global economy was in recession and many were questioning the ethicality of business. By examining what it means to be just and examining relationships between justice and ethicality, the authors have provided conceptual models for understanding ethical challenges facing organizations. Whether these challenges are actual or perceived, models grounded in organizational justice theory provide powerful insights and suggest new ways of looking at leadership ethics.

## REFERENCES

Greenberg, J., & Colquitt, J. A. (2005). *Handbook of organizational justice: Fundamental questions about fairness in the workplace*. Mahwah, NJ: Erlbaum.

# PART I

## EXPANDING MODELS OF ORGANIZATIONAL JUSTICE

CHAPTER 1

# JUSTICE IN ORGANIZATIONS

## A Person-Centric Perspective

**Jing Guo, Deborah E. Rupp,
Howard M. Weiss, and John P. Trougakos**

The purpose of this chapter is to articulate a vision for a person-centric approach to the study of organizational justice. We diverge from the prevailing paradigm by advocating a focus on individuals' subjective experiences of justice—beginning with momentary states and continuing to longer processes of rumination and including the anticipation of justice-related events. We highlight the importance of considering individuals' in situ cognitive, affective, and physiological responses to justice-related events, and consider how these event-based justice experiences influence the mental representations of potential transgressors. The acknowledgment of a priori memory structures allows for the consideration of further questions related to the retrieval and/or reconstruction of narratives about transgressors, significant justice events, and past justice evaluations. Following the proposal of several research questions within each of these areas, we briefly discuss specific research methods that hold promise for person-centric investigations of justice-related phenomena.

Justice researchers can investigate phenomena in various ways. One approach might be to explore the relationships between constructs at a given point in time. Here, the focus is on the constructs themselves; for

*Emerging Perspectives on Organizational Justice and Ethics*
pp. 3–32

example employees' perceptions of procedural justice, and their covariation with other constructs, say job performance or job satisfaction. We might explore these relationships via correlational designs, such as through the use of employee surveys; or we might design experiments where justice is manipulated and its effects on attitudes and behaviors explored (or alternatively contextual elements are manipulated and their effects on justice perceptions explored). Such approaches might yield results that guide managers and organizations in developing employment systems that optimize the productivity and well-being of the workforce.

Another approach might have as its goal a deep understanding of the psychological processes individuals go through as they experience work and interpret their experiences through a lens of justice. Such an approach is not aimed at predicting variance in attitudes and behaviors, nor does it necessarily focus on between-person variation at all. It does not have as a central focus a constellation of constructs, but rather seeks to map experiential processes, as they are occurring, and over time. The primary goal is not to uncover implications for human resource management, but rather to uncover the role of fairness in the actual experience of work.

This contrast parallels the prevailing and person-centric paradigms articulated by Weiss and Rupp (2011), who argue that organizational psychology has primarily been focused on cross-sectional, between-persons investigations of construct covariation, and in the process, has focused less on how working adults approach, experience, and navigate themselves through the organizational milieu (see also Tripp & Bies, 2007). They have called for shifting from a paradigm where the individual is treated as a collection of properties, to one where the focus is on how individuals experience work (i.e., an explicit focus on the lived through experience of working).

In this chapter, we attempt to articulate a vision of what a truly person-centric study of organizational justice might look like. We assert that a shift in focus may uncover many insights not currently conceived of within the current paradigm. We call for direct evidence as to how justice is experienced by employees, and for that matter, what *experienced* justice really is. We posit that there is a need to explore how justice is subjectively experienced, and whether justice is a discrete experience, or a more complex evaluation that includes both momentary reactions to justice related events and a much longer process of anticipating, experiencing, and ruminating about ethics-related experiences.

Contemporary justice research has, to be "fair," taken strides to consider the salience of events, affective reactions to events, and to some extent, the counterfactual thinking that occurs following justice-related events. The literature is sprinkled with discussions of "hot" emotions, anger, deontic rage, guilt/shame, and so on. However, there is little focus on the true, naturally occurring, subjective experiences of employees, conducted for the sole purpose of understanding the experience itself—not to better understand decision making—not to predict ethical behavior in organizations—but rather to more fully understand how people experience fairness at work. Such an investigation might begin with developing an understanding of the unfolding of justice experiences. For example, we know little about what launches cognitive and emotional processing in a direction that is encoded as justice-related in the human mind; the role of rumination in the solidifying of mental representations of those who might later treat us (un)fairly; the targeted retrieval of past events when new fairness-related events are encountered; memory decay and distortion; forecasting, et cetera.

These questions cannot be answered via the methods of the prevailing paradigm. Filling out surveys of distributive, procedural, and interactional justice are themselves events, events that are subjectively experienced by participants, and that frame and prime recalled encounters in less than negligible ways. Research has shown that retrospectively reported affective responses are rarely correlated with true emotions experienced during the events referenced in our questionnaires (e.g., Fredrickson & Kahneman, 1993; Redelmeier & Kahneman, 1996). A true investigation of justice experience would require the observation and measurement of individuals in situ and over periods of time, long enough in duration to track cognitive processes (encoding, retrieval, forecasts), emotional spikes, trends, and cycles, and the occurrence and patterns of normal-spectrum psychopathological responses (e.g., paranoia, anxiety, rumination, antisocial behavior, etc.). This could involve verbal protocol analysis, autobiographical/life narrative methods, ethnography, phenomenology, experience sampling, ongoing physiological measurement, and the like. The goal of such investigations would *not* be to predict behaviors or attitudes, but rather to more fully articulate what justice is, to map thoroughly the processes it implies, and to generate knowledge about the true experience of injustice.

Thus, in this chapter, we seek to make a first attempt at conceptualizing a person-centric approach to the study of employee justice. We seek to: (a) articulate what justice research in the person-centric work psychology paradigm (as described by Weiss and Rupp) would look like; (b) review existing justice theories that are more person-centric in flavor; (c) offer propositions and research questions for future justice research within this paradigm to explore; and (d) describe methodologically how we might go about exploring these issues.

## PERSON-CENTRIC WORK PSYCHOLOGY

Although the fields of organizational psychology and organizational behavior have uncovered a number of insights regarding the relationships between workplace constructs, paradoxically, employees' subjective experience of work, the meaning employees derive from work, and the process by which workers reflect on their work experiences have gone largely unexplored (Hulin, 2010). Weiss and Rupp (2011) attribute this neglect to aspects of the dominant paradigm which influences the collective research agenda within organizational psychology and organizational behavior.

Two characteristics are argued to depict the prevailing paradigm. The first is a "between entities" approach, where workers are objectified by virtue of being treated as receptacles of data, used for the purpose of studying the association of static constructs (e.g., traits, job performance, job satisfaction). This practice treats workers as variance providers, as points suspended in multidimensional space, with axes corresponding to different attributes that are more often than not treated as stable qualities. In this case, we aren't exploring the experience of workers, but rather the relationship between attribute A and attribute B, and the effect of moderator C or mediator D, for whatever sample is available.

The second characteristic that has been used to describe the prevailing paradigm is a "collective purpose agenda." As journals continue to require us to describe the practical implications of our results, we continue to frame the impetus of our research as one of purpose--of increasing organizational performance, or influencing the well-being of workers. This is in contrast with an alternative purpose, which would be simply to understand how employees experience work. Within the justice domain, we typically ask, "What is the relationship between perceptions of justice and employee attitudes and behaviors?" rather than "What does justice feel like?" or "How are events encoded into memory as fairness-related, and how are past experiences used to construct visualizations of the future?"

Although the prevailing paradigm has produced research that has enriched our theory and improved the quality of management practices, it has simultaneously immunized us against the organic emergence of other sorts of research questions which, while self-evident to a study of work psychology, lay dormant due to paradigmatic constraints. Weiss and Rupp (2011) argue that a central point missing from the prevailing paradigm is a focus on the subjective experiences of people at work. From moment to moment, to longer experience segments and the recall of the past, true worker experience has received little attention.

Consequently, the person-centric approach has been presented as a complement to the current paradigm. This approach is explicitly devoted to the study of workers' subjective experiences, with a particular interest in dynamic processes. It would necessarily include affective, cognitive, and physiological experience, as well as patterns of change in sensation, perception, attention, and memory, as work events occur and are imagined over time.

## PERSON-CENTRIC ORGANIZATIONAL JUSTICE

### Justice Research Under the Prevailing Paradigm

The organizational justice literature has not been spared the influence of the prevailing paradigm within organizational psychology and organizational behavior, as a between-entities approach and collective purpose frame have loomed large across the decades. To illustrate, consider the recent analysis by Greenberg (2009), who classified the body of organizational justice research into four categories: *Basic research* (i.e., research focused on uncovering the psychological process inherent to perceptions of justice as well as correlates of justice perceptions), *implication research* (i.e., research examining the relationship between employee justice perceptions and specific aspects of organizational functioning), *intervention research* (i.e., research testing the efficacy of justice interventions in organizations), and *case studies* (research that describes post hoc efforts to promote justice in organizations).What strikes us is that *all* of these categories are imbued with both the between-entities approach, as well as the collective purpose agenda used to describe the prevailing research paradigm.

This observation is further strengthened by follow-up analyses by Bauer and colleagues, revealing that among these categories, implication research is by far the most prevalent (i.e., 411 of the 545 studies published between 1994 and 2008; Bauer et al., 2009).[2] Also related to the current thesis is the fact that the use of surveys to collect retrospective and cross-sectional data characterizes a large majority of the current justice research. In fact, recent meta-analyses report that of the entire set of empirical studies conducted between the years 1984 and 2009, approximately 80% were correlational in nature (Rupp, Shao, Jones, & Liao, 2011).

Said differently, it seems that although the study of justice seems to imply a focus on the plight of workers, and despite the fact that justice has predominantly taken a "first person" approach (i.e., employees are asked to respond to items such as, "My supervisor treats me fairly"), there lacks any systematic investigation of lived-through justice experience,[3] such as the pain and sorrow felt by mistreated workers, the emotional responses and evaluations toward a supervisor that change as time goes by, or the tears and joys that are remembered and recollected as employees look back on their work experiences. The extant justice research has been largely concerned with the influence of context on justice perceptions, and how justice perceptions corelate with various attitudes and behaviors. To better understand how justice is experienced by workers *as they experience their working lives*, a person-centric perspective is necessary.

## Justice Research Under a Person-Centric Paradigm

Although a large proportion of organizational justice research to date is characteristic of the prevailing paradigm, the literature is not completely absent of theoretical models possessing a person-centric flavor.

### *Uncertainty Management/Fairness Heuristic Theory*

Fairness heuristic theory (FHT; Lind, 2001) has argued that virtually every social relationship begins with the dilemma that individuals lack adequate information to accurately calculate their risk of exploitation or exclusion by others. A central premise of FHT is that fairness judgments are used as heuristics to guide social decisions and to interpret new information. According to FHT, fairness judgments are formed quickly, remain relatively stable, and are used heuristically for making subsequent predictions involving the trustworthiness of exchange partners. According to this theory, justice processes are episodic. Individuals use early events to form justice judgments, and then apply these judgments to interpret subsequent events. Original judgments will continue to be used heuristically until phase-shifting events occur, signaling that the original judgment should be adjusted.

FHT has been more fully elaborated into a broader uncertainty management theory (UMT), which speaks to the fundamental angst caused by the high levels of uncertainty employees face, as well as the power of (in)justice perceptions to exacerbate or curb work-related existential discomfort (Lind & van den Bos, 2002; van den Bos & Lind, 2002). Together, these perspectives (FHT and UMT) have highlighted not only *how* justice judgments are formed and used, but also *why* justice is of fundamental importance to working people. That is, people care about fairness because fairness helps them deal with uncertainty, and they use cognitive shortcuts when forming fairness judgment under uncertainty (e.g., the priming and substitutability effect).[4]

### *A Temporal Model of Information Aggregation and Judgment*

Within the constraints of the prevailing paradigm, the justice literature has amassed a large number of surveys with which to measure a broad array of justice dimensions. That is, researchers have investigated different types of justice (distributive justice, procedural justice, interactional justice; Colquitt, Conlon, Wesson, Porter, & Ng, 2001), justice perceptions about different foci (e.g., supervisor justice, coworker justice; Rupp & Cropanzano, 2002; Rupp & Spencer, 2006), and even overall justice (Ambrose & Schminke, 2009; Jones & Martens, 2009). This proliferation of dimensions and surveys leads to fundamental questions about what justice really is, and what it isn't, as well as how these various perceptual categories are related to each other. Rupp and Paddock (2010, see also Rupp, 2011) have argued that the missing link that can connect these justice constructs is *time*. According to their temporal model of information aggregation and judgment, employees are thought to encounter justice related-events on a daily basis, and these event histories, coupled with event-level affective and cognitive reactions, are encoded into memory and used as input for higher-level judgments as needed.

As such, this model describes how employees *look in* (i.e., how fairly they judge themselves to be treated), *look around* (i.e., how fairly they view people around them, such as coworkers, to be treated) and *look out* (i.e., how fairly they view their organization to have treated external stakeholders, such as offshore workers and the environment). This model therefore suggests not only a complex informational network, but also a complex social network from which information is encoded. It acknowledges socialization, attraction-selection-attrition, and social information processing as playing a role as employees make sense of their working environments and build narratives around their work experiences (Cardador & Rupp, 2010).

### *Affective Context and Fairness Perceptions*

Scholars largely agree that justice-related events elicit both cognitive and emotional reactions (Barsky, Kaplan, & Beal, 2011; Maas & van den Bos, 2009; Weiss, Suckow, & Cropanzano, 1999), with some work events being more affect inducing than others. Researchers have investigated the different types of emotions elicited by justice (e.g., sadness, anger; Barclay, Skarlicki, & Pugh, 2005; Weiss et al., 1999), the moderating role of affect intensity (Murphy, 2009), the effect of state affect on justice judgments (van den Bos, 2003), as well as the mediating role of emotion in reactions to treatment perceived of as unfair (Rupp, McCance, Spencer, & Sonntag, 2008; Schoefer & Diamantopoulos, 2008). Although this research has enriched our understanding of the relationship between cognitive and emotional aspects of justice reactions, much of this research continues to be characteristic of the prevailing paradigm, and falls short of truly integrating the vast literatures on justice and affect.

Recently, Barsky et al. (2011) have attempted to fill this gap by proposing an integrated model that discusses the various ways in which events, the experience of emotion, and perceptions of justice influence each other. Building on work by Weiss and colleagues (1999), they suggest that a first influence comes from the appraisal of justice-related events. Following general appraisal models (e.g., Lazarus, 1991), it is thought that when people encounter justice-related events, they engage in fast, relatively automatic appraisals ("primary appraisals") about the valence of the events (i.e., good vs. bad), as well as the relevance of the events to current goals. These primary appraisals are thought to give rise to emotional reactions as well as to automatic justice perceptions. More deliberative appraisals ("secondary appraisals") follow, which deal with the meaning and implications of the events to the individual, including evaluations about who is responsible for the events, what could have happened under alternative conditions, and what normative ethical frameworks imply should have taken place (see also Folger & Cropanzano, 2001).

In addition to affective reactions stemming from justice-related events (integral affect), affect caused by reasons unrelated to the focal events (incidental affect) is also said to influence employees' justice perceptions. Incidental affect is thought to influence justice perceptions by influencing the occurrence of justice related events (termed a formative influence) as well as via the appraisals of those events (the substantive influence). Employees' expressions of emotions or mood not only convey information about their own emotions, intentions, and relational orientations (e.g., being trustworthy), but can also evoke affect and behavior from others. In other words, one employee's incidental affect might implicitly predispose the appraisal dimensions of future events (known previously as appraisal tendencies, Lerner & Tiedens, 2006). A third influence on justice-affect relationships proposed by Barsky et al. (2011), termed deliberative influence, deals with the influence of affect on the encoding of justice related events, as well as the aggregation of justice perceptions over time. Differential emotions are thought to stimulate differential forms of information processing. Emotions associated with uncertainty (e.g., sadness, fear) are expected to stimulate deep level processing, whereas high-certainty feelings (e.g., anger, happiness) are thought to stimulate the use of more heuristic processing. Therefore, when individuals are asked to make more holistic judgments of workplace fairness, their current affective states might play an important role in what (and how many) events are retrieved and aggregated.

## OTHER AVENUES FOR A PERSON-CENTRIC STUDY OF EMPLOYEE JUSTICE

Although we see promise in the contemporary perspectives reviewed above, and indeed, these approaches certainly point to new, more person-centric research questions involving employee perceptions of justice, we feel that a breaking away from the prevailing paradigm, and an explicit embracing of a person-centric approach, could take us well beyond this set of ideas. In this section, we pose some additional research questions that our person-centric considerations have led us to wonder about.

To review, we feel the central question for person-centric justice research to consider is how justice is experienced by workers, *as they experience their everyday working lives*. From our perspective, workers react to justice-related events, tell other people about what happened to them and their coworkers, form evaluations about the various parties with whom they interact, and reflect on their justice-related experiences in order to obtain insights and wisdom. We depict these activities in Figure 1. Upon experiencing (and witnessing) events, employees respond cognitively, emotionally, and physically. We see these reactions as potentially moderated by employees' previous mental representations of the parties involved (e.g., supervisors, coworkers, customers), which might be updated according to the employees' new experiences of justice related events (as suggested by all three perspectives reviewed in the last section). We conceptualize mental representation broadly, as including memories of specific events, reactions to those events, as well general evaluations of those events and the people associated with them. Considering justice in this way allows for the exploration of how workers experience justice at work, from momentary reactions to justice events, to mental representations of a particular justice perpetrator, to the formation of fairness-imbued narratives spanning extended periods of time.

### How do Employees Experience Justice-Related Events?

First, we feel it necessary to understand how justice-related events are experienced phenomenologically, as they are occurring, prior to subsequent appraisal, sense-making, and other postevent processes. The social cognition literature has much to say about "hot" experiential feelings and phenomenal experiences (Schwarz & Clore, 1996, 2007). Such experience includes affective (e.g., anger, sadness, happiness), cognitive (e.g., surprise, familiarity, fluency, ease-of-retrieval), as well as bodily (e.g., pain, hunger, physiological arousal) phenomena. According to the componential appraisal model of emotion (Grandjean, Sander, & Scherer, 2008),

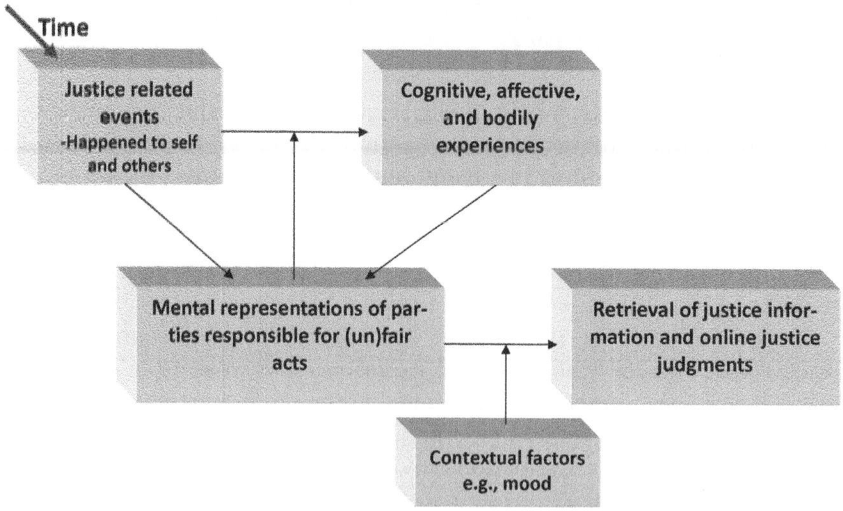


Figure 1.1. A person-centric model of organizational justice.

subjective feeling is viewed as a component of an emotional episode, similar to other components including appraisals (relevance, implications, coping potential, and normative significance), motivational urges (action tendencies), physiological responding (e.g., shorter breaths) and motor expressions (e.g., facial expression and change in voice). According to Scherer (2009), there can be an unlimited number of subjective experiences resulting from interactions among these components, which are subject to further categorization and verbal labeling (e.g., anger, sadness, and anxiety). It would be interesting to understand if employees, while experiencing a justice-related event, consciously label their feelings as anger or sadness, or if such labels only emerge upon recall (e.g., when asked on a survey) or later reflection.

As for in situ physiological experience, we have even less justice research from which to draw, although there have been some promising breakthroughs within social psychology that may aid such an investigation. For example, Zhong and his colleagues (e.g., Zhong, Bohns, & Gino, 2010; Zhong & Leonardelli, 2008) have shown that our social experiences are not independent of our bodily perceptions. That is, this research has found that people literally feel cold (estimating the room temperature as lower and asking for more warm food and drinks) when they are socially excluded (Zhong & Leonardelli, 2008). According to the theory of embodied cognition (Barsalou, 1999), it is possible that on an abstract level, the psychological experience of social exclusion may cooccur with the physiological experiences of coldness. If the experience of coldness is an integral part of social exclusion, we wonder what kind of somatic experiences are associated with experiences of unfairness, which in part deals with issues of inclusion and exclusion, but also involves automatic perceptions of moral indignation and a discretionary act of a perpetrator that leads to an individual or group of individuals being harmed in some way (Folger & Cropanzano, 2001). Not only could an exploration of the true experience of justice apply research from other areas of psychology, but it could also uncover additional insights that might inform these fields.

The in situ cognitive process involved in the processing of justice-related events is also an area in need of further inquiry. Whereas affective events theory (Weiss & Cropanzano, 1996), as well as some of the new advances summarized above, speaks to the reciprocal cognitive-affective processes involved in justice judgment formation, there is far more theory than empirical evidence within this domain. We know little about the exact point at which a situation is labeled unfair, the role of retrieved past experience, the cognitive-affective relay system, or the role of rumination in the development and stability of fairness judgments.

We also know little about how an individual's experience of a particular justice-related event is affected by his or her history of experience with the same or similar events. The experience of a transgression, via the same transgressor and with the same contextual elements, is likely not experienced similarly the first, second, and twentieth time it occurs. It has been shown that participants use previous justice experiences as frames of reference to interpret subsequent events (van den Bos et al., 2005). Similarly, the judgment and emotions associated with a previous party can be automatically transferred to a new party filling the same role (e.g., from an old to a new supervisor; Ritter & Lord, 2007). Based on this research, we expect that previous fairness perceptions influence the intensities of affective, cognitive, and physiological experiences of justice-related events.

Another question of interest involves emotion regulation in the midst of a justice-related event. One determinant of emotional intensity is regulation and the relationship between regulation and emotional intensity is probably complex and reciprocal as "emotional intensity presumably determines how much regulation is needed, but successful regulation will decrease that intensity" (Sonnemans & Frijda, 1995, p. 483). According to Gross's (1998) model of emotional regulation, there are two strategies of regulation: reappraisal and suppression. The regulation method used may also influence the duration of the emotional reactions resulting from the justice-related event. Might the use of differential forms of regulation influence how a justice event is experienced (and subsequently perceived)? Future research might consider exploring such a question.

## How do Mental Representations Guide the Judgment Process?

Given the critical role of memory to individual sense-making (Bluck, 2009), the paucity of research exploring its role in justice perception formation and workers' judgments of work experience over time is most peculiar and potentially results from the constraints imposed by the prevailing paradigm operating in organizational psychology. As mentioned above, we use the term "mental representation" to denote encoded events, reactions to those events, and subsequent evaluations, categorized into memory according to the party held responsible for the set of events (i.e., the perpetrator/transgressor; see Rupp, 2011; Rupp & Paddock, 2010). As such, an employee, at any given time, may hold mental representations of his or her supervisor, the human resources department as a unit, individual clients or clients as a group, et cetera, and each of these mental representations may vary in the amount of "evidence" stored in memory supporting the summary judgments the individual holds about each party. We purport that these mental representations are the pillars supporting individuals' work narratives. They are what is recalled as people discuss their days with one another, resolve conflicts, and even fill out the questionnaires of justice researchers. We wonder why such elements, which seem so very fundamental to an understanding of the work experience of individuals, have received little attention in the literature.[5] We certainly feel such an exploration would be a fruitful endeavor.

According to social cognitive theories of memory, observed events are often encoded according to the focal "experiencing" individual (Fiske & Taylor, 1991). This is even more likely for familiar individuals with whom the encoder expects to have future interactions. Andersen and Chen (2002) also argued in their social-cognitive theory of self, that the multiple selves a person holds (e.g., social self, student self, daughter self; Markus & Wurf, 1987) are inherently tied to the relationships the person holds with various parties. According to this model, relational information is stored in memory, leading to the development of mental representations for each party, which can be activated automatically to guide cognitive, emotional, and motivational processes inherent to the development of new relationships. A recent application of the theory showed that the evaluation of a new leader is influenced by the mental representation of a previous leader, such that if the new leader is perceived as similar to the previous leader, the expectations and affections associated with the previous leader are transferred to the new leader (Ritter & Lord, 2007).

The justice literature has pointed to the complex web of social relationships employees engage in at work (Rupp & Paddock, 2010). Integrating this research with that reviewed above would suggest that employees hold mental representations of supervisors, coworkers, clients/customers, and the like, which contain memories of detailed events, abstractions of general events, the life period context within which encounters with these parties were experienced, as well as more abstract evaluations associated with each party. These multifoci mental representations then influence subsequent encounters with these parties, as well as future encoding and appraisal.

## How Are Justice-Related Autobiographical Memories Formed?

Following the call of Weiss and Rupp (2011), we call for a consideration of justice from the workers' point of view. We ask the questions: How do people experience specific justice related-events? How do they listen and respond to others' (un)fair experiences? Do they reflect on those events? Do they tell people about their justice experiences? According to the self-memory system (SMS) model of autobiographical memory (Conway & Pleydell-Pearce, 2000; Conway, Singer, & Tagini, 2004), meaningful segments of experiences, lasting seconds, minutes, or hours, are the building blocks of episodic memories. These episodic memories contain "experience-near, event-specific, sensory-perceptual-cognitive-affective details" (Conway et al., p. 496), making recall a very present-feeling experience (i.e., the memory feels as if it is happening right now). For example, after a day's work, an employee may recall a specific meeting he/she had with his/her supervisor, with vivid details of his/her feelings and thoughts, as well the reactions displayed by others (e.g., supervisor's facial expressions). Many of the detailed episodic memories are lost as time goes by, but some, due to the relevance to people's current goals and concerns (Carver & Scheier, 1998), are gradually incorporated into the autobiographical knowledge base, from which autobiographic memories are drawn. The autobiographical knowledge base consists of information about life period (when I was in my first job), general events (my supervisor gave me a lot of autonomy), event-specific knowledge (one time, we had a technical problem, he came to me …). So according to the self-memory system model, we organize our past life experiences in meaningful structures.

According to autobiographic research, a specific type of autobiographic memory is self -defining memory (Blagov & Singer, 2004; Conway et al., 2004; Moffitt & Singer, 1994; Thorne, McLean, & Lawrence, 2004). There are several dimensions of self-defining memory that have been studied, including specificity (detailed recollection or general events/abstractions), meaning (whether the individual derived any meaning from the event), content (types of events), and affect (the emotions felt when recalling; Blagov & Singer, 2004). The meaning aspect is especially important for the memory to be "self-defining." For example, individuals are very likely to rely on self-defining memory to derive lessons and self insights (Thorne et al., 2004), which might be a turning point for the individual (McAdams, 2001, 2008b). Conway (1995) also identified variables that characterize self-defining memory: surprise, consequentiality, importance, and emotion.

Based on this research, we feel a potentially fruitful line of research would be one that explores how justice-related events cause self-defining memories and how these events are encoded into broader autobiographical memory structures. Because the experience of injustice has been shown to induce strong emotions, we suspect such experiences to provide many self-defining inputs to autobiographical memory. Such a proposition is consistent with recent findings within neuroscience, which show how the experiences of strong emotion both during and following events have a positive influence on their long term retention (Ferree & Cahill, 2009). It would be interesting to explore the relative effects of more impactful, idiosyncratic events, such as the gain/denial of a promotion, versus more repetitive, lower intensity events (ongoing disrespect from customers). Certainly issues of regulation would be pertinent here.

Finally, we suspect, as Rupp and Paddock (2010) have implied, that justice-related events are encoded according to the party held responsible for the event, that events are categorized by party, leading to the development of more stable mental representations of various parties, and that these mental representations form the building blocks of justice related output. This output would include the justice-laden autobiographical memories and other justice-related evaluations.

## How Are Justice-Related Memories Retrieved From Memory?

When we hand an employee a justice survey, we catalyze a recall process. However, the natural recall of justice-related events, coupled with the mental representations of the enactors of (in)justice, may be critical to the processes by which individuals navigate their working lives. Despite this fact, virtually no research exists exploring justice retrieval processes. That is, we have yet to understand *when* people recall justice evaluations, whether such recall is event-based (e.g., when with trusted others) or time-based (e.g., during dinner), whether frequency of recall solidifies mental representations, or what role emotion and mood serve in retrieval processes. We expect different cues (e.g., a survey, a justice-related event) to produce different retrieval results and different contextual variables (e.g., stress, uncertainty, amount of past information stored on perpetrator) to moderate the quantity and quality of the information retrieved. Again we can look to the memory literature for ideas on what sorts of cues and contextual variables might be most influential for such processes.

According to Conway and Pleydell-Pearce (2000), memories are mostly retrieved through generative retrieval, where a cue is elaborated and the memories that match this cue are verified according to some criterion. The cues can be of all types and at all levels of specificity, for example, a taste experience, a piece of music, or a question asked by others (e.g., "how was your day?"; "what do you think of your boss?"). The different cues usually imply different verification criteria. For example, an employee may recall different memories when ruminating about his/her relationship with his/her supervisor, versus when talking to several coworkers about their shared supervisor. A person-centered study of justice might consider the different types of memory output that are formed due to different verification criteria, including justice-defining memory, narratives about a particular justice perpetrator, justice-related evaluations, and so on.

In terms of contextual moderators, individuals' state affect at the time of memory retrieval is an important factor influencing memory recall. It is well-known that people exhibit mood-state dependent memory of daily experiences, such that people recall higher percentages of positive events when in a positive mood, while recalling higher percentages of negative events in a negative mood (Bower, 1981). Thus, it is likely that experimentally induced mood or mood states caused by unrelated factors will influence the types of justice-related event/evaluations recalled by employees.

Another important contextual factor is the time point of the memory retrieval. There is evidence that people appraise current emotions as more intense than previous ones (Van Boven, White, & Huber, 2009), possibly due to the salience of the current emotion and the relatively more information available for current emotion episodes. Thus, the events retrieved in order to form a justice judgment may be biased by their time stamp. Anticipatory justice (Shapiro & Kirkman, 2001) has been defined as the expectation of (un)just treatment in the context of a future event (e.g., Rodell & Colquitt, 2009). We argue that it is possible that employees also anticipate how they are going to be treated not only in the context of a particular event, but in general. For example, on a Sunday night, one employee may think, "My boss is going to humiliate me again tomorrow." The mere act of anticipation may influence later justice perceptions. There are studies from other research areas showing this anticipated effect: Across several studies, Galak and Meyvis (2011) found that if people are exposed to an uncomfortable experience (e.g., irritating sounds), and come to anticipate continued exposure to discomfort, they will rate the previously experienced discomfort as greater. In a related vein, these authors also found women to report their most recent menstrual experience as more painful when their next period is close in time. This suggests that an employee anticipating injustice may respond very differently to survey items compared to an employee who is not.

Employees may naturally recall or reevaluate their justice judgments from time to time (or quite often) and as discussed above, the justice judgments are likely to be influenced by different contextual factors. On the other hand, employees' justice judgments may change over time as more events are incorporated into mental representations. Thus, the temporal fluctuation of justice evaluations may be a true reflection of the latent justice construct; however, these fluctuations may also reflect the effect of contextual factors on the retrieval of justice mental representations. The true effect of change in justice perceptions, as well as artificial effects due to contextual factors, may be investigated by measuring justice perceptions across multiple time points as well as contextual factors at the time of recall. If no significant justice-related events happened during the measurement periods, then the variance of justice evaluations due to contextual factors can be evaluated.

Some longitudinal studies of justice perceptions exist, which have investigated people's justice perceptions about one particular event over several time points (Ambrose & Cropanzano, 2003; Lilly, Virick, & Hadani, 2010). From these types of studies we gain more understanding about the change in justice perceptions toward a particular event over time. Another type of longitudinal research investigates change in overall justice perceptions across time. For example, one recent study found that intraindividual variance accounted for 29% of the total variance in supervisory justice, when the measurement was taken at three time points within 8 weeks (Holtz & Harold, 2009). The contribution of contextual variables to within-person variability in justice perceptions may be one important factor to consider in future longitudinal studies of justice.

## PERSON-CENTRIC METHODOLOGIES

In the previous sections, we listed a number of currently unanswered research questions that take a person-centric approach to the study of organizational justice. In this section, we propose a number of methodological approaches that could aid the pursuit of such questions.

The person-centric model of organizational justice presented here and elsewhere points to two broad research questions involving (a) how employees experience justice-related events, and (b) how employees make sense of justice-related events that they experience, over time. Such questions require methods that can capture momentary states, as well as employees' mental representations of various parties (actors, observers, victims). A fundamental argument of the person-centric approach is that workers' subjective experiences are highly relevant; therefore, a focus on how people live, experience, and make sense of their work lives is essential.

## Phenomenology

This argument is not unlike that made in phenomenology (Burrell & Morgan, 1979; Creswell, 1994; Lincoln & Guba, 1985), an approach that calls for the consideration of subjective perception and conscious experiences in all psychological research. The corresponding methodology, interpretative phenomenological analysis, attempts to explore and understand people's subjective experiences, while acknowledging the perceptual biases created by the act of inquiry (J. A. Smith & Osborn, 2004). A commonly used data elicitation method in interpretative phenomenological analysis involves semistructured interviews. Qualitative interview data are subjected to theme analysis, with the goal of detecting themes both within and between persons. The interpretative phenomenological analysis method is especially useful when the aim is to understand the subjective experiences of research participants, and when the research topic is novel, complex, or involves processes and changes.

For example, Smith (2010) used a transcendental phenomenology approach to understand the meaning and essence of fairness in the workplace. In depth qualitative data from correctional officers revealed five properties of workplace fairness expressed by the workers: place, contribution, situation, relationships with others, and relationship with one's own work. Unique qualities were defined for each property, and they were accompanied by descriptors of valence indicating the workers' polarity toward fairness and unfairness. This analysis also provided evidence that the temporality of workplace fairness extends in time beyond organizational boundaries.

## Autobiographical/Life Narrative Methods

To explore the development, adjustment, and stability of perpetrator mental representations, autobiographical memory/life story interview methods may also be useful. There are a number of ways that this approach might be carried out (Schrauf & Rubin, 1998). For example, researchers may employ free or cued recall (e.g., ask employees to describe their working lives vs. asking them about memories pertaining to "workplace fairness"). McAdams and colleagues have used a technique whereby participants are first asked to view their lives as a book or novel and to give an overall summary of their life stories chapter by chapter (McAdams, Reynolds, Lewis, Patten, & Bowman, 2001). Participants are then asked to describe key scenes, including high points and low points. The interview also asks participants to envision their future, and talk about past challenges, their personal ideologies, and so on (McAdams, 2008a).

This type of interview could easily be carried out for individuals' working lives. Studs Terkel's *Working* (1974) is essentially a collection of such narratives, and even a cursory read of this work reveals that justice, fairness, and the meaning of work to people's lives emerge without the need of cues or surveys. Indeed such data are rich with insights into the ways in which individuals carry issues of justice throughout their working lives.

## Ethnography

Ethnography is another qualitative research method that could aid in exploring person-centric justice questions. A brief history of organizational ethnography (Eberle & Maeder, 2011) can be found in Zickar and Carter (2010). Although multiple methods of data collection are used in ethnography, including observation, interviews, and archival records, the one characteristic that distinguishes it from other qualitative methods is its primary reliance on direct observations. Researchers often spend a long period of time in the field, blending themselves into the workplace, making extensive observations about how the actors work and interact with each other in their natural working environment. For example, Pratt (2000) spent almost 2 years studying identification at Amway, systematically collecting data through semiovert participant observation, interviews, and the analysis of archival data. Although his "coworkers" were aware that he was a researcher, Pratt took on the tasks of an actual employee. Ethnographic writing usually provides a more holistic picture of people in work contexts, and seeks to confirm their observations via field notes or direct quotes from interviews.

Another example is Barley (1996), who used technicians' work drawings as an ethnographic dataset, from which insights regarding the relational and nonrelational aspects of technical work, as well as the changing nature of work in a postindustrial economy, were highlighted. Further it revealed dangers of selection practices that do not make efforts to understand the work context. Similarly, Fine (1996) conducted observations of cooks' use of occupational rhetoric to define their work and their identity. Based on observations and interviews, Fine described four types of occupational selves with which cooks identify, depending on working conditions (professionals, artists, businessmen, or manual laborers).

## Experience Sampling

Ecological momentary assessment or the experience sampling method (Beal & Weiss, 2003), as well as more general diary methods (Bolger, Davis, & Rafaeli, 2003), also provide techniques for detecting justice-related processes as they are occurring over time. Experience sampling method usually samples participants several times a day over 1 or 2 weeks, whereas diary methods often collect participant recollections once a day or week, over a longer time interval. Both methods can be used to capture close to live experiences over a time period, which are very important to answer how employees' justice perceptions change over time and how previous experiences influence later ones.

A related method is the day reconstruction method (DRM, Kahneman, Krueger, Schkade, Schwarz, & Stone, 2004). In DRM, respondents are first asked to reconstruct a previous day by segmenting that day into intervals or episodes, which might last from 15 minutes to 2 hours. Then they are asked about the context of those episodes (e.g., at home or at work, with other people or not), their affective experiences, and other reactions. By using DRM, rare events that might not be captured by experience sampling method can be detected. Also, by asking respondents to reconstruct the previous day into different episodes, the day is more fully reconstructed than with the dairy method. Using DRM may help researchers better understand individuals' working lives and discover how they are influenced by experiences over time. A recent study using the DRM method by Miron-Shatz (2009) asked participants to segment their previous day into episodes of various lengths and rate their feelings during those episodes. Miron-Shatz's research question was about how people arrive at an overall, retrospective evaluation of a day when they experience multiple episodes. The results of the study indicate that the retrospective evaluation of the day was predicted more by the average ratings of emotions during each episode (the normative model) rather than by the end episode (one example of using heuristic evaluation). Certainly this method could be used to study how overall justice perceptions are formed via the incorporation of information from multiple events.

## Verbal Protocol Analysis

Another method that could potentially assist researchers in uncovering how justice is *actually* experienced by workers is verbal protocol analysis. This method involves training participants to voice their cognitions while "working" (actual work or laboratory task work). These voiced cognitions are then transcribed and subjected to content analysis. By asking participants to voice their thoughts and feelings while experiencing work in real time, researchers may gain insight regarding the processing and retrieval of justice-related information that is not possible via traditional cross-sectional, retrospective survey designs.

For example, Roch, Lane, Samuelson, Allison, and Dent (2000) asked participants to voice their cognitions while working on a resource sharing task. While requesting resources, participants' voiced cognitions were recorded and the verbal protocol were coded along the rules used for resource sharing (i.e., equality, self-serving, etc.). It was found that participants under high cognitive load verbalized more equality-based cogntions, whereas those under low load expressed more self-serving cognitions, suggesting equality as a heuristic tool for maximizing fairness when cognitive resources cannot be strategically allocated to different tasks. Similarly, Rupp and Bell (2010) used voiced cognitions to reveal the complexity of individuals' thought processes when responding to third-party injustice. Whereas past research has argued that individuals show a slight tendency to punish those observed to be unfair to others, it has generally been thought that self-focused and relational concerns often trump such motivations. However, by using voiced cognition data, Rupp and Bell showed that oftentimes individuals engage in moral self-regulation, concluding that the act of punishing a transgressor is in itself unfair. These individuals therefore choose not to punish, not out of selfish or relational concerns, but as the result of complex moral reasoning. These results suggested that prior tests of morality-based judgments may have been quite conservative in nature.

## Physiological Measures

As pointed out in the previous section, people not only react to justice related events cognitively and emotionally, but they also react physiologically. Commonly used physiological measures include heart rate (e.g., Van der Molen, Boomsma, Jennings, & Nieuwboer, 1989), skin conductance level (e.g., Chao, Chen, Roisman, & Hong, 2007), and blood pressure/stroke volume (e.g., Tomaka, Blascovich, Kibler, & Ernst, 1997). These measures are easily taken via equipment such as heart rate monitor, blood pressure meter, and other devices that connect to computers with data acquisition software (e.g., the Snapmaster Data Acquisition System, 2000; Chao et al., 2007).

Another physiological variable that could prove useful for testing person-centric justice questions is cortisol level. Cortisol is one of the stress responsive hormones that can alter people's moods or even damage the brain (Herbert, 1997). When facing stressful events, higher levels of cortisol are released, which prepares people for "fight or flight" responses. Cortisol can be detected from samples of saliva and blood. For example, Creswell et al. (2005) collected participants' saliva following a stressful event, finding that those participants who affirmed their values before the stressful event had lower levels of cortisol concentration.

Very little justice research has employed physiological measurement, although a few exceptions exist. For example, Vermunt and Steensma (2003) measured participants' heart rate and blood pressure after engaging in a stressful activity. The participants were then treated either fairly or unfairly. Results indicated that fair treatment was associated with reduced levels of cardiovascular activity, indicating lower levels of stress. In another study by Vermunt and colleagues (Vermunt, Peeters, & Berggren, 2007), saliva cortisol was measured as an indicator of stress following manipulations both of mental pressure (high or low) and fairness (present or not). The results supported the prediction that fair treatment reduces stress.

## Functional Magnetic Resonance Imaging

Over the past 2 decades, there has been an enormous expansion of the field of functional magnetic resonance imaging (fMRI; Buxton, 2002). fMRI is a tool used to understand the functional organization of the human brain by locating the metabolic activity and blood flow changes in the brain that follow neural activity. Researchers have started to investigate which areas of the brain show activation as individuals engage in mental activities. For example, an fMRI study of social exclusion found that the pain felt due to social exclusion activated similar regions in the brain to those activated by felt physical pain (Eisenberger, Lieberman, & Williams, 2003). This explains why people feel hurt due to loss of loved ones, psychologically as well as physically. Similarly, an fMRI study of justice showed fairness to activate several reward regions in the brain, whereas the acceptance of unfair offers was aligned with increased activity in brain regions associated with emotion regulation (Tabibnia, Satpute, & Lieberman, 2008). Tabibnia et al.'s study also shows that fairness itself, rather than the material gain due to fair treatment, can be rewarding.

## CONCLUSION

In this chapter, we sought to describe what justice research conducted according to a person-centric paradigm might look like, and in the process, to present a number of research questions that future person-centric justice research might seek to answer (see Table 1.1). Whereas the prevailing paradigm can be characterized by both a between-entity assumption and a collective purpose agenda, we feel that a dearth of research has given attention to individuals' subjective experience of working life. Weiss and Rupp's (2011) call for more research focused on workers' subjective experiences, momentary states, and the experience of events certainly shaped our propositions regarding person-centric justice, as did the existing justice theories that are more person-centric in nature.

Specifically, we proposed that justice-related events and associated cognitive, affective, and physiological reactions are incorporated into mental representations of potential transgressors, based on which, justice judgments, narratives about transgressors, and significant justice events are recalled and/or constructed. We believe that a person-centric justice

**Table 1.1. A Small Sample of Research Questions Emerging From a Person-Centric Focus on Organizational Justice**

| | |
|---|---|
| Experience | • What cognitive, affective, and somatic experiences occur during events that are later categorized in memory as justice-related?<br>• When do individuals label affective experience as justice-related?<br>• How do current mental representations influence subsequent fairness perceptions of potential transgressors?<br>• How do regulation strategies influence the intensity and duration of emotional reactions to justice-related events? |
| Mental representations | • How is justice represented in memory?<br>• What type of justice information is stored in memory?<br>• What types of events most strongly influence mental representations?<br>• What are the characteristics of self-defining justice memories?<br>• Is justice perception shaped by one prominent event or the repetition of similar less-prominent events? |
| Retrieval | • When do people recall justice events and justice evaluations?<br>• Do individuals recall justice information more often on a particular occasion (e.g., at friend's gathering) or at a particular time (e.g., Sunday night, when people think about Monday)?<br>• Does the frequency of recall influence justice-related mental representations?<br>• Does mood influence recall of justice-related events? |

approach will aid justice researchers in asking important questions that are related to individuals' justice experiences at work. The questions we pose are just a start, as there are certainly plenty more that are yet to be posited. Our hope is that over time, we will gain a better understanding of what it means to experience justice, and we will use optimal methodologies to investigate new and exciting research questions within this domain.

Finally, while the present discussion has focused on the person-centric perspective, it is important to acknowledge the potential for this approach to incorporate between-person elements typically examined in more traditional justice research. In order to achieve this, researchers will need to combine the various methodologies discussed in this chapter with more traditional ones. Integration of these perspectives and methodologies should provide us with a greater understanding of the intricacies of justice experiences, both over the course of a single justice episode, as well as over greater periods of time. This integration should provide excellent opportunities for future research; undoubtedly resulting in a better understanding of the antecedents, components, and consequences, at multiple levels of analysis, of the phenomenon we call justice.

## NOTES

1. For example, Weiss et al. (1999) studied participants' happiness, pride, guilt, and anger reactions under experimental manipulations of outcome favorability and procedural fairness. Other examples include the study of shame, guilt, anger, and hostility among workers being laid off (Barclay, Skarlicki, & Pugh, 2005).
2. Examples of implication research include Bell, Wiechmann, and Ryan (2006), who examined the relationship between job applicants' expectations of justice and their reactions to the selection system; or Johnson, Selenta, and Lord (2006), who examined how justice perceptions relate to outcomes such as job attitudes and citizenship behavior.
3. Exceptions include a study by Barclay and Skarlicki (2009) wherein the effectiveness of expressive writing on reducing the negative result of workplace injustice was investigated (see also Smith, 2010).
4. Whereas they are cognitive perspectives in a broad sense, FHT and UMT are not necessarily experiential as described by Weiss and Rupp (2011). Like the evolutionary models of reciprocal altruism proposed by Trivers (1971), we could use UMT to explain the behavior of lower level organisms as well. We feel a potential new avenue for UMT is to explore the true experience of uncertainty as it naturally occurs throughout the working lives of people.
5. This is tangentially related to the research on social exchange theory (Blau, 1964; Organ, 1990), and to some extent, the relational model (Tyler &

Lind, 1992), both which focus on the "exchange partnerships" created between employees and other parties such as supervisors, coworkers, et cetera. This research considers the impact of relational quality on worker and organizational outcomes. Despite the relational tone of this research, we do not find it to be completely person-centric, in that more attention has been placed on between-persons correlations with outcomes driven by a collective purpose rather than on the subjective experience of said relations.

## REFERENCES


Ambrose, M. L., & Cropanzano, R. (2003). A longitudinal analysis of organizational fairness: An examination of reactions to tenure and promotion decisions. *Journal of Applied Psychology, 88*(2), 266-275.

Ambrose, M. L., & Schminke, M. (2009). The role of overall justice judgments in organizational justice research: A test of mediation. *Journal of Applied Psychology, 94*(2), 491-500.

Andersen, S. M., & Chen, S. (2002). The relational self: An interpersonal social-cognitive theory. *Psychological Review, 109*(4), 619-645.

Barclay, L. J., & Skarlicki, D. P. (2009). Healing the wounds of organizational injustice: Examining the benefits of expressive writing. *Journal of Applied Psychology, 94*(2), 511-523.

Barclay, L. J., Skarlicki, D. P., & Pugh, S. D. (2005). Exploring the role of emotions in injustice perceptions and retaliation. *Journal of Applied Psychology, 90*(4), 629-643.

Barley, S. R. (1996). Technicians in the workplace: Ethnographic evidence for bringing work into organization studies. *Administrative Science Quarterly, 41*(3), 404-441.

Barsalou, L. W. (1999). Perceptual symbol systems. *Behavioral and Brain Sciences, 22*(4), 577-660.

Barsky, A., Kaplan, S. A., & Beal, D. J. (2011). Just feelings? The role of affect in the formation of organizational fairness judgments. *Journal of Management, 37*(1), 248-279.

Bauer, J., Saboe, K., Cho, E., Yang, L., Johnson, R. E., Erol, H. T. G., et al. (2009). How prevalent are the different types of organizational justice research? *Industrial and Organizational Psychology: Perspectives on Science and Practice, 2*(2), 196-198.

Beal, D. J., & Weiss, H. M. (2003). Methods of ecological momentary assessment in organizational Research. *Organizational Research Methods, 6*(4), 440-464.

Bell, B. S., Wiechmann, D., & Ryan, A. M. (2006). Consequences of organizational justice expectations in a selection system. *Journal of Applied Psychology, 91*(2), 455-466.

Blagov, P. S., & Singer, J. A. (2004). Four dimensions of self-defining memories (specificity, meaning, content, and affect) and their relationships to self-restraint, distress, and repressive defensiveness. *Journal of Personality, 72*(3), 481-511.

Blau, P. (1964). *Exchange and power in social life*. New York, NY: Wiley.

Bluck, S. (2009). Introduction: Baddeley revisited: The functional approach to autobiographical memory [Special issue]. *Applied Cognitive Psychology, 23*(8), 1050-1058.

Bolger, N., Davis, A., & Rafaeli, E. (2003). Diary methods: Capturing life as it is lived. *Annual Review of Psychology, 54*, 579-616.

Bower, G. H. (1981). Mood and memory. *American Psychologist, 36*(2), 129-148.

Burrell, G., & Morgan, G. (1979). *Sociological paradigms and organizational analysis*. Aldershot, England: Ashgate.

Buxton, R. B. (2002). *Introduction to functional magnetic resonance imaging: Principles and techniques* (2nd ed.). New York, NY: Cambridge University Press.

Cardador, M. T., & Rupp, D. E. (2010). Organizational culture, multiple needs, and the meaningfulness of work. In N. M. Ashkanasy, C. P. M. Wilderom, & M. F. Peterson (Eds.), *The handbook of organizational culture and climate* (2nd ed., pp. 158-180). Thousand Oaks, CA: Sage.

Carver, C. S., & Scheier, M. F. (1998). *On the self-regulation of behavior*. New York, NY: Cambridge University Press.

Chao, M. M., Chen, J., Roisman, G. I., & Hong, Y. -Y. (2007). Essentializing race: Implications for bicultural individuals' cognition and physiological reactivity. *Psychological Science, 18*(4), 341-348.

Colquitt, J. A., Conlon, D. E., Wesson, M. J., Porter, C. O. L. H., & Ng, K. Y. (2001). Justice at the millennium: A meta-analytic review of 25 years of organizational justice research. *Journal of Applied Psychology, 86*(3), 425-445.

Conway, M. A. (1995). *Flashbulb memories*. Hove, East Sussex, England: Erlbaum.

Conway, M. A., & Pleydell-Pearce, C. W. (2000). The construction of autobiographical memories in the self-memory system. *Psychological Review, 107*(2), 261-288.

Conway, M. A., Singer, J. A., & Tagini, A. (2004). The self and autobiographical memory: Correspondence and coherence. *Social Cognition, 22*(5), 491-529.

Creswell, J. W. (1994). *Research design: Qualitative & quantitative approaches*. Thousand Oaks, CA: Sage.

Creswell, J. D., Welch, W. T., Taylor, S. E., Sherman, D. K., Gruenewald, T. L., & Mann, T. (2005). Affirmation of personal values buffers neuroendocrine and psychological stress responses. *Psychological Science, 16*(11), 846-851.

Eberle, T. S., & Maeder, C. (2011). Organizational ethnography. In D. Silverman (Ed.), *Qualitative research. Theory, method and practice* (pp. 54-73). Thousand Oaks, CA: Sage.

Eisenberger, N. I., Lieberman, M. D., & Williams, K. D. (2003). Does rejection hurt? An fMRI study of social exclusion. *Science, 302*(5643), 290-292.

Ferree, N. K., & Cahill, L. (2009). Post-event spontaneous intrusive recollections and strength of memory for emotional events in men and women. *Consciousness and Cognition: An International Journal, 18*(1), 126-134.

Fine, G. A. (1996). Justifying work: Occupational rhetorics as resources in restaurant kitchens. *Administrative Science Quarterly, 41*(1), 90-115.

Folger, R., & Cropanzano, R. (2001). Fairness theory: Justice as accountability. In J. Greenberg & R. Cropanzano (Eds.), *Advances in organizational justice* (pp. 1–55). Stanford, CA: Stanford University Press.

Fiske, S. T., & Taylor, S. E. (1991). *Social cognition* (2nd ed.). New York, NY: Mcgraw-Hill Book Company.

Fredrickson, B. L., & Kahneman, D. (1993). Duration neglect in retrospective evaluations of affective episodes. *Journal of Personality and Social Psychology, 65*(1), 45-55.

Galak, J., & Meyvis, T. (2011). The pain was greater if it will happen again: The effect of anticipated continuation on retrospective discomfort. *Journal of Experimental Psychology: General, 140*(1), 63-75.

Grandjean, D., Sander, D., & Scherer, K. R. (2008). Conscious emotional experience emerges as a function of multilevel, appraisal-driven response synchronization. *Consciousness and Cognition: An International Journal, 17*(2), 484-495.

Greenberg, J. (2009). Everybody talks about organizational justice, but nobody does anything about it. *Industrial and Organizational Psychology: Perspectives on Science and Practice, 2*(2), 181-195.

Gross, J. J. (1998). The emerging field of emotion regulation: An integrative review [Special Issue]. *Review of General Psychology, 2*(3), 271-299.

Herbert, J. (1997). Fortnighly review: Stress, the brain, and mental illness. *British Medical Journal, 315*(7107), 530-535.

Holtz, B. C., & Harold, C. M. (2009). Fair today, fair tomorrow? A longitudinal investigation of overall justice perceptions. *Journal of Applied Psychology, 94*(5), 1185-1199.

Hulin, C. L. (2010). *Work, being, and nothingness: The roles and meanings of work* (Working paper). Champaign, IL: Author.

Johnson, R. E., Selenta, C., & Lord, R. G. (2006). When organizational justice and the self-concept meet: Consequences for the organization and its members. *Organizational Behavior and Human Decision Processes, 99*(2), 175-201.

Jones, D. A., & Martens, M. L. (2009). The mediating role of overall fairness and the moderating role of trust certainty in justice-criteria relationships: The formation and use of fairness heuristics in the workplace. *Journal of Organizational Behavior, 30*(8), 1025-1051.

Kahneman, D., Krueger, A. B., Schkade, D. A., Schwarz, N., & Stone, A. A. (2004). A survey method for characterizing daily life experience: The day reconstruction method. *Science, 306*(5702), 1776-1780.

Lazarus, R. S. (1991). *Emotion and adaptation*. New York, NY: Oxford University Press.

Lerner, J. S., & Tiedens, L. Z. (2006). Portrait of the angry decision maker: How appraisal tendencies shape anger's influence on cognition [Special issue: The role of affect in decision making]. *Journal of Behavioral Decision Making, 19*(2), 115-137.

Lilly, J. D., Virick, M., & Hadani, M. (2010). The dynamic nature of justice: Influential effects of time and work outcomes on long-term perceptions of justice. *Social Justice Research, 23*(1), 37-59.

Lincoln, Y., & Guba, E. (1985). *Naturalistic inquiry*. Newbury Park, CA: SAGE.

Lind, E. A. (2001). Fairness heuristic theory: Justice judgments as pivotal cognitions in organizational relations. In J. Greenberg & R. Cropanzano (Eds.), *Advances in organizational justice* (pp. 56-88). Stanford, CA: Stanford University Press.

Lind, E. A., & van den Bos, K. (2002). When fairness works: Toward a general theory of uncertainty management. In B. M. Staw & R. M. Kramer (Eds.), *Research in organizational behavior: An annual series of analytical essays and critical reviews* (pp. 181-223). New York, NY: Elsevier Science/JAI Press.

Maas, M., & van den Bos, K. (2009). An affective-experiential perspective on reactions to fair and unfair events: Individual differences in affect intensity moderated by experiential mindsets. *Journal of Experimental Social Psychology, 45*(4), 667-675.

Markus, H., & Wurf, E. (1987). The dynamic self-concept: A social psychological perspective. *Annual Review of Psychology, 38*, 299-337.

Miron-Shatz, T. (2009). Evaluating multiepisode events: Boundary conditions for the peak-end rule. *Emotion, 9*(2), 206-213.

McAdams, D. P. (2001). The psychology of life stories [Special issue: Autobiographical memory]. *Review of General Psychology, 5*(2), 100-122.

McAdams, D. P. (2008a). *The life story interview.* Retrieved from http://www.sesp.northwestern.edu/foley/instruments/interview/

McAdams, D. P. (2008b). Personal narratives and the life story. In O. P. John, R. W. Robins, L. A. Pervin (Eds.), *Handbook of personality psychology: Theory and research* (pp. 242-262). New York, NY: The Guidford Press.

McAdams, D. P., Reynolds, J., Lewis, M., Patten, A. H., & Bowman, P. J. (2001). When bad things turn good and good things turn bad: Sequences of redemption and contamination in life narrative and their relation to psychosocial adaptation in midlife adults and in students. *Personality and Social Psychology Bulletin, 27*(4), 474-485.

Moffitt, K. H., & Singer, J. A. (1994). Continuity in the life story—Self-defining memories, affect, and approach avoidance personal strivings. *Journal of Personality, 62*(1), 21-43.

Murphy, K. (2009). Procedural justice and affect intensity: Understanding reactions to regulatory authorities. *Social Justice Research, 22*(1), 1-30.

Organ, D. W. (1990). The motivational basis of organizational citizenship behavior. In B. M. Staw & L. L. Cummings (Eds.), *Research in organizational behavior* (Vol. 12, pp. 43-72). Greenwich, CT: JAI.

Pratt, M. G. (2000). The good, the bad, and the ambivalent: Managing identification among Amway distributors. *Administrative Science Quarterly, 45*(3), 456-493.

Redelmeier, D. A., & Kahneman, D. (1996). Patients' memories of painful medical treatments: Real-time and retrospective evaluations of two minimally invasive procedures. *Pain, 66*(1), 3-8.

Ritter, B. A., & Lord, R. G. (2007). The impact of previous leaders on the evaluation of new leaders: An alternative to prototype matching. *Journal of Applied Psychology, 92*(6), 1683-1695.

Roch, S. G., Lane, J. A. S., Samuelson, C. D., Allison, S. T., & Dent, J. L. (2000). Cognitive load and the equality heuristic: A two-stage model of resource overconsumption in small groups. *Organizational Behavior and Human Decision Processes, 83*(2), 185-212.

Rodell, J. B., & Colquitt, J. A. (2009). Looking ahead in times of uncertainty: The role of anticipatory justice in an organizational change context. *Journal of Applied Psychology, 94*(4), 989-1002.

Rupp, D. E. (2011). An employee-centered model of organizational justice and social responsibility. *Organizational Psychology Review, 1*, 72-94.

Rupp, D. E., & Bell, C. M. (2010). Extending the deontic model of justice: Moral self-regulation in third-party responses to injustice. *Business Ethics Quarterly, 20*(1), 89-106.

Rupp, D. E., & Cropanzano, R. (2002). Multifoci justice and social exchange relationships. *Organizational Behavior and Human Decision Processes, 89*, 925-946.

Rupp, D. E., McCance, A. S., Spencer, S., & Sonntag, K. (2008). Customer (in)justice and emotional labor: The role of perspective taking, anger, and emotional regulation? *Journal of Management, 34*(5), 903-924.

Rupp, D. E., & Paddock, E. L. (2010). From justice events to justice climate: A multilevel temporal model of information aggregation and judgment. *Research on Managing Groups and Teams, 13*, 239-267.

Rupp, D. E., Shao, R., Jones, K. S., & Liao, H. (2011). *Multifoci justice and the target similarity model: A meta-analysis* (Unpublished manuscript). Purdue University, West Lafayette, IN.

Rupp, D. E., & Spencer, S. (2006). When customers lash out: The effect of customer interactional injustice on emotional labor and the mediating role of discrete emotions. *Journal of Applied Psychology, 91*, 971-978.

Scherer, K. R. (2009). The dynamic architecture of emotion: Evidence for the component process model [Special issue: Individual differences in emotion]. *Cognition and Emotion, 23*(7), 1307-1351.

Schoefer, K., & Diamantopoulos, A. (2008). The role of emotions in translating perceptions of (in)justice into postcomplaint behavioral responses. *Journal of Service Research, 11*(1), 91-103.

Schrauf, R. W., & Rubin, D. C. (1998). Bilingual autobiographical memory in older adult immigrants: A test of cognitive explanations of the reminiscence bump and the linguistic encoding of memories. *Journal of Memory and Language, 39*(3), 437-457.

Schwarz, N., & Clore, G. L. (1996). Feelings and phenomenal experiences. In E. T. Higgins & A. W. Kruglanski (Eds.), *Social psychology: Handbook of basic principles* (1st ed., pp. 433-465). New York, NY: The Guilford Press.

Schwarz, N., & Clore, G. L. (2007). Feelings and phenomenal experiences. In A. W. Kruglanski & E. T. Higgins (Eds.), *Social psychology: Handbook of basic principles* (2nd ed., pp. 385 -407). New York, NY: The Guilford Press.

Shapiro, D. L., & Kirkman, B. L. (2001). Anticipatory injustice: The consequences of expecting injustice in the workplace. In J. Greenberg & R. Cropanzano (Eds.), *Advances in organizational justice* (pp. 152–178). San Francisco, CA: New Lexington.

Smith, J. A., & Osborn, M. (2004) Interpretative phenomenological analysis. In G. M. Breakwell (Ed.), *Doing social psychology research* (pp. 229-254). Oxford, England: BPS Blackwell.

Smith, R. S. (2010). *The meaning and essence of fairness in the workplace: A phenomenological study of organizational justice* (Doctoral dissertation). George Washington University, Washington, DC.

Snapmaster Data Acquisition System [Computer software]. (2000). Southfield, MI: HEM Data Corp.

Sonnemans, J., & Frijda, N. H. (1995). The determinants of subjective emotional intensity. *Cognition and Emotion, 9*(5), 483-506.

Tabibnia, G., Satpute, A. B., & Lieberman, M. D. (2008). The sunny side of fairness: Preference for fairness activates reward circuitry (and disregarding unfairness activates self-control circuitry). *Psychological Science, 19*(4), 339-347.

Terkel, S. (1974). *Working: People talk about what they do all day and how they feel about what they do*. New York, NY: Pantheon Books.

Thorne, A., McLean, K. C., & Lawrence, A. M. (2004). When remembering is not enough: Reflecting on self-defining memories in late adolescence. *Journal of Personality, 72*(3), 513-541.

Tomaka, J., Blascovich, J., Kibler, J., & Ernst, J. M. (1997). Cognitive and physiological antecedents of threat and challenge appraisal. *Journal of Personality and Social Psychology, 73*(1), 63-72.

Tripp, T. M., & Bies, R. J. (2007). Scholarly bias in studying justice and emotion: If we don't ask, we don't see. In D. De Cremer (Ed.), *Advances in the psychology of justice and affect* (pp. 175-190). Charlotte, NC: Information Age.

Trivers, R. L. (1971). The evolution of reciprocal altruism. *Quarterly Review of Biology, 46*, 35-57.

Tyler, T. R., & Lind, E. A. (1992). A relational model of authority in groups. In M. P. Zanna (Ed.), *Advances in experimental social psychology* (Vol. 25, pp. 115-191). San Diego, CA: Academic Press.

Van Boven, L., White, K., & Huber, M. (2009). Immediacy bias in emotion perception: Current emotions seem more intense than previous emotions. *Journal of Experimental Psychology: General, 138*(3), 368-382.

van den Bos, K. (2003). On the subjective quality of social justice: The role of affect as information in the psychology of justice judgments. *Journal of Personality and Social Psychology, 85*(3), 482-498.

van den Bos, K., Burrows, J. W., Umphress, E., Folger, R., Lavelle, J. J., Eaglestone, J., et al. (2005). Prior experiences as temporal frames of reference in social justice: The influence of previous fairness experiences on reactions to new and old supervisors. *Social Justice Research, 18*(2), 99-120.

van den Bos, K., & Lind, E. A. (2002). Uncertainty management by means of fairness judgments. In M. P. Zanna (Ed.), *Advances in experimental social psychology* (Vol. 34, pp. 1-60). San Diego, CA: Academic Press.

Van der Molen, M. W., Boomsma, D. I., Jennings, J. R., & Nieuwboer, R. T. (1989). Does the heart know what the eye sees? A cardiac/pupillometric analysis of motor preparation and response execution. *Psychophysiology, 26*(1), 70-80.

Vermunt, R., Peeters, Y., & Berggren, K. (2007). How fair treatment affects saliva cortisol release in stressed low and high type-A behavior individuals. *Scandinavian Journal of Psychology, 48*(6), 547-555.

Vermunt, R., & Steensma, H. (2003). Physiological relaxation: Stress reduction through fair treatment. *Social Justice Research, 16*(2), 135-149.

Weiss, H. M., & Cropanzano, R. (1996). Affective events theory: A theoretical discussion of the structure, causes and consequences of affective experiences at work. In B. M. Staw & L. L. Cummings (Eds.), *Research in organizational behavior* (pp. 1-74). Greenwich, CT: JAI Press.

Weiss, H., & Rupp, D. E. (2011). Experiencing work: An essay on a person-centric work psychology. *Industrial and Organizational Psychology, 4*, 83-97.

Weiss, H. M., Suckow, K., & Cropanzano, R. (1999). Effects of justice conditions on discrete emotions. *Journal of Applied Psychology, 84*(5), 786-794.

Zhong, C. -B., Bohns, V. K., & Gino, F. (2010). Good lamps are the best police: Darkness increases dishonesty and self-interested behavior. *Psychological Science, 21*(3), 311-314.

Zhong, C. -B., & Leonardelli, G. J. (2008). Cold and lonely: Does social exclusion literally feel cold? *Psychological Science, 19*(9), 838-842.

Zickar, M. J., & Carter, N. T. (2010). Reconnecting with the spirit of workplace ethnography: A historical review. *Organizational Research Methods, 13*(2), 304-319.

CHAPTER 2

# THE ROLE OF MEMORY IN JUDGMENTS OF ORGANIZATIONAL JUSTICE

**Irina Cojuharenco, Jan-Willem van Prooijen, and David Patient**

We discuss the role of memory in judgments of organizational justice. Building on memory and cognition research, we suggest that self-relevance biases in justice judgments are partly due to differential availability in memory of information about past experiences. We predict that self-relevance biases are stronger in memory-based judgments than in judgments immediately following events. Consequently, the greater the extent to which others are central to self, the more likely it is that memory-based judgments of fairness take into account the experiences of others. We present research designs that can be used for the study of memory effects and report preliminary findings from 2 studies. We conclude by emphasizing the importance of considering the malleability of justice judgments as a function of memory biases over time.

Imagine that someone asks "*Has* your supervisor *treated* you with dignity?" (Colquitt, 2001), "*showed* concern for your rights as an employee?" (Moorman, 1991), or "*given* you an opportunity to express your side?" (Konovsky, Folger, & Cropanzano, 1987). You will probably think back to meetings and conversations with your supervisor that you have experienced or observed, such as his or her handling of a layoff last month. This suggests that judgments of organizational justice are frequently memory

*Emerging Perspectives on Organizational Justice and Ethics*
pp. 33–48

based. It is therefore surprising that, in spite of research indicating that people are prone to severe biases in their recollection of social events (Schacter, 2001), the effect of memory on justice judgments has received little research attention. In this chapter, we propose that effects of memory on justice judgments can have important theoretical and practical implications.

Several studies of organizational justice phenomena have explicitly acknowledged the role of memory in justice judgments. Messick and colleagues (Messick, Bloom, Boldizar, & Samuelson, 1985; Liebrand, Messick, & Wolters, 1986) showed self-serving biases in memory for fair and unfair treatment. In their studies, individuals were more likely to recall fair behaviors of their own rather than of others, but recall unfair behaviors of others rather than of their own. Bashshur and Cojuharenco (2009) found that memory-based judgments of organizational fairness are subject to a negativity bias. In particular, unfair aspects of situations are more memorable than fair aspects, and bias downwards people's evaluation of the whole situation. Cojuharenco, Patient, and Bashshur (in press) showed that people's recollection of unfair events at work is influenced by whether they construe the employment relationship at a general, abstract level or at a more specific, concrete level. In particular, recalling distant past events leads to a more general and abstract view of employment and more distributive versus interactional unjust events being brought to mind, whereas recalling recent past events leads to a more specific and concrete view of employment and a greater proportion of interactional unjust events being brought to mind. The above research on self-serving biases, negativity biases, and construal effects in memory demonstrates that insights can be gained from applying research in memory and cognition to organizational justice phenomena.

A fundamental feature of memory is that it becomes less accurate over time (Schacter, 2001). Therefore, many memory biases represent mechanisms by which the mind compensates for memory decay. For example, people use what is more memorable and what they believe to be true to "fill in the gaps" when recalling the past (Loftus & Palmer, 1974; Ross, 1989; Skowronski & Carlston, 1987). When judgments about past events need to be made, people search their memory, especially when they did not anticipate having to judge the event or when they need to use details of what happened to justify a decision (Hastie & Park, 1986). However, the greater the time since the event, the more likely it is that memory might not be able to provide an accurate and detailed account. Indeed, a variety of memory phenomena exist that call into question the assumption that recollections of past events are always accurate, including: simply forgetting, biased recall, generation of false memories, or attributing events to an incorrect source (Schacter, 1999).

Exploring the effects of memory on justice judgments can help us better understand how justice perceptions develop over time. In particular, understanding memory processes can enhance the empirical rigor and practical relevance of findings in organizational justice research by offering a framework for understanding *when* effects occur (Mitchell & James, 2001). In this chapter, we focus on a specific memory bias: the selectivity of people's memory for unfair events, depending on how self-relevant the target of injustice is. We examine how memory can affect perceptions of organizational justice depending on whether people remember justice-relevant events that were experienced by self, a close friend or colleague, or a more socially distant other. First, we review research on self-relevance biases in judgements of organizational justice. Second, we examine the literature on the relationship between self-relevance of information and its availability in memory. Following this, research propositions are advanced regarding the susceptibility of justice judgments to self-relevance biases over time. Fourth, the results of two preliminary studies are reviewed. To conclude, we discuss promising directions for future research and emphasize the importance of memory to better understanding and managing organizational justice perceptions.

## Self-Relevance and Perceptions of Organizational Justice

Research in organizational justice has demonstrated that the unfair treatment experienced by others can have a substantial impact on one's own fairness perceptions (e.g., Brockner et al., 1994). Cooley's (1902) classic research on queue jumping showed that people not only react strongly against a person who cuts in line in front of them, but also against someone who cuts in line behind them. Skarlicki and Kulik (2005) point out that most injustices have many onlookers and observers, and the reactions of onlookers and observers, in turn, affect the broader organization. For example, third-party reactions to layoffs affecting others can include retributive intentions toward the organization if the procedures and treatment are regarded as unjust (Skarlicki, Ellard, & Kelln, 1998).

People tend to respond more strongly to the unfair treatment of others to the extent that these other people are more central to the self concept. This is consistent with the idea that people extend justice considerations more to those inside their "circle of moral regard," and less to those who fall outside (Reed & Aquino, 2003; cf. Opotow, 1990). For instance, layoff survivors respond most negatively to perceived unfair treatment of layoff victims when they identify strongly with those victims (Brockner, Grover, Reed, DeWitt, & O'Malley, 1987), or when the layoff victims are included within survivors' scope of justice (Brockner, 1990). Researchers have looked at constructs such as justice orientation, justice sensitivity, and compassion and empathy, to differentiate between individuals whose perceptions of justice are more versus less likely to be affected by others' experiences (Goetz, Keltner, & Simon-Thomas, 2010; Liao & Rupp, 2005; Patient & Skarlicki, 2010; Schmitt, Gollwitzer, Maes, & Arbach, 2005). Yet, little is known about how the passage of time and reliance on memory might change the extent to which a person's justice perceptions can be influenced by the observed experiences of others.

In this chapter, we examine how the passage of time can heighten self-relevance biases in justice judgments. For example, would the effect of unfair treatment experienced by others on one's own justice judgments differ depending on whether the event has just been witnessed versus if it is recalled at a later time?

## Self-Relevance and Memory

Memory and cognition research suggests that self-relevance is a powerful principle for predicting the availability of information in memory. For example, people generally recall their own (versus others') statements and contributions to a group interaction more easily and more frequently (Ross & Sicoly, 1979). On tasks such as memorizing lists of adjectives, encoding by self-relevance (respondents consider how well each adjective describes themselves) leads to superior recall compared to other types of encoding (Rogers, Kuiper, & Kirker, 1977; Schacter, 2001). Wagenaar (1986) recorded daily experiences in terms of "who," "what," "where," and "when" for a period of 5 years and later tested his recall using the same words as clues. Relevant to our investigation of justice perceptions, his analysis showed that experiences rated as "self-related, very unpleasant" were remembered particularly well. Moreover, past actions that conflict with a person's self-definition are typically recalled from a more distant, third-person (observer) perspective (Libby & Eibach, 2002). This suggests that people, presumably without being aware of it, dissociate from the self memories that are inconsistent with self-definitions.

Effects of self-relevance should differ among individuals who define their relationships to others in markedly different ways. For example, individuals can vary in the extent to which others are "included in the self." For instance, partners in close relationships feature more centrally in each other's self-concepts than is the case for two strangers (Aron, Aron, Tudor, & Nelson, 1991). People may also differ dispositionally in their tendency to perceive the self as connected to others, depending on whether they emphasize the individual self, the relational self, or the collective self (e.g., Markus & Kitayama, 1991; Sedikides & Brewer, 2001).

People who emphasize their individual self particularly value their uniqueness, distinctiveness, and separateness from others. People who emphasize their relational self tend to define themselves in terms of roles they play in relation to specific others, for example, being somebody's parent, teacher, or friend. Finally, people who emphasize their collective self focus on their membership in social groups, as in "U.S. citizen" or "IBM employee."

Because people who emphasize their interdependent (i.e., relational or collective) self attach greater importance to relationships than do people who emphasize their independent (i.e., individual) self, interdependent self-definition facilitates memory for contextual information. In an intriguing example, Kuhnen and Oyserman (2002) primed participants with either independence or interdependence and then tested their recall of twenty eight objects presented in the rows and columns of a matrix. Whereas the recall of individual objects by interdependence and independence-primed participants was similar, interdependence-primed participants were significantly better at recalling the location of objects in the matrix, that is, in relation to other objects. These findings illuminate the concern for relations that is associated with the interdependent self, even to the extent that this concern is reflected in a better memory for relations between nonliving objects.

One way in which recall is affected by self-relevance is in greater recall of others who are close versus distant, suggesting that a close other can be as prominent in memory as the self (Aron et al., 1991). Very similar self- and other-related judgments can be expected to result if memory about self becomes confused with memory about a close other. We therefore expect memory to play an important role in self- and other-related justice judgments, depending on the extent to which the other is central to the self concept.

## RESEARCH PROPOSITIONS

When individuals are evaluating workplace fairness, they have to weight their own experience and the events experienced by their coworkers. An individual's sense of self is likely to guide his or her search, evaluation, and recall of fairness-related information at work (Ham & Van den Bos, 2008; Johnson, Selenta, & Lord, 2006; Skitka, 2003). We advance two interrelated propositions about the relationship between the self-relevance of events and their effect on judgments of overall fairness over time. First, the passage of time can blur the distinction between self- and other-focused events, depending on the extent to which the other is included in one's self-definition. Second, because self-relevant events are more available in memory, events happening to others will more likely affect judgments of overall fairness over time when others are included in one's self-definition. We consider each of these propositions in turn.

When initially experiencing an event, an organizational actor is likely to notice numerous details of what is happening, including specific details regarding what is happening to oneself versus what is being experienced by coworkers: "Yes, you are not allowed to talk to the boss, but he is! They are considering his opinion"; or, "Yes, he is not allowed to talk to the boss, but you are! They are considering your opinion." As the event takes place, an attentive individual can *see* what is happening and to whom, and should be able to distinguish between fairness received by others and fairness directly affecting the self. Therefore, we would expect in-the-moment or relatively recent evaluations of fairness to clearly distinguish between own and others' experiences.

When an event is later recalled from memory, however, the details and richness of the actual experience are often stripped away. One way in which we expect this to happen is a relative loss in detail regarding others' versus own experiences. More versus less self-relevant aspects of the experience will be more accessible and more easily retrieved for evaluating a past experience. As our review of memory and cognition research suggests, with the passage of time people are less likely to bring to mind and accurately remember what others experienced and more likely to remember how they themselves were affected. Self-relevant events would then become relatively more prominent (versus events experienced by others) in overall fairness judgments.

In the present chapter, however, we propose that the effects of memory are somewhat more complex. Self-definition can play an important role in this process, as people vary in the extent to which they include others in their self-concept (Aron et al., 1991). For example, if Ellen considers herself "John's friend," she is more likely to retrieve John's experiences as "Ellen's." To the extent that John's experiences are self-relevant to Ellen she will be able to recall these easily, along with her own experiences. Thus, the fact that Ellen's supervisor yelled at John in a meeting is going to matter to Ellen even if at a later date she no longer remembers exactly who the supervisor yelled at. If what happens to John is self-relevant to Ellen, it may even matter more to her after the passage of time blurs many of the distinctions between events that are referenced "John" and those that are referenced "Ellen."

Thus, we propose that whether an individual includes others in the self to a greater versus lesser extent can influence the relationship between the self-relevance of events and the passage of time, in the following way. When an individual relates closely to another person who experiences unfairness, then the other's experience can become available in memory, as if the event to some extent happened to self. As a consequence, justice judgments for events that happened to others are likely to become more strongly related to justice judgments for events that happened to self as time passes by. No such assimilation effects should occur in the case of individuals who do not include others in their self-definition. Hence,

> ***Proposition 1:*** For individuals who include others in their self-definition, the passage of time will blur the distinction between treatment received by the individual himself or herself and treatment received by others. This effect will not occur for individuals who do not include others in their self-definition.

The extent to which individuals include others in their self-definition is also expected to moderate the relationship between the passage of time and the extent to which others' experiences are accounted for in judgements of overall justice. For the reasons given above, experiences that are more versus less self-relevant are expected to become more prominent and available the greater the passage of time since the event. However, for individuals who include others in the self, others' experiences will matter more for judgments of overall fairness over time, because these experiences are more likely to be recalled as one's own. This effect is not likely to emerge for individuals who do not include others in the self, given the decreased availability in memory of events that are not self-relevant. Hence,

> ***Proposition 2:*** For individuals who include others in their self-definition, the passage of time will increase the effect of treatment of others on overall justice judgments. For individuals who do not include others in their self-definition, the passage of time will decrease the effect of treatment of others on overall justice judgments.

## PRELIMINARY STUDIES AND FINDINGS

We report here results of two studies examining the relationship between memory, self-relevance, and justice judgments regarding past events. We first conducted a quasi-experiment using employees in various organizations recruited through a U.S. market research firm (Study 1). In this experiment, our aim was to test Proposition 1 described above. We used the work setting to explore the possibility that the passage of time blurs the distinction between the treatment received by self versus the treatment received by coworkers.

Respondents in the "low memory decay" condition were asked to report on the fairness of treatment that they received and that their coworkers received *in the past 2 weeks* at work. In the "high memory decay" condition, respondents were asked to do the same for *the past month* at work. Respondents' collectivism was measured as a proxy for the extent to which they include coworkers in their self-concept. Thus, we were able to test whether the centrality of others to self-definition moderated the relationship between memory decay (low versus high) and whether reports of treatment of the self (e.g., "I was treated fairly by my organization") were affected by the fair or unfair treatment of others.

Our Study 1 results showed that coworker treatment affected perceptions of justice to the self in the ways predicted. A significant three-way interaction was found between memory decay, coworker experienced justice, and collectivism. For participants who scored high on collectivism, the relationship between fair treatment of coworker and perceptions of justice to the self was stronger when memory decay was high as opposed to low. Thus, people were more likely to incorporate the treatment of others in their evaluations of how fairly they themselves were treated if they remembered a more (versus less) temporally distant event. In contrast, no such effect was found for participants low on collectivism. These findings are consistent with Proposition 1: greater memory decay leads people to mentally confuse justice-related events that happened to self versus others, but only if the other people affected are relatively central to the observer's self-concept.

An additional study (Study 2) was conducted to complement and extend these findings by testing Proposition 2. In Study 2, we also addressed some of Study 1's limitations. First, whereas Study 1 relied on measurements at a fixed point in time—thus not allowing for a direct tracking of changes in perceptions of fairness over time—in Study 2 we measured justice perceptions at two different points in time. Thus, in Study 2 we sought to more clearly incorporate the temporal aspect of memory decay in our research set-up. Second, in Study 1 we had no control over the type of justice-based memories that participants brought to mind as the basis for their judgments. It is therefore possible that the experiences referred to by participants differed in terms of severity, perpetrator, and type of unfair treatment. Moreover, in Study 1 we were unable to verify that the treatment that respondents received differed from the treatment received by their coworkers. To address this limitation, all Study 2 participants read, recalled, and responded to the same justice-related incident.

Study 2 was a longitudinal laboratory experiment in which participants considered a specific justice-based event at Time 1, and were asked 2 weeks later to recall the event. Participants read the scenario at Time 1 and were asked to imagine that they and one other person had applied for an important scholarship. We implemented a design in which the final outcome of the process (awarding of the scholarship) was fair to participants themselves but unfair to the other person. Thus, accounting for the treatment of the other would manifest itself in judgments of lower overall fairness. To manipulate inclusion of the other person in the self, we varied whether this other person was a friend, with whom they interacted frequently, or a stranger, with whom they had not previously interacted. Time was included as a within-subjects factor. Participants reported their Time 1 perceptions of overall fairness of the scholarship decision. In particular, we used the following items (1 = *strongly disagree*, 7 = *strongly agree*): "I believe the final decision was fair," and "The way things worked out in this situation was unfair" (reverse coded). To make sure that participants understood the scenario, we also measured their perceptions of fairness to self and fairness to the other person. Two to 3 weeks later (Time 2), participants were contacted again and asked to recall as much of the scenario as possible and, based on what they remembered, to again report their fairness perceptions of the scholarship decision. This was a Time 2 analogue of the dependent variable that we collected at Time 1.

As expected, we found that with the passage of time, judgments of overall fairness become affected by whether the other person is a friend or a stranger. Time 1 fairness judgments did not differ according to whether the other person experiencing (in)justice was a friend or a stranger. However, Time 2 fairness judgments were more negative when it was a friend rather than a stranger who experienced injustice at Time 1. The effect was primarily due to somewhat more positive Time 2 perceptions of overall fairness in the stranger condition (compared to Time 1, this being consistent with a self-relevance bias focusing the attention of participants on the fair treatment that they received). Thus, the effect of the unfair treatment of the stranger on overall justice judgments decreased over time, which is consistent with Proposition 2. Also, Time 2 perceptions of fairness to self remained stable in the stranger condition, but decreased in the friend condition (compared to Time 1), consistent with the argument that blurring of treatment to self and the other occurs over time when others are included in self-definition. Thus, when injustice happens to a friend, the impact of that treatment on judgment of overall fairness increases over time. These results provide support for Proposition 2 and show that it may take time before the unfair treatment of others impacts overall justice judgments.

## DISCUSSION

The studies presented in this chapter address an important topic in the field of organizational justice—how does memory influence individuals' tendency to integrate others' experiences in their judgments of organizational justice? The justice literature has clearly shown that events that are relevant to the self affect justice judgments more than events that are less relevant to the self (Brockner & Greenberg, 1990; Brockner et al., 1987; Lind, Kray, & Thompson, 1998). However, whether the effects of self-relevance on justice judgments can be affected by memory processes has not received research attention. In this chapter we begin to explore how the effects of self-relevance biases can become more pronounced as time passes between an event and judgments concerning it. Given that self-relevance is a powerful principle for the availability of information in memory, we argue that it can be expected to affect justice judgments more when accurate recall of past experiences becomes more difficult.

Future research should explore whether memory effects occur due to the encoding, retrieval, or rehearsal of target events. For example, it might be that when friends are treated unfairly, we remember the injustice they experience because we think back to the original events time and again. Yet, when strangers are treated unfairly, we do not rehearse the unfair events as much. Not only would this provide a mechanism behind memory biases in recalling and judging the treatment received, it would also suggest a novel way in which injustice affects people over time. An alternative possibility, however, is that unfair experiences are stored differently in memory for friends than for strangers during the encoding phase. As people feel more strongly connected to friends than to strangers—due to stronger inclusion of others in the self (Aron et al., 1991)—it is plausible that people have a better eye for detail, experience more emotions, or simply pay more attention as an unfair event unfolds when it concerns a friend instead of a stranger. Such a difference in the mental resources that people spend during the encoding phase may then make their perception of an unfair event less vulnerable to memory decay in the case of a friend.

Finally, it would be interesting to explore moderators of the effects that we observe. Perhaps, highly intense injustice can override the effects that we find (Lind et al., 1998), such that self-relevance effects would not develop over time, but rather the other's (highly intense) injustice would impact our fairness evaluations as much in immediate observation as in retrospect. The phenomena of enduring survivor guilt and posttraumatic stress disorder speak to this possibility (Ozer, Best, Lipsey, & Weiss, 2003).

The present ideas have implications for both research and practical application. For instance, the insight that people's justice-based experiences are subject to memory biases may stimulate scholars to appreciate the fact that post-hoc descriptions of unfair events do not necessarily reflect what actually happened. This consideration may suggest that managers frequently need to search for additional—preferably more objective—information when they try to reconstruct the causes of employee-reported violations of justice standards in their organization. In addition, the present propositions may hold implications for evaluations of the reliability of testimonies given by eyewitnesses and victims in court trials. Such testimonies are typically memory based, and are characterized by perceptions that fundamental justice norms were violated. Although it is widely established that eyewitness testimonies are not necessarily very reliable in all circumstances (Wells & Loftus, 2003), our preliminary findings may add to this field of research by suggesting that people may even confuse their own and other's experiences when a close other was victimized, or when they are strongly oriented toward including others in their self-concept.

## Theoretical Implications

The temporal aspect in justice judgments has been largely ignored in theoretical accounts of organizational justice. To the best of our knowledge, only fairness heuristic theory has an explicit temporal aspect, which is that an employee's first fairness-related experience will set a standard that helps them determine how subsequent experiences should be evaluated (Van den Bos, Vermunt, & Wilke, 1997). For instance, fairness heuristic theory proposes that justice judgments are formed quickly in an early encounter with a superior, and then used as a mental shortcut to decide whether or not to trust powerful others at work. These ideas are reminiscent of more general knowledge on primacy effects, whereby first impressions are often used as a cognitive anchor to interpret subsequent events as they unfold. Our findings suggest an additional temporal aspect to theorizing about justice: that justice judgments are prone to memory biases. It thus seems that employees' first justice-based experience in an organization may serve as an interpretational framework for future events (Van den Bos et al., 1997), while at the same time being transformed through memory processes. These considerations illustrate the complex dynamics that are at play when people's present-day justice judgments are shaped by past events.

An interesting avenue for future research is to explore the effects of accountability of justice judgments over time. Accountability is known to make people process information more thoroughly, and thereby to help them avoid judgmental biases. Accountability manipulations typically involve making participants aware of the need to announce their judgments publicly or justify these judgments in front of an authority figure (Tetlock, 2002; Tetlock & Henik, 2004). Future research should investigate whether raising accountability of those who report on fair or unfair treatment at work may matter for judgments of recent versus more temporally distant experiences. We believe it will, because details of more recent experiences are more likely to be recalled and subjected to careful examination, enabling people to clearly distinguish what happened to whom (i.e., to others versus to self). In contrast, when experiences lie farther away in time details relating to them are more likely to be forgotten, making a more detailed and careful examination of them difficult, if not impossible.

For example, Ellen might remember it was unfair that her boss yelled once at a meeting, but she might forget what the meeting was about, where it took place, who was present, and even whether the boss yelled at her or at John, a person that Ellen identifies with. If directly following the event, Ellen was asked whether she and others were treated unfairly, Ellen should have been able to report that the boss yelled at John and not at her. However, at a later time Ellen may no longer be able to remember who (whether it was her or a friend) was shouted at. To the extent that she in this way blurs the line between her experience and a friend's experience, she can report having been treated unfairly *herself*. In such a case, holding Ellen accountable is unlikely to change her judgment because she is simply unable to recall details of an event that lies in the more distant past. Only for more recent events, when the effort to recall details is likely to be fruitful, should accountability lead to a person more accurately distinguishing between their own and another's experience. In fact, greater accountability in the reporting of recently experienced events should help reverse not only the effects of self-relevance, but also the effects of other memory biases, such as the self-serving bias and negativity, discussed earlier.

Importantly, biases are not the only manifestations of how memory affects judgment and behavior. Organizational justice researchers may benefit from exploring the implications and patterns of other memory-related phenomena, from the mere forgetting of fair and unfair events at work to the possibility of intrusive memories and false memories affecting perceptions of fairness and reactions to the experience of injustice.

## Methodological Implications

Our aim was to shed light on the temporal dimension of organizational justice judgments. Recognition of this temporal dimension is of importance, particularly given that contemporary measures of organizational justice typically refer to past events (e.g., Colquitt, 2001; Konovsky et al., 1987; Moorman, 1991). Most empirical work on organizational justice thus relies on participants' memory-based judgments, and we suggest that these judgments may differ from people's evaluations directly following a justice-based incident. Further research investigating *when* changes in justice judgments occur and what principles underlie such changes may help in the design of studies in the field that would more broadly and accurately capture the effects of fair and unfair treatment.

One reason that this area has received little attention to date might lie in methodological challenges. The study of how justice judgments evolve over time is difficult without the use of longitudinal research designs, such as the "friend or stranger" experiment we described, with their attendant difficulties. In the field study we demonstrate how cross-sectional designs can be adapted to study the effects of memory. Hopefully, organizational justice researchers can explore further approaches to conducting controlled and cost-efficient studies on time-related phenomena of relevance to the field.

Another reason might lie in the popularity of organization-centric rather than person-centric approaches to the study of organizational justice (Guo, Rupp, Weiss, & Trougakos, in press). As in the broader field of organizational behavior (Weiss & Rupp, 2011), often "the "individual" is treated as a collection of properties placed in a system" with little focus on the experience of that individual and on the role that memory plays in shaping individual experience.

## Concluding Remarks

In the present chapter we sought to illuminate the memory-based nature of many justice judgments. We believe that the insight that memory structurally alters people's justice judgments underscores the need to appreciate the subjective nature of such judgments, as they may easily deviate from the way that a specific event actually took place. The present propositions may contribute to the question of when and why do people differ substantially in how they experience the fairness of the same social event, providing the basis for negative emotions, disobedience, and conflict escalation.

## ACKNOWLEDGMENT

This research was funded by a grant of the Portuguese Foundation for Science and Technology-FCT with funds cofinanced by the state budget through the program PIDDAC.

## REFERENCES

Aron, A., Aron, E., Tudor, M., & Nelson, G. (1991). Close relationships as including other in the self. *Journal of Personality and Social Psychology, 60*, 241-253.

Bashshur, M., & Cojuharenco, I. (2009, August). When fair is unfair: Halo, negativity and uniqueness biases in justice perceptions over time. Paper presented at the annual meeting of the Academy of Management, Chicago, IL.

Brockner, J. (1990). Scope of justice in the workplace: How survivors react to coworker layoffs. *Journal of Social Issues, 46*, 95-106.

Brockner, J., & Greenberg, J. (1990). The impact of layoffs on survivors: An organizational justice analysis. In J. Carroll (Ed.), *Advances in applied social psychology and organizational settings* (pp. 45-75). Hillsdale, NJ: Erlbaum.

Brockner, J., Grover, S., Reed, T., DeWitt, R., & O'Malley, M. (1987). Survivors' reactions to layoffs: We get by with a little help for our friends. *Administrative Science Quarterly, 32*, 526-542.

Brockner, J., Konovsky, M., Cooper-Schneider, R., Folger, R., Martin, C., & Bies, R.J. (1994). The interactive effects of procedural justice and outcome negativity on the victims and survivors of job loss. *Academy of Management Journal, 37*, 397-409.

Cojuharenco, I., Patient, D., & Bashshur, M. (in press). Seeing the "forest" or the "trees" of organizational justice: Effects of temporal perspective on employee concerns about unfair treatment at work. *Organizational Behavior and Human Decision Processes*.

Colquitt, J. A. (2001). On the dimensionality of organizational justice: A construct validation of a measure. *Journal of Applied Psychology, 86*, 386-400. doi:10.1016/j.obhdp.2011.05.008

Cooley, C. H. (1902). *Human nature and social order.* New York, NY: Scribner's.

Goetz, J. L., Keltner, D., & Simon-Thomas, E. (2010). Compassion: An evolutionary analysis and empirical review. *Psychological Bulletin, 136*, 351-374.

Guo, J., Rupp, D. R., Trougakos, J., & Weiss, H. (in press). Organizational justice: A person-centric approach. *Research in Social Issues in Management*.

Ham, J., & Van den Bos, K. (2008). Not fair for me! The influence of personal relevance on social justice inferences. *Journal of Experimental Social Psychology, 44*, 699-705.

Hastie, R., & Park, B. (1986). The relationship between memory and judgment depends on whether the judgment is memory-based or on-line. *Psychological Review, 93*, 258-268.

Johnson, R., Selenta, C., & Lord, R. (2006). When organizational justice and the self-concept meet. *Organizational Behavior and Human Decision Processes, 99*, 175-201.

Konovsky, M. A., Folger, R., & Cropanzano, R. (1987). Relative effects of procedural and distributive justice on employee attitudes. *Representative Research in Social Psychology, 17*, 15-24.

Kuhnen, U., & Oyserman, D. (2002). Thinking about the self influences thinking in general: Cognitive consequences of salient self-concept. *Journal of Experimental Social Psychology, 38*, 492-499.

Liao, H., & Rupp, D. (2005). The impact of justice climate and justice orientation on work outcomes: A cross-level multifoci framework. *Journal of Applied Psychology, 90*, 242-256.

Libby, L. K., & Eibach, R. P. (2002). Looking back in time: Self-concept change and visual perspective in autobiographical memory. *Journal of Personality and Social Psychology, 82*, 167-179.

Liebrand, W. B. G., Messick, D. M., & Wolters, F. J. M. (1986). Why we are fairer than others: A cross-cultural replication and extension. *Journal of Experimental Social Psychology, 22*, 590-604.

Lind, E. A., Kray, L., & Thompson, L. (1998). The social construction of injustice: Fairness judgments in response to own and others' unfair treatment by authorities. *Organizational Behavior and Human Decision Processes, 75*, 1-22.

Loftus, E. F., & Palmer, J. C. (1974). Reconstruction of auto-mobile destruction: An example of the interaction between language and memory. *Journal of Verbal Learning and Verbal Behaviour, 13*, 585-589.

Markus, H., & Kitayama, S. (1991). Culture and the self: Implications for cognition, emotion, and motivation. *Psychological Review, 98*, 224-253.

Messick, D. M., Bloom, S., Boldizar, J., & Samuelson, C. D. (1985). Why we are fairer than others. *Journal of Experimental Social Psychology, 21*, 480-500.

Mitchell, T. R., & James, L. R. (2001). Building better theory: Time and the specification of when things happen. *Academy of Management Review, 26*, 530-547.

Moorman, R. H. (1991). Relationship between organizational justice and organizational citizenship behaviours: Do fairness perceptions influence employee citizenship? *Journal of Applied Psychology, 76*, 845-855.

Opotow, S. (1990). Moral exclusion and injustice: An introduction. *Journal of Social Issues, 46*, 1-20.

Ozer E. J., Best, S. R., Lipsey, T. L., & Weiss, D. S. (2003). Predictors of posttraumatic stress disorder and symptoms in adults: A meta-analysis. *Psychological Bulletin, 129*, 52-73.

Patient, D., & Skarlicki, D. (2010). Increasing interpersonal and informational justice when communicating negative news: The role of the manager's empathic concern and moral development. *Journal of Management, 36*, 555-578.

Reed, A., & Aquino, K. (2003). Moral identity and the circle of moral regard towards out-groups. *Journal of Personality and Social Psychology, 84*, 1270-1286.

Rogers, T. B., Kuiper, N. A., & Kirker, W. S. (1977). Self-reference and the encoding of personal information. *Journal of Personality and Social Psychology, 35*, 677-688.

Ross, M. (1989). Relation of implicit theories to the construction of personal histories. *Psychological Review, 96*, 341-357.

Ross, M., & Sicoly, F. (1979). Egocentric biases in availability and attribution. *Journal of Personality and Social Psychology, 37*, 322-336.

Sedikides, C., & Brewer, M.B. (2001). *Individual self, relational self, collective self.* Philadelphia, PA: Psychology Press.

Schacter, D. L. (1999). The seven sins of memory: Insights from psychology and cognitive neuroscience. *American Psychologist, 54*, 182-203.

Schacter, D. (2001). *The seven sins of memory: How the mind forgets and remembers.* Boston, MA: Houghton Mifflin.

Schmitt, M., Gollwitzer, M., Maes, J., & Arbach, D. (2005). Justice sensitivity: Assessment and location in the personality space. *European Journal of Psychological Assessment, 21*, 202-211.

Skarlicki, D. P., Ellard, J. H., & Kelln, B. R. C. (1998). Third-party perceptions of a layoff: Procedural, derogation, and retributive aspects of justice. *Journal of Applied Psychology, 83*, 119-127.

Skarlicki, D. P., & Kulik, C. (2005). Third party reactions to employee mistreatment: A justice perspective. In B. Staw & R. Kramer (Eds.) *Research in organizational behavior* (Vol. 26, pp.183-230). New York, NY: Elsevier.

Skitka, L. (2003). Of different minds: An accessible identity model of justice reasoning. *Personality and Social Psychology Review, 7*, 286-297.

Skowronski, J., & Carlston, D. (1987). Social judgment and social memory: the role of cue diagnosticity in negativity, positivity, and extremity biases. *Journal of Personality and Social Psychology, 52*, 689-699.

Tetlock, P. E. (2002). Social-functionalist frameworks for judgment and choice: The intuitive politician, theologian, and prosecutor. *Psychological Review, 109*, 451-472.

Tetlock, P. E., & Henik, E. (2004). Accountability. In N. Nicholson, P. Audia, & M. Pillutla (Eds.). *Blackwell encyclopedic dictionary of organizational behavior.* Cambridge, MA: Blackwell.

Van den Bos, K., Vermunt, R., & Wilke, H. A. M. (1997). Procedural and distributive justice: What is fair depends more on what comes first than on what comes next. *Journal of Personality and Social Psychology, 72*, 95-104.

Wagenaar, W. (1986). My memory: A study of autobiographical memory over six years. *Cognitive Psychology, 18*, 225-252.

Weiss, H., & Rupp, D. E. (2011). Envisioning person-centric work psychology. *Industrial and Organizational Psychology: Perspectives on Science and Practice, 4*, 138-143.

Wells, G. L., & Loftus, E. F. (2003). Eyewitness memory for people and events. In A. M. Goldstein (Ed.), *Handbook of psychology: Forensic psychology* (Vol. 11, pp. 149-160). New York, NY: John Wiley.

CHAPTER 3

# MOVING BEYOND (IN)JUSTICE PERCEPTIONS

## Examining the Roles of Experience and Intensity

**Laurie J. Barclay and David B. Whiteside**

In this chapter, we argue that the emphasis on *perceptions* of (in)justice in contemporary research has limited our ability to fully understand individuals' experience of and reactions to (in)justice. In order to capture the richness of individuals' experiences, we argue that justice scholars should consider a broader approach that includes an examination of the dynamic interplay between perceptions, affect, and beliefs. We also propose a new construct that can help shed light on the relationship between (in)justice experiences and employee reactions. Termed *(in)justice intensity*, this construct is defined as the strength or force with which (in)justice is experienced. We identify factors that contribute to this construct in an exploratory qualitative study. We argue that (in)justice intensity provides additional insight into when and why (un)fairness exerts an impact. We close the chapter by suggesting new directions that emerge when this broader approach is adopted.

Organizational justice has been the focus of an extensive amount of research over the past 30 years. During this time, the study of organiza-

*Emerging Perspectives on Organizational Justice and Ethics*
pp. 49–74

tional justice has been dominated by employee *perceptions* of (in)justice. Central research issues have included identifying what is being appraised, how it is being appraised, under what circumstances appraisals are likely to occur, and how these appraisals are related to employee attitudes and behaviors (e.g., Colquitt, Conlon, Wesson, Porter, & Ng, 2001; Cropanzano, Byrne, Bobocel, & Rupp, 2001). This approach has been ingrained in the literature with the development and pervasive use of standardized scales, which focus on specific sets of fairness criteria (e.g., Colquitt, 2001).

Although this approach has generated tremendous insights, a number of interesting findings have emerged which suggest that simply studying *perceptions* may be insufficient. First, research has demonstrated that the same level of event (in)justice can produce different responses in different circumstances (Cropanzano et al., 2001). That is, similar justice perceptions can produce a wide range of responses both *between* victims (i.e., two different coworkers experiencing the same event) and *within* victims (i.e., the same employee experiencing the same injustice at two different time periods). This suggests that perceptions are not the only consideration that impacts responses to (un)fairness. Second, justice scholars have argued that rather than focusing on perceptions of specific justice dimensions, individuals often focus on and react to their overall sense or experience of (in)justice (Ambrose & Arnaud, 2005; Ambrose & Schminke, 2009; Greenberg, 2001; Lind, 2001; Shapiro, 2001). Although some scholars have fruitfully responded to this critique by examining overall justice perceptions (e.g., Ambrose & Schminke, 2009), we propose that the justice literature can reap significant benefits by further broadening our approach.

The objectives of this paper are two-fold. First, we argue for a broader and more comprehensive conceptualization of the (in)justice experience.[1] Drawing on other literatures, we argue that there are at least three integral components inherent in the experience of (in)justice—perceptions, affect, and beliefs. While empirical justice research has tended to focus on the perceptual, and to a lesser extent, belief-based aspects of justice, affect has been underemphasized and lacked systematic study (Breugelmans & De Cremer, 2007; Weiss, Suckow, & Cropanzano, 1999). As a result, we place particular emphasis on the integral role of affect in the (in)justice experience. In contrast to previous research, which has primarily examined the role of affect as a precursor or as an outcome to justice perceptions, we argue that affect is also a defining characteristic of the experience of (in)justice. Taken together, we argue that *all three* components (i.e. perceptions, affect, and beliefs) are needed in order to understand the overall experience of (in)justice.

Second, we introduce the construct *(in)justice intensity*, defined as the overall strength or force with which (in)justice is experienced. We argue

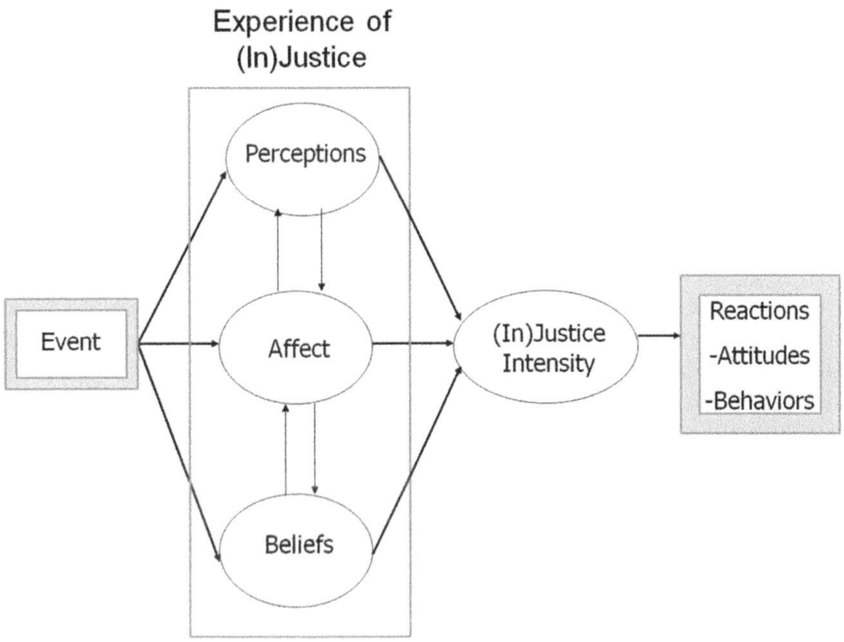


Figure 3.1. The relationship between events, the experience of (in)justice, intensity, and reactions.

that this construct can help explain why the *experience* of (in)justice impacts employee attitudes and behaviors (see Figure 3.1). Specifically, we propose that individuals can respond to the same (in)justice event differently because the intensity of the overall experience can vary across individuals and across time, even when perceptions of unfairness are the same. In order to further understand (in)justice intensity, we conduct an exploratory qualitative study to help identify factors that contribute to intensity.

## MOVING BEYOND PERCEPTIONS: UNDERSTANDING (IN)JUSTICE AS AN EXPERIENCE

Although initial justice research focused on more holistic assessments of justice experiences (e.g., I feel unfairly treated), contemporary empirical research has tended to focus on justice as a cognitive process in which individuals assess whether an outcome (i.e., distributive justice), procedure (i.e., procedural justice), or interpersonal treatment (i.e., interactional justice) followed a fairness rule (e.g., equity, equality, or need), met a justice-related criterion (e.g., consistency, accuracy, lack of bias), or adhered to a moral standard (e.g., human dignity). The creation and pervasive use of standardized scales that focus on specific sets of fairness criteria has further solidified the treatment of justice as a "cold" cognitive appraisal (i.e., an appraisal derived from the careful weighing of information and that is essentially devoid of emotion; Abelson, 1963; Kunda, 1999). As an example, consider commonly used items that assess distributive (e.g., Does your outcome reflect the effort you have put into your work?), procedural (e.g., Have the procedures used to determine your outcome been applied consistently?), and interactional justice (Has your supervisor treated you with respect?) (cf. Colquitt, 2001). These measures shed light on criteria that can be used in forming justice perceptions; however, they lack the capacity to tap into how individuals actually *experience* (un)fairness.

In an effort to capture the richness and depth of individuals' justice experiences, several justice scholars have suggested that overall justice judgments should be considered. Specifically, these researchers have argued that overall justice judgments are important because (a) individuals have a tendency to make holistic judgments when forming impressions of fairness (Greenberg, 2001), (b) individuals' reactions tend to be driven by an overall sense of fairness (Lind, 2001; Shapiro, 2001), and (c) these judgments are likely to have a more proximal influence on outcomes than individual justice dimensions (Ambrose & Arnuad, 2005; Ambrose & Schminke, 2009). Building on this line of reasoning, Ambrose and Schminke (2009) recently developed a measure of "overall justice judgments" that examines global assessments of fairness (e.g., Overall, I'm treated fairly by this organization). The authors found that these judgments mediate the relationship between judgments about the specific justice dimensions (e.g., distributive, procedural, and interactional) and employee attitudes and behaviors. Although examining overall justice judgments can provide a more holistic view of fairness than examining the specific justice dimensions, these judgments are still primarily conceptualized as "cold" cognitive appraisals. The items, for example, focus on cognitive evaluations such as: "In general, I can count on this organization to be fair" and "For the most part, this organization treats its employees fairly."

Although these cold cognitive processes are informative, they are limited in at least two ways. First, research has demonstrated that affect can impact judgments during the appraisal process (van den Bos, 2007). Specifically, justice judgments are often formed through a "hot cognitive process" in which both cognitive and affective factors play a role in forming the overall judgment (van den Bos, 2003, 2007). Thus, focusing on cold cognitive processes fails to provide a comprehensive account of how justice judgments are formed. Second, employees who experience justice, and in particular injustice, often describe an emotionally laden experience (Bies & Tripp, 2002). In other words, the cognitive aspects of the justice appraisal do not fully represent how individuals *experience* (in)justice and the role of affect should be considered.

In addition to cognitive and affective factors, research in other domains suggests that it can be fruitful to examine the role of beliefs in the formation of global assessments or judgments. Weiss (2002), for example, argued that at least three components should be considered when studying global assessments: cognition (i.e., the evaluative judgment made with regard to a target or an event), affect (i.e., moods, discrete emotions), and beliefs (i.e., propositional statements regarding an object). Beliefs are important because they can activate schemas and impact individuals' interpretations of situations and their affective responses (Weiss, 2002). Ultimately, we argue that all three components are important to study since they are conceptually distinct with different causes and consequences (Eagly & Chaiken, 1993) and each component makes a meaningful contribution to the *experience* of (in)justice.

Taken together, we argue that by focusing on perceptions, organizational justice research has underemphasized two key aspects of the experience of (in)justice—affect and beliefs. To address this gap, we propose that a broader and more comprehensive approach that includes all three components is needed in order to capture the richness of individuals' experiences. In the following subsections, we briefly overview the roles of beliefs and affect in the experience of (in)justice.

## Beliefs

Beliefs are critical to individuals' interpretations and experiences of events (Lazarus, 1991). Regardless of whether beliefs arise from personal or culturally-shared experiences, beliefs can reflect individuals' evaluations of themselves, their worldviews, and their expectations for the future (Tomaka & Blascovich, 1994). Moreover, beliefs can impact both cognitions and affect (Lazarus, 1991; Lazarus & Folkman, 1984). With respect to cognitions, beliefs can focus the individual on salient aspects of the situation, as well as, serve as a lens through which the situation is interpreted. With respect to affect, beliefs can impact affective reactions, as well as, how affective factors influence cognitive appraisal processes and coping responses. For example, an individual who believes that the world is fair and people get what they deserve is likely to interpret and affectively experience an unfair event (e.g., failure to receive a promotion) differently than someone who does not hold this belief (Lerner, 1980; Tomaka & Blascovich, 1994). Moreover, these beliefs will also impact how individuals cope with the event in both the short and long term (Lazarus, 1991). For example, belief in a just world has been shown to impact the types of behavioral and cognitive coping mechanisms used by victims of injustice (Lerner, 1980).

Although justice researchers have examined the role of beliefs, they are typically not studied as part of justice judgments or the experience of (in)justice. Given the potential impact of beliefs on cognitions and affect, failure to consider the role of beliefs undoubtedly results in an incomplete picture of the individual's experience and how they will react to the (in)justice.

## Affect

Within the justice literature, affect has primarily been conceptualized as either an antecedent or an outcome of justice perceptions (see Cohen-Charash & Byrne, 2008 for an extensive review of these research streams). When viewed as an antecedent, researchers have largely emphasized an "affect-as-information" model, which implies that affect (typically mood) impacts justice perceptions by influencing individuals' motivation to scrutinize information and by serving as heuristic cues (Schwarz, 1990; Schwarz & Clore, 1983). Mood can also influence the types of justice criteria individuals prefer. For instance, Sinclair and Mark (1991) found that individuals are more likely to endorse egalitarian preferences and less likely to endorse equity preferences when they are in a positive mood than when they are in a negative mood.

While research has explored affect as an antecedent to justice perceptions, the majority of research examining affect and justice has focused on affect (typically discrete emotions) as an outcome of justice perceptions (Cohen-Charash & Byrne, 2008; Greenberg & Ganegoda, 2007). A variety of theories have been used to understand this relationship, including appraisal theories (e.g., Lazarus, 1991), affective events theory (Weiss & Cropanzano, 1996), fairness theory (Folger & Cropanzano, 1998, 2001), and deontic justice (Folger, 2001). With the exception of deontic models, these theories typically suggest that individuals cognitively appraise an event and then experience an emotional reaction based on this appraisal (i.e., cognition comes first and emotion arises from the cognition). In contrast, deontic models suggest that moral emotions can arise from perceptions but this approach also suggests that emotional reactions (e.g., moral outrage, righteous indignation) can sometimes accompany perceptions of injustice (Folger, 2001).

Overall, research has supported the role of affect as a cause and a consequence of justice perceptions. However, less is known about the role of affect *during* the appraisal process (De Cremer, 2007). As noted above, we argue that affect is important for at least two reasons. First, affect is an essential component of the (in)justice experience (Bies & Tripp, 2002). Second, justice judgments are often formed through a "hot-cognitive process" in which there is a dynamic interplay between cognition and affect (van den Bos, 2007). With respect to the first point, Bies and Tripp (2002, p. 211) compellingly argued that (in)justice is "not just a judgment; it also is an emotional and physiological experience." Using qualitative data that delved into individuals' experiences, these authors found that emotions permeate the experience of injustice, with individuals often reporting strong visceral responses, a deep sense of violation, as well as feelings of helplessness, terror, and obsession. In other words, affect was a core aspect of the experience of injustice. Rather than focusing on specific sets of criteria that had or had not been violated, individuals expressed a deeper experience that impacted them at a fundamental level. Thus, exploring the "emotional terrain" of injustice would seem critical for understanding individuals' experiences of (in)justice.

With respect to the second point, van den Bos (2007) challenged the notion that individuals engage in a careful evaluation of relevant information in order to form a justice judgment. Instead, he argued that individuals sometimes rely on "gut reactions" and make snap judgments. Thus, rather than being a "cold-cognitive process" (e.g., Abelson, 1963; Kunda, 1999), justice judgments are formed through a "hot-cognitive process" in which cognition and affect work together (van den Bos, 2007). Moreover, emotions are likely to play a particularly influential role in justice judgments under conditions of uncertainty (van den Bos, 2003, 2007). Specifically, individuals may rely on the emotions they experience during a violation to determine whether something is (un)fair when they lack appropriate information to make justice judgments (van den Bos, 2007).

Barsky and colleagues extended this argument by suggesting that affect and justice perceptions interact in a reciprocal and dynamic manner (Barsky & Kaplan, 2007; Barsky, Kaplan, & Beal, 2011). Specifically, Barsky and Kaplan (2007, p. 287) argued that justice perceptions are the result of an "interplay between fundamental cognitive and social-information processes (i.e., memory, schemata) and phenomenological states of feeling" (Barsky & Kaplan, 2007, p. 287). Moreover, when viewed as an accompaniment to justice perceptions, Barsky et al. (2011) suggested that affect is intertwined in the appraisal of justice events such that affect influences the generation of justice appraisals and connects justice perceptions across multiple situations to create aggregate justice perceptions of entities.

Building on these findings, we argue that focusing on perceptions as a cold cognitive appraisal is insufficient since it does not reflect how individuals experience (in)justice, nor does it reflect how affect can infuse perceptions and play a central role in how justice judgments are formed. In other words, rather than viewing affect solely as a cause or a consequence of justice, we propose that affect should also be viewed alongside perceptions and beliefs as an integral part of the (in)justice experience.

## Bringing It All Together: Moving Toward (In)Justice as an Experience

Taken together, we argue that justice researchers should adopt a broader and more comprehensive approach to studying (in)justice by delving into how individuals *experience* (in)justice rather than focusing solely on *perceptions*. Moreover, we propose that the experience of (in)justice is likely to include a dynamic interplay between cognitions, affect, and beliefs. By adopting this experience-based approach, we argue that researchers will be better able to tap into the depth and richness of how individuals are interpreting and experiencing (in)justice as well as understand when and why employees are likely to react to (in)justice.

> ***Proposition 1:*** Experiences of (in)justice will be more predictive of employee reactions to (in)justice than perceptions of (in)justice.

In addition to providing a more comprehensive conceptualization of justice, this approach also raises a number of new research questions. Sample questions that might be explored include: How do perceptions, affect, and beliefs combine to form the overall (in)justice experience? Does this differ for fairness versus unfairness? What individual and situational factors moderate the relationships between these components? When are beliefs particularly likely to impact the cognitive and/or affective elements of a justice judgment and does this differ from other types of judgments? These are only a few of the questions that might be raised by adopting this approach; many more opportunities exist to expand our understanding of (in)justice.

As noted above, a central objective of this chapter is to further understand how and why the same level of event (in)justice can produce different responses in different circumstances. An important step toward this end is to explore (in)justice as an "experience" rather than simply as a perception. In the next section, we suggest that it is also important to explore when and why an experience of (in)justice relates to attitudinal and behavioral outcomes. Further to this end, we introduce the concept of *(in)justice intensity* and propose that this construct can help explain why experiences of (in)justice are likely to impact employee reactions.

## (IN)JUSTICE INTENSITY: A DRIVING FORCE OF EMPLOYEE REACTIONS

One of the goals of justice research is to understand how justice shapes individuals' attitudes and behaviors. Although examining individuals' judgments and experiences can shed light on attitudinal and behavioral reactions, other literatures have demonstrated that it can also be fruitful to explore the strength of these assessments. Within the emotions literature, for example, affect can vary in the degree of arousal and/or intensity experienced by the individual, which can impact other reactions (e.g., Feldman, 1995; Larsen & Diener, 1987). Within the attitudes literature, research has demonstrated that it is important to consider the strength of an attitude (Raden, 1985). Specifically, early research exploring the attitude-behavior relationship found that the predictive ability of attitudes was rather limited. Further investigation revealed that not all attitudes are alike; whereas some attitudes are characterized as strong (i.e., firmly crystallized with consequential outcomes), others are characterized as weak (i.e., flexible and relatively inconsequential) (Raden, 1985). Strong attitudes have been argued to be persistent over time, resistant to change, and have a strong impact on information processes as well as behaviors (Krosnick & Petty, 1995). This research suggests that the predictive ability of attitudes rests in the *strength* of the attitude, which can be differentiated from attitude direction (Krosnick, Boninger, Chuang, Berent, & Carnot, 1993). Thus, in order to understand when attitudes will have an impact, the strength of the attitude must also be considered (Krosnick & Abelson, 1992).

Analogous to the way attitudes have strength and affect has arousal or intensity, we argue that experiences of (in)justice can vary in intensity. We define *(in)justice intensity* as the strength or force with which an (in)justice is experienced. We propose that (in)justice intensity represents a motivational state in which individuals attempt to process what an experience of (in)justice means to them and experience driving forces geared toward helping them manage their environment (e.g., by withdrawing, escaping, or attacking in the case of defensive states, or promoting and engaging with the environment in the case of appetitive states; Lang, Bradley, & Cuthbert, 1997). We contend that intensity plays a more proximal role in predicting attitudinal and behavioral outcomes than experiences of (in)justice. In other words, we argue that (in)justice intensity captures the vibrancy of an experience of (in)justice and provides a unifying explanation for *why* experiences of (in)justice result in attitudinal and behavioral reactions.

## EXPLORING INTENSITY: A PRELIMINARY QUALITATIVE STUDY

In order to understand the nature of intensity within the context of justice, we conducted an exploratory study that delved into individuals' experiences of injustice. Although the concept of intensity is likely to be relevant for experiences of fairness and unfairness, we focused only on intensity related to unfairness. Bies and Tripp (2002) noted that focusing on injustice can often yield insights into the dynamics of justice since this is often how people conceptualize their experiences.

Data was collected using three different samples: (1) full-time working adults ($N$ = 589) in the United States, (2) undergraduate students ($N$ = 241) at an Eastern Canadian university and (3) undergraduate students ($N$ = 85) at a Western Canadian university. We utilized the critical incident technique (Flanagan, 1954) with all of the samples. Each participant was instructed to think about a time when they experienced unfairness at work and then answer a series of questions about the nature of the violation, why they felt unfairly treated, how they experienced the violation, and what factors they believed impacted the relative intensity of the experience.

Content coding of this data revealed a number of factors that can contribute to intensity. Interestingly, several of the factors relate to the attitude strength dimensions. Within the attitudes literature, at least ten different dimensions related to attitude strength including *attitude extremity, importance, intensity, accessibility, certainty, direct experience, interest in relevant information, knowledge, latitudes of rejection/noncommitment*, and *affective-cognitive consistency* (cf. Krosnick et al., 1993). We found evidence that (in)justice intensity is also characterized by several of these factors including *extremity, importance, intensity, accessibility, certainty*, and *direct experience*.[2] We also identified factors that were unique to injustice intensity including *ongoing, isolation/pervasiveness*, and *powerlessness*. Drawing upon the results from our qualitative study and supplementing with findings from the justice literature, we overview each of the identified factors and discuss similarities/differences between (in)justice intensity and attitude strength. Table 3.1 presents a summary of these factors.

### Extremity

Within the attitude strength literature, attitude extremity refers to the extent to which an attitude deviates from neutrality on an evaluative continuum that ranges from strongly positive to strongly negative (Abelson, 1995; Judd & Johnson, 1981). Similar to attitude strength extremity, the degree to which individuals feel that their treatment is either extremely

**Table 3.1. Results of Exploratory Study Identifying Factors That Contribute to (In)Justice Intensity**

| *Factor* | *Definition* |
|---|---|
| Extremity | Degree to which the experience of (in)justice is particularly fair or unfair (i.e., the degree it deviates from neutrality on an evaluative continuum that ranges from strongly positive to strongly negative). |
| Importance | The subjective significance that individuals attach to a given experience. |
| Emotional intensity | The relative breadth, depth, and intensity of the emotional reactions generated as a *consequence* of experiencing (in)justice. |
| Accessibility | The extent to which an injustice is retrievable from memory, including the degree to which individuals ruminate on the experience and/or feel like the experience psychologically weighs on them or dominates their thoughts. |
| Certainty | The degree to which individuals felt confident that an (in)justice had occurred. |
| Direct experience | The extent to which an individual has had personal contact with similar experiences or issues with similar themes (e.g., from childhood or personal lives). |
| Ongoing | The degree to which an individual feels like the experience is enduring. |
| Isolation/pervasiveness | Relates to how the (in)justice was experienced not only by the individual but within the broader context (e.g., whether the injustice was only experienced by the individual or by others). |
| Powerlessness | Relates to the degree that individuals feel that they have the ability to impact or change the situation. |

fair or extremely unfair is likely to contribute to intensity. Gilliland (2008), for example, argued that experiencing (un)fairness can be highly influential in shaping behavioral reactions when it is extremely fair or extremely unfair. This was also supported by our participants, who indicated that extreme unfairness made the experience seem more intense.

## Importance

Within the context of attitude strength, importance relates to the subjective significance that individuals attach to a given attitude and/or the degree to which an individual is personally invested in a given attitude (Boninger, Krosnick, Berent, & Fabrigar, 1995). Importance is also noteworthy for (in)justice intensity. Within our study, participants indicated that intensity was increased to the degree that the injustice was highly salient and/or the experience had significant consequences for them. However, it is imperative to distinguish how importance related to intensity differs from the concepts of valence or severity, which have been shown to impact perceptions of (in)justice.

Within our data, deservingness, attributions of blame, and valence were frequently mentioned as factors that enhanced perceptions of injustice *and* intensity. Ample research has demonstrated that perceptions of injustice can be enhanced when individuals feel that the injustice was undeserved (e.g., Deutsch, 1985; Feather, 1999), someone is to blame (e.g., Folger & Cropanzano, 2001), and that the injustice is related to something that they cared deeply about (Greenberg, 1994). However, these factors can also relate to intensity because they have broader repercussions for the individual. Once individuals have made the overall judgment that they have been unfairly treated, these factors can impact how they manage their experience of injustice.

For example, if someone else is to blame for the injustice, individuals will perceive that they are unfairly treated but they will also need to understand and assess how this injustice impacts themselves (e.g., manage identity and self-worth concerns and consider whether they need to reassess how they view themselves) as well as their relationships with the transgressor(s) and others who have may have witnessed the violation (e.g., consider how this violation will impact or alter these relationships moving forward). Moreover, they must manage the ramifications of experiencing this injustice if it spills over into other domains, such as their family or personal life (Judge & Colquitt, 2004). In other words, these factors enhance intensity by increasing uncertainty and requiring individuals to devote cognitive and emotional resources toward managing the situation, including making sense of how the situation impacts their broader experiences and identifying ways to cope with the situation and the ramifications that can occur across multiple domains (e.g., work and personal life). Taken together, this suggests that intensity can be enhanced when the violation has ramifications for the individual that go beyond the violation itself.

## Emotional Intensity

Within the context of attitude strength, intensity refers to the strength of the emotional reaction provoked by the event and is often operationalized by how strongly individuals felt about an issue (Cantril, 1944; Stouffer et al., 1950). Within the context of (in)justice, our results indicated that intensity reflected the breadth, depth, and intensity of the emotional reactions generated as a *consequence* or *outcome* of experiencing (in)justice. It is important here to distinguish between affect that is a part of the experience of (in)justice and affect that results from the justice judgment. As noted above, affect is important within experiences of (in)justice because it has a dynamic interplay with cognition and beliefs to form justice judgments and characterizes the experience of (in)justice. Affect, however, is not limited to the initial precipitating event or experience. Frijda (1993), for example, argued that individuals often experience emotional episodes, in which they remain in a heightened level of arousal and have a series of emotional transactions with the environment. Within these episodes, individuals can experience a variety of emotions, which are typically organized around a theme. For example, when an individual experiences an emotional episode organized around the theme of grief, this episode will likely endure for a significant period of time beyond the initial precipitating event. During this time, individuals may feel a variety of other emotions that are related to the overall experience of grief (e.g., sadness, anger, guilt).

Within our study, many features of emotional episodes were apparent. For example, participants described being consumed with a broad range of emotions including anger, disappointment, humiliation, shame, and embarrassment. Moreover, these emotions were often deeply felt and persisted for a meaningful period of time. These emotions also had significant implications. For example, the emotions of humiliation and shame led some individuals to feel that they had lost a significant amount of self-worth as a result of the experience. Notably, many participants mentioned a "sense of injustice" that was pervasive and deeply experienced.

## Accessibility

Within the context of the attitude strength literature, accessibility refers to the extent to which an attitude object and its evaluation can be retrieved from memory (Fazio, 1986). This might include how often individuals thought about an issue or the frequency with which the issue arose (e.g., in conversations with others) (Krosnick et al., 1993). Within the context of injustice, our participants discussed accessibility in terms of the degree to which they ruminated on the experience and/or felt like the experience would not dissipate. Specifically, our results indicated that intensity increases when individuals ruminate about their experiences, particularly when they engaged in anger-focused rumination. This type of rumination is often characterized by the activation of past memories, the amplification of emotional intensity and duration, and the instigation of counterfactual processes (Sukhodolsky, Golub, & Cromwell, 2001). By engaging in anger-focused rumination, individuals can feel that the experience of injustice "weighs" on them and dominates their thoughts.

Additionally, individuals experienced an injustice as intense when they were unable to make sense of the situation or understand why it occurred. Research has demonstrated that the negative effects or intensity of an experience can dissipate when individuals form meaning of an event and/or integrate it into their broader experiences (Rimé, Finkenauer, Luminet, Zech, & Philippot, 1998). Failure to make sense of the situation, however, can lead individuals to cognitively revisit and reappraise the event in an attempt to find meaning. Moreover, when individuals lack understanding of an event, they can fail to habituate or develop strategies to effectively manage the situation, which can increase anticipation or fear of a reoccurrence. In other words, individuals can feel like the event continues to psychologically weigh on them and that the event is highly accessible in memory (i.e., it frequently comes to mind and is easily retrieved from memory). Taken together, rumination and failure to make sense of the situation can increase the intensity of the experience.

## Certainty

Within the attitude strength literature, certainty reflects the degree to which individuals feel confident or sure about their position on an issue (Budd, 1986; Gross, Holtz, & Miller, 1995). This is often operationalized as the degree to which individuals believed that they were "right" or had a firm opinion related to the attitude object (e.g., Krosnick et al., 1993). Within the context of injustice, our participants indicated that intensity was heightened to the degree that individuals felt certain that an injustice had occurred. In these instances, individuals had no doubt that what they experienced was unfair and would be judged by others to be unfair as well. Said differently, in contrast to the typical approach to justice in which fairness is viewed as being subjective and "in the eye of the beholder", individuals believed that the injustice was so blatantly unfair that it took on an objective quality in which no one would dispute the unfairness of their treatment.

## Direct Experience

Direct experience involves the extent to which an individual has had contact or personal experience with an object (Regan & Fazio, 1977).

Within the context of (in)justice, we found evidence that an individual's personal history can increase intensity in at least two different ways. First, some individuals indicated that unfairness can raise or re-open other issues related to their past, or issues that are impacting them in other domains (e.g., issues related to their childhood or other aspects of their personal life). In some cases, an injustice that appeared relatively minor on the surface was experienced intensely because it tapped into the individual's history and the "baggage" that accompanied these previous experiences. In other words, the experience had a depth or gravity that went beyond the experience at hand.

Second, some individuals indicated that injustice can be experienced more intensely when they did *not* have prior experience with similar transgressions. In these instances, lack of personal experience contributes to intensity because individuals did not understand what was happening or why. Additionally, these victims often perceived that they lacked the appropriate resources and strategies necessary to cope with the experience (see above discussion on rumination). Overall, individuals indicated that their personal histories and previous experiences were strongly associated with (in)justice intensity.

## Ongoing

Ongoing relates to the degree that the individual felt that the experience was enduring or unending. Participants indicated that injustice is more intense when it is experienced across a range of situations or as a long-term issue. For example, when the unfairness is constant, persistent, left uncorrected, or poorly dealt with (i.e., their manager ignores or avoids the issue or alienates the victim) it can increase the intensity of the experience. Intensity can be enhanced for a variety of reasons. For example, victims may begin to feel that the unfairness will never be resolved or dealt with appropriately, which can make them unsure of whether they have the resources needed to cope with the unfairness in the long-term. Individuals may also feel like the current injustice is simply a continuation of previous injustices or that it is setting the stage for future injustices. This can increase feelings of helplessness and make individuals feel like they are fighting a losing battle. Although this factor is likely related to direct experience in that the presence of multiple injustices can raise deeper issues, it is also distinct because it focuses on individuals' ability to manage these experiences moving forward. In other words, it focuses on individuals coping ability and whether they need to be continually vigilant and prepared to deal with unfairness.

### Isolation/Pervasiveness

Isolation/pervasiveness relates to how the injustice was experienced not only by the individual but also within the broader context. Specifically, some individuals indicated that the intensity of the experience was increased when they felt singled out by the injustice experience (i.e., intensity was enhanced because they felt like they were suffering alone). In contrast, other individuals indicated that the intensity of the experience was increased because *many* of their colleagues were also experiencing the unfairness (i.e., the unfairness was insidious and pervasive across the group). In both instances, individuals may feel that they lack the ability to cope with the situation. In the former, individuals may feel like they lack support whereas in the latter instance, they may feel that they incapable of effecting change since the injustice is so pervasive. This is likely related to the next dimension, powerlessness.

### Powerlessness

Participants indicated that powerlessness contributed to intensity, particularly when individuals felt that they lacked the power to change the situation, confront the aggressor, or withdraw from the situation. In these cases, participants often noted that they had to protect themselves but that there was a severe lack of support within the system (e.g., the organization did not have the policies in place to help them deal with the situation) or among their colleagues (e.g., no one else wanted to "stick their neck out").

## BRINGING IT ALL TOGETHER: UNDERSTANDING INTENSITY AND OPENING NEW RESEARCH AVENUES

Drawing upon an exploratory qualitative study and complementing these results with findings from the justice literature, we identified a variety of situational and individual difference factors that can contribute to intensity including extremity, importance, emotional intensity, accessibility, certainty, direct experience, ongoing, isolation/pervasiveness, and powerlessness. By integrating situational and individual difference variables into a unifying construct, we argue that (in)justice intensity provides a coherent explanation that can further our understanding of why experiences of (in)justice can impact employees' attitudes and behaviors. That is, (in)justice intensity can shed light on why reactions to the same (in)justice event can vary across individuals and within individuals over time.

Taken together, we propose that (in)justice intensity is a more proximal driver of attitudinal and behavioral outcomes than experiences of (in)justice.

> ***Proposition 2:*** (In)justice intensity mediates the relationship between experiences of (in)justice and employee attitudinal as well as behavioral outcomes.

In addition to the advantages discussed above, the notion of intensity also creates exciting new opportunities for justice researchers. Below, we briefly discuss two of these opportunities: (a) the implications of intensity for health and buffering effects and (b) increasing the effectiveness of recovery attempts by focusing on reducing injustice intensity.

## The Implications of (In)Justice Intensity for Health and Buffering Effects

Throughout the chapter, we focused on attitudinal and behavioral reactions. However, (in)justice intensity may also be critical for understanding outcomes that are particularly important to employees (e.g., physical and psychological health). Research has demonstrated that experiencing injustice can profoundly impact individuals long after the violation has occurred. Some individuals, for example, may ruminate about the injustice for years (Matthews, 1988), whereas others may feel the symbolic impact of an injustice for the remainder of their life (Hansson, Jones, & Fletcher, 1990). Given these pervasive effects, it is not surprising that experiencing unfairness has been associated with long-term health consequences, including psychiatric disorders (Kivimaki, Elovainio, Vahtera, & Ferrie, 2003; Kivimaki, Elovainio, Vahtera, Virtanen, & Stansfeld, 2003) and coronary heart disease (Kivimaki et al., 2005).

We argue that (in)justice intensity can help explain why experiences of (in)justice can also have such persistent and long-lasting health implications. Within the context of injustice, intensity can consume a significant amount of psychological energy as individuals try to manage the uncertainty raised by an experience and make sense of the incident within the context of their broader life experiences. This can place a burden on individuals' cognitive and emotional resources, which in turn can significantly impact their psychological health (Pennebaker, 1997).

> ***Proposition 3:*** (In)justice intensity mediates the relationship between experiences of (in)justice and physical as well as psychological health outcomes.

Although we have focused on intensity associated with injustices, we argued above that intensity is also associated with fair experiences. When individuals experience an intense sense of fairness, it is likely to have a number of beneficial effects. Specifically, we propose that these experiences may help buffer individuals from the detrimental consequences associated with future negative events. Research in the emotions literature, for instance, has demonstrated that positive emotions and experiences can help individuals find meaning in and rebound from stressful encounters (e.g., Tugade & Fredrickson, 2004). We suggest that justice intensity can build individuals' coping resources and generate positive emotions, which can make it easier for them to manage future stressful encounters.

> ***Proposition 4:*** Individuals who have experienced an intensely fair experience will be better able to cope with an unfair event than individuals who have not experienced an intensely fair experience.

## Recovering From Injustice: Targeting Intensity Rather Than Perceptions

Injustice intensity might also be particularly important in helping individuals recover from injustice. Specifically, a point of intervention for preventing deleterious effects on individuals (e.g., detrimental effects on physical and psychological health) may be to focus on reducing the intensity associated with experiences of (in)justice. Research often advocates the use of apologies and/or social accounts to manage fairness violations. Explanations, for instance, have been found to help legitimatize the transgressor's actions, alter causal attributions, manage impressions, reframe negative consequences, and/or are often seen as simply the "fair thing to do" (Colquitt & Chertkoff, 2002). Attributions and perceptions, however, are often incredibly resistant to change. As a result, explanations are not always effective at decreasing the overall level of unfairness that the victim perceives and individuals often continue to perceive some unfairness in the situation. The concept of (in)justice intensity suggests that effectively recovering from justice violations might be less about managing *perceptions* and more about managing the *intensity* of the experience. In other words, it might be more effective to focus on reducing the intensity with which the injustice is experienced rather than attempting to change perceptions. Ultimately, while the victim may still deem the event to be unfair, reducing the intensity of the experience might mitigate the negative effects of the injustice on attitudes and behaviors as well as make it more likely that the victim will recover from and move past the injustice.

*Proposition 5:* Interventions that target intensity will be more effective at helping individuals cope with and move past an injustice than interventions that target perceptions.

## (IN)JUSTICE INTENSITY: MOVING FORWARD AND ADDRESSING THE GAPS

Although examining intensity can create a variety of exciting research avenues, much work still needs to be done in order to develop this construct within the justice literature. In this section, we explore some of the challenges and gaps that must be addressed in order for this construct to reach its potential.

### Injustice Intensity Versus Justice Intensity

Although we argued that intensity is important for justice and injustice, we focused on the factors that can influence intensity in the case of *injustice* in our exploratory study. While we argue that intensity is also relevant in the case of justice, more research is required to determine whether the dimensions of justice intensity are the same as injustice intensity. Moreover, future research should consider whether intensity impacts behaviors and attitudes differently in fair versus unfair situations.

### Measuring (In)Justice Intensity

Although more work is first needed to develop this construct (e.g., to determine whether injustice intensity differs from justice intensity, to ensure that a comprehensive list of factors has been identified), it will also be important to create a measure that can assess this construct in order to fully capitalize on the opportunities presented in this chapter. In this section, we briefly discuss two measurement strategies that might be fruitful to explore: aggregation and global assessments.

First, we conceptualize (in)justice intensity as an aggregate multidimensional construct, such that the overall construct can be formed from its dimensions (cf. Law, Wong, & Mobley, 1998). This suggests that a measure of this construct might be created by aggregating the identified dimensions. Sample items for this approach might include: "This experience involves something that I deeply care about"; "This experience has significantly impacted me as a person"; "This experience is extremely emotional for me"; "This experience keeps coming to mind"; "There is no doubt in my mind that this experience was fair/unfair"; "This experience reminds me of incidents from my past"; "It feels like this experience will never end"; "This experience makes me feel powerful/powerless." A key question to address with this approach, however, is whether all of the dimensions should be provided with equal weighting or whether some dimensions are more influential than others.

A second alternative to measuring measure intensity is to adopt a more global approach. Sample items for this approach might include: "This is an intense experience"; and "This experience makes me feel an intense sense of (in)justice." The advantage of this approach is that it allows individuals to define how they are experiencing intensity within that particular situation (cf. Ambrose & Schminke, 2009).

Although both approaches have their benefits and drawbacks, we hope that the differences between measures of perceptions and intensity are clear. Whereas current scales measuring justice perceptions examine the extent to which an individual perceives something to be fair or unfair (e.g., Colquitt, 2001), a measure of (in)justice intensity would explore how *powerfully* an individual experienced an (in)justice.

## Distinguishing Intensity From Other Related Constructs

In order to establish (in)justice intensity as a construct in its own right, it is also important to distinguish it from other constructs in the literature including affect intensity and emotional arousal. Affect intensity refers to stable individual differences in the potency of individuals' emotional reactions (e.g., Larsen & Diener, 1987; Larsen, Diener, & Cropanzano, 1987). Within the context of fairness, individuals who possess high levels of affective intensity tend to experience stronger emotional reactions to perceptions of unfairness than individuals low on this dimension (van den Bos, Maas, Waldring, & Semin, 2003). Emotional arousal, on the other hand, is a situational variable that refers to the degree to which an emotion is associated with feelings of activation (e.g., from calm to intense) (Feldman, 1995; Russell, 1980).

We argue that these constructs differ from (in)justice intensity in a number of ways. First, whereas affect intensity is an individual difference variable and emotional arousal is a situational variable, (in)justice intensity incorporates both individual and situational components. That is, it provides a more comprehensive approach than either affect intensity or emotional arousal. Second, appraisal theories of emotion indicate that emotional arousal results from a situational appraisal (e.g., Lazarus, 1991). (In)justice intensity, however, is not an appraisal; rather intensity can be enhanced to the degree that the individual is uncertain about the meaning of the experience. Thus, (in)justice intensity is distinct from emotional arousal due to the differences in the nature of how emotions are generated.[3] Taken together, there are theoretical differences between these constructs. Future research should empirically explore these differences.

## SUMMARY AND CONCLUSION

Although the justice literature has gained numerous insights from studying perceptions of justice, there has been increasing discontentment due to the limitations of this approach. We argued that it is important to move beyond perceptions and delve into individuals' *experiences*. In doing so, we are able to understand not only how individuals perceive justice but also how their affect and beliefs combine with perceptions to create an overall experience of (in)justice. Moreover, we explored how the intensity of the experience can help (a) advance our understanding of why individual reactions can vary so widely in response to the same justice event and (b) increase the precision with which we can predict attitudinal and behavioral reactions. Although much research is needed to further develop these constructs, we believe that they have the potential to create exciting new research opportunities and avenues that are certain to increase our understanding and ability to manage fairness in the workplace.

## NOTES

1. We use the term *(in)justice experience* for two reasons. First, the term *experience* represents a more holistic approach to global assessments. As we argue below, within the justice literature the term "judgment" often refers to a cold cognitive appraisal which is too narrow for our purposes. Second, we are interested in how individuals not only interpret (in)justice but how they fundamentally *experience* it.
2. Although participants identified six factors that were similar to attitude strength, we did not find evidence for four dimensions in our study: *latitudes of rejection and noncommitment* (i.e., the parts of an attitude continuum that individuals find objectionable versus acceptable; Sherif, Sherif, & Nebergall, 1965), *affective-cognitive consistency* (i.e., the match between one's feelings and beliefs about an object's attributes; Chaiken & Baldwin, 1981), *interest in relevant information* (i.e., the degree to which an individual is motivated to gather information or attend to information about an attitude object; Bradburn & Caplovitz, 1965), and *knowledge* (i.e., the amount of information that an individual has about an attitude object (Krosnick et al., 1993). We believe that these factors did not appear in the results due to the qualitative differences between experiencing (in)justice versus an attitude. This suggests that drawing upon attitude strength can be helpful as a first step but we should not equate attitude strength and (in)justice intensity.

3. We thank an anonymous reviewer for this point.

## REFERENCES


Abelson, R. P. (1963). Computer simulation of "hot cognitions." In S. S. Tomkins & S. Messick (Eds.), *Computer simulation and personality: Frontier of psychology theory* (pp. 277-298). New York, NY: Wiley.

Abelson, R. P. (1995). Attitude extremity. In R. E. Petty & J. A. Krosnick (Eds.), *Attitude strength: Antecedents and consequences* (pp. 25-42). Mahwah, NJ: Erlbuam.

Ambrose, M. L., & Arnaud, A. (2005). Distributive and procedural justice: Construct distinctiveness, construct interdependence, and overall justice. In J. Greenberg & J. Colquitt (Eds.), *The handbook of organizational justice* (pp. 59-84). Mahwah, NJ: Erlbaum.

Ambrose, M. L., & Schminke, M. (2009). The role of overall justice judgments in organizational justice research: A test of mediation. *Journal of Applied Psychology, 94,* 491-500.

Barsky, A., & Kaplan, S. A. (2007). If you feel bad, it's unfair: A quantitative synthesis of affect and organizational justice perceptions. *Journal of Applied Psychology, 92,* 286-295.

Barsky, A., Kaplan, S. A., & Beal, D. J. (2011). Just feelings? The role of affect in the formation of organizational fairness judgments. *Journal of Management, 37,* 248-279.

Bies, R. J., & Tripp, T. M. (2002). "Hot flashes and open wounds": Injustice and the tyranny of its emotions. In S. W. Gilliland, D. D. Steiner, & D. P. Skarlicki (Eds.), *Emerging perspectives on managing organizational justice* (pp. 203-221). Greenwich, CT: Information Age.

Boninger, D. S., Krosnick, J. A., Berent, M. K., & Fabrigar, L. R. (1995). The causes and consequences of attitude importance. In R. E. Petty & J. A. Krosnick (Eds.), *Attitude strength: Antecedents and consequences* (pp. 159-190). Mahwah, NJ: Erlbaum.

Bradburn, N. M., & Caplovitz, D. (1965). *Reports on happiness: A pilot study of behavior related to mental health.* Chicago, IL: Aldine.

Breugelmans, S., & De Cremer, D. (2007). The role of emotions in cross-cultural research. In D. De Cremer (Ed.), *Advances in the psychology of justice and affect* (pp. 85-106). Charlotte, NC: Information Age.

Budd, R. J. (1986). Predicting cigarette use: The need to incorporate measures of salience in the theory of reasoned action. *Journal of Applied Social Psychology, 16,* 633-685.

Cantril, H. (1944). *Gauging public opinion.* Princeton, NJ: Princeton University Press.

Chaiken, S., & Baldwin, M. W. (1981). Affective-cognitive consistency and the effect of salience behavioral information on the self-perception of attitudes. *Journal of Personality and Social Psychology, 41,* 1-12.

Cohen-Charash, Y., & Byrne, Z. S. (2008). Affect and justice: Current knowledge and future directions. In N. M. Ashkanasy & C. L. Cooper (Eds.), *Research companion to emotion in organizations* (pp. 360-391). Cheltenham, England: Edward Elgar.

Colquitt, J. A. (2001). On the dimensionality of organizational justice: A construct validation of a measure. *Journal of Applied Psychology, 86,* 386-400.

Colquitt, J. A., & Chertkoff, J. M. (2002). Explaining injustice: The interactive effect of explanation and outcome on fairness perceptions and task motivation. *Journal of Management, 28,* 591-610.

Colquitt, J. A., Conlon, D. E., Wesson, M. J., Porter, C., & Ng, K. Y. (2001). Justice at the millennium: A meta-analytic review of 25 years of organizational justice research. *Journal of Applied Psychology, 86,* 425-445.

Cropanzano, R., Byrne, Z. S., Bobocel, D. R., & Rupp, D. E. (2001). Moral virtues, fairness heuristics, social entities, and other denizens of organizational justice. *Journal of Vocational Behavior, 58,* 164-209.

De Cremer, D. (2007). Justice and affect: When two friends met. In D. De Cremer (Ed.), *Advances in the psychology of justice and affect* (pp. 1-14). Charlotte, NC: Information Age.

Deutsch, M. (1985). *Distributive justice: A social-psychological perspective.* New Haven, CT: Yale University Press.

Eagly, A. H., & Chaiken, S. (1993). *The psychology of attitudes.* Fort Worth, TX: Harcourt Brace Jovanovich College.

Fazio, R. H. (1986). How do attitudes guide behavior? In R. M. Sorrentino & E. T. Higgins (Eds.), *The handbook of motivation and cognition: Foundations of social behavior* (pp. 204-243). New York, NY: Guilford Press.

Feather, N. T. (1999). *Values, achievement, and justice: Studies in the psychology of deservingness.* New York, NY: Kluwer.

Feldman, L. A. (1995). Valence focus and arousal focus: Individual differences in the structure of affective experience. *Journal of Personality and Social Psychology, 69,* 153-166.

Flanagan, J. C. (1954). The critical incident technique. *Psychological Bulletin, 51,* 327-358.

Folger, R. (2001). Fairness as deonance. In S. W. Gilliand, D. D. Steiner, & D. P. Skarlicki (Eds.), *Theoretical and cultural perspectives on organizational justice* (pp. 3-33). Thousand Oaks, CA: SAGE.

Folger, R., & Cropanzano, R. (1998). *Organizational justice and human resource management.* Beverly Hills, CA: SAGE.

Folger, R., & Cropanzano, R. (2001). Fairness theory: Justice as accountability. In J. Greenberg & R. Cropanzano (Eds.), *Advances in organizational justice* (pp. 1-55). Stanford, CA: Stanford University Press.

Frijda, N. H. (1993). Moods, emotion episodes, and emotions. In M. Lewis & J. M. Haviland (Eds.), *Handbook of emotions* (pp. 381-403). New York, NY: Guilford Press.

Gilliland, S. (2008). The tails of justice: A critical examination of the dimensionality of organizational justice constructs. *Human Resource Management Review, 18,* 271-281.

Greenberg, J. (1994). Using socially fair treatment to promote acceptance of a work site smoking ban. *Journal of Applied Psychology, 79,* 288-297.

Greenberg, J. (2001). Setting the justice agenda: Seven unanswered questions about "what, why, and how." *Journal of Vocational Behavior, 58,* 210-219.

Greenberg, J., & Ganegoda, D. B. (2007). Justice and affect: Where do we stand? In D. De Cremer (Ed.), *Advances in the psychology of justice and affect* (pp. 261-292). Charlotte, NC: Information Age.

Gross, R. A., Holtz, R., & Miller, N. (1995). Attitude certainty. In R. E. Petty & J. A. Krosnick (Eds.), *Attitude strength: Antecedents and consequences* (pp. 215-246). Mahwah, MJ: Erlbaum.

Hansson, R. O., Jones, W. H., & Fletcher, W. L. (1990). Troubled relationships in later life: Implications for social support. *Journal of Social and Personal Relationships, 7,* 451-463.

Judd, C. M., & Johnson, J. T. (1981). Attitudes, polarization, and diagnosticity: Exploring the effects of affect. *Journal of Personality and Social Psychology, 41,* 25-36.

Judge, T. A., & Colquitt, J. A. (2004). Organizational justice and stress: The mediating role of work-family conflict. *Journal of Applied Psychology, 89,* 395-404.

Kivimaki, M., Elovainio, M., Vahtera, J., & Ferrie, J. E. (2003). Organizational justice and health of employees: Prospective cohort study. *Occupational Environmental Medicine, 60,* 27-34.

Kivimaki, M., Elovainio, M., Vahtera, J., Virtanen, M., & Stansfeld, S. A. (2003). Association between organizational inequity and incidence of psychiatric disorders in female employees. *Psychological Medicine, 33,* 319-326.

Kivimaki, M., Ferrie, J. E., Brunner, E., Head, J., Shipley, M. J., Vahtera, J., & Marmot, M. G. (2005). Justice at work and reduced risk of coronary heart disease among employees: The Whitehall II study. *Archives of Internal Medicine, 165,* 2245-2251.

Krosnick, J. A., & Abelson, R. P. (1992). The case for measuring attitude strength in surveys. In J. M. Tanur (Ed.), *Questions about questions: Inquiries into the cognitive bases of surveys* (pp. 177-203). New York, NY: SAGE.

Krosnick, J. A., Boninger, D. S., Chuang, Y. C., Berent, M. K., & Carnot, C. G. (1993). Attitude strength: One construct or many related constructs? *Journal of Personality and Social Psychology, 65,* 1132-1151.

Krosnick, J. A., & Petty, R. E. (1995). Attitude strength: An overview. In R. E. Petty & J. A. Krosnick (Eds.), *Attitude strength: Antecedents and consequences* (pp. 1-24). Mahwah, NJ: Erlbaum.

Kunda, Z. (1999). *Social cognition: Making sense of people.* Cambridge, MA: MIT Press.

Lang, P. J., Bradley, M. M., & Cuthbert, B. N. (1997). Motivated attention: Affect, activation, and action. In P. J. Lang, R. F. Simons, & M. T. Balaban (Eds.), *Attention and orienting: Sensory and motivational processes* (pp. 97-135). Hillsdale, NJ: Erlbaum.

Larsen, R. J., & Diener, E. (1987). Affect intensity as an individual difference characteristic: A Review. *Journal of Research in Personality, 21,* 1-39.

Larsen, R. J., Diener, E., & Cropanzano, R. (1987). Cognitive operations associated with individual differences in affect intensity. *Journal of Personality and Social Psychology, 53,* 767-774.

Law, K. S., Wong, C., & Mobley, W. H. (1998). Toward a taxonomy of multidimensional constructs. *Academy of Management Review, 23,* 741-755.

Lazarus, R. S. (1991). *Emotion and adaptation.* New York, NY: Oxford University Press.

Lazarus, R. S., & Folkman, S. (1984). *Stress, appraisal and coping.* New York, NY: Springer.

Lerner, M. (1980). *The belief in a justice world: A fundamental delusion.* New York, NY: Plenum.

Lind, E. A. (2001). Thinking critically about justice judgments. *Journal of Vocational Behavior, 58,* 220-226.

Matthews, C. (1988). *Hardball: How politics is played—Told by one who knows the game.* New York, NY: Summit Books.

Pennebaker, J. W. (1997). *Opening up: The healing power of expressing emotions.* New York, NY: Guilford Press.

Raden, D. (1985). Strength-related attitude dimensions. *Social Psychology Quarterly, 48,* 312-330.

Regan, D. T., & Fazio, R. H. (1977). On the consistency between attitudes and behavior: Look to the method of attitude formation. *Journal of Experimental Social Psychology, 13,* 28-45.

Rimé, B., Finkenauer, C., Luminet, O., Zech, E., & Philippot, P. (1998). Social sharing of emotion: New evidence and new questions. In W. Stroebe & M. Hewstone (Eds.), *European review of social psychology* (Vol. 9, pp. 145-189). Chichester, England: Wiley.

Russell, J. A. (1980). A circumplex model of affect. *Journal of Personality and Social Psychology, 39,* 1161-1178.

Schwarz, N. (1990). Feelings as information: Informational and motivational functions of affective states. In E. T. Higgins & R. Sorrentino (Eds.), *Handbook of motivation and cognition: Foundations of social behavior* (Vol. 2, pp. 527-561). New York, NY: Guilford Press.

Schwarz, N., & Clore, G. L. (1983). Mood, misattribution, and judgments of well-being: Informative and directive functions of affective states. *Journal of Personality and Social Psychology, 45,* 513-523.

Shapiro, D. (2001). The death of justice theory is likely if theorists neglect the "wheels" already invented and the voices of the injustice victims. *Journal of Vocational Behavior, 58,* 235-242.

Sherif, C. W., Sherif, M., & Nebergall, R. E. (1965). *Attitude and attitude change.* Philadelphia, PA: Saunders.

Sinclair, R. C., & Mark, M. M. (1991). Mood and the endorsement of the egalitarian macrojustice versus equity-based microjustice principles. *Personality and Social Psychology Bulletin, 17,* 369-375.

Stouffer, S. A., Guttman, L., Suchman, E. A., Lazarsfeld, P. F., Star, S. A., & Clausen, J. A. (1950). *Measurement and prediction.* Princeton, NJ: Princeton University Press.

Sukhodolsky, D. G., Golub, A., & Cromwell, E. N. (2001). Development and validation of the anger rumination scale. *Personality and Individual Differences, 31,* 689-700.

Tomaka, J., & Blascovich, J. (1994). Effects of justice beliefs on cognitive appraisal of and subjective, physiological, and behavioral responses to potential stress. *Journal of Personality and Social Psychology, 67,* 732-740.

Tugade, M. M., & Fredrickson, B. L. (2004). Resilient individuals use positive emotions to bounce back from negative emotional experiences. *Journal of Personality and Social Psychology, 86,* 320-333.

van den Bos, K. (2003). On the subjective quality of social justice: The role of affect as information in the psychology of justice judgments. *Journal of Personality and Social Psychology, 85,* 482-498.

van den Bos, K. (2007). Hot cognitions and social justice judgments: The combined influence of cognitive and affective factors on the justice judgments process. In D. De Cremer (Ed.), *Advances in the psychology of justice and affect* (pp. 61-84). Charlotte, NC: Information Age.

van den Bos, K., Maas, M., Waldring, I. E., & Semin, G. R. (2003). Toward understanding the psychology of reactions to perceived fairness: The role of affect intensity. *Social Justice Research, 16,* 151-168.

Weiss, H. M. (2002). Deconstructing job satisfaction: Separating evaluations, beliefs, and affective experiences. *Human Resource Management Review, 12,* 173-194.

Weiss, H. M., & Cropanzano, R. (1996). Affective events theory: A theoretical discussion of the structure, cases, and consequences of affective experiences at work. In B. M. Staw & L. L. Cummings (Eds.), *Research in organizational behavior* (Vol. 18, pp. 1-74). Greenwich, CT: JAI Press.

Weiss, H.W., Suckow, K., & Cropanzano, R. (1999). Effects of justice conditions on discrete emotions. *Journal of Applied Psychology, 84,* 786-794.

CHAPTER 4

# OPENING A NEW CONVERSATION IN ORGANIZATIONAL JUSTICE

## A Conceptual Model of Offender Reintegration in Organizations

**Jerry Goodstein, Karl Aquino, and Daniel Skarlicki**

In this chapter, we introduce into the organizational justice conversation the topic of offender reintegration—the psychological willingness of others to maintain or develop new working relationships with an individual who has violated social and moral norms valued by an organization. We develop a conceptual model that emphasizes the role of moral, social, and instrumental considerations, as reflected in important social and psychological variables, on the decision to reintegrate an offender. We close with a discussion of a number of possibilities for empirical research motivated by our model and the broader topic of offender reintegration in organizations.

A recent *New York Times* article (Wade, 2010) brought to light the case of a prominent scholar at Harvard University, Dr. Marc Hauser. Dr. Hauser was placed on leave because of evidence gathered by the faculty of arts

*Emerging Perspectives on Organizational Justice and Ethics*
pp. 75–104

and sciences at Harvard that he had fabricated experimental data in 2002 for a study subsequently published in the journal, *Cognition*. *Times* reporter Nicholas Wade wrote in his article, "Some forms of scientific error, like poor record keeping or even mistaken results, are forgivable, but fabrication of data, if such a change were to be proved against Dr. Hauser, is usually followed by expulsion from the scientific community." Wade went on to note that, "Dr. Hauser's case is unusual however because of his substantial contributions to the fields of animal cognition and the basis of morality." Wade suggested further that there may be the possibility of "redemption." As affirmed by the editor of the journal *Cognition*, Dr. Gerry Altman, "If he were to give a full and frank account of the errors he made, then the process can start repatriating him into the community in some form."

When individuals like Dr. Hauser commit serious workplace transgressions, such as violations of procedural justice involving breaches of professional codes of conduct, the possibility of redemption and reintegration might or might not be an option. But when it is, what factors enable it to occur? And even if the offender is permitted to rejoin the workplace community, what determines whether his or her coworkers will be willing to maintain harmonious and productive relations with him or her?

To date, considerable attention has been devoted to the "dark side" of organizational justice; that is, to how feelings of injustice motivate negative reactions such as punishment or revenge toward the transgressor. Less discussed are the factors that might heal damaged relationships between offenders, victims, and third parties, often labeled restorative justice. Restorative justice involves healing through both material and symbolic restitution, rebuilding the self-respect of offenders, and allowing them back into the community (Braithwaite, 2002; Wenzel, Okimoto, Feather, & Platow, 2008). In the present chapter we focus on a specific aspect of restorative justice: offender reintegration. An offender is defined as someone who has violated one or moral and social norms valued by the organization. We define offender reintegration as other employees' psychological willingness to maintain or develop working relationships with the offender. These employees can include victims of mistreatment or third parties who become aware of the mistreatment.

Offender reintegration has received limited discussion in the management literature. In light of this lack of attention, one might ask, "Why should we care about offenders and their reintegration in organizations?" First, it is important to note that offending happens frequently in the workplace. Pearson and Porath (2005), for instance, reported that 20% of employees polled in their study have experienced incivility and 10% report being mistreated every day. A report by the Ethics Resource Center (2009) indicated that 57% of employees surveyed in 2007 and 49% surveyed in 2009 witnessed acts of employee misconduct such as lying and conflicts of interest. Those who are victims at one point in time may also fall prey to human frailty and become offenders themselves who might see the importance of reintegration. Second, the reintegration of offenders has important implications for offenders and organizations. Criminal justice (Maruna, 2001) and restorative justice (Strang, 2004) researchers note that when offenders can rely on factors such as social bonds in a community and victim forgiveness to facilitate reintegration, they are less likely to repeat criminal behavior. From an organizational perspective, offender reintegration may also lessen the likelihood that an offender leaves the organization either voluntarily or involuntarily. This can be particularly important when the offenders are potentially important contributors to the organization and difficult to replace, such as in the case of disruptive physician behavior (Rosenstein & O'Daniel, 2005, 2008). An interesting corollary of our chapter is that the violator who takes steps to come clean and seek redemption can become the target of punishment by the victim and third parties (i.e., the transgressor becomes the victim). This perspective warrants considering. Third, victims and third parties are not the only ones to whom justice is due. Goodstein and Aquino (2010) argued that offenders are due justice as well, particularly with respect to having an opportunity to make amends and earn redemption and reintegration. Reintegration can provide the potential for strengthened bonds between employees and between employees and their companies.

For these reasons, we propose that offender reintegration is an important topic that has the potential to expand the scope of organizational justice research by addressing new questions and drawing from theoretical and practical perspectives that have seldom been used by organizational scholars. Our broad goal in this chapter is to shift the organizational justice conversation from one of rejecting and punishing the transgressor to looking for ways to reintegrate the offender into the workplace community. A second goal is to propose a framework for explaining what factors might contribute to successful offender reintegration. We begin our discussion with a brief review of the current lens through which organizational justice is studied, and we contrast that view with a restorative justice perspective. From there we focus specifically on offender reintegration. We then present a model that identifies moral, social, and instrumental considerations that influence offender reintegration. The third section of our chapter extends the conversation by considering the theoretical, empirical, and practical implications of our model and the restorative justice perspective.

## REACTIONS TO UNFAIRNESS: A REVIEW OF ORGANIZATIONAL JUSTICE RESEARCH

Organizational justice refers to people's reactions to fairness and unfairness in the workplace. To date, the conversation on organizational justice has focused on the antecedents and consequences of workplace (un)fairness from the victim's (e.g., Greenberg & Colquitt, 2005) and the third party's perspective (O'Reilly & Aquino, 2011; Skarlicki & Kulik, 2005). Discussions about justice have focused on its dimensions (i.e., distributive, procedural, interpersonal and informational justice) (Colquitt, 2001), measurement issues (Colquitt & Shaw, 2005), and various theories for why individuals care about fairness in the first place. Among the prominent justice theories are those that identify instrumental (Thibaut & Walker, 1978), relational (Tyler & Blader, 2002), uncertainty management (Lind & van den Bos, 2002), and moral (Folger, 2001) concerns underlying fairness.

A sizable body of justice research over the last 2 decades has explored how mistreatment leads victims and third parties to seek revenge against transgressors (Aquino, Tripp, & Bies, 2001; Skarlicki & Folger, 1997) or to engage in antisocial behaviors like theft (Greenberg, 1993) and sabotage (Ambrose, Seabright, & Schminke, 2002) directed against the perceived source of the mistreatment. Sources of mistreatment can include the organization, individuals and authorities inside the organization, and its customers (e.g., Skarlicki, van Jaarsveld, & Walker, 2008). A commonly mentioned explanation for such behaviors is based on some variant of equity theory (Adams, 1965), which predicts that when individuals experience unfair treatment to themselves, they address the inequity psychologically and/or attempt to even the score using physical means, including theft or quitting. The moral perspective, in contrast, proposes that certain kinds of mistreatment can violate norms of moral and social conduct and motivate individuals, including third parties, to seek retribution against transgressors for their wrongdoings (Cropanzano, Goldman, & Folger, 2003, 2005). The moral perspective relies less on social comparison processes than equity or self-interest-based models, assuming instead that responses to injustice are driven by evolved moral intuitions about right and wrong that transcend self-interested concerns (O'Reilly & Aquino, in press).

Although negative reactions and punishing someone who has violated principles of justice can have positive consequences (e.g., discouraging future transgressions and preserving a sense of moral order) (Tripp, Bies, & Aquino, 2002), these reactions can also have certain drawbacks. Revenge behaviors such as theft and sabotage can be risky in that the avenger can get caught (Cropanzano et al., 2003). Moreover, punishing the harm doer can escalate conflict and lead to costly feuds (Folger & Baron, 1996; Tripp & Bies, 2009). When feuding erupts in organizations, it can heighten distrust within a group, increase emotional tension, and undermine team performance and morale (De Dreu & Weingart, 2003).

As mentioned above, we propose to shift the conversation concerning organizational justice research. First, inspired by the "positive psychology" movement (Seligman & Csikszentmihalyi, 2000) we seek to turn the justice conversation from negative reactions to transgressors (e.g., revenge, punishment, retaliation) toward alternative, relationship-restoring responses. We are not the first in this endeavor. For example, Aquino and colleagues (Aquino, Tripp, & Bies, 2006; Bradfield & Aquino, 1999) identified forgiveness and reconciliation as (in)justice reactions. Similarly, Barclay and Skarlicki (2009) explored the benefits of expressive writing in helping victims heal their wounds of mistreatment. Our chapter builds on the work of these writers by presenting a more comprehensive model that includes victims, the offender, and third parties as actors in the attempt to achieve justice.

Second, we aim to shift attention from focusing solely on the victim to take into account third party and transgressor perspectives. The latter in particular has received little attention in the justice literature, leaving a sizable gap in the understanding of alternatives to punishment and revenge. It is perhaps understandable that the field would be less sympathetic to the plight of transgressors than to the victim. In fact, punishing a transgressor appears to have evolutionary roots (e.g., Wiessner, 2005). However, our contention is that transgressors are not always motivated to intentionally harm others and that perhaps, more often than not, they experience regret over their actions. For this reason, it seems worthwhile to explore ways for allowing at least some transgressors to make up for their wrongs and be reintegrated back into the workplace community. We believe that doing so represents a more humane approach to dealing with harm doing in organizations than solely emphasizing punishment and retribution. Similarly, third parties who are not direct victims but are potentially affected by a transgression have also received limited attention from management scholars in terms of their role in restorative justice. As we explain below, the support of third parties may be essential for facilitating reintegration, and so their perspective also needs to be considered.

Our chapter develops a model of offender reintegration in the workplace following an acknowledged act of wrongdoing. Our model incorporates the victim, the offender, and third parties into the process of justice restoration, and identifies some of the underlying motivations and influences on offender reintegration.

## RESTORATIVE JUSTICE THEORY AND RESEARCH

Braithwaite conceptualized restorative justice as "a process whereby all the parties with a stake in a particular offense come together to resolve collectively how to deal with the aftermath of the offense and its implications for the future" (1999, p. 5). Braithwaite (2002) argued that restorative justice has been the dominant model of criminal justice for most of human history, although many people in modern Western societies are probably more familiar with a contrasting retributive model of justice that emphasizes punishment. Restorative justice concepts and practices such as forgiveness, reconciliation, and redemption have roots in ancient Greek, Roman, and Arab civilization, a variety of indigenous cultures (e.g., Native American, African, Australian Aborigine), and various religious traditions, including Confucianism, Taoism, Buddhism, Hinduism, and early Christianity. The shift to more modern retributive justice systems is a relatively recent development. According to Braithwaite, the rise of retributive justice began in medieval Europe, "transforming crime as a matter of fealty to and felony against the king, instead of a wrong done to another person" (2002, p. 5).

Perspectives on criminal justice have bounced back and forth between rehabilitation and retribution for much of the past century (Zehr, 1990). Critics of both of these approaches, however, argue that they focus on the past, are detached from the direct participants, suffer from an overreliance on due process, and ignore the victim (e.g., Kidder, 2007). In response to growing frustration with these approaches, a revival of restorative justice practices began across much of Western society in the 1970s, most notably in Canada, Australia, New Zealand, the United States, South Africa, and the United Kingdom (Braithwaite, 2002). Restorative justice offers an alternative approach to wrongdoing, one where the emphasis is placed on being forward-looking, solving problems, actively involving all participants, and repairing relationships (Braithwaite, 2002; Kidder, 2007; Strang, 2004; Zehr, 1990). Moreover, restorative justice offers an alternative view of wrongdoing itself, conceptualizing it as "first and foremost a violation of people and their relationships, rather than merely a violation of the law" (Roche, 2003).

Restorative justice focuses on the interactions between the offender, victim, and third parties who might have a stake in the wrongdoing and who are indirectly affected. Three core principles are at the heart of restorative justice. The first key principle for offenders is that they are motivated to make amends with those who have been harmed, which allows the offender a chance at earned redemption and reintegration (Goodstein & Aquino, 2010). The process of making amends involves accepting responsibility and accountability for the wrongdoing, expressing remorse, seeking forgiveness from the victim and other affected parties, and offering a sincere apology and/or other restitution (e.g., Braithwaite, 1999, 2002; Roche, 2006).

Second, for victims, restorative justice often involves forgiveness (Goodstein & Aquino, 2010). Forgiveness is defined as a process involving affective, cognitive, and behavioral responses in which negative emotions toward and judgments about the offender are diminished by trying to view the offender with compassion, understanding, and perhaps even love (Aquino, Grover, Goldman, & Folger, 2003; Enright, Gassin, & Wu, 1992; McCullough, Worthington, & Rachal, 1997; North, 1987). As Walker (2006) argued, forgiveness can help victims relieve themselves of the burden of resentment, anger, vengefulness, and other negative feelings toward the offender, by restoring damaged or broken relations between victim and offender, and by settling a wrong from the past "while releasing the future from its impact" (2006, p. 154). Bradfield and Aquino (1999) noted that forgiveness can play a powerful a role in restoring a sense of justice in the workplace.

Third, offender reintegration involves individuals who are affected indirectly by a particular act of wrongdoing. In workplaces, for instance, this could include coworkers, supervisors, or customers. The latter group of third parties becomes highly relevant when considering that customers can be involved in task forces or committees designed to further an organization's goals. Third parties play an important part in the reintegration process by providing offenders with an opportunity to earn redemption and reintegrate back into the community through mechanisms such as restorative justice conferences (Goodstein & Aquino, 2010). While offender reintegration is related to the notion of offender rehabilitation, the focus for rehabilitation has a longer time horizon. These longer-term goals involve reducing the risk of offender recidivism, through specific targeted correctional interventions and promoting offender well-being by providing offenders with skills, attitudes, and resources to lead a meaningful life that does not involve inflicting harm on others (Ward & Langlands, 2009). For the purposes of this chapter, we limit our attention to offender reintegration.

Although restorative justice has a long tradition in disciplines such as criminal justice (e.g., Braithwaite, 1999, 2002; Daly & Immarigeon, 1998; Zehr, 1990), social welfare (e.g., Roche, 2006), and education (e.g., Karp & Conrad, 2005), it has only recently begun to receive attention in the management literature. Bradfield and Aquino (1999) initially introduced restorative justice when they examined the enactment of revenge and forgiveness in the workplace. Kidder (2007) explored restorative justice as an alternative method of resolving workplace disputes and healing damaged or broken relationships in the workplace. According to Kidder (2007), restorative justice can mitigate against future deviant behavior by improving interpersonal relations, rebuilding trust, and fostering perceptions of organizational justice.

More recently, Goodstein and Aquino (2010) and Goodstein and Butterfield (2010) examined restorative justice in the aftermath of wrongdoing in organizations. Goodstein and Aquino (2010) directed attention to considering how offenders (making amends), victims (extending forgiveness), and organizations (fostering reintegration) restore justice in the workplace. Goodstein and Butterfield (2010) developed a conceptual framework to illustrate how restorative justice can contribute to the business ethics literature. Their model examines potential interrelationships between making amends, extending forgiveness, and fostering reintegration, specifically in the aftermath of an ethical transgression. Goodstein and Butterfield (2010) also explored potential moderators of these relationships (e.g., whether the offender intended to commit the unethical act), as well as outcomes of the restorative justice process (e.g., perceived justice in the workplace, and interpersonal trust).

Trust researchers have similarly written about how relationships marred by trust violations can be repaired. Dirks, Lewicki, and Zaheer (2009), for instance, reviewed three processes: attribution based (attempts to repair the relationship via using social accounts, apologies, denial, and penance), social equilibrium (restoring into equilibrium the status of the aggrieved party), and structural processes (legalistic remedies to limit future violations). These perspectives attempt to understand the processes through which relationship repair can occur. From an attribution-based perspective, in order to repair trust, "the wronged party must perceive that the transgression does not reflect the violator's true nature, or must perceive that the violator has experienced redemption following the transgression" (Dirks et al., 2009, p. 71). This is consistent with work in the impression management literature suggesting that apologies and other efforts to make amends can maintain the reputation of offenders following transgressions such as breaches of cooperation (Bottom, Gibson, Daniels, & Murninghan, 2002). For the social equilibrium process, repairing trust is a matter of restoring social order through the performance of rituals to make amends such as apologies, penance, and punishment (e.g., Ren & Gray, 2009). Kim, Ferrin, Cooper, and Dirks (2004), for example, found that trust was repaired more successfully when the mistrusted parties apologized for violations concerning matters of competence, but denied culpability regarding violations of integrity. A more structurally oriented approach to restoring trust (e.g., Sitkin & Roth, 1993) involves the use of legalistic remedies such as policies, procedures, and contracts as control mechanisms that increase the reliability of future interactions and restore trust (Dirks et al., 2009).

In summary, the organizational justice, trust repair, and to a lesser extent, the empirical research on restorative justice, tend to emphasize the restoration of justice for victims. Our specific perspective, in contrast, focuses primarily on the transgressor.

## A MODEL OF OFFENDER REINTEGRATION

Having explained why people in organizations should pay heed to or care about offenders, we turn to some of the key boundary conditions of our model. At the outset, it is important to remind the reader that we are not advocating restorative justice as universally applicable. We believe it can be extremely beneficial in certain cases, but given the demands it places on managers, the offender, fellow coworkers, and his or her victims to move toward reintegration, it is necessary to identify the specific conditions to which we believe it can be most effective in a workplace setting. We view these conditions as setting the boundaries of our model. Three boundary conditions must be met to make a violation amenable to offender reintegration.

First, the violation should not rise beyond a level of severity that would make it extremely unlikely for an individual to consider offender reintegration. Thus we do not include in our model violations that are generally recognized as heinous (e.g., sexual abuse, rape, grievous injury, wanton destruction of property, premeditated murder) or illegal. If the offense is one that violated legal codes, then the transgressor needs to have paid his or her dues and served a sentence as determined by the criminal justice system. Second, the violator should have publicly acknowledged wrongdoing, expressed remorse, and shown a willingness to make amends for what he or she has done. We view this second condition as being critical for pursuing restorative justice because in the absence of any acknowledged wrongdoing or expression of remorse, the likelihood of the offender being welcomed back into the workplace community is low. Moreover, because pursuing restorative justice requires the willing cooperation of the violator, a violator who is not strongly motivated to make amends is also unlikely to invest the time or effort into the processes required to achieve partial or full reintegration. Third, organizational authorities and those members of the workplace community most directly affected by the transgression must be at least somewhat motivated to pursue a reintegrative process. Their motivation might stem from various sources that are elaborated more fully below, including purely instrumental ones (e.g., the violator is a high performer) as well as those based on moral concerns (e.g., everyone who expresses remorse deserves a second chance).

We propose that these three conditions are likely necessary but not sufficient for reintegration to occur. If these conditions are satisfied, then organizational authorities and employees can *consider* pursuing restorative justice. As the model we present shows, however, subsequent offender reintegration is likely to depend on a host of other factors. Our analysis of offender reintegration builds on a foundation of existing research in organizational justice and restorative justice that highlights the central role of perceptions of moral, social, and instrumental considerations in influencing responses to injustice and harm doing in the workplace. We develop below a model that identifies, within each of the domains of moral, social, and instrumental considerations, important variables likely to affect offender reintegration in a workgroup and workplace context.

Our proposed model of reintegration is shown in Figure 4.1. The model offers an initial framework for exploring important perceived psychological and social factors, reflecting broad moral, social, and instrumental considerations that influence the willingness of individual employees, in particular in the role of third parties, to accept a transgressor back into the workplace community. Thus, the unit of analysis to which our model applies is an individual and his or her perceptions of these moral, social, and instrumental considerations, whether he or she is a superior, coworker, subordinate or customer who may be faced with the

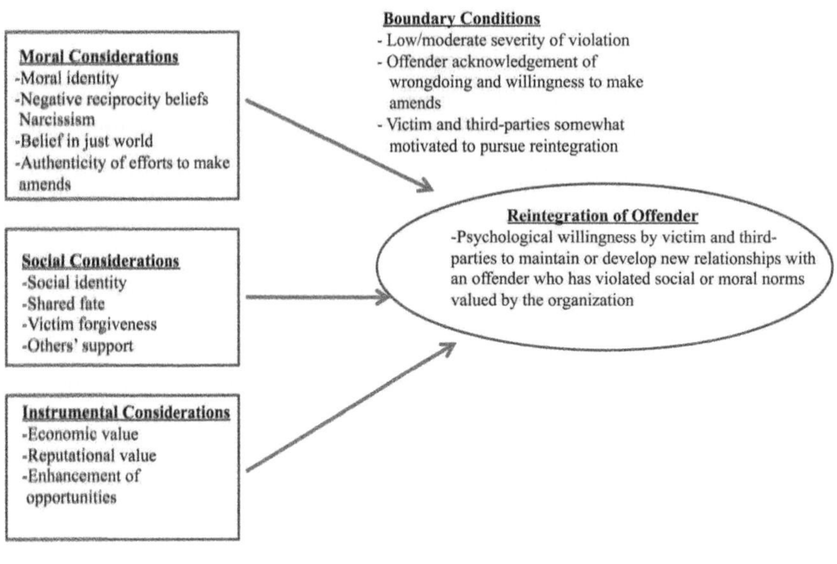


Figure 4.1. A model for exploring offender reintegration in the workplace.

decision whether or not to agree to work with someone who has violated a moral or social norm. We acknowledge that reintegration can take various forms that may change over time, moving from the more superficial and instrumental willingness to work with the person, to those that are more affective and personal, such as trusting the person and having positive feelings toward him or her. We also recognize that offender reintegration can involve taking specific actions, such as providing emotional support and encouragement. However, for the purposes of this initial model of offender reintegration, we limit our emphasis to psychological willingness to work with the offender. We also distinguish forgiveness, which is oriented to what has happened in the past and which arguably is something that can only be offered by victims, from offender reintegration which is focused on future interactions and includes third parties who may not have been directly affected by the offense. Once again, the model holds only when three conditions described above have been satisfied.

## The Role of Moral Considerations in Offender Reintegration

In this chapter, we do not attempt to offer an exhaustive list of constructs that might influence an employee's perspective on reintegration. Instead, we call attention to descriptive moral, social, and instrumental considerations that can motivate employees to participate in the reintegration process. We summarize our main arguments below in the form of propositions that relate these considerations to offender reintegration. The propositions are specifically framed from the perspective of those in a position to reintegrate offenders—victims and third parties.

In making a judgment as to whether to reintegrate a coworker who has committed a workplace offense an individual might be prompted to ask, "What is the right thing to do in this situation?" The response to this question is likely to depend on the employee's sensitivity to moral issues (i.e., issues that have implications for how people treat one another). It might also be affected by the employee's beliefs about the appropriate response to wrongdoers.

### *Moral Identity*

Moral identity has been defined as the mental representation a person holds about their moral character (Aquino & Reed, 2002). Following other theorists (e.g., Aquino & Freeman, 2009; Blasi, 1984), we propose that the extent to which a person's moral identity is more rather than less central to his or her self-concept can influence the degree to which he or she will take a moral perspective into account when making decisions and acting on social information. The role of moral identity centrality could support or oppose reintegration depending upon contextual factors (Aquino, Freeman, Reed, Lim, & Felps, 2009) as well as the particular moral frameworks that a person adopts (Aquino & Freeman, 2009). According to Aquino and Freeman (2009), moral identity provides the motivational impetus for acting in ways that are consistent with one's moral viewpoint, but it does not provide a direction for behavior. Consequently, what is needed along with moral identity to account for why people might or might not support reintegration is another variable. We suggest that an important set of beliefs concerns the degree to which people endorse a norm of negative reciprocity.

### *Negative Reciprocity Beliefs*

Negative reciprocity norms can be found in every culture (Gouldner, 1960). These norms stipulate that people are justified, and perhaps even morally obligated, to punish or seek revenge against those who treat them inappropriately or unfairly. The most obvious behavioral prescription associated with the endorsement of the negative reciprocity norm is an antagonistic response toward harm doers. Empirical research supports this relationship (Eder, Aquino, Turner, & Reed, 2006; Eisenberger, Lynch, Aselage, & Rohdieck, 2004; Gallucci & Perugini, 2003; Mitchell & Ambrose, 2007; Perugini, Gallucci, Presaghi, & Ercolani, 2003) and suggests that people who endorse this norm are likely to view revenge as a practical and perhaps even a moral imperative. For people who endorse the negative reciprocity norm, a punitive response to people who violate organizational norms may be viewed as morally desirable because it reaffirms and validates standards about how people should be treated while also deterring future violations (Eisenberger et al., 2004; Vidmar, 2002).

If negative reciprocity can be construed as being a moral imperative, then people for whom moral goals and concerns are central to their self-definitions—that is, people high in moral identity centrality—should be the least supportive of efforts to reintegrate transgressors into the workplace community. In other words, while moral identity sensitizes individuals to take a moral perspective when thinking about reintegration, their belief in the negative reciprocity norm will likely lead them to either support or oppose it. Our argument suggests that both variables need to be taken into account at the individual level to understand their influence on reintegration.

> ***Proposition 1a:*** A person whose moral identity is central to his or her self-definition and who also strongly endorses negative reciprocity will be the least supportive of offender reintegration, whereas a person whose moral identity is central and who does not

strongly endorse negative reciprocity beliefs will be the most supportive of offender reintegration.

### *Narcissism*

Narcissism has been shown to be an impediment to forgiveness (Exline, Baumeister, Bushman, Campbell, & Finkel, 2004). Narcissism as an individual-difference construct is defined as the tendency to have a grandiose and inflated sense of self and to hold beliefs about one's uniqueness and entitlement (Emmons, 1987; Raskin & Terry, 1988). We postulate that narcissism may influence an employee's willingness to support offender reintegration because employees who are high in narcissism are more likely to interpret the actions of others through the lens of their own inflated self-regard. As a result, they may be less likely to concede that people who commit transgressions may be as deserving of opportunities for redemption as they would be. It is also possible that narcissism prevents an employee from empathizing with a transgressor or feeling compassion toward him or her. It has been consistently shown that feelings of empathy can motivate more conciliatory and forgiving responses toward an offender (McCullough, Kilpatrick, Emmons, & Larson, 2001).

> ***Proposition 1b:*** Individuals who are high in narcissism will be the least supportive of offender reintegration.

### *Belief in a Just World*

Whether offender reintegration is perceived as morally appropriate may depend upon the individual's "belief in a just world." Belief in a just world refers to an individual's belief that people get what they deserve and deserve what they get (Lerner & Simmons, 1966). This process involves victim derogation—the tendency to blame a victim for their fate, framed in terms of deservingness, as a way to sustain a belief that the world is just. Individuals with high versus low levels of belief in a just world are more likely to deem the transgressor worthy of punishment, and less likely to consider reintegrating the offender.

> ***Proposition 1c:*** The stronger one's belief in a just world, the less supportive they will be of offender reintegration.

As explained above, the list of proposed individual difference variables is intended to be illustrative not exhaustive. We propose them to begin the conversation on how individual characteristics could influence the success of workplace reintegration efforts. We leave it to future research to test, expand on, or modify the list depending on what the data show. But regardless of what psychological characteristics an individual employee may possess, it seems likely that whether an individual reintegrates a transgressor back into the community will depend a great deal on how the transgressor behaves in the aftermath of his or her violation. In particular, the expression of remorse, an offer of apology, and a desire to make amends would seem to be critical for easing his or her path toward redemption and, in fact, we viewed these actions as being essential conditions for facilitating reintegration. Yet there are different kinds of apologies and attempts to make amends, so in the next section, we consider the role of these factors in more detail as they are among those in our model that are under the transgressor's control.

### *The Role of the Apology*

An individual's response to an offender may depend as well on a moral judgment regarding the perceived authenticity of the offender's efforts to make amends. Wenzel et al. (2008) suggest that taking steps to make amends has moral significance, "If a transgression is primarily seen as the violation, questioning, or undermining of values that are presumed to be shared in the relevant community, then the most effective undoing of the incident should be the offenders' reendorsement of those values." (2008, p. 381). When apologies are deemed to be window dressing (i.e., not seen as sincere), they can backfire, undermining restorative possibilities and resulting in even higher levels of punishment tendencies (Skarlicki, Folger, & Gee, 2004).

At issue then is whether steps taken to make amends, including offering an apology, extend beyond a surface level response to wrongdoing to fulfill moral expectations as to what constitutes an authentic effort to make amends and reaffirm workplace values. Summarizing a large literature on apologies, Radzik (2009) noted that apologies should involve an admission of responsibility for the offense, a condemnation of the wrong, a commitment not to reoffend, and respect for others who have been harmed. Exploring the role of apologies and the making of amends in an experimental context, Bottom et al. (2002) found in prisoner dilemma scenarios that apologies, in combination with other substantive efforts to make amends, were most effective in protecting the reputation of transgressors and restoring breaches of cooperation. Apologies gain greater authenticity as well when they convey a range of emotions including regret, shame, and guilt. In short, having made an apology that is deemed as sincere is likely to enhance the likelihood of offender reintegration because an apology reaffirms social norms, and provides a claim by the transgressor that he or she will not reoffend.

After having apologized and perhaps trying to make amends, obstacles to reintegration can still remain because acceptance back into a community will also depend upon social considerations that might not be under the total control of either the transgressor or the individual employees with whom he or she might interact.

> ***Proposition 1d:*** The greater the perceived authenticity of an offender's efforts to make amends, the greater the likelihood of offender reintegration.

## The Role of Social Considerations in Offender Reintegration

We propose that the success of offender reintegration can be a function of several social factors that can strengthen or weaken social bonds between the offender and employees directly and indirectly affected by a workplace offense.

### *Social Identity*

Wenzel et al. (2008) argued that people endorse restorative responses to wrongdoing when they perceive a shared social or group identity, because of the expectation of shared values. When individuals perceive themselves as sharing a common social identity and set of values with the offender, they are likely to be concerned with the harm the transgression does to their social identity and the underlying values shared by the group. These concerns will motivate individuals to take steps (i.e. the reintegration of the offender) that attempt to restore these values and shared identity in order to guide future interaction. Tyler, Sherman, Strang, Barnes, and Woods (2007) underscored the importance of offender reintegration for future interactions, "The reintegration with the social ties within which they live creates a set of interpersonal expectations that they are committed to following into the future" (2007, p. 555).

It is important to acknowledge the possibility that shared social identity can operate in a way that weakens social bonds and hinders offender reintegration. Gromet and Darley (2009) pointed out that violations of shared values among "in-group members" can lead to moral loss (Wenzel et al., 2008) and a sense of anger and moral outrage (Vidmar, 2002). These feelings of moral loss and moral outrage can overwhelm existing social bonds and motivate "calls for retribution" (Gromet & Darley, 2009, p. 54), as well as efforts to exclude the offender from the in-group as a means to protect group reputation.

> ***Proposition 2a:*** The greater the perception of shared social identity, the greater the likelihood of offender reintegration.

### Shared Fate

In addition to shared identity, shared fate (i.e. interdependence in work roles), can also influence the possibilities for reintegration. Greater interdependence may be associated with a greater investment and commitment to a working relationship (Green, Burnett, & Davis, 2008; Thibaut & Kelley, 1959). A coworker who must work closely with the transgressor, can therefore be more motivated to want to sustain the working relationship in the aftermath of a workplace transgression. On the other hand, interdependence, particularly if established over time, can represent an obstacle to reintegration. Examining cooperative behavior in an experimental prisoners dilemma context, Bottom et al. (2002) found that the longer two individuals interacted, the greater the difficulty in reestablishing cooperative relationships after a breach. Morrison and Robinson (1997) pointed out that at a more general level, when transgressions occur in lengthier relationships, they can represent betrayals of trust. These betrayals in turn may inhibit the potential for healing and reintegration.

> ***Proposition 2b:*** The greater the perception of shared fate, the greater the likelihood of offender reintegration.

### Forgiveness by the Victim(s)

Reintegration is not only a function of the social relationship between employee and offender, the motivation to reintegrate an offender can depend on the actions and perceptions of others. The actions of the victim or victims, in particular, can be extremely influential for facilitating reintegration. If the victim(s) acknowledge the efforts by the offender to make amends and publicly forgive the offender, the likelihood of reintegration will increase. One procedural mechanism for allowing this to occur is the restorative justice conference where people publicly forgive others (Strang, 2004).

> ***Proposition 2c:*** The greater the perception of forgiveness by the victim(s), the greater the likelihood of offender reintegration.

### Others' Support

The perceived support of other coworkers and workgroup norms can also play an important role. Edmondson (1999) and Tucker and Edmondson (2003) noted the potential for a culture of "psychological safety" to be created when members of work groups establish norms that allow for mistakes and errors to be acknowledged. Edmondson (1999) found that reintegration of clinicians into health care departments, specifically in the aftermath of committing a medical error, is facilitated by "psychologically safe" team environments characterized by "a shared belief that the team is safe for interpersonal risk taking" (Edmondson, 1999). Within these units, team members provide encouragement to individuals who make medical errors and work with them to resolve the error and associated harms, without stigma or shame (Edmondson, 1999). Psychologically safe work groups may also be places where team members are more likely to provide each other with support in the reintegration of offenders involved in more intentional transgressions.

Support can also come from outside the workgroup context. A strong advocate or champion within the organization can have a positive influence on offender reintegration. For instance, someone who has referent power in the work community—someone who is liked and trusted by the work group—is likely to help sway individuals to give the transgressor a second chance. The values of an organization, as reflected in its mission statement and embedded in the culture of the organization, can also reinforce a social context supportive of offender reintegration. Bazemore (1998) and Walker (2006) argued for the importance of values such as compassion, collective mercy, and hope in supporting the principles and practices of restorative justice within communities and societies. These broader cultural values, in combination with others such as respect for the dignity of employees, can be important in creating and sustaining the norms within an organization that emphasize the restoration of relationships for the offender, victim, and others in the organization in the aftermath of a transgression.

***Proposition 2d:*** The greater the perceived support of others, the greater the likelihood of offender reintegration.

To this point, we have emphasized how moral and social factors might influence employee's willingness to welcome an offender back into the workplace community. However, it may also be that in many organizations, the factor that might ultimately tip the balance in favor or reintegration is simply whether the offender is viewed as adding significant value to the organization. And the more value they add, either economically or in terms of reputation or prestige, the more likely individuals such as coworkers and customers will be to accept the transgressor back into the workplace.

## The Role of Instrumental Considerations in Offender Reintegration Economic value

Wenzel et al. (2008) argued that when individuals do not have a sense of shared social identity, for example based on age, family, or race, their response to wrongdoing will be influenced primarily by a focus on furthering self-interest. Under these conditions, a central issue is whether offender reintegration is in the individual's and organization's self-interest. In organizations whose principal goal is profitability, the most salient aspect of self-interest is likely to be the economic value of the offender, as reflected in the resources they bring into the organization. For example, in considering how to respond to physicians who engage in disruptive behaviors in health care organizations, a relevant consideration in terms of reintegration may be the physician's ability to attract patients and/or grant resources and the difficulty in replacing the physician.

> ***Proposition 3a:*** The greater the perceived economic value of the offender, the greater the likelihood of offender reintegration.

### Reputational Value

Another dimension of self-interest is the reputational value of the offender. Highly skilled individuals—whether physicians, executives, or R&D engineers, for example—may have high levels of reputational capital that provide these individuals with a greater degree of mobility, even in situations where they may have been involved in various kinds of transgressions. Halgin (2006), for example, found that coaches with winning team records were more likely than those with losing records to be able to continue coaching at colleges and universities, and to secure new positions at other similar-tier institutions, even after their programs had received National Collegiate Athletic Association sanctions for a variety of violations. More recently, Mark Hurd, former chief exectutive of Hewlett-Packard, was quickly hired soon after his resignation from Hewlett-Packard. Hurd resigned from Hewlett-Packard after violating the company's code of ethics in regard to accounting for business expenses (Worthen & Lublin, 2010). Hurd had been instrumental in helping Hewlett-Packard in recent years enhance its profitability and market leadership. Oracle Corporation hired Hurd within weeks of his resignation offering him a position as president with a salary of $950,000 and incentives worth close to $10,000,000.

> ***Proposition 3b:*** The greater the perceived reputational value of the offender, the greater the likelihood of offender reintegration.

### Ability to Enhance Success

Related to the above factors is the degree to which the offender's presence enhances an individual's own opportunities for success. It may be that employees who benefit from interacting with an offender will be more willing to advocate for and accept a coworker's reintegration in the workplace, than those who are either in direct competition with the transgressor for organizational rewards, or who derive no benefit from continued association with him or her.

> ***Proposition 3c:*** The greater the perceived ability of the offender to enhance one's success in the organization, the greater the likelihood of offender reintegration.

In summary, we propose that offender reintegration is a decision influenced by moral (e.g., personality traits, the response to actions taken by the offender such as making an apology), social (e.g., a shared fate, whether others decide to reintegrate), and instrumental considerations (e.g., ability to contribute to the organization's and individual's goals, reputational value).

## IMPLICATIONS FOR RESEARCH

Viewing injustice and mistreatment from the perspective of offender reintegration broadens the types of factors and processes that can come into play relative to the scope currently studied by justice researchers. For example, this perspective also has the potential to shift the focus from backward (the need to punish a transgressor for a wrongdoing) to forward looking (What can be done to make things better?) and shift attention from concerns solely about the victim to concerns about the transgressor as well. It seems to us that although reintegration might not be the first reaction to a violation, there are several advantages for doing so that we discussed previously. Our perspective, which emphasizes ways to retain potentially valuable organizational members who may have made a one-time error in judgment, is consistent with research on enhancing psychological capital (Luthans, Youssef, & Avolio, 2007) as a way to gain an organizational competitive edge. This perspective also brings to the foreground the social influence of third parties on a subject's decision whether to reintegrate an offender in the work group. Social information processing theory (Salancik & Pfeffer, 1978) proposes that employees' attitudes and behavior are affected by their coworkers who communicate setting-specific norms, values, and expectations. Indeed, information from one's peers might help employees clarify the fairness of events (DeGoey, 2000). Moreover, in studies of organizational justice, peers' opinions about fairness can be highly diagnostic (Folger & Kass, 2000) and collective experiences of justice provide more events to consider than do personal experiences alone (Lind, Kray, & Thompson, 1998). Jones and Skarlicki (2009) found that merely overhearing third parties talk about a transgressor can influence an individual's fairness perceptions and retaliation tendencies independent of how the individual was personally treated. Research is needed to explore whether third parties similarly influence reintegration efforts.

Moreover, we propose that offender reintegration provides research advantages over the forgiveness perspective. One of the challenges facing researchers studying forgiveness is that it is difficult to define and measure. We would argue in contrast that making a decision to allow someone back on the team is measurable, does not necessitate complete forgiveness, and opens opportunities for work groups to function despite having experienced conflict. It is also a more observable phenomenon than forgiveness, which is an intrapersonal experience. Third, there is the potential for offender reintegration to lead to stronger bonds among group members than existed prior to the reintegration process. Consumer research, for instance, has found that restoring customer service after a service failure resulted in higher levels of customer trust, loyalty, and commitment relative to before the service failure—labeled a service recovery paradox (see de Matos, Henrique, & Rossi, 2007, for a review). Whether this phenomenon might be associated with offender reintegration, warrants testing.

With regard to our model of offender reintegration, an important theoretical and empirical issue is to understand contextual differences in the relative influence of moral, social, and instrumental considerations on offender reintegration. One might expect that in highly competitive corporate contexts, such as investment banks, sales units of corporations, or in high technology firms (as reinforced by Mark Hurd's experience), instrumental considerations might be of greatest importance. In health care and university contexts, as brought out by the Dr. Marc Hauser case, considerations of social and professional identity, along with instrumental value, may be particularly salient in influencing responses to transgressions.

An additional contextual issue to consider is how individual and organizational preferences for retributive and restorative measures might influence offender reintegration. Research (Carlsmith, Darley, & Robinson, 2002) supports the inclination of people to desire retribution when confronted with wrongdoing by an offender, particularly for high severity crimes. However, recent research also supports that when people are given an opportunity to include restorative responses to wrongdoing, as well as retributive responses, they prefer both, rather than the forced choice of one or the other (Gromet & Darley, 2009). Gromet and Darley (2009) explained why a combination of punishment and restorative measures could facilitate offender reintegration. They noted,

> The use of an option that combines both restorative and retributive elements allows for respondents to show their condemnation by inflicting retribution upon the offender, as well as reestablish value consensus with the offender and repair the harm caused to the victim through the restorative measures. (2009, p. 55)

Thus, a reintegration option might also include certain punishment as a condition of reintegration.

Karp and Conrad (2005) presented an example of a formalized organizational system that combines punitive and restorative measures to address offenders who violate integrity standards in a higher education context. They profiled Skidmore College and its integrity board. Skidmore College employs a five-stage process to address violations of integrity standards. The process employed is typical of many restorative justice conferences. It involves establishing common ground between the victim, offender, and community (university and local), determining responsibility, having the offender apologize and accept responsibility, identifying the impact of the offense, and collectively strategizing repair and reintegration. In order to conduct an integrity board hearing a group is brought together consisting of four students, one staff member and one or two faculty depending on whether the integrity issue is one of academic integrity (requires two faculty members). Members of the Integrity Board participate in a series of weekly 1-hour meetings over the course of fall semester that involve readings, role plays, guest speakers, and review of prior cases.

Karp and Conrad (2005) point to a number of examples that illustrate how the Integrity Board promotes offender reintegration. In one case a college student was suspended for using cocaine. The student served time in a state prison, reapplied to Skidmore to complete his senior year, and then was readmitted with the understanding that the student would be involved in leading conferences/workshops on campus related to drug abuse. The student created a 30-minute video that provided a foundation for discussing on campus the risks of using and dealing drugs. The Skidmore Integrity Board can encourage reintegration in other ways. Violators of academic integrity might participate in orientations and share with new students the importance of not cheating, while someone who engages in hate speech might be encouraged to work with others to organize a campus-wide event on diversity and multicultural issues.

The integrity board at Skidmore represents one possibility for introducing restorative justice practices into corporate settings and facilitating offender reintegration. To date, however, there has been little integration of restorative justice practices and structures such as the integrity board at Skidmore College. Kidder (2007, p. 16) has argued that utilizing restorative justice practices such as conferences could be employed to address workplace offenses, including conflicts and offenses traditionally handled through alternative dispute resolution processes, "if an organization has a mandatory [alternative dispute resolution] clause in their employment contract, any dispute that calls for arbitration could be effectively handled by the restorative justice process."

Although our model also presents different categories of factors, each factor offers the opportunity to explore relationships between these factors. For example, one might expect that an offender's authentic apology (moral consideration) would positively influence victim forgiveness (social consideration) and increase the likelihood of offender reintegration. Some of these variables may also act as moderating variables. For example, instrumental considerations, such as perceptions of the offender's ability to enhance success, might moderate social considerations such as increasing the perception of shared fate.

Related situational and personality factors can also be integrated into our model. We noted above that the importance of the offender's perceived instrumental value on the likelihood of reintegration might depend on the organizational/industry context. We also proposed that individuals are likely to engage in offender reintegration when their social network does so. We would speculate, for example, that individuals high on external locus of control would be particularly susceptible to social network cues. Thus, in addition to the main effects described above, there exists the potential to explore how these factors interact to predict offender integration.

We also recognize that there are other important main effects to explore and researchers should draw on relevant literatures in building on our model. For example, McCarter and Caza (2009) drew attention to the role that power can play in the formal process of reinstatement (i.e., the formal return of privileges to an employee by a manager following disciplinary action). They suggested that power, specifically in the form of regulatory and stakeholder pressure can positively influence managers to reinstate employees. They also noted, however, that this coercive influence can potentially undermine trust and positive affect between the manager and offender. Similarly, if a manager employed power to coerce employees into reintegrating an offender, one might expect this to inhibit the full integration of the offender by the workgroup.

We encourage researchers as well to expand the model and take into consideration variables that may influence whether psychological willingness to reintegrate offenders leads to direct actions such as extending emotional and social support to offenders or speaking to others on behalf of the offender. For example, high status individuals may have the respect of others and be in a better position to act on behalf of the offender. Providing emotional support may be dependent on an individual's communication skills. Also important to consider would be the structural and contextual features of organizations. For example, it may be that flatter as opposed to more hierarchical organizations make it easier to implement reintegration since the offending employee may have had more opportunities to interact with his or her coworkers at various times. Turning to culture, there are multiple contextual attributes that might facilitate reintegration and it is beyond the scope of our paper to identify all of them. However, as we noted earlier, we believe that the extent to which the organization is perceived as having a climate of psychological safety could be an important factor in this regard (Edmondson, 1999). Psychologically safe work group contexts can reinforce norms and values that encourage extending forgiveness and second chances to those not only who have made errors, but to those who have committed transgressions.

When testing for the effects described in this chapter, scholars have numerous research options. Laboratory experiments, for instance, provide a basis for understanding what individuals *are capable of doing*, but without the context of many of the factors discussed in our model, they can fail to inform us as to what individuals *actually will do* in the workplace. Said differently, it is one thing for participants to report that they would reintegrate an offender, it is quite another for them to actually do so. Thus while it will be important to test some of these effects in the laboratory, field research will be important to flesh out our theorizing.

Field research might be particularly important given that the decision of whether to reintegrate an offender into a work group is likely to involve considerable social information processing. This is because, in many cases, the individuals deciding whether or not to readmit an offender into a work group could be doing so without having directly observed the transgression. Individuals often rely on vicarious information and their assessments are likely to be heavily informed by the opinions of others (Lind et al., 1998; Umphress, Labianca, Brass, Kass, & Scholten, 2003). Accordingly, there is an opportunity for network theory to aid this research direction. Knowing who talks to whom and knowing characteristics of the network itself can provide important information regarding offender reintegration. Individuals' decisions are likely to be both affected by and have an impact on their social network.

Building on the above point about a lack of first hand information about a transgression, field research could enhance understanding of how people talk about organizational events. Storytelling is a common mechanism by which people share and make sense of events around them (DeGoey, 2000; Martin, Feldman, Hatch, & Sitkin, 1983). Stories provide an interpretive account of an event's sequences, and convey information in a concentrated and concrete manner. Narratives can have a significant impact on the reintegration process because while some information is included, other information is left out. Storytelling is also critical artifact in shaping and reinforcing organizational culture (Schein, 1990). Narratives also carry information regarding what a just world should look like. Thus, an interesting line of research would be to explore how individuals make reintegration decisions when faced with contradictory versions of an event from different sources. Policy-capturing studies might be an effective method for discovering which cues are most influential in determining, for example, an individual's assessment of authentication.

Finally, field research could allow for exploring offender reintegration over time. Judgments as to not only whether to reintegrate offenders, but changes in one's level of respect and affect for a given offender, may change over time in light of new information from one's coworkers, the actions of the offender, and even changes in the offender's instrumental value. Restorative justice scholars reference the notion of "earned redemption" (Braithwaite, 2002) and this type of longitudinal research on offender reintegration could provide a deeper understanding of the factors that influence judgments as to what constitutes the conditions of earned redemption and full reintegration.

## SUMMARY

A primary goal of this chapter is to shift the organizational justice conversation from one that emphasizes the punishment of offenders to one that explores the possibilities of reintegrating offenders into the workplace. We used the restorative justice literature as a foundation for drawing attention to the importance of healing and repairing relationships between the offender, victims, and others in the workplace. We developed a conceptual model incorporating a number of important psychological and social influences on offender reintegration. As our closing discussion suggests, we believe that as the justice conversation begins to taken into greater account offenders and their reintegration, there will be opportunities for researchers to build on this model and pursue a variety of promising research directions.

## REFERENCES

Adams, J. S. (1965). Inequity in social exchange. In L. Berkowitz (Ed.), *Advances in experimental social psychology* (Vol. 2, pp. 267-299). New York, NY: Academic Press.

Ambrose, M. L., Seabright, M. A., & Schminke, M. (2002). Sabotage in the workplace: The role of organizational injustice. *Organizational Behavior and Human Decision Processes, 89,* 947-965.

Aquino, K., & Freeman, D. (2009). Moral identity in business situations: A social-cognitive framework for understanding moral functioning. In D. Narvaez & D. Lapsley (Eds.), *Personality, identity, and character: Explorations in moral psychology* (pp. 375-395). New York, NY: Cambridge University Press.

Aquino, K., Freeman, D., Reed, A., II, Lim, V. K. G., & Felps, W. (2009). Testing a social-cognitive model of moral behavior: The interactive influence of situations and moral identity centrality. *Journal of Personality and Social Psychology, 97,* 123-141.

Aquino, K., Grover, S. L., Goldman, B., & Folger, R. (2003). When push doesn't come to shove: Interpersonal forgiveness in workplace relationships. *Journal of Management Inquiry, 12,* 209-216.

Aquino, K., & Reed, A. (2002). The self-importance of moral identity. *Journal of Personality and Social Psychology, 83,* 1423-1440.

Aquino, K., Tripp, T. M., & Bies, R. J. (2001). How employees respond to personal offense: The effects of blame attribution, victim status, and offender status on revenge and reconciliation in the workplace. *Journal of Applied Psychology, 86,* 52-59.

Aquino, K., Tripp, T. M., & Bies, R. J. (2006). Getting even or moving on? Power, procedural justice, and types of offense as predictors of revenge, forgiveness, reconciliation, and avoidance in organizations. *Journal of Applied Psychology, 91,* 653-668.

Barclay, L. J., & Skarlicki, D. P. (2009). Healing the wounds of organizational injustice: Examining the benefits of expressive writing. *Journal of Applied Psychology, 94,* 511-523.

Bazemore, G. (1998). Restorative justice and earned redemption: Communities, victims, and offender reintegration. *American Behavioral Scientist, 41,* 768-813.

Blasi, A. (1984). Moral identity: Its role in moral functioning. In W. M. Kurtines & J. L. Gewirtz (Eds.), *Morality, moral behavior, and moral development* (pp. 128-139). New York, NY: Wiley.

Bottom, W. P., Gibson, K., Daniels, S. E., & Murnighan, J. K. (2002). When talk is not cheap: Substantive penance and expressions of intent in rebuilding cooperation. *Organization Science, 13,* 497-513.

Bradfield, M., & Aquino, K. (1999). The effects of blame attributions and offender likableness on forgiveness and revenge in the workplace. *Journal of Management, 25,* 607-631.

Braithwaite, J. (1999). Restorative justice: Assessing optimistic and pessimistic accounts. *Crime and Justice, 25,* 1-127.

Braithwaite, J. (2002). *Restorative justice and responsive regulation.* New York, NY: Oxford University Press.

Carlsmith, K. M., Darley, J. M., & Robinson, P. H. (2002). Why do we punish?: Deterrence and just deserts as motives for punishment. *Journal of Personality and Social Psychology, 83,* 284-299.

Colquitt, J. A. (2001). On the dimensionality of organizational justice: A construct validation of a measure. *Journal of Applied Psychology, 86,* 386-400.

Colquitt, J. A., & Shaw, J. C. (2005). How should organizational justice be measured. In J. Greenberg & J. A. Colquitt (Eds.), *Handbook of organizational justice* (pp. 113-152). Mahwah, NJ: Erlbaum.

Cropanzano, R., Goldman, B., & Folger, R. (2003). Deontic justice: The role of moral principles in workplace fairness. *Journal of Organizational Behavior, 24,* 1019-1024.

Cropanzano, R., Goldman, B., & Folger, R. (2005). Self-interest: Defining and understanding a human motive. *Journal of Organizational Behavior, 26,* 985-991.

Daly, K., & Immarigeon, R. (1998). The past, present, and future of restorative justice: Some critical reflections. *Contemporary Justice Review, 1,* 21-45.

De Dreu, C. K. W., & Weingart, L. R. (2003). Task versus relationship conflict, team performance, and team member satisfaction: A meta-analysis. *Journal of Applied Psychology, 88,* 741-749.

de Matos, C. A., Henrique, J. L., & Rossi, C. A. V. (2007). Service recovery paradox: A meta-analysis. *Journal of Service Research, 10,* 60-77.

DeGoey, P. (2000). Contagious justice: Exploring the social construction of justice in organizations. In B. M. Staw & R. I. Sutton (Eds.), *Research in organizational behavior* (Vol. 22, pp. 51-102). New York, NY: Elsevier Science.

Dirks, K. T., Lewicki, R. J., & Zaheer, A. (2009). Repairing relationships within and between organizations: Building a conceptual foundation. *Academy of Management Review, 34,* 68-84.

Eder, P., Aquino, K., Turner, C., & Reed, A. (2006). Punishing those responsible for the prison abuses at Abu Ghraib: The influence of the Negative Reciprocity Norm (NRN). *Political Psychology, 27,* 807-821.

Edmondson, A. (1999). Psychological safety and learning behavior in work teams. *Administrative Science Quarterly, 44,* 350-383.

Eisenberger, R., Lynch, P., Aselage, J., & Rohdieck, S. (2004). Who takes the most revenge? Individual differences in negative reciprocity norm endorsement. *Personality and Social Psychology Bulletin, 30,* 787-799.

Emmons, R. A. (1987). Narcissism: Theory and measurement. *Journal of Personality and Social Psychology, 52,* 11-17.

Enright, R. D., Gassin, E. A., & Wu, C.-R. (1992). Forgiveness: A developmental view. *Journal of Moral Education, 21,* 99-114.

Ethics Resource Center. (2009). *National business ethics survey.* Arlington, VA: Author.

Exline, J. J., Baumeister, R. F., Bushman, B. J., Campbell, W. K., & Finkel, E. J. (2004). Too proud to let go: Narcissistic entitlement as a barrier to forgiveness. *Journal of Personality and Social Psychology, 87,* 894-912.

Folger, R. (2001). Fairness as deonance. In S. W. Gilliland, D. D. Steiner & D. P. Skarlicki (Eds.), *Research in social issues in management: Theoretical and cultural perspectives on organizational justice* (Vol. 1, pp. 3-33). Greenwich, CT: Information Age.

Folger, R., & Baron, R. A. (1996). Violence and hostility at work: A model of reactions to perceived injustice. In G. R. Van den Bos & E. Q. Bulatao (Eds.), *Violence on the job: Identifying risks and developing solutions* (pp. 51-85). Washington, DC: American Psychological Association.

Folger, R., & Kass, E. E. (2000). Social comparison and fairness: A counterfactual simulations perspective. In J. Suls & L. Wheeler (Eds.), *Handbook of social comparison: Theory and research* (pp. 423-441). New York, NY: Plenum Press.

Gallucci, M., & Perugini, M. (2003). Information seeking and reciprocity: A transformational analysis. *European Journal of Social Psychology, 33,* 473-495.

Goodstein, J., & Aquino, K. (2010). And restorative justice for all: Redemption, forgiveness, and reintegration in organizations. *Journal of Organizational Behavior, 31,* 624-628.

Goodstein, J., & Butterfield, K. D. (2010). Extending the horizon of business ethics: Restorative justice and the aftermath of unethical behavior. *Business Ethics Quarterly, 20,* 453-480.

Gouldner, A. W. (1960). The norm of reciprocity: A preliminary statement. *American Sociological Review, 25,* 161-178.

Green, J. D., Burnett, J. L., & Davis, J. L. (2008). Third-party forgiveness: (Not) forgiving your close other's betrayer. *Personality and Social Psychology Bulletin, 34,* 407-418.

Greenberg, J. (1993). The social side of fairness: Interpersonal and informational classes of organizational justice. In R. Cropanzano (Ed.), *Justice in the workplace: Approaching fairness in human resource management* (pp. 79-103). Hillsdale, NJ: Erlbaum.

Greenberg, J., & Colquitt, J. A. (2005). *Handbook of organizational justice*. Mahwah, NJ: Erlbaum.

Gromet, D. M., & Darley, J. M. (2009). Retributive and restorative justice: Importance of crime severity and shared identity in people's justice responses. *Australian Journal of Psychology, 61,* 50-57.

Halgin, D. L. (2006). *The influence of legitimacy on career trajectories of individuals in leadership positions: NCAA basketball.* Paper presented at the Academy of Management Best Paper Conference Proceedings, Atlanta, GA.

Jones, D., & Skarlicki, D. P. (2005). The social construction of justice: The effects of overhearing peers discuss an authority's fairness reputation on reactions to subsequent treatment. *Journal of Applied Psychology, 90,* 363-372.

Karp, D., & Conrad, S. (2005). Restorative justice and college student misconduct. *Public Organization Review: A Global Journal, 5,* 315-333.

Kidder, D. L. (2007). Restorative justice: Not "rights," but the right way to heal relationships at work. *International Journal of Conflict Management, 18,* 4-22.

Kim, P. H., Ferrin, D. L., Cooper, C. D., & Dirks, K. T. (2004). Removing the shadow of suspicion: The effects of apology versus denial for repairing competence—Versus integrity-based trust violations. *Journal of Applied Psychology, 89,* 104-118.

Lerner, M. J., & Simmons, C. H. (1966). Observer's reaction to the "innocent victim": Compassion or rejection? *Journal of Personality and Social Psychology, 4,* 203-210.

Lind, E. A., Kray, L., & Thompson, L. (1998). The social construction of injustice: Fairness judgments in response to own and others unfair treatment by authorities. *Organizational Behavior and Human Decision Processes, 75,* 1-22.

Lind, E. A., & van den Bos, K. (2002). When fairness works: Toward a general theory of uncertainty management. In B. M. Staw & R. M. Kramer (Eds.),

*Research in organizational behavior* (Vol. 24, pp. 181-223). Oxford, England: Elsevier Science.

Luthans, F., Youssef, C. M., & Avolio, B. J. (2007). *Psychological capital: Developing the human competitive edge*. New York, NY: Oxford University Press.

Martin, J., Feldman, M. S., Hatch, M. J., & Sitkin, S. B. (1983). The uniqueness paradox in organizational stories. *Administrative Science Quarterly, 28*, 438-453.

Maruna, S. (2001). *Making good: How ex-convicts reform and rebuild their lives*. Washington, DC: American Psychological Association.

McCarter, M., & Caza, A. (2009). Toward a theory of reinstatement: Seven motivations for reinstatement as relationship repair. *Employee Responsibilities and Rights Journal*. Retrieved from http://www.springerlink.com/content/105548/

McCullough, M. E., Kilpatrick, S. D., Emmons, R. A., & Larson, D. B. (2001). Is gratitude a moral affect? *Psychological Bulletin, 127*, 249-266.

McCullough, M. E., Worthington, E. L., Jr., & Rachal, K. C. (1997). Interpersonal forgiving in close relationships. *Journal of Personality and Social Psychology, 73*, 321-336.

Mitchell, M. S., & Ambrose, M. L. (2007). Abusive supervision and workplace deviance and the moderating effects of negative reciprocity beliefs. *Journal of Applied Psychology, 92*, 1159-1168.

Morrison, E. W., & Robinson, S. L. (1997). When employees feel betrayed: A model of how psychological contract violation develops. *The Academy of Management Review, 22*, 226-256.

North, J. (1987). Wrongdoing and forgiveness. *Philosophy, 62*, 499-508.

O'Reilly, J., & Aquino, K. (2011). A model of third parties' morally-motivated responses to mistreatment in organizations. *Academy of Management Review, 36*, 526-543.

Pearson, C. M., & Porath, C. L. (2005). On the nature, consequences and remedies of workplace incivility: No time for "nice"? Think again. *Academy of Management Executive, 19*, 7-18.

Perugini, M., Gallucci, M., Presaghi, F., & Ercolani, A. P. (2003). The personal norm of reciprocity. *European Journal of Personality, 17*, 251-283.

Radzik, L. (2009). *Making amends: Atonement in morality, law, and politics*. New York, NY: Oxford University Press.

Raskin, R., & Terry, H. (1988). A principal-components analysis of the narcissistic personality inventory and further evidence of its construct validity. *Journal of Personality and Social Psychology, 54*, 890-902.

Ren, H., & Gray, B. (2009). Repairing relationship conflict: How violation types and culture influence the effectiveness of restoration rituals. *Academy of Management Review, 34*, 105-126.

Roche, D. (2003). *Accountability in restorative justice*. New York, NY: Oxford University Press.

Roche, D. (2006). Dimensions of restorative justice. *Journal of Social Issues, 62*, 217-238.

Rosenstein, A. H., & O'Daniel, M. (2005). Disruptive behavior and clinical outcomes: Perceptions of nurses and physicians. *American Journal of Nursing, 105*, 54-64.

Rosenstein, A. H., & O'Daniel, M. (2008). Managing disruptive physician behavior: Impact on staff relationships and patient care. *Neurology, 70,* 1564-1570.

Salancik, G. R., & Pfeffer, J. (1978). A social information processing approach to job attitudes and task design. *Administrative Sciences Quarterly, 23,* 224-252.

Schein, E. (1992). *Organizational culture and leadership.* San Francisco, CA: Jossey Bass.

Seligman, M. E. P., & Csikszentmihalyi, M. (2000). Positive psychology: An introduction. *American Psychologist, 55,* 5-14.

Sitkin, S. B., & Roth, N. L. (1993). Explaining the limited effectiveness of legalistic "remedies" for trust/distrust. *Organization Science, 4,* 367-392.

Skarlicki, D. P., & Folger, R. (1997). Retaliation in the workplace: The roles of distributive, procedural, and interactional justice. *Journal of Applied Psychology, 82,* 434-443.

Skarlicki, D. P., Folger, R., & Gee, J. (2004). When social accounts backfire: The exacerbating effects of a polite message or an apology on reactions to an unfair outcome. *Journal of Applied Social Psychology, 34,* 322-341.

Skarlicki, D. P., & Kulik, C. T. (2005). Third-party reactions to employee (mis)treatment: A justice perspective. In B. M. Staw & R. M. Kramer (Eds.), *Research in organizational behavior: An annual series of analytical essays and critical reviews* (Vol. 26, pp. 183-229). Oxford, England: Elsevier.

Skarlicki, D. P., van Jaarsveld, D. D., & Walker, D. D. (2008). Getting even for customer mistreatment: The role of moral identity in the relationship between customer interpersonal injustice and employee sabotage. *Journal of Applied Psychology, 93,* 1335-1347.

Strang, H. (2004). *Repair or revenge: Victims and restorative justice.* New York, NY: Oxford University Press.

Thibaut, J. W., & Kelley, H. H. (1959). *The social psychology of groups.* New York, NY: John Wiley.

Thibaut, J. W., & Walker, L. (1978). A theory of procedure. *California Law Review, 66,* 541-566.

Tripp, T. M., & Bies, R. J. (2009). *Getting even: The truth about workplace revenge—And how to stop it.* San Francisco, CA: Jossey-Bass.

Tripp, T. M., Bies, R. J., & Aquino, K. (2002). Poetic justice or petty jealousy? The aesthetics of revenge. *Organizational Behavior and Human Decision Processes, 89,* 966-984.

Tucker, A. L., & Edmondson, A. C. (2003). Why hospitals don't learn from failures: Organizational and psychological dynamics that inhibit system change. *California Management Review, 45*(2), 55-72.

Tyler, T. R., & Blader, S. L. (2002). Autonomous vs. Comparative status: Must we be better than others to feel good about ourselves? *Organizational Behavior and Human Decision Processes, 89,* 813-838.

Tyler, T. R., Sherman, L., Strang, H., Barnes, G. C., & Woods, D. (2007). Reintegrative shaming, procedural justice, and recidivism: The engagement of offenders' psychological mechanisms in the Canberra RISE drinking-and-driving experiment. *Law & Society Review, 41,* 553-586.

Umphress, E. E., Labianca, G., Brass, D. J., Kass, E., & Scholten, L. (2003). The role of instrumental and expressive social ties in employees' perceptions of organizational justice. *Organization Science, 14,* 738-753.

Vidmar, N. (2002). Retributive justice: Its social context. In M. Ross & D. T. Miller (Eds.), *The justice motive in everyday life* (pp. 291-317). New York, NY: Cambridge University Press.

Wade, N. (2010, August 27). Harvard researcher may have fabricated data. *The New York Times.* Retrieved from http://www.nytimes.com

Walker, M. U. (2006). *Moral repair: Reconstructing moral relations after wrongdoing.* New York, NY: Cambridge University Press.

Ward, T., & Langlands, R. (2009). Reparing the rupture. Restorative justice and the rehabilitation of offenders. *Aggression and Violent Behavior, 14,* 205-214.

Wenzel, M., Okimoto, T. G., Feather, N. T., & Platow, M. J. (2008). Retributive and restorative justice. *Law & Human Behavior, 32,* 375-389.

Wiessner, P. (2005). Norm enforcement among the ju/'hoansi bushmen: A case of strong reciprocity? *Human Nature, 16,* 115-145.

Worthen, B., & Lublin, J. S. (2010, September 7). Mark Hurd hired by H-P rival Oracle. *Wall Street Journal,* pp. A1-A2.

Zehr, H. (1990). *Changing lenses: A new focus for crime and justice.* Scottsdale, PA: Herald Press.

CHAPTER 5

# ORGANIZATIONAL JUSTICE AND MULTIPLE LEVELS OF SOCIAL CAPITAL

**Keith James, Damon Drown, and Gabriela Burlacu**

We present a model of different types of organizational justice as major influences on social capital in the workplace. Our model positions interorganizational, organizational, team, and individual social capital as being determined by multilevel organizational justice (interorganizational, organizational, interteam and intrateam, individual). All major subtypes of organizational justice—distributive, procedural, and interactional—are characterized in the model as multilevel and as important to social capital development. Research propositions and applied implications of our justice-to-social-capital model are outlined.

In their seminal paper on organizational social capital, Nahapiet and Ghoshal (1998) stated that "the central proposition of social capital theory is that networks of relationships constitute a valuable resource (that provides organizations and their members with) a 'credential' which entitles them to credit, in the various senses of the word." In this paper, we propose that multilevel organizational justice may be a critical mechanism for creating—or destroying—social capital, and that the latter plays a major role in transmitting organizational justice effects to major individual and organizational outcomes. Our thesis in this paper is that fair

*Emerging Perspectives on Organizational Justice and Ethics*
pp. 105–134

behavior in and by organizations is a generator of social capital, and unjust behavior in or by organizations promotes degeneration of social capital. Further, we view organizational justice as a multilevel phenomenon in which justice at each different level has its own distinctive influence on social capital formation and use. In addition, we propose that organizational social capital occurs at multiple levels: interorganizational, organizational, team, and individual. Therefore, we examine factors and processes by which multilevel justice shapes multilevel social capital; and how social capital then influences outcomes (e.g., individual health; team efficacy; organizational learning) at multiple levels. To some, but a lesser, extent we also examine influences of the opposite sort—how existing patterns of social capital influence organizational-justice processes and outcomes.

Empirical research over the last decade has demonstrated that organizational justice is related to a number of social capital components and measures such as: network ties (Lamertz, 2002); collective esteem (Colquitt, 2001); trust (Sunshine & Tyler, 2003; Tyler & DeGoey, 1995); felt organizational obligation (Aquino, 1995; Colquitt, 2001; Sunshine & Tyler, 2003); and group identification (Lind, Kray, & Thompson, 2001; Tyler & DeGoey, 1995). An examination of this research suggests that social capital and organizational justice are distinct but mutually influential constructs with differing relationships dependant on the level of analysis and how each construct is operationalized.

Our model in Figure 5.1 indicates, therefore, multiple levels of organizational justice (left side of Figure 5.1) affecting social capital processes (center, Figure 5.1) and outcomes (right side, Figure 5.1) *within* each organizational level. It also indicates justice-based linkages *among* the various levels of justice, social capital formation, and social-capital outcomes.

## SOCIAL CAPITAL: DEFINITION AND LEVELS

Coleman (1988) distinguishes between *human capital*—made up of the knowledge, skills and abilities that individuals (or teams) carry within them—versus social capital, which covers all types of *social* assets that are derived from the social networks of individuals, teams or organizations. Nahapiet and Ghoshal (1998) focused on social capital as a *mechanism* for the creation of other organizational outcomes (e.g., organizational learning; organizational innovation; organizational resource acquisition). Putnam (2007, p. 137 defined social capital as "social networks and the associated norms of reciprocity and trustworthiness." In that definition, social capital consists of social relationships and networks that are based on social cooperation among people or entities and that are *mutually*

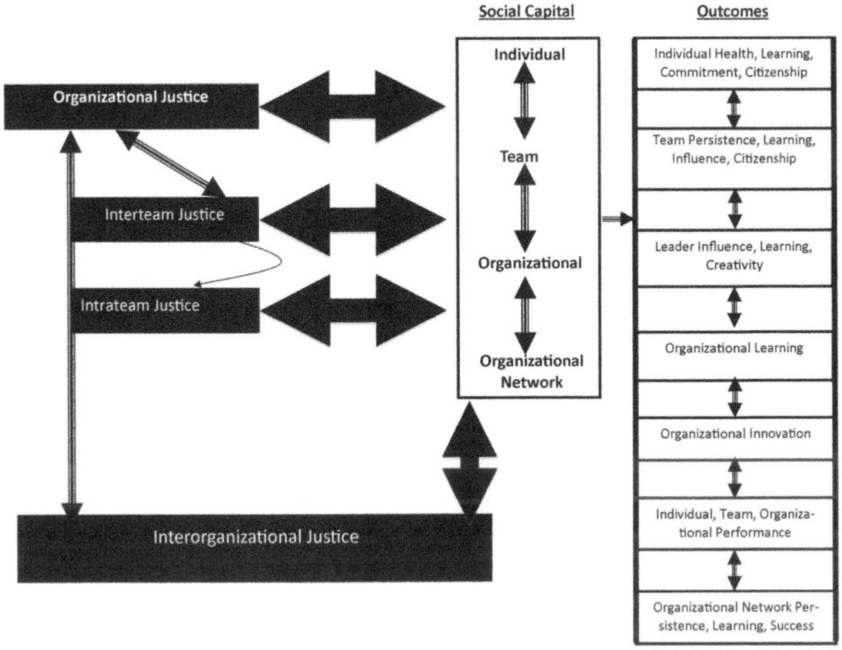


Figure 5.1. Organizational justice and multiple levels of social capital.

*advantageous*. By "mutually advantageous," we are following Putnam (2007) and Nahapiet and Ghosal (1998) in seeing social capital as partially defined by the positive benefits for one or more target entities that result from being embedded in a "social network (characterized by) reciprocity and trustworthiness" (Putnam, 2007, p. 137)

Lamertz (2002) and Putnam (2007) have also focused on social capital as either an individual or a collective process. That is, the network of relationships can be among individuals, or among groups, and the positive outcomes that results can be at the individual, group, organizational, or organizational-network, level. Recent works, for instance, have examined social capital formation and outcomes among networks of organizations (e.g., Bunderson & Sutcliffe, 2002; Caldwell & Evaerhart, 1996). In line with those works, our model in Figure 5.1 shows organizational social capital as a multilevel construct that applies to individuals, work teams, organizations, and organizational networks.

All of the authors cited above sought to understand the *societal and organizational mechanisms* that help to create social capital. In this chapter, we propose that organizational justice, as it occurs at multiple levels, influences organizational social capital formation, as well as the outcomes that social capital shapes. Nahapiet and Ghoshal (1998) describe a *relational* dimension of social capital that is composed trust, identification, norms, and obligations. The calculus-based form of social capital, on the other hand, is shaped more by perceptions of *equity of social exchanges*—in the workplace, that is, by distributive organizational justice.

The distinction between calculus-based versus relational social capital is very similar to the two major theories of organizational-justice processes: the group-value or relational model of justice, and social-exchange theory. According to the group-value or relational model of justice, individuals feel that they are valued and respected members of the organization when they are treated justly (Tyler, 1989). The basic premise is that the fairness of procedures and practices signify the relationship that workers have with leaders and collectives (Tyler & DeGoey, 1995). In this model, when procedures are fair the message is conveyed that one is respected as a community member, which tends to increase many aspect and levels of social capital: self-esteem (individual level—e.g., Koper, Van Knippenberg, Bouhuijs, Vermunt, & Wilke, 1993); identification with a group (team level—e.g., Brewer, 1991; Messick & Mackie, 1989), and trust in, engagement with, and commitment to, the organization (organizational level—Saks, 2006). Increased engagement in the workplace seems to result in increased development of social capital—that is, *from* perceptions of justice (left-side Figure 5.1) *to* social capital (center box Figure 5.1) for the individual, group, organization or network *to* outcomes (right box) for individuals, work teams, organizations, and organizational networks. We propose, therefore that:

> ***Proposition 1:*** Social capital (center box, Figure 5.1) mediates between organizational justice (left side, Figure 5.1) and the multilevel outcomes displayed at the right side of Figure 5.1.

## ORGANIZATIONAL JUSTICE: DEFINITIONS AND LEVELS

Initially, organizational justice theorists and researchers focused on *distributive* justice (Adams, 1965; Greenberg, 1982), but soon *procedural* justice was added as another major category of workplace fairness (Folger & Konovsky, 1989; Sweeney & McFarlin, 1993). Distributive justice refers to whether an outcome received is viewed as fair, while procedural justice refers to the fairness of decision and allocation *processes* in the workplace (Colquitt, 2001). Research on distributive and procedural justice perceptions has shown that employee perceptions of the degree to which these justice elements are present in an organization impacts their thinking, affect, and behavior toward work, supervisors, coworkers, teams, and organizations (Colquitt, 2001; Erdogan, 2002; Rupp, Bashshur, & Liao, 2007; Sweeney & McFarlin, 1993; Umphress, Labianca, Brass, Kass, & Scholten, 2011).

More recently, the construct of procedural justice has been separated into two distinct categories: procedural justice, per se, and *interactional* justice, the latter of which refers broadly to "the quality of interpersonal treatment received during the enactment of organizational procedures" (Masterson, Byrne, & Mao, 2005). Interactional justice has been further divided into two categories: *informational* justice, which refers to the degree to which relevant information regarding an organizational procedure or outcome is fairly provided; and *interpersonal* justice, which refers to whether an organizational entity (for instance, a supervisor), treats another entity (e.g., a single employee; a team) with respect and care (Colquitt, Conlon, Wesson, Porter, & Ng, 2001; Masterson et al., 2005). One widely used measure of informational justice can be found in Colquitt's (2001) organizational justice scale. One example item requires respondents to indicate the degree to which an entity within his or her organization (for instance, the supervisor) provides reasonable explanations regarding an outcome. As the use of the word "entity" above indicates, distributive, procedural and interactional (both subtypes) justice can be evaluated at different organizational levels: supervisors, coworkers, units within an organization of which one is not a member, organizations as a whole, or networks of organizations (Caldwell & Evaerhart, 1996; Colquitt, 2001; Lavalle, Rupp & Brockner, 2008; Rupp, Bashur & Liao, 2007).

Certain types of justice (e.g., interpersonal), however, implicate only entities at some levels, that is, interpersonal addresses interindividual relationships such as those with supervisors or individual coworkers, but excludes collectives). For instance, Aryee, Budhwar, and Chen (2002) found that distributive, interactional and procedural organizational justice were all related to trust in the organization as a whole, but that only interactional justice was related to trust in supervisor. Similarly, Walumbwa, Cropanzano, and Hartnell (2009) produced evidence that effects of supervisory interpersonal and informational justice on individual learning were mediated by employees' ratings of leader-member exchange relationships.

Liao and Rupp (2005) found that team membership had a differential effect on justice perceptions at multiple levels with individual justice perceptions controlled for; and that, while team-level supervisor-focused procedural and interpersonal justice perceptions predicted supervisory commitment and satisfaction, supervisor-focused *informational justice* did not significantly relate to either of those outcomes. On the other hand,

Liao and Rupp (2005) also found that organization-focused procedural justice climate predicted organizational commitment and organizational citizenship behavior; while organization-focused informational justice predicted only organizational citizenship. Organization-focused interpersonal justice did not have significant relationships with any *organization*-focused outcome. Thus, we propose that:

> ***Proposition 2:*** Distributive justice at each level will be more strongly associated with calculus-based organizational social capital mechanisms than with relational social-capital mechanisms; and calculus-based organizational social capital mechanisms at a given level will mediate calculus-driven outcomes (e.g., individual performance).

And that:

> ***Proposition 3:*** Procedural and interactional organizational justice at a given level will be most closely associated with relational social capital mechanisms (e.g., trust; identification); and relational social capital will mediate relational outcomes (e.g., citizenship behaviors; team identification; organizational learning).

## Individual-Level Justice and Individual Social Capital

Justice at multiple organizational levels is crucial to individual social-capital processes and outcomes in the workplace. For instance, Pastoriza, Arino, and Ricart (2008) muster evidence that a leader's degree of ethical behavior shapes employee trust, commitment, and social-capital inputs (to the organization) and outputs (from the organization and work group). The ethical behaviors that Pastoriza et al. describes are largely those that others have labeled as components of interactional justice—for example, displaying concern for subordinates' well-being. Lamertz (2002) examined the same constructs more explicitly and directly. He found that employees' degrees of social capital were significantly positively associated with their perceptions of interactional fairness in their workplace. James (1997), in fact, provides evidence that even when supportive behaviors from supervisors or coworkers occur, perceptions of relatively high general unfairness may make them ineffective.

On the other hand, researchers using the two-factor model of organizational justice have suggested that distributive justice, or the fair distribution of desired or expected outcomes from group authorities, is more related to *person*-referenced (as opposed to organizational- or group-level) outcomes. They posit, in contrast, that procedural justice—the fairness of the decision-making process—will have a greater influence on system-referenced outcomes (Folger & Konovsky, 1989). In a comprehensive test of this model Sweeny and McFarlin (1993) examined four different models of the relationship between distributive justice and procedural justice and employee reactions. They found the most support for a two-factor model of distributive justice predicting person-referenced outcomes (e.g., pay satisfaction), and procedural justice predicting system-referenced outcomes (e.g., organizational commitment). This prediction has been supported in several studies on legitimacy or evaluation of authorities (e.g., Ball, Trevino, & Sims, 1993; Sunshine & Tyler, 2003). We address, therefore, organizational justice in a separate section and address mainly individual worker to supervisor justice patterns here.

Positive relationships (e.g., perceived interactional justice, for purposes of this chapter) with organizational insiders have also been indicated to result in organizational newcomers' learning more about the organization's goals and norms, better understanding of the organization's historical narrative, and the learning of more inside information (Chao, O'Leary-Kelly, Wolf, Klein, & Gardner, 1994). Through mastery of a shared language and narrative, individuals are able to communicate more effectively with other organizational members, and to act in ways that enhances the likelihood of their long-term success in the organization (Fisher, 1986; Schein, 1968). We propose, therefore, that:

> ***Proposition 4:*** Interactional justice from supervisor will especially strongly influence long-term individual-level social capital formation, as well as the outcomes (e.g., health, learning) that such social capital promotes.

## Team-Level Justice and Social Capital

Brickman, Folger, Goode, and Schul (1981) introduced the distinction between microjustice, or a focus on justice at the individual-level, and macrojustice, or a focus on justice at the collective level. A focus on microjustice or macrojustice reflects different foci for justice experiences: when one is focused on the justice experiences and outcomes of unique individuals, microjustice is being evaluated. When one identifies oneself primarily as part of a collective, the overall sense of collective justice becomes more important. Individual-level and intrateam justice, then, both have individuals as a focal target. They differ, however, in the entities whose justice behaviors are being evaluated; leaders' or organizations' summary justice behaviors toward individual employees, in the case of individual-level justice (as the term is used in this chapter); versus within-team coworkers' summary justice behaviors toward each other, in the case of intrateam justice; versus perceived justice *toward a team as a unit* as a construct, for interteam justice.

## Intrateam Justice

*Intrateam* justice is somewhat different from individual justice. While the latter deals with individual-variations in perceptions of leader or organizational justice actions, outcomes, or systems, *intra*team justice concerns *how individuals within a distinct organizational group perceive justice behaviors procedures, outcomes, and interactions from ingroup members* (Cropanzano, Li, & James, 2007, emphasis added). According to Rupp, Bashshur, and Liao (2007), intrateam justice deals with justice patterns that occur *within* a given work team but that typically differs *across* teams in the same organization. While it is individual, to some extent in that it occurs between coworkers, it differs from individual-justice in that it is a collective, team-level construct (Cropanzano et al., 2007; Mitchell, Cropanzano, & Quisenberry, in press). Gardner and Avolio (1998) similarly discuss *social contagion* processes that produce substantial sharing of reactions among coworkers who are in some way bound together in an organization. Readers may wonder if the concept of "team" feelings about justice makes sense. Recent works (e.g., Elovainioa, Kivimaki, Steen, & Vahtera, 2004; Liao & Rupp, 2005; Rupp & Cropanzano, 2002) seem to indicate that it does.

Similar to Lamertz (2002) study of supervisor-employee fairness, Umphress et al. (2011) found that interactional fairness from coworkers predicted individual health outcomes. Intrateam interactional fairness, we therefore conjecture, promotes social support and acceptance of social support from coworkers (James, 1997). Coworkers typically have less to do with determining decision processes or distributive outcomes, however, than do supervisors or *organizations as a whole. We propose, therefore, that:*

> ***Proposition 5:*** Intrateam (coworker) interactional and informational justice will promote formation of the individual-level social capital and individual-level outcomes such as learning and health.

## Interteam Justice

*Interteam* justice reflects substantially shared perceptions by members of a team of justice directed *at the team* by either the organization as a whole or by other work teams within it. It has sometimes also been called *justice climate*, defined as a "group-level cognition about how a work group as a whole is treated" (Naumann & Bennett, 2000, p. 882; see also Cropanzano, et al., 2007; James, 2006; Rupp & Liao, 2007; Roberson & Colquitt, 2005). Interteam justice reflects the perceived status of one's in-group as a whole within an organization (Cropanzano et al., 2007; James, 2006; Tyler, 1989).

If an organization is going to use performance teams some or all of the time, a system of purely individual rewards will prove effective. Traditionally, organizations have had reward systems that focus on individual inputs and outputs, but effective team performance requires use of team-level evaluation and reward systems, operated with procedural justice and resulting in distributive justice (Hülsheger, Anderson, & Salgado, 2009; Wageman, 1995). Teams do have to be evaluated for performance, and do need to differ in performance outcomes (rewards) for high levels of performance to result. Yet, even low and moderate distributive outcome groups need to see performance evaluation *procedures* and *practices* as inherently fair for good performance to ensue. Purely group-level evaluation or group-level rewards probably are not a good idea, though—see the social loafing literature (Asmus & James, 2005; Jackson & Harkins, 1985).

Colquitt (2001) also found that increased informational justice (the degree to which justice distributions and procedures are adequately explained) resulted in increased *collective* esteem. Lower levels of workplace secrecy reduced ambiguity about distributions and procedures, increased trust in the collective, and enhanced collective esteem. All of those outcomes should increase positive feeling toward and engagement with work teams and organizations as collectives (Korsgaard, Schweiger, & Sapienza, 1995; Murrell & Dietz, 1992). We propose, therefore, that:

> ***Proposition 6:*** Higher levels of informational justice about (inter-) team-level distributions and procedures will be associated with positive affect (including collective esteem) toward one's team and organization. This will motivate affect-driven social capital (e.g., group attachment and low turnover) that will, in turn, support development of team and organizational-level effectiveness.

In general, researchers need to examine both intra- and interteam justice more as potentially major types of macrojustice perceptions that occur in organizations. Organizational-level justice and justice in interorganizational networks are two other important collective-level constructs. We turn to the former next.

## Organizational-level Justice

Organizational-level justice is the component of shared perceptions among *all organization members* of the justice in their organization, overall. It has also been called organizational justice climate (Cropanzan et al., 2007; Rupp & Liao, 2007). In particular, Katz and Kahn (1978) and Jacobs and Jacques (1987) indicate a key role for organizations' communication systems (i.e., technologies) and procedures. Executive leaders must, according to systems theory, use organizational systems both to communicate their own (for our purposes, justice-related) values and direct actions, as well as to effectively communicate the justice norms and procedures they have created for the organization. Executive leaders' own justice actions become symbolic of organizational justice values and principles, and their decisions about their organizations' procedural and distributive justice systems must be articulated in persuasive communications.

While the two-factor model (Sweeny & McFarlin, 1993) has been frequently supported, it has sometimes been contradicted in others (e.g., Conlon, 1993; Taylor, Tracy, Renard, Harrison, & Carrol, 1995). In particular, individual health outcomes have been shown to be negatively impacted by both organizational procedural and distributive justice (James, 1997; Tepper, 2001). Tepper, in fact, found in two studies that (perceived) unfair organizational distributions interacted with perceived unfairness to organizational procedures to negatively impact the health of individual workers.

> ***Proposition 7:*** Distributive justice from organizations will most strongly influence development of relatively immediate types of individual-level social capital (e.g., pay satisfaction) and procedural justice from organizations will most strongly determine the social capital drivers of longer-term individual outcomes (e.g., learning; health impacts).

A meta-analysis by Colquitt et al. (2001) suggested that these results might be due to whether workers view authority as vested in the organization or in a supervisor. A study by Masterson, Lewis, Goldman, and Taylor (2000) supports this suggestion. They found that procedural justice affects organizational-related outcomes (e.g., organizational-directed citizenship behaviors, intentions to quit), via the mediation of perceived organizational support, but was *not* related to supervisor-related outcomes (e.g., supervisor-directed citizenship behaviors). Instead they found that interactional justice, or the quality of interpersonal treatment, affects supervisor-related outcomes, through the mediation of leader-member exchange. These results suggest that different mechanisms occur when referring to a leader of an organization, versus the organization as a whole. The findings from Masterson et al. (2000) and the meta-analysis by Colquitt et al. (2001) suggest that there are different organizational justice processes and results for social capital contributions to individual leaders versus social capital contributions to organizations.

It seems, then, that when organizations need to draw on a given type of social capital more than another, their justice systems and strategies will need to be adjusted. For instance, when individuals focus mainly on overall organizational procedural justice, and it is relatively high, they will direct their social capital efforts largely toward the benefit of the overall organization. In contrast, when individuals are focused mainly on interpersonal justice, they will direct benefits of social capital toward supervisor- (and, possibly, interteam-) related outcomes. An army platoon may, as an example, need to focus more on a general deployment mission and a broad strategy when either no immediate fighting is underway, or circumstances demand high levels of coordination with other platoons. When engaged in a "hot," localized battle, on the other had, the platoon will probably need to be more concerned with adhering to immediate goals and tactics determined by the platoon leader. In the former case, organizational procedural justice systems should be dominant. In the latter case, procedures may need to be relaxed and interpersonal made the main justice focus. We propose, therefore, that:

> ***Proposition 8:*** Environmental conditions for an organization determine which types of social capital are more critical at a given time and, therefore, the balance of justice levels and types to emphasize.

## Interorganizational Justice

Neither public nor private sector organizations operate in a contextual vacuum. Rather, they are part of a community of collaborating and competitive corporate bodies. Many form cooperative networks (Koput, Smith-Doerr, & Powell, 1997; Provan & Sebastian, 1998). Potentially, these networks can help their members deal with institutional pressures (Provan, Isett & Milward, 2004), improve firm performance (Powell, Koput, Smith-Doerr & Owen-Smith, 1999), promote organizational learning (Powell, Koput, & Smith-Doerr, 1996; Suarez, 2005), and produce innovations (Smith-Doerr, Owen-Smith, Koput, & Powell, 1999).

Research on interorganizational networks has only begun to take a workplace-justice perspective, though such early work as has been done seems promising. A study by Provan, Lamb, and Doyle (2004) suggests that network growth is facilitated by factors that build a sense of network legitimacy among member organizations. Social justice, of course, has been found to promote legitimacy of decision-makers (Tyler, 1997) and institutions (Tyler, 1990).

In a more direct test, Luo (2005) examined 124 cross-national organizational alliances operating in China. When alliance partners perceived justice among partners to be relatively high, alliance profitability was superior to that obtained when justice perceptions were relatively low. More recently, Beugre and Acar (2008) proposed a model of cultural influences on interorganizational justice perceptions and outcomes. They argue that cultural similarity among the boundary spanners (i.e., individual or team go-betweens for two or more focal organizations) who link the organizations in a network will lead to relatively positive perceptions of distributive, procedural, and interactional justice among the organizations. Positive perceptions of interorganizational justice among boundary spanners is, then, in Beugre and Acar's (2008) model a driver of commitment by individual organizations to the network, and positive performance by the network in its collaborative efforts.

Nooteboom (1999) proposed that boundary spanners might serve any of six roles that aid the development and utility of network social capital. At least three of those roles seem justice related (the quoted phrases are from Nooteboom, 1999, p. 341): "monitoring and controlling compliance" (i.e., providing the mechanisms of procedural justice); "mediate the building of trust" (i.e., providing and facilitating "interpersonal"/interorganizational justice, as well as belief in social-exchange equity and procedural adequacy and consistency). We propose, therefore, that:

> ***Proposition 9:*** Relatively high distributive, procedural and interactional justice among organizations in a network will promote development of network social capital (e.g., information exchange; cooperative efforts) which will, in turn, predict strength of network ties, network goal achievement, and network persistence.

## CASCADE EFFECTS OF MULTILEVEL JUSTICE AND MULTILEVEL SOCIAL CAPITAL

Figure 5.1 shows cascading effects of organizational justice across levels, of social capital across organizational levels, and crossovers between justice and social capital at different levels. There are, that is, spillover effects among levels of organizational justice, among levels of social capital, and across levels of organizational-justice-to-social-capital relationships. For instance, we described in the team-level section, above, how informational justice promotes collective esteem and how that can build the team and organization levels of social capital. At the same time, individuals who have higher levels of collective esteem also tend to experience positive results such as reductions in stress (James, 1997) and better learning (Cho & McLeod, 2007). Reduced stress at the individual level is associated with lower health-related costs for organizations (James, 1997).

On the individual side, workers who are highly engaged in the workplace are more involved in their work roles (Nahapiet & Ghoshal, 1998; Saks, 2006) and expend more effort networking, accessing network resources, sharing information, or providing help. Workers receiving relatively high perceived organizational justice seem to also exhibit relatively high levels of workplace engagement (Clayton & Opotow, 2003). Increased willingness to develop new, and more fully engage with existing, work relationships results in increased network size, enhanced network strength, and improved organizational trust. According to Nahapiet and Ghoshal (1998; see also Keller & Holland, 1983; Teece, 1998), those types of employee actions and inputs are what build the organizational-level social capital that is the source of organizational learning, organizational innovation, and new profit sources, as well as a source of buffering against turbulence in organizational environments. We propose, therefore, that serving in a third-party role can also increase individual, team, or organizational social capital. For individuals, serving in a third-party role generates social capital that may be of particular value for leadership emergence and leaders' own success (Fleming & Waguespack, 2007). Fleming and Waguespack (2007) reported that individuals in boundary-spanning positions (i.e., who are part of two or more intersecting groups) are more likely to emerge as the leaders of their groups than are individuals not in boundary-spanning positions. Interestingly, Fleming and Waguespack also found that trust in individuals was not predictive of leadership emergence among boundary spanners, but *was* predictive of leadership emergence among individuals who were *brokers* between groups. Brokers, unlike boundary spanners, mediate between/among groups *without* being an actual member of all of those groups. We can speculate from the latter finding that procedural and distributive justice behaviors are more critical to the social capital of brokers than to that of boundary spanners. A final example is that learning by individual workers is a related to organizational-level justice, but also predicts organizational knowledge development. Thus, organizational procedures and leader behaviors that build social capital at the individual level aid creation of social capital at both the individual and collective levels.

## MEDIATORS OF ORGANIZATIONAL JUSTICE INFLUENCES ON SOCIAL CAPITAL

Some mechanisms through which organizational justice impacts on social capital in the workplace have already been alluded to or sketched briefly in the preceding sections on justice and capital types and levels. A few key mechanisms are discussed next in greater detail as ways of better detailing the nomological network of organizational justice and social capital, supporting the posited multilevel nature of their relationship to each other, and suggesting mediators that should be subjected to additional research.

### Social Identity

When a particular type and level of group-based identity is active (i.e., cognitively prominent *and* evocative of an emotional attachment to the group), an individual should be most likely to focus on justice outcomes from or for that group and social capital processes are likely to be directed toward it (Triandis, 1989; see also Turner, 1985; and Tyler, 1999). When individual identities are salient and important, on the other hand, individuals should be most likely to focus on individual-level justice and individual social capital.

Fair or unfair treatment by a given entity is, itself, a activator of identity(ies). In the relational model, fair treatment by a group helps promote group identification while unfair treatment triggers perceptions of separation of self from group (Tyler, 1990, 1999). Similarly, leader-member exchange (LMX) theory indicates that perceived fairness of treatment by a leader shapes identification (or lack of same) with her and her in-group, and that this can occur at multiple organizational levels (Graen & Uhl-Bien, 1995; Walumbwa et al., 2009). More on this point follow in the Leadership as a mediator section later in this chapter.

### Trust

Putnam's definition of social capital explicitly implicates trust. Although trust and social capital are *not* the same thing, theories of trust in organizations, leaders or coworkers (organizational trust, like organizational justice and organizational social capital, is multifocal) typically define and detail trust in ways that are very similar to conceptions of social capital. Rousseau, Sitkin, Burt, and Carmerer (1998, p. 395), for instance, concluded that the common core of conceptions of trust from psychology, sociology, organizational behavior, and other scholarly disciplines is that they involve a state of interdependence where the "interests of one party cannot be achieved without reliance upon another." This is very close to the concept of social capital, as previously defined, as involving a sense of mutual obligation.

Relatively high levels of organizational justice are associated with outcomes such as trust in management (Konovsky & Cropanzano, 1991) and toward an organization, in general (Leung, Su, & Morris, 2001). Lavelle, Rupp and Brockner (2007) make explicit and review evidence to support the key role that organizational justice plays in promoting trust which, in turn, they indicate triggers such effects as identification with colleagues and the organization; positive social exchange among organization members and between members and the organization as an entity; and citizenship behavior toward colleagues and the organization. The latter three outcomes are also identified in the literature as key indicators and components of social capital. Lavelle et al. (2007, p. 852) state that: "In other words, the ... trust of the organization that organizational justice creates" leads to identification, positive social exchange, and citizenship.

Organizational justice of different types and at different levels may differentially impact on trust at different levels, however, such that social capital generation and social-capital derived outcomes will also vary across levels (e.g., Mitchell et al., in press). Justice-based impacts on trust in coworkers should, for instance, shape behaviors directed toward individual or clusters of coworkers, such as willingness to engage and support group-level identity, work-team cohesiveness, reciprocal support within teams, more so than trust in supervisor or trust in the organization as a whole.

Rousseau et al. (1998) joined other theorists (e.g., Lewicki, Wiethoff, & Tomlinson, 2005) in differentiating between *calculus-based* trust and *identity-* (or affective-) based trust. The former is based on evaluations of social exchanges. The latter is characterized, according to Lewicki et al. (2005) by "shared goals, values, and close emotional attachment." Others point out, though, that calculus-based trust can form a basis for the development of identity-based trust (Mitchell et al., in press; Lavelle et al., 2008). Moreover, the two types of trust may also interact such that high relational trust, for instance, alters exchange calculations (Mitchell et al., in press). For example, DeCremer and Van Vugt (1999) found that either dispositional or situationally induced group identification increased cooperative interpersonal behavior in a social dilemma. Similarly, Van Vugt (2001) showed that structural incentives promoting conservation behavior mattered less when community identification was high. His interpretation of this finding was that when community identification was strong, motivation for behavior that enhanced the well-being of the collective was already so high that additional incentives were redundant.

Trust at the organizational level seems to be particularly influenced by perceptions of the justice of the rules and laws that govern that organization (Tyler, 1990). Korsgaard et al. (1995) found evidence that employee's organizational commitment, attachment, and trust were promoted by worker perceptions of high *procedural* justice (i.e., fair procedures used to arrive at an outcome). People examine the rules and procedures used by an organization to infer what values define the organization. The way these laws are created and the input that people have in the decision outcome also influences feelings of identification with the organization (Tyler & DeGoey, 1995). Previous research has shown that people are more likely to feel obligated to follow general rules and laws when they feel that laws have been applied fairly (Thibaut & Walker, 1975; Tyler, 1990; Tyler & DeGoey, 1995). Procedural justice should, by way of promoting trust in the organization, have a significant relationship with felt obligation to the organization (Aquino, 1995; Bies & Moag, 1985; Tyler et al., 1996). The use of fair procedures buttresses the belief that one should willingly contribute inputs (Colquitt, 2001). Thus, organizations that use methods that increase feelings of procedural justice will also increase feelings of organizational identification and promote inputs toward organizational-level social capital. Others point out, though, that calculus-based trust can form a basis for the development of relational (identity-based) trust (Mitchell et al., in press; Lavelle et al., 2008). Over time, reciprocal obligations based on prior social exchange can develop into trusting, and loyal commitments (Cropanzano & Mitchell, 2005) resulting in increased engagement and inclinations to contribute to positive outcomes for the organization or its other members (Saks, 2006). Thus, through good social exchange experiences, social capital is built at the individual, inter-individual, and collective levels. Moreover, the two types of trust may also interact such that high relational trust, for instance, alters exchange calculations (Mitchell et al., in press). For example, DeCremer and Van Vugt (1999) found that either dispositional or situationally-induced group identification increased cooperative interpersonal behavior in a social dilemma. Similarly, Van Vugt (2001) showed that structural incentives promoting conservation behavior mattered less when community identification was high. His interpretation of this finding was that when community identification was strong, motivation for behavior that enhanced the well-being of the collective was already so high that additional incentives were redundant. We propose, therefore that (for every level of organizational entity):

There are also likely, of course, to be indirect effects such attachment to an organization as a whole being increased (or undermined) by way of degree of attachment to a component work group. Since relational trust promotes identification, increased group- or individual-level (supervisor, coworker) trust should promote organizational identification, for instance, and promote social-capital outcomes at the organizational level.

## LEADERSHIP, JUSTICE, AND COLLECTIVE SOCIAL CAPITAL

Leadership is a major source of intra-team-level, inter-team-level, and organizational-level justice influences on social capital formation. Scandura (1999) proposed a somewhat different model of justice-to-social-capital patterns than did Korsgaard or what is implied in the work of Colquitt (2001) or Masterson et al. (2000). Along with Masterson et al. (2000), Scandura (1999) positions leadership as a key moderator of the justice-type to social-capital-inputs relationship. In particular, Scandura proposed that employees who are members of their leaders' ingroups (employees who have positive emotional attachments and a shared sense of identity with leaders) use interactional justice to judge *organizational* characteristics and attractiveness; while employees who are part of their leaders' outgroups us *distributive* justice rules to judge their organizations.

The logic behind Scandura's (1999) conclusion is essentially that leader-ingroup relationships operate on principles of identity-based trust, while leader-outgroup relationships operate on calculus-based trust. Identity-based trust, as Scandura employs the term, seems to be synonymous with organizational social capital a la Putnam: strength of individuals' social networks *plus* strength of perceived norms of network reciprocity *and* trust in the values and ethics of network members. According to Scandura (1999), with greater degrees of identity-based trust came greater organizational commitment, higher levels of organizational citizenship behaviors, and improved learning. Thus, leader-member and member-member interpersonal justice (identity-based trust) enhanced the inclination of workers to contribute a relatively high volume of *organizational*-level inputs.

These ideas are very similar to those of LMX theory. Note, however, that LMX largely deals with supervisory-level leadership. LMX (whether one is part of a leader's ingroup or outgroup) may also influence the type of justice that becomes the focus of decision-making about organizational fairness: interactional justice, among ingroup members, and distributive justice among outgroup members. LMX studies show us that ingroup and outgroup members differ in outcomes such as pay levels and promotion opportunities, and in procedures such as experiences with politicized decision making (James, 2006). Those LMX social-capital derived outcomes seem to shape future justice foci and judgments (Ho, Rousseau, & Levesque, 2006; Masterson et al., 2000). We propose, therefore, that:

> ***Proposition 10:*** Individuals relatively high on perceived membership in the ingroup of their immediate supervisor will contribute to organizational social capital to the extent that interpersonal justice is also perceived to be high.

Organizational-systems theory (Jacobs & Jaques, 1987; Katz & Kahn, 1978) and transformational leadership theory (e.g., Bass, 1998; Bass & Avolio, 2000) may provide mechanisms for resolving the differing results and ideas of Masterson et al. (2000) and Scandura (1999). Katz and Kahn (1978) state that, by behaving in ways that epitomize prosocial values and engendering identification from employees, organizational leaders can draw followers into organizational commitment. Interactional justice behaviors seem to be a major type of behavior that leaders can use to model prosocial values and engender identification by employees. That is, behavior that models positive organizational values and that promotes identification between a leader and followers creates social capital for organizations. Organizational values are "a justification and idealization of its functions" (Katz & Kahn, 1978, p. 755).

Transformational and charismatic leadership theories (e.g., Bass, 1996, 1998; Conger & Kanungo, 1998; House, 1977) directly address how leadership behavior can model values and generate subordinate identification. A large body of accumulated empirical evidence supports the general contention that transformational leadership is effective. Meta-analyses and other reviews have shown that ratings of charismatic leadership are related to followers' work and organizational attitudes, as well as to followers' performance (Bass & Avolio, 1993; Lowe, Kroeck, & Sivasubramaniam, 1996; Shamir, House, & Arthur., 1993). Transformational leaders (intended to subsume charismatic leadership, for the purposes of this paper) are seen as *trusted*, respected role models such that followers identify with, and to emulate, those leaders (James & Lahti, 2011; Kirkpatrick & Locke, 1996).

In addition, however, organizational-system theory specifies that leaders' *level in an organization* influences the impact that any given leader's behavior has on subordinates (Jacobs & Jaques, 1987). A primary leadership-level dichotomy is between what are variously labeled *leadership* versus *management* or *executive* versus *nonexecutive* (middle and supervisory) levels of leaders. Executive leaders in an organization tend to develop the organization's mission, strategy, policies and values. They also tend to take the lead in efforts to make organizational ideology and systems, and in making employees adhere to them. Thus, justice behaviors by executive-level leaders should be most important toward using organizational systems to align individual, team, and interteam goals and actions with organizational-level goals. The justice types most relevant to executive-level leadership for most employees may be procedural justice and (design and monitoring of systems for) distributive justice.

Nonexecutive leaders however, while not generally responsible for developing their organizations' mission, policies and values, *are* responsible for *promoting* and *modeling* that vision directly to workers (Bass, 1996; Hater & Bass, 1988). Their justice behaviors should, therefore, mainly be of the interpersonal variety and mainly influence leader-member (i.e., individual-level) identification, trust, and social capital reciprocity, as well as team-level identification and social capital contributions.

Dirks and Ferrin's (2002) meta-analytic review distinguished between the same two leadership levels (executive leadership versus nonexecutive) in their impacts on worker trust and reciprocity inclinations. They found that trust in *executive* leadership is likely to be more strongly related to organizational-level reciprocation, such as organizational commitment. On the other hand, trust in *nonexecutive* leadership was more strongly related to dyadic leader-follower reciprocity. We propose, therefore, that:

> ***Proposition 11:*** Executive leaders' informational and procedural justice behaviors will be most important to influencing social capital formation, and do so most strongly and directly at the organizational level.

Executive leaders are also, however, responsible for using *organizational systems* (procedural and distributive) to align goals across levels, and to align cross-level social capital to organizational mission and goals. One way that executive leaders can achieve the preceding is through their interpersonal relationships with key middle managers and other (e.g., executive assistants) employees. The executive-level leaders of even relatively sizable organizations should have fairly consistent interpersonal interactions with a subset of lower-level leaders and other nonexecutive employees. Relative to that subset of employees, executive-level interpersonal justice behaviors should be significant influences. Through those interpersonal-justice behaviors, executive leaders can attempt to capture social capital that exists at lower (i.e., team and individual) levels and direct it toward organization-level goals. Executive leaders can also use their interpersonal relationships with selected nonexecutive leaders to promote identification among the latter with executive-leaders' and organization's identities. If such identification is achieved, nonexecutive leaders' interactional justice behaviors will tend to align with and effectively enact the values and justice norms and systems that executive-level leaders articulate. Through these means, social-capital inputs and outcomes might be brought into alignment across its three main organizational types (individual-level, team-level, organizational-level).

Organizational system theory also indicates another mechanism for promoting linkage of social capital across organizational levels. As was noted above, organizational systems theory posits a key role for organizational communication systems in promoting integrated justice norms and value (Katz & Kahn, 1978; Jacobs & Jacques, 1987). In this perspective, as Barnard (1938, p. 184) stated "All communication relates to the formulation of purpose and the transmission of coordinating prescriptions for action." The extent to which that is done effectively will partially determine how well social capital inputs and outcomes align across organizational levels in ways that support the organization's mission, strategy, and goals (Baum, Locke & Kirkpatrick, 1998).

House, Hanges, Javidan, Dorfman, and Gupta (2004) used the term *institutional collectivism* to reflect similar ideas about alignment across organizational levels. They found that institutional systems that reinforce collective ideals and collective action at the organizational level seem to be distinct from, but potentially complementary to, group-level collectivism (i.e., identification with either a nonexecutive leader or with a team of coworkers). They argued that leader characteristics and behaviors that promote organizational success are effective only to the extent that an organization's systems are also effective at promoting institutional collectivism. We propose, therefore, that:

## Reward Systems

Reward systems (procedural justice norms and policies for organizational distributions) are a major tool that can be used to align social capital inputs across levels. Rewards and sanctions are major forces that organizations and leaders use to promote values and goals, and influence employee effort and motivation (House et al., 2004; Katz & Kahn, 1978; Nanus, 1992). Organizations' reward systems must align with and reinforce a vision if employees are to be inspired to act on it. Effective design and use of reward systems help integrate individuals and teams into a collaborative collective by supporting social expectations of behavior (i.e., visions, goals, norms) as guides and motivations to action. This is substantially what is involved in creating institutional collectivism (House et al., 2004). The same is likely true for justice in the reward systems of interorganizational networks.

Organizational system theory also discusses reward-systems and reward outcomes as major mediators of effective binding of teams and individuals to an organizational identity and to contributing to organizational-level social capital. Organizational-identity and system-integration directed rewards "make people want to stay in the organization" (Katz &

Kahn, 1978, p. 78), and may serve to effect more acceptance of organizationally defined roles, norms, and values. Katz and Kahn (1978) also propose that one way that organizational rewards and systems can promote organizational-level identities (institutional collectivism) is through the "sharing of rewards from common effort" (p. 288). In other words, when individuals and teams feel justly rewarded for inputs to organizational success, they are more likely to internalize the organization's identity as their own, which, in turn, increases their inclination to contribute further social-capital inputs to the organization

## HOW SOCIAL CAPITAL INFLUENCES ORGANIZATIONAL JUSTICE

In addition to organizational justice influencing social capital, social capital outcomes also seem to impact organizational justice perceptions. Thus the arrow-heads pointing *from* the social-capital box at the center of Figure 5.1 *toward* the organizational justice types at the left of the figure. Structural social capital can have either positive or negative impacts on justice perceptions. Based on experienced social capital, individuals are also prompted with interpretations and explanations of organizational events and circumstances (Burt, 2002; Lamertz, 2002). This is an effect of the perceived quality of social networks. For instance, social capital influences workers' psychological-contract beliefs (Ho et al., 2006), or more specifically, their beliefs about what they *should* expect of their organization, their leader, and other organization members, as well as what is expected of them. Through this route, social-capital levels impact individuals' perceptions of how fair exchange outcomes are.

We noted earlier that justice in organizations helps influence activation of different levels of identity. At the same time, the justice climate associated with an identity that is active for whatever reason will be most important in determining an individual's justice-related thinking, affect, and behavior. That is, that work-identity activation may not only mediate the effects of justice climates at different levels but other organizational influences identity activation should also help shape individuals' perceptions of justice climate at every organizational level. So, justice climate at different levels (organizational versus group versus individual) will be evaluated differently, and have different impacts on organizational outcomes, depending on whether the identity active for a person is individual, group, organization or network. Variations in active identity may, therefore, moderate the accuracy of assessments of justice climate, themselves, as well as moderate the outcomes of empirical tests of the impacts of assessed justice climate on other organizational outcomes. It may be, that is, that it will only be possible to accurately assess justice climate (and, by extension, to test the implications of justice climate for other things) only be when we know what identity is active for study participants.

Finally, identities have emotional components that can both affect motivations (Van Knippenberg, 2000) and shape evaluations (Brown, 2000; Hogg & Terry, 2000; Tyler, 1999). Justice climates have similar emotional components and potential implications. Social identity theory/social cognitive theory (SIT/SCT) knowledge of the emotional elements of identity may, therefore, help inform a multilevel justice approach. Tyler (1999), for instance, argues that individual and group-level identities are each related to a distinct cluster of emotions that differs between them. Because of this, Tyler proposed and provides supportive evidence for differential (procedural) justice concerns and justice implications between identities of the two types (individual versus group—with the latter including organizational-level identity). Similarly, James (in press) argues that differences in group subcultures and affective norms mean that different group identities will channel justice evaluations and justice behaviors in different directions. The role of affect, therefore, provides another bridge between theories of identity and theories of multilevel justice climate. SIT/SCT conceptions and findings about the mechanisms and implications of affect might, therefore, usefully inform a multilevel justice perspective.

The specific knowledge, information, and other inputs from each particular level and aspect of social network that an individual is part of influences that person's justice perceptions. According to the social identity theory people have a need to have positive regard for the groups that they belong to (Messick & Mackie, 1989). Employees who maintain a large number of network ties are likely to feel valued and identify with the organization (Lamertz, 2002).

Additionally, the cognitive dimension of social capital deals directly with the development of trust and identification with the group (Nahapiet & Ghoshal, 1998). According to SIT, individuals who receive higher levels of social capital (self-esteem, in SIT) from a workplace identity will tend to have their perceptions skewed more by that identity than will individuals who receive less social capital from their identity. Similarly, the just world hypothesis and evidence supporting it indicate that receiving good results from environments leads to a general belief in the fairness of procedures and outcomes, as well as a sense of deservingness (Lerner & Miller, 1977).

Organizational justice is a key to accessing the social capital that is potentially available from one's network, with the "one" in this case referring to any focal entity—an individual, a team, or an organization. Specifically, each entity's maximum social capital potential is determined by that entity's position in a network, and justice is both a major determinant of network position, and a major mechanism through which potential social capital is turned into usable social capital.

All of the preceding points need to be examined further empirically. In addition, space constraints allowed us to only briefly outline the potential general connections between SIT/SCT and multilevel organizational justice climates, and also limited us to providing only a few examples of a larger number of possible specific mechanisms and outcomes implicated by links between SIT/SCT and the concept of multilevel organizational justice. Clearly, therefore, much additional conceptual/theoretical work is also needed on the topics touched on in this section.

## CONCLUSIONS

We proposed and examined the components of a model of organizational justice influences on multiple levels of social capital, as well as some influences of social capital on organizational justice. We considered the individual-, team-, organizational-, and interorganizational levels of social capital as being linked to each other, but still somewhat distinct from each other in mechanism and outcomes. We proposed that leader-based justice plays a major role in both the generation of social capital and the degree of integration across levels of social capital.

Overall the research review suggests that organizational justice has a positive impact on the development of social capital formation at multiple levels, and that social capital is, in turn, associated with a variety of important individual, team, and organizational outcomes. Future research should more directly examine all of the preceding points, as much of the evidence that we mustered for them comes from indirect sources and results. The other potential influences (than, i.e., leader behaviors or collective identification) on the development of social capital shown at the left side of Figure 5.1 should be elaborated further conceptually, and investigated further empirically. Additional potential moderators of justice relationships to the differently types (levels) of social capital, as well as the role of different justice sources and types to integration of social-capital levels, should also be considered and investigated. Organizational systems theory, which we invoked in places in this paper, provides some insights about potential moderators. Thus, justice and social capital theories should incorporate more of a systems perspective, and future studies might fruitfully expand on the organizational-system constructs examined relative to organizational justice and social capital relationships and outcomes.

The types of future directions for research that we outline above would provide scientifically and practically useful information. The model and discussion here do, however, provide the beginnings to an understanding of the role of organizational justice in the generational of social capital at different levels, and the role of justice in the relationship between social capital and various important organizational outcomes. As such, they support the contention that this is an issue that requires future attention by organizational scientists, and provide a heuristic spark for future work on them.

## REFERENCES


Adams, J. S. (1965). Inequity in social exchange. In L. Berkowitz (Ed.), *Advances in experimental social psychology* (Vol. 2, pp. 267-299). New York, NY: Academic Press.

Aquino, K. (1995). Relationships among pay inequity, perceptions of procedural justice, and organizational citizenship. *Employee Responsibility and Rights Journal, 8*(1), 21-33.

Aryee, S., Budhwar, P. S., & Chen, Z. X. (2002). Trust as a mediator of the relationship between organizational justice and work outcomes: Test of a social exchange model. *Journal of Organizational Behavior, 23*, 267-286.

Asmus, C., & James, K. (2005). Group structure, individual social loafing, and creativity in task teams. *Creativity Research Journal, 17*, 349-355.

Ball, G. A., Trevino, L. K., & Sims, H. P., Jr. (1993). Justice and organizational punishment: Attitudinal outcomes of disciplinary events. *Social Justice Research, 6*(1), 39-67.

Barnard, C. I. (1938). *The functions of the executive*. Cambridge, MA: Harvard University Press.

Bass, B. M. (1996). *A new paradigm of leadership: An inquiry into transformational leadership*. Alexandria, VA: U.S. Army Research Institute for the Behavioral and Social Sciences.

Bass, B. M. (1998). *Transformational leadership: Industry, military, and educational impact*. Mahwah, NJ: Erlbaum.

Bass, B. M., & Avolio, B. J. (1993). Transformational leadership: A response to critiques. In M. M. Chemers & R. Ayman (Eds.), *Leadership theory and research: Perspectives and directions* (pp. 49-80). San Diego, CA: Academic Press.

Baum, J. R., Locke, E. A., & Kirkpatrick, S. A. (1998). A longitudinal study of the relation of vision and vision communication to venture growth in entrepreneurial firms. *Journal of Applied Psychology, 83*(1), 43-54.

Beugre, C. D., & Acar, W. (2008). Offshoring and cross-border interorganizational relationships: A justice model. *Decision Sciences, 39*(3), 445-468.

Bies, R. J., & Moag, J. F. (1986). Interactional justice: Communication and fairness. In R. J. Lewicki, B. H. Sheppard, & M. H. Bazerman (Eds.), *Research on negotiations in organizations* (Vol. 1, pp. 43-55). Greenwich, CT: JAI Press.

Brickman, P., Folger, P., Goode, E., & Schul, Y. (1981). Microjustice and macrojustice. In M. J. Lerner & S. C. Lerner (Eds.), *The justice motive in social behavior* (pp. 173-202). New York, NY: Plenum.

Brown, R. (2000). Social identity theory: Past achievements, current problems, and future challenges. *European Journal of Social Psychology, 30*(6), 745-778.

Bunderson, J. S., & Sutcliffe, K. M. (2002). Why some teams emphasize learning more than others: Evidence from business unit management teams. In H. Sondak (Ed.) *Toward phenomenology of groups and group membership* (pp. 49-84). New York, NY: Elsevier Science.

Burt, R. S. (1995). *Structural holes: The social structure of competition.* Boston, MA: Harvard University Press.

Caldwell, B. S., & Evaerhart, N. C. (1996). Information flow and development of coordination in distributed supervisory teams. *International Journal of Human-Computer Interaction, 10*, 51-70.

Chao, G. T., O'Leary-Kelly, A. M., Wolf, S., Klein, H. J., & Gardner, P. D. (1994). Organizational socialization: Its content and processes. *Journal of Applied Psychology, 79*(5), 730-743.

Cho, J., & McLeod, D. M. (2007). Structural antecedents to knowledge and participation: Extending the knowledge gap concept to participation. *Journal of Communication, 57*(2), 205-228.

Clayton, S., & Opotow, S. (2003). Justice and identity: Changing perspectives on what is fair. *Personality and Social Psychology Review, 7*(4), 298-310.

Coleman, J. S. (1988). Social capital in the creation of human capital. *American Journal of Sociology, 94*(3.5), 95-120.

Colquitt, J. A. (2001). On the dimensionality of organizational justice: A construct validation of a measure. *Journal of Applied Psychology, 86*(3), 386-400.

Colquitt, J. A., Conlon, D. E., Wesson, M. J., Porter, C. O. L., & Ng, K. Y. (2001). Justice at the millennium: A meta-analytic review of 25 years if organizational justice research. *Journal of Applied Psychology, 86*(3), 425-445.

Conger, J. A., & Kanungo, R. N. (1998). *Charismatic leadership in organizations.* Thousand Oaks, CA: SAGE.

Conlon, D. E. (1993). Some tests of the self-interest and group value models of procedural justice: Evidence from an organizational appeal procedure. *Academy of Management Journal, 36*(5), 1109-1124.

Cropanzano, R., Li, A., & James, K. (2007). Intraunit justice and interunit justice and the people who experience them. In F. Dansereau & F. J. Yammarino (Eds.), *Research in multilevel issues* (Vol. 6, pp. 415-438). Englewood Cliffs, NJ: Erlbaum.

DeCremer, D., & Van Vugt, M. (1999). Social identification effects in social dilemmas: A transformation of motives. *European Journal of Social Psychology, 29*(7), 871-893.

Dirks, K. T., & Ferrin, D. L. (2002). Trust in leadership: Meta-analytic findings and implications for research and practice. *Journal of Applied Psychology, 87*(4), 611-628.

Dumdum, U. R., Lowe, K. B., & Avolio, B. J. (2002). A meta-analysis of transformational and transactional leadership correlates of effectiveness and satisfaction: An update and extension. In B. J. Avolio, & F. J. Yammarino (Eds.), *Transformational and charismatic leadership: The road ahead* (pp. 35-66). London, England: JAI Press.

Elovainioa, M., Kivimaki, M., Steen, N., & Vahtera, J. (2004). Job decision latitude, organizational justice and health: Multilevel covariance structure analysis. *Social Science & Medicine, 58*(9), 1659-1669.

Erdogan, B. (2002). Antecedents and consequences of justice perceptions in performance appraisals. *Human Resource Management Review, 12*, 555-578.

Fisher, C. D. (1986). Organizational socialization: An integrative review. *Research in Personnel and Human Resource Management, 4*(1), 101-145.

Fleming, L., & Waguespack, D. M. (2007). Penguins, camels, and other birds of a feather: Brokerage, boundary spanning, and leadership in open innovation communities. *Organization Science, 18*(2), 165-180.

Folger, R., & Konovsky, M.A. (1989). Effects of procedural and distributive justice on reactions to pay raise decisions. *Academy of Management Journal, 32*(1), 115-130.

Graen, G. B., & Uhl-Bien, M. (1995). Relationship-based approach to leadership: Development of leader-member exchange (LMX) theory of leadership over 25 years: Applying a multi-level multi-domain perspective. *Leadership Quarterly, 6*, 219-247.

Greenberg, J. (1982). Approaching equity and avoiding inequity in groups and organizations. In J. Greenberg & R. L. Cohen (Ed.), *Equity and justice in social behavior* (pp. 389-435). New York, NY: Academic Press.

Hater, J. J., & Bass, B. M. (1988). Superiors' evaluations and subordinates' perceptions of transformational and transactional leadership. *Journal of Applied Psychology, 73*(4), 695-702.

Hezlett, S. A., & Gibson, S. K. (2007). Linking mentoring and social capital: Implications for career and organization development. *Advances in Developing Human Resources, 9*(3), 384-412.

Ho, V., Rousseau, D., & Levesque, L. (2006). Social networks and the psychological contract: structural holes, cohesive ties, and beliefs regarding employer obligations. *Human Relations, 59*(4), 459-81.

Hogg, M. A. & Terry, D. J. (2000). Social identity and self-categorization processes in organizational contexts. *Academy of Management Review, 25*(1), 121-140.

House, R. J., & Aditya, R. N. (1997). The social scientific study of leadership: Quo vadis? *Journal of Management, 23*(3), 409-473.

House, R. J., Hanges, P. J., Javidan, M., Dorfman, P. W., & Gupta, V. (2004). *Culture, leadership and organizations: The GLOBE study of 62 societies*. Thousand Oaks, CA: SAGE.

Hülsheger, U. R., Anderson, N., & Salgado, J. F. (2009). Team-level predictors of innovation at work: A comprehensive meta-analysis spanning three decades of research. *Journal of Applied Psychology, 94*, 1128–1145.

Jackson, J. M., & Harkins, S. G. (1985). Equity in effort: An explanation of the social loafing effect. *Journal of Personality and Social Psychology, 49*, 1199-1206. Process variables and team performance: A team-level analysis in a field setting. *Small Group Research, 33*, 121-150.

Jacobs, T. O., & Jaques, E. (1987). Leadership in complex systems. In J. Zeidner (Ed.), *Human productivity enhancement* (pp. 7-65). New York, NY: Praeger.

James, K. (1997). Worker social identity and health-related costs for organizations: A comparative study between ethnic groups. *Journal of Occupational Health Psychology, 2(2)*, 108-117.

James, K. (2006). Antecedents, processes, and outcomes of collective (group-level) politics in organizations. In E. Vigoda-Gadot & A. Drory (Eds.), *The handbook of organizational politics* (pp. 53-74). Cheltenham, England: Elgar.

James, K., & Lahti, K. (2011). Organizational vision and system influences on employee inspiration and organizational performance. *Creativity and Innovation Management Journal, 20*, 1-14.

Katz, D,. & Kahn, R. J. (1978). *The social psychology of organizations* (2nd ed.). New York, NY: Wiley.

Keller, R. T., & Holland, W. E. (1983). Communicators and innovators in research and development organizations. *Academy of Management Journal, 26*(4), 66-74.

Kirkpatrick, S. A., & Locke, E. A. (1996). Direct and indirect effects of three core charismatic leadership components on performance and attitudes. *Journal of Applied Psychology, 81*(1), 36-51.

Konovsky, M. A., & Cropanzano, R. (1991). Perceived fairness of employee drug testing as a predictor of employee attitudes and job performance. *Journal of Applied Psychology, 76*(5), 698-707.

Koper, G., Van Knippenberg, D., Bouhuijs, F., Vermunt, R. & Wilke, J. (1993). Procedural fairness and self-esteem. *European Journal of Social Psychology, 23*(3), 313-325.

Koput, K. W., Smith-Doerr, L., & Powell, W. W. (1997). Strategies of learning and industry structure: The evolution of networks in biotechnology. In A. Huff (Ed.), *Advances in strategic management research* (Vol. 14, pp. 229-254). Greenwich, CT: JAI Press.

Korsgaard, M. A., Schweiger, D. M., & Sapienza, H. J. (1995). Building commitment, attachment, and trust in strategic decision-making teams: The role of procedural justice. *Academy of Management Journal, 38*(1), 60-84.

Lamertz, K. (2002). The social construction of fairness: Social influence and sense making in organizations. *Journal of Organizational Behavior, 23*(1), 19-37.

Lavelle, J. J., Rupp, D. E., Brockner, J. (2008). Taking a multifoci approach to the study of justice, social exchange, citizenship behavior: The target similarity model? *Journal of Management, 33*(6), 841-866.

Lerner, M. J., & Miller, D. T. (1977). Just world research and the attribution hypothesis: Looking back and ahead. *Psychological Bulletin, 85*(5), 1030-1051.

Leung, K. Su, S. & Morris, M. M. (2001). When is criticism not constructive? The roles of fairness perceptions and dispositional attributions in employee acceptance of critical supervisory feedback. *Human Relations, 54*(9), 1155-1187.

Lind, A. E., Kray, L., Thompson, L. (2001). Primacy effects in justice judgments: Testing predictions from fairness heuristic theory. *Organizational Behavior & Human Performance, 85*(2), 189-210.

Lewicki, R. J., Wiethoff, C., & Tomlinson, E. C. (2005). What is the role of trust in organizational justice? In J. Greenberg & J. A. Colquittt (Eds.), *Handbook of organizational justice* (pp. 247-270). Mahwah, NJ: Erlbaum.

Liao, H., & Rupp, D. E. (2005). The impact of justice climate and justice orientation on work outcomes: A cross-level multifoci framework. *Journal of Applied Psychology, 90*(2), 242-256.

Lowe, K., Kroeck, K. G., & Sivasubramaniam, N. (1996). Effectiveness correlates of transformational and transactional leadership: A meta-analytic review of the MLQ literature. *Leadership Quarterly, 7(3)*, 385-425.

Luo, Y. (2005). How important are shared perceptions of procedural justice in cooperative alliances? *Academy of Management Journal, 48*, 695-709.

Masterson, S. S., Byrne, Z. S., & Mao, H. (2005). Interpersonal and information justice: Identifying the differential antecedents of interactional justice behaviors. In S. W. Gilliland, D. D. Steiner, D. P. Skarlicki, & K. van den Bos (Eds.), *What motivates fairness in organizations?* (pp. 79-103). Greenwich, CT: Information Age.

Masterson, S. S., Lewis, K., Goldman, B. M., Taylor, M. S. (2000). Integrating justice and social exchange: The differing effects of fair procedures and treatment on work relationships. *Academy of Management Journal, 43*(4), 738-748.

Messick, D. M., & Mackie, D. M. (1989). Intergroup relations. *Annual Review of Psychology, 40*, 45-81.

Mitchell, M. S., Cropanzano, R., & Quisenberry (in press). Social exchange theory, exchange resources and interpersonal relationships: A modest resolution of theoretical difficulties. In K. Tornblom & A. Kazemi (Eds.), *Handbook of social resource theory.* New York, NY: Springer-Verlag.

Murrell, A. J., & Dietz, B. (1992). Fan support of sport teams: The effect of a common group identity. *Journal of Sport & Exercise Psychology, 14*(1), 28-39.

Nahapiet, J., & Ghoshal, S. (1998). Social capital, intellectual capital, and the organizational advantage. *Academy of Management Review, 23*(2), 242-266.

Nanus, B. (1992). *Visionary leadership: Creating a compelling sense of direction for your organization.* San Francisco, CA: Jossey-Bass.

Naumann, S. E., & Bennett, N. (2000). A case for procedural justice climate: Development and test of a multilevel model. *Academy of Management Journal, 43*(5), 881-889.

Nooteboom, B. (1999). The triangle: Roles of the go-between. In R. T. A. J. Leenders & S. M. Gabbay (Eds.), *Corporate social capital liability* (pp. 341-355). Boston, MA: Kluwer.

Pastoriza, D., Arino, M. A., & Ricart, J. E. (2008). Ethical managerial behaviour as an antecedent of organizational social capital. *Journal of Business Ethics, 78*(3), 329-341.

Powell, W. W., Koput, K.W., & Smith-Doerr, L. (1996). Interorganizational collaboration and the locus of innovation: Networks of learning in biotechnology. *Administrative Science Quarterly 41*(1), 116-145.

Powell, W. W., Koput, K. W., Smith-Doerr, L., & Owen-Smith, J. (1999). Network position and firm performance: Organizational returns to collaboration in biotechnology. In D. Knoke (Ed.), *Research in the sociology of organizations* (Vol. 15, pp. 129-160). Stamford, CT: JAI Press.

Provan, K. G., Isett, K. R., & Milward, H. B. (2004). Cooperation and compromise: A network response to conflicting institutional pressures in community mental health. *Nonprofit and Voluntary Sector Quarterly, 33*(3), 489-514.

Provan, K. G., Lamb, G., & Doyle, M. (2004). Building legitimacy and the early growth of health networks for the uninsured. *Health Care Management Review, 29*(2), 117-128.

Provan, K. G., & Sebastian, J. G. (1998). Networks within networks: Service link overlap, organizational cliques, and network effectiveness. *Academy of Management Journal, 41*, 453-463.

Putnam, R. D. (2007). *E pluribus unum*: Diversity and community in the twenty-first century: The 2006 Johan Skytte Prize lecture. *Scandinavian Political Studies, 30*(2), 137-174.

Roberson, Q., & Colquitt, J. A. (2005). Shared and configural justice: A social network model of justice in teams. *Academy of Management Review, 30*(3), 595-607.

Rothbard, N. P. (2001). Enriching or depleting? The dynamics of engagement in work and family roles. *Administrative Science Quarterly, 46*(4), 655-84.

Rousseau, D. M., Sitkin, S. B., Burt, R. S., & Camerer, C. (1998). Not so different after all: A cross-discipline view of trust. *Academy of Management Review, 23*(3), 393-404.

Rupp, D. E., Bashshur, M. R., & Liao, H. (2007). Justice climate: Consideration of the source, target, specificity, and emergence. In F. Dansereau & F. J. Yammarino (Eds.), *Research in multi-level issues* (Vol. 6, pp. 439-459). Oxford, England: Elsevier.

Rupp, D. E., & Cropanzano, R. (2002). Multifoci justice and social exchange relationships. *Organizational Behavior and Human Decision Processes, 89*(1), 925-946.

Saks, A. (2006). Antecedents and consequences of employee engagement. *Journal of Managerial Psychology, 21*(7), 600-619.

Scandura, T. A. (1999). Rethinking leader-member exchange: An organizational justice perspective. *Leadership Quarterly, 10*(1), 25-40.

Schein, E. H. (1968). Organizational socialization and the profession of management. *Industrial and Management Review, 9*(1), 1-16.

Shamir, B., House, R. J., & Arthur, M. (1993). The motivational effects of charismatic leadership: A self-concept based theory. *Organization Science, 4*(4), 577-594.

Sunshine, J., & Tyler, T. R. (2003). The role of procedural justice and legitimacy in shaping public support for policing. *Law & Society Review, 37*(3), 513-547.

Sweeney, P. D., & McFarlin, D. B. (1993). Workers' evaluation of the "ends" and the "means": An examination of four models of distributive and procedural justice. *Organizational Behavior and Human Decision Processes, 55*(1), 23-40.

Taylor, M. S., Tracy, K. B., Renard, M. K., Harrison, J. K., & Carroll, S. J. (1995). Due process in performance appraisal: a quasi-experiment in procedural justice. *Administrative Science Quarterly, 40*(3), 495-523.

Teece, D. J. (1998). Capturing value from knowledge assets: The new economy, markets for know-how, and intangible assets. *California Management Review, 40*(1), 55-79.

Tepper, B. J. (2001). Health consequences of organizational injustice: Tests of main and interactive effects. *Organizational Behavior and Human Decision Processes, 86*(2), 197–215.

Thibaut, J., & Walker, L. (1975). *Procedural justice: A psychological analysis.* Hillsdale, NJ: Erlbaum.

Triandis, H. C. (1989). The self and social behavior in differing cultural contexts. *Psychological Review, 96*(3), 506-520.

Triandis, H. C. (1995). *Culture and social behavior.* New York, NY: McGraw-Hill.

Turner, J. C. (1985). Social categorization and the self-concept: A social-cognitive theory of group behavior. In E.J. Lawler (Ed.), *Advances in group processes* (Vol. 2, pp. 77-122). Greenwich, CT: JAI Press.

Tyler, T. R. (1989). The psychology of procedural justice: A test of the group-value model. *Journal of Personality and Social Psychology, 57*(5), 830-838.

Tyler, T. R. (1990). *Why people obey the law.* New Haven, CT: Yale University. Press.

Tyler, T. R. (1997). The psychology of legitimacy: A relational perspective on voluntary deference to authority. *Personality and Social Psychology Review, 1*(4), 323-345.

Tyler, T. R. (1999). Why people cooperate with organizations: An identity-based perspective. In B. M. Staw & R. Sutton (Eds.), *Research in organizational behavior* (Vol. 21, pp. 201-246). Greenwich, CT: JAI Press.

Tyler, T. R., & DeGoey, P. (1995). Collective restraint in social dilemmas: Procedural justice and social identification effects on support for authority. *Journal of Personality and Social Psychology, 69*(3), 482-497.

Umphress, E. E., Labianca, G, Brass, D. J., Kass, E. & Scholten, L. (2011). The role of instrumental and expressive social ties in employees' perceptions of organizational justice. *Organization Science, 14*(6), 738-753.

Wageman, R. (1995). Interdependence and group effectiveness. *Administrative Science Quarterly, 40*, 145-180.

Walumbwa, F. O., Cropanzano, R., & Hartnell, C. A. (2009). Organizational justice, voluntary learning behavior, and job performance: A test of the mediating effects of identification and leader-member exchange. *Journal of Organizational Behavior, 30*(8), 1103-1126.

Van Kippenberg, D. (2000). Work motivation and performance: A SIT perspective. *Applied Psychology: An International Review, 49*, 357-371.

Van Vugt, M. (2001). Community identification moderating the impact of financial incentives in a natural social dilemma: Water conservation. *Personality and Social Psychology Bulletin, 27*, 1440–1449.

# PART II

## APPLYING JUSTICE TO DEVELOP MODELS OF ETHICAL BEHAVIOR

CHAPTER 6

# PERCEPTIONS OF GREED

## A Distributive Injustice Model

**Stephen W. Gilliland and Jennifer S. Anderson**

People generally have strong intuitive understanding of the concept of greed, and perceived greed prompts public outcry, political action, and retributive measures. Despite the widespread use of greed in public dialog, relatively little attention has been directed toward studying this topic. In this chapter, we review the literature, develop a working definition, and develop a theoretically grounded conceptual model of perceptions of greed. Based on distributive justice and attribution theories, we suggest that greed is perceived when a person views 1 or more people as being responsible for seeking more than they deserve and need, while others are losing out. Theoretical and empirical implications of this model are discussed and we conclude that greed is an interesting and important construct that deserves greater research attention.

*Greed is right, greed works. Greed clarifies, cuts through, and captures the essence of the evolutionary spirit. Greed, in all of its forms; greed for life, for money, for love, knowledge has marked the upward surge of mankind.*

—Gordon Gekko (in the movie *Wall Street*, 1987)

*Emerging Perspectives on Organizational Justice and Ethics*
pp. 137–166

Despite the fact that Gordon Gekko is a fictitious character, his sentiments appear to have taken root in American society. Relatively strong cultural norms of individual achievement may have resulted in a higher tolerance for what otherwise would be labeled greedy behavior. However, recently many have questioned the "greed is good" mentality, and the popular press is filled with criticisms of excessive greed in business (e.g., Colvin, 2006; Sarna, 2010). The dot-com boom, corporate accounting scandals like Tyco and Enron, and the behavior of business moguls like Gary Winnick and Bernie Madoff all have prompted attributions of greed. People expressed outrage at the greed of Wall Street when Goldman Sachs offered billions in bonuses while the economy was collapsing and the U.S. government was bailing out the banking sector (Ausick, 2010). Even the 2010 sequel to the movie *Wall Street* has Gordon Gekko questioning, "is greed good?"

When asked to define greed, people have little trouble doing so and there appears to be remarkable consistency in definitions. We recently asked a class of executive master of business administration (MBA) students to define greed in their own words. The following quotes (and other quotes throughout this chapter) represent excerpts from their definitions.

> Greed is a selfish uncontrolled ambition to accumulate wealth, power, and possessions.

> Greed in my opinion is ... going above and beyond what most would think is sufficient.

> Greed is the desire to have more of something no matter how much you already have.

Although most people seem to have an intuitive understanding of how greed is defined, the academic literature has not given much attention to this definition. It is interesting that the business literature has been relatively silent on what the Catholic Church lists as one of the seven "deadly" or "Cardinal" sins. Vecchio (2007) makes a similar observation about the lack of research on another deadly sin, envy. We believe the implicit notion of greed is nuanced and that developing the perceptual construct represents a unique and interesting contribution to the management literature.

How do people define greedy behavior? What is the process by which people determine that an individual or an organization is greedy? The formal definition sheds some light on underlying constructs that may lead to perceptions of greed. Merriam-Webster (2010) defines greed as "a selfish and excessive desire for more of something than is needed," clearly highlighting elements of attribution theory (attributing selfishness) and distributive justice (more than is needed). At their core, perceptions of greed are judgments about the appropriateness of others' behavior. Our own perceptions of greed are colored by the circumstances of the situation, our values, and the relevant norms involved. Greed goes beyond ambition, self-interest, and even selfish behavior to incite visceral reactions in people. In many ways, it is a moral judgment, and most commonly a pejorative one.

Clearly, few people strive to be judged as greedy. Over time and repetition, perceptions of greedy behavior can develop into assessments of individuals, and even of professions and organizations as greedy, embedding negative attitudes toward these entities in the minds of observers. Whether these perceptions are transitory and based on one incident, or stable and based on a pattern of observations, a number of negative consequences arise not only from perceptions of greedy behavior, but also from the actual behavior itself that is labeled as greedy. The consequences include calls for legal and regulatory action, reputational loss, and public denigration (Sarna, 2010).

In addition to these large-scale consequences of greed, employees and business partners regularly experience and deal with everyday consequences of what is perceived to be greedy behavior. The unfairness inherent in perceptions of greed certainly can lead to negative attributions about an individual or organization (Grégoire, Laufer, & Tripp, 2010). It can also cause a decrease in cooperative behavior and an increase in competitive behavior among individuals within a group, fracturing otherwise productive relationships (Coombs, 1973; Dawes, Fowler, Johnson, McElreath, & Smirnov, 2007). Research in experimental economics has shown that greedy behavior in repeated games can invite retributive behaviors (Dawes et al., 2007), even at a significant personal cost. In the marketing literature, perceived greed has been shown to lead to customer revenge (Grégoire et al., 2010). Greed in business deals can leave one organization at an unjustified financial disadvantage, or can even cause a business to fail (Colvin, 2006).

In this chapter, we advance a theoretically-grounded working definition of perceptions of greed and present a model that integrates distributive justice with attribution theory to explain when and how individuals arrive at these perceptions. We first discuss the treatment of greed in four associated research fields: economics, negotiations, political science, and applied psychology. We then build a definition that highlights many of the underlying characteristics of greed. With this definition, we present a model of how individuals arrive at perceptions of greedy behavior and discuss the implications of this model. Our goal is to introduce management researchers to a theoretically grounded way of looking at this timely and important construct.

## EXISTING LITERATURE

Despite its widespread treatment in the popular press (e.g., Colvin, 2006; Goldfarb, 2009; Green, 2010), the topic of greed has not been addressed in the management literature in a systematic way. The concept has yet to be clearly defined using fundamental psychological or social psychological concepts, even though there have been discussions in a number of areas, such as the economics, negotiations, political science, and very recently, applied psychology literatures. Greed appears to be universally understood, and its treatment in these areas of literature provides some insight into the underlying psychological mechanisms.

### Experimental Economics

Greed has been addressed in the literature on experimental economics and is used to describe both profit maximizing and free riding behaviors, albeit in different contexts. The underlying motivation is described as individual utility maximization, with greed used in general terms as a synonym for profit maximization attitudes and behaviors, and used specifically to describe free riding behavior associated with public goods games. The idea that individuals will act in ways that yield the best possible advantages to themselves, given the constraints of the situation, is a long-held belief within the field of economics (Smith, 1776/1991). While the universality of this concept has been successfully challenged (Kahneman & Tversky, 1984), it does retain explanatory power when examining human behavior. Early explorations of the limits of profit maximizing behavior identified fairness as a constraint (Kahneman, Knetch, & Thaler, 1986; Samuelson, Messick, Rutte, & Wilke, 1984), which suggests a relationship between the concept of greed, defined as profit maximization, and justice.

Samuelson et al. (1984) proposed three factors—greed, a desire for efficient use of resources, and a desire for fairness—that determine an individual's decision to pursue overharvesting, a behavior that can be perceived as greedy. This framework integrates rational and nonrational antecedents to behavior, and seeks to further explain profit maximizing behavior. In this framework, greed is defined as a desire to maximize one's own benefit, however this model also acknowledges the role of factors that are not economically driven (fairness) and not rational from an individual utility maximization standpoint (efficient use of resources). Wilke (1991) then refined this concept into his greed-efficiency-fairness (GEF) hypothesis, which states that while greed is the dominant motivator for acquisition of resources, this is tempered by a desire for efficiency and a desire to realize fairness, all three of which can coexist. It should be noted that Wilke's (1991) GEF hypothesis is set within the context of environmental uncertainty and relative resource scarcity. Later in this chapter, we propose that resource scarcity is a key element to perceptions of greed. It should also be noted that both Samuelson et al. (1984) and Wilke (1991) address greed from the perspective of the recipient rather than the perceiver.

In public goods games, greed is typically understood as a desire to free ride on the contributions of others (Rapoport & Eshed-Levy, 1989). Building on the concept of profit maximization, free riding is a form of utility maximization wherein individuals choose to refrain from contributing to a public pool, despite the known potential for greater benefits should everyone contribute. Public goods games provide an interesting context within which to understand the relationship of greed and justice perceptions, in that the structure of these games requires that each participant contribute their "fair share" in order to maximize payouts to all participants. Should even one participant withhold contributions, the entire group is penalized with a final payout that is less than optimal. As may be expected, free riding in public goods games has been shown to contribute to negative attitudes and behaviors toward the individual targeted as greedy (Coombs, 1973; Dawes et al., 2007).

Building on earlier work, Eek and Biel (2003) studied the impact of factors identified in Wilke's (1991) GEF hypothesis within the context of public goods games. They manipulated the extent to which decisions were based on greed, efficiency, or fairness. In one specific experiment, they found that prompting participants to consider the collective nature of the task increased cooperative behavior, supporting Wilke's proposed mechanism. While this work is important in that it demonstrates that these factors constrain greedy behavior, it does not specifically address the process by which behavior is labeled as greedy.

## Negotiation

In negotiation, a process whereby two or more parties decide on the distribution of scarce resources (Bazerman & Neale, 1983), there is the possibility for perceptions of greed to emerge. In general, parties in a negotiation are assumed to adopt either a cooperative or a competitive posture during the negotiation activities. Within the negotiations literature, these two viewpoints are termed integrative and distributive. An integrative strategy seeks to generate a larger or broader set of outcomes for the parties in the negotiation, thereby maximizing the total amount of resources available to all parties, similar to the mechanism of public goods games. On the other hand, the distributive approach seeks to divide the current set of resources among the parties through concessions (Weingart, Brett, Olekalns, & Smith, 2007), inferring a zero-sum situation. Under a distributive negotiation strategy, each party seeks to maximize outcomes for themselves, often at the expense of another party or parties in the negotiation. In the negotiations literature, this is referred to as value claiming, and can be associated with the concept of profit or utility maximization from economics. Indeed, the negotiation literature has drawn considerably from the behavioral economics literature, picking up themes of individual profit maximization (Bazerman, Curhan, Moore, & Valley, 2000).

Although not discussed explicitly as such, themes associated with greed are present in the negotiations literature. For example research has found that attributions of negotiating parties' intent to claim value have resulted in negative attitudinal and behavioral outcomes. Tinsley, O'Connor, and Sullivan (2002) found that those with a reputation for being an expert at value claiming, or individual outcome maximization, were perceived negatively by opposing parties within a negotiation. This value claiming framing has also been shown to result in negative attributions, which in turn develop into a self-fulfilling prophecy of suboptimal outcomes through the interactions of negotiating parties (Bazerman et al., 2000).

Interestingly, Hegtvedt and Killian (1999) identified both cognitive and emotional outcomes resulting from justice perceptions emergent in negotiation activities. They found that individuals receiving the smaller outcome in a bargaining session experienced both procedural and distributive injustice as well as negative emotions (Hegtvedt & Killian, 1999). Although not explicitly addressed as such, if perceptions of greed are accompanied by both cognitive and affective processes as we propose, perceptions of greed may be common in negotiation and bargaining situations.

## Political Science

Within in the political science literature, as with the experimental economics literature, the underlying social psychological mechanisms of greed are not specifically articulated. Nevertheless, an intriguing story unfolds when greed is examined in this context. The concept of greed is most often covered in the political science literature in reference to antecedents of war and instability. In combination with grievance, greed is seen as a motivator for conflict and rebellion (Collier, 2000). The general model stipulates that a contextual inequality creates a general sense of grievance, which if not resolved, leads to antistate attitudes and behaviors

(Collier, 2000). Once individuals are organized and motivated for action, this can escalate to conflict, war, and even revolution. Taxation without representation is an example of an inequality that has lead to conflict on a number of occasions throughout history, two examples of which are the northern barons' uprising against King John of England that lead to the signing of the Magna Carta and the taxation on various goods including tea, that ignited the American Revolution.

At its inception, the underlying mechanism for unrest is the group's grievance over the inequality it is experiencing, but as antistate attitudes are expressed and their related behaviors emerge, feelings of grievance are neutralized (Collier, 2000). As the group's motivation for further action begins to wane, an individual level motivator is needed for conflict activities to continue (Regan & Norton, 2005). It is at this point that greed becomes a motivator for continued activities. Collier (2000) defines greed as an economically self-interested behavior that motivates individuals to engage in conflict. This grievance and greed dynamic has been further refined by Regan and Norton (2005) through the illumination of the use of greed as a mobilizing force for individuals engaged in antistate activity. It is interesting to note the presence of both justice and attribution theories in the process described in this literature. Later, we also touch on the assertion that greed is a motivator of retributive and rebellious behavior, as has been discussed in the political science literature.

## Applied Psychology

There has been recent interest in perceptions of greed within the applied psychology literature (Crossley, 2009; Grégoire et al., 2010), although the question of how people arrive at perceptions of greed has yet to be addressed here as well. Crossley (2009) examines the role of perceived greed and malice in determining victim responses to social undermining in both a laboratory and a field study. In his laboratory study, participants were presented with scenarios describing socially undermining treatment targeted toward themselves on the part of a hypothetical actor. In the greed condition, participants "came to realize that their offender acted 'in a selfish effort to get a raise'" (Crossley, 2009, p. 17), effectively defining greed as selfishness. The use of undeserved raises as outcomes in this scenario highlights again the role that distributive justice plays in perceptions of greed. In his field study, Crossley (2009) deployed a critical incident technique to survey perceived greed and malice motives behind victims' experienced social undermining. He found a strong relationship between perceived greed and perceived offense severity.

Extending the idea of justice antecedents to greed perceptions, Grégoire et al. (2010) present a model of customer revenge that includes perceptions of firm greed as a driver for the desire for revenge. They identify procedural, interactional, and distributive justice as antecedents of perceived greed along with blame attributions, which have been traditionally studied in the customer revenge literature as a trigger for either desire for revenge or actual revenge behaviors. In their extended customer revenge model, Grégoire and colleagues also incorporate anger as an outcome resulting from perceptions of firm greed. Interestingly, Grégoire et al. (2010) tested their proposed sequence of unfairness followed by blame leading to perceived greed against the reverse sequence, as this reverse sequence could be a viable alternative explanation for the observed behaviors. They found that their originally proposed sequence had the superior fit. This argues effectively for a specific cognitive process that includes both justice and attributions as key components of greed perceptions.

### Conclusions

The construct of greed has been touched on in a number of literatures, four of which are highlighted here, and yet there is no explicit definition of greed in terms of fundamental psychological concepts. We note that distributive justice is implied in all areas of literature discussed above, and that an attributional process is implied in both the political science and applied psychology literatures. We argue below for a more generalized model describing how individuals arrive at judgments of greed outside of any specific organizational context. A key challenge in examining greed as a phenomenon in organizations is the lack of a clear definition for what individuals perceive as greedy. Before we outline our model, we share some insights that lead to our definition of greed.

## TOWARD A DEFINITION OF GREED

*"Of course, none of us are greedy, it's only the other fellow who's greedy."*

—Milton Friedman

As Milton Friedman aptly suggests, greed is fundamentally a people-centered perception, a label that observers apply to actors and their behavior. We note that people tend to focus on others when thinking about greed, rather than themselves. Whether through cognitive dissonance or some other self-justifying attribution process, people do not readily perceive greed in themselves. Consequently, we focus our definition and model on perceived greed in others.

Greedy behavior is often ascribed to individual actors, but this perception may also be extended to entities such as professions and organizations. Through an individual's repetitive behavior, a permanent judgment of greed may eventually be assigned to that individual. Aggregations of greedy people may lead to judgments of greed directed at specific professions, as is sometimes the case with investment bankers. This same mechanism may be applied to entire industries as well, such as Wall Street, based on an aggregated perception of greed on the part of those associated with Wall Street. Aggregations may also be institutionalized, resulting in judgments of greed applied to organizations, as was the case with Enron.

Perceptions of greed also involve the assignment of a certain responsibility to the focal actor; that is, the perception is based on an observation that the focal actor is actively pursuing or taking an over-reward. Presented another way, when an over-reward is given without focal actor pursuit of the reward, we are less likely to judge that focal actor as greedy.

It is interesting to note that greed may be ascribed to behavior that directly impacts the observer, or it may be assigned by a third party observing the impact of an actor's behavior on another individual. In other words, the person who observes and judges the behavior may or may not be directly involved in or impacted by the behavior of the greedy actor. We propose that the underlying perceptual and attributional mechanisms are the same in either case.

In general, we believe that people's feelings about what is considered greedy behavior are fairly clear, but if one aspect of the situation is changed, that perception may be invalidated. Actual or perceived need on the part of the focal actor is one example. If the observer perceives need, then there is less likely to be an attribution of greed. Greedy individuals who help themselves to what might be perceived as more than their fair share of food at a buffet restaurant become deserving when we find out that they are a construction workers who work long hours performing physical work and that they skipped lunch earlier in the day. Social norms may also make the relative judgment different, as in the case of free items given away at conferences or trade fairs. If someone takes more than one branded pen from a display, this is not necessarily viewed as greedy behavior, perhaps due to the low value of the item and the assumption that there are plenty to go around. As suggested by the construction worker example, we find that perceptions of greed are tied to judgments of deservingness. If the observer feels that the focal actor is deserving of the outcome, even if the actor is pursuing it, then the actor is less likely to be perceived as greedy.

Situational deservingness highlights the role of relative deprivation as pertinent to judgments of greed, as it appears that greed is often assigned when one party experiences a gain at the expense of another. In reflecting on circumstances where greed is perceived, there are often two or more parties involved in the situation, with one party receiving more than the others.

We also observe that judgments of greed are most commonly assigned in cases where the relevant outcomes are valuable and scarce resources. This may include money, power, status, food, and other situationally relevant scarcities. For example, if an individual takes 20 cookies from a plate left in the office break room, leaving only four for the rest of the office staff, this person is quite likely to be judged as greedy, even more so if the cookies are particularly delicious. On the other hand, consider an individual who is observed checking out 20 books at the library. Even if it is reasonable to assume that the average person will be unable to finish reading all 20 books by the time they come due, this individual is nevertheless not likely to be perceived as greedy, unless some of the titles are particularly coveted.

We also acknowledge that perceptions of greed are tied to cultural and organizational norms that touch on themes of individualism, competitiveness, ambition, and achievement. In the United States, for example, greed is not always discouraged, nor does it always have a negative connotation. The U.S. capitalist economy is structured to incentivize individual wealth creation, accumulation, and maintenance, largely through competitive market forces. Within this system, a certain amount of selfish ambition is encouraged and valued, and it is accepted and often times expected that when one person gains, another person loses. On the other hand, collectivist societies are probably less tolerant of greedy behavior, as taking more than one's fair share is inherently antithetical to the collective benefit. Research studying greed in cross-cultural settings may provide important information about the boundary conditions for perceptions of greed, and the circumstances under which perceptions of greed gain the most traction.

Similarly, the values embedded within different organizational cultures also likely impact the extent to which greed is encouraged, tolerated, or discouraged. Competitive, individualistic, and excessive behavior that is rewarded in some investment banks is detrimental and discouraged in nonprofits and social services. Big banks and oil industry firms continue to reward senior executives for amassing multibillion dollar profits, while laying off thousands of employees.

Regardless of the cultural and organizational context, and whether assigned to people, professions, entities, or formal organizations, we do not expect greed to vary along more than one dimension. People or behaviors are generally considered more, less, or not at all greedy, making this a unidimensional construct.

Lastly, judgments of greed assigned to behaviors appear to be accompanied by an emotional response. Grégoire et al. (2010) touch on this by identifying anger as an outcome of perceptions of greed. We question whether emotional reactions follow from or accompany perceptions of greed, and therefore, propose that perceived greed has both cognitive and affective components.

### Greed Defined

Based on the preceding discussion, we propose the following definition of greed:

> Greed is a culturally bound and emotionally charged negative perception of others who are seen as responsible for trying to take more of a scarce resource than they need and deserve, to the relative disadvantage of others.

With this working definition, we now consider the psychological processes that underlie our definition of greed. We develop these theoretical underpinnings to present a model of greed perceptions.

## A DISTRIBUTIVE INJUSTICE MODEL OF GREED

Two psychological theories that address fundamental principles in our definition of greed are distributive justice (Deutsch, 1975) and attribution theory (Weiner, 1985). Distributive justice theory addresses the perceived fairness of resource allocation decisions, recognizing that many different principles govern fair allocations (Deutsch, 1975). Attribution theory addresses the cognitive process of inferring causes and responsibility for events and behavior (Weiner, 1985). These causes can be internal to the actor or externally driven by environmental factors and can be incidental or stable. We discuss each of these theories and the implications of these theories for greed.

### Distributive Justice

As our definition of greed highlights, greed is fundamentally about someone taking a disproportionally unfair allocation or outcome. When evaluating the fairness of outcomes, people examine allocations with respect to one or more rules or principles of fairness. Deutsch (1975) discussed three distributive rules: Equity, needs, and equality. The equity principle suggests that outcomes should be commensurate with contributions relative to what others are receiving for their contributions. For example, merit increases should differentiate individuals based on performance and contributions. The needs principle suggests that some outcomes should be allocated to those who are neediest. Reasonable accommodations to individuals with disabilities tend to be allocated on the basis of needs. Whereas both equity and need are differentiating distributive principles, equality is a nondifferentiating principle and suggests that outcomes should be allocated equally. Employee benefits are usually nondifferentiating, as are across the board cost-of-living increases.

All three distributive justice rules have been discussed in the management literature (e.g., Colquitt, Greenberg, & Zapata-Phelan, 2005; Gilliland, 1993), although the equity principle has received far more research attention than the other principles. Research in social psychology demonstrates that while equity is the dominant distributive rule (in North America), needs and equality may become more dominant when people are exposed to rule violations (e.g., Schwinger, 1986). Gilliland (2008) suggested that all justice principles carry the greatest importance to people as treatment becomes more extreme. That is, we are more concerned with justice principles when those principles are severely violated. Extending this theorizing, we suggest that greed generates such negative reactions because it represents a violation of equity, needs, and equality.

It is important to acknowledge that distributive justice theory has tended be examined from the perspective of either the allocator (Leventhal, 1980) or the recipient (Adams, 1965). Our application of distributive justice to understanding perceptions of greed adopts an additional, third-party perspective in which the perceiver is neither the allocator nor the greedy recipient, but rather someone who passes judgment on the greedy recipient. The perceiver in our model can either be a person directly impacted by the greedy focal actor or a third-party not directly impacted. Organizational justice research has demonstrated that third-party experiences of procedural injustice are similar to those of victims of injustice, except with a somewhat lessened impact (Kray & Lind, 2002; Skarlicki, Ellard, & Kelln, 1998). For example, Skarlicki et al. (1998) studied third-party observers' reactions to layoffs described in a newspaper article and found that procedural fairness perceptions and retributive intentions were influenced by the extent to which victims of the layoff were provided with voice opportunities and adequate explanations. To our knowledge, third-party reactions have not been studied when the recipient receives overcompensation rather than a procedural or economic disadvantage.

Although our focus in this chapter is on distributive justice, we are not intending to suggest that other types of justice (i.e., procedural, informational, or interpersonal) are not important in shaping perceptions of greed. Indeed, unfair allocations obtained through unfair procedures are likely to be viewed as particularly greedy, as exemplified by a dealer who stacks the deck. However, since procedural injustices are likely to impact greed perceptions through their influence on distributive injustice, we have chosen to focus our discussion in this chapter on the distributive justice foundation of greed perceptions. In the following sections, we discuss each of the three distributive justice principles with respect to greed and then discuss the process by which the principles may combine to form perceptions of greed.

### *Equity*

Adams (1965) developed equity theory to explain emotional, attitudinal, and behavioral reactions to underpayment and overpayment. According to equity theory people evaluate the outcomes they received relative to their inputs, in comparison to the outcomes and inputs of referent others. If one's ratio of outcomes to inputs is less than that for the referent other, perceptions of underpayment inequity result, and these perceptions lead to anger, dissatisfaction, and a number of behaviors attempting to balance the equation (e.g., decrease inputs, increase outcomes) or to withdraw from the situation. If one's ratio is greater than the referent other's, equity theory suggests that dissatisfaction and attempts to restore equity also result, but Homans (1961) suggested the underlying emotion is guilt rather than anger. Generally, research has been more supportive of the underpayment hypothesis than the overpayment hypothesis (Greenberg, 1982), although both have received support (e.g., Greenberg, 1988).

Recent research questions whether guilt is an emotional reaction that follows from overpayment (Van den Bos, Peters, Bobocel, & Ybema, 2006). They found that overpayment results in positive affective reactions (satisfaction) at receiving a relatively good outcome, but negative fairness-based cognitive reactions of being unfairly advantaged. Further, they found that people are more satisfied with overpayment inequity when they were cognitively "busy." The implication is that the fairness-based considerations require cognitive attention, and without sufficient attention, the egoism-based positive reactions dominate reactions to overpayment.

A number of important implications of equity theory contribute to an understanding of how perceptions of greed may be formed. First, inequity can be created based on outcomes, inputs, or both. Perceiving that someone is receiving a disproportionately large outcome and is not contributing their fair share both contribute to perceptions of inequity. Second, equity is a perceptual construct and is therefore based on perceptions of outcomes, inputs, and comparisons to referent others. It is therefore possible to perceive inequity even when none actually exists if inputs or outcomes are misperceived. Third, individuals can choose from a variety of referent others, including those in the same department/firm, those in other organizations, or even one's own prior experiences. As a consequence of these implications, two people can perceive the same situation differently depending on whom they identify as their referent comparison. Investment bankers receiving millions of dollars in bonuses may perceive the bonuses as equitable relative to other investment bankers, but outsiders relying on referents outside the industry can perceive the same bonuses as overpayment inequity.

> Greed is when you take more than you deserve.
>
> I think greed is ... overcompensating.
>
> I believe greed is when a person or entity seeks to gain [an] unfair or unbalanced amount of resources (at the expense or detriment of others).

These quotes from MBA students and our definition of greed suggest that greed is a result of someone receiving more than they deserve. This clearly represents a violation of equity, with the greedy person receiving more in outcomes than is warranted based on their inputs. This perception of inequity can exist for someone who is directly losing out as a result of the greedy person's overcompensation, or can exist for an observer who is not directly impacted by the greedy person. In the latter case, inequity still exists when one considers the ratio of one's own outcomes and inputs relative to that of the greedy person. For example, a school teacher or nurse can question whether the inputs of investment bankers really justify outcomes that are several hundred times greater than their own, even when the investment bankers' outcomes are in no way impacting the teacher's own financial situation. This mechanism has been supported by research; Wade, O'Reilly, and Pollock (2006) found that when CEOs are overpaid relative to lower level managers, those managers were more likely to leave the organization.

Outcome inequity also helps explain the concept of greed discussed in the economic literature on free riders. When one refrains from contributing to a public goods pool and yet benefits from the outcomes of this pool, the free rider can be described as greedy (Rapoport & Eshed-Levy, 1989). In this case, greed is not the result of gaining more outcomes than others, but instead is the result of contributing fewer inputs and receiving the same outcomes. From an equity theory perspective, free riding results in overcompensation inequity.

Based on equity theory, we propose that perceptions of greed will result from overpayment inequity based on either inputs or outcomes:

> ***Proposition 1:*** Greed is perceived when individuals view others as seeking more than they deserve relative to comparison others, or as trying to contribute less while receiving the same as comparison others.

At least three points are important to note in this proposition. First, we are not suggesting that all cases of overpayment inequity will result in perceptions of greed, rather that overpayment inequity is one of the conditions that contribute to perceptions of greed. Other conditions include violations of needs and equality. Second, actual overpayment is not necessarily required to perceive greed; simply the act of trying to get overcompensated (without success) could be viewed as greedy. Finally, we highlight the active or intentional role of the greedy person in trying to get overcompensated. Being given more without involvement in the decision is not likely to be seen as greedy. We address this issue further when we discuss attribution theory.

### *Needs*

Violations of distributive justice also exist when those with the greatest needs do not receive outcomes they deserve (Deutsch, 1975). When organizations allocate outcomes in a manner that fulfills individual needs, those individuals can then focus their efforts on organizational goals rather than personal goals (Folger, Sheppard, & Buttram, 1995). A number of studies have demonstrated the importance of the needs principle as a component of distributive justice associated with employee benefits (e.g., Grandey, 2001; Tremblay, Sire, & Pelchat, 1998). The use of family-friendly policies, such as maternity leave, can satisfy the needs principle, and these policies are viewed to be fairer by those with needs (e.g., individuals having children or being of childbearing age) than those without, and by those who hold positive attitudes toward women (Grover, 1991). Research demonstrates that people are most likely to allocate outcomes on the basis of needs when those needs are made salient and when needs are externally and unintentionally caused (Schwinger, 1986; Skitka & Tetlock, 1992).

Distributive justice theory suggests that a violation of the needs principle exists when someone with clear needs does not receive outcome allocations to address those needs. However, we also believe that needs violations can exist when someone receives far more than they need. Consider the following quotes from our MBA students:

> In my opinion, "greed" is wanting more when you already have plenty—even more than you need to satisfy your needs.
>
> Greed is ... when you covet and accumulate more than you will ever have a use for.
>
> Greed is when you have an intense desire to acquire or purchase material possessions that are extremely above necessity.
>
> Greed is taking more than you morally need.

Just as overpayment exists with the equity principle, we are suggesting a similar overpayment condition exists when outcomes exceed individual needs. Grover (1991) found that women perceived parental leave policies to be fairer than men did. While this result could suggest that women perceive a greater need for these policies than men, it is also possible that men are more likely to see these policies as being unfair because they provide more leave than is needed. That is, men may be more likely to see these policies as an unfair overcompensation on the basis of needs. Anecdotally, most people can recall a feeling of outrage when hearing news reports of need-based distributions of food and financial aid being diverted to those who are not truly needy. We propose that witnessing overpayment that violates the needs principle contributes to perceptions of greed.

> ***Proposition 2:*** Greed is perceived when individuals view others as seeking more than they need relative to comparison others.

### *Equality*

The equality principle suggests that outcomes should be allocated equally, regardless of inputs, performance, or other differentiating information (Deutsch, 1975). In situations in which cooperation, social relations, and cohesion are primary goals, equality tends to be the dominant social principle (Kabanoff, 1991). Meindl (1989) had managers evaluate different allocation scenarios and found that when solidarity was a stated goal, managers tended to prefer allocations based on equality, whereas equity was preferred when productivity was emphasized. He also found that when both productivity and solidarity were emphasized, managers tended to rely on equality rather than equity. Mannix, Neale, and Northcraft (1995) manipulated the cultural context of an organization in a negotiation exercise and found that students were more likely to negotiate based on equality when the culture emphasized relationships and mutual respect. Colquitt and Jackson (2006) directly examined different distributive rules and had participants rate the importance of equity, equality, and needs in either an individual or team context. Equality was rated as more important in the team context than in the individual context. Collectively, these results demonstrate that individuals are sensitive to the equality distributive rule in organizational contexts.

Gilliland (1993) suggested that equality becomes a more salient distributive justice principle when outcomes clearly violate the equality principle. Individuals have been shown to be more sensitive to equality violations based on discrimination after seeing clear-cut examples of discrimination (Crosby, Burris, Censor, & MacKethan, 1986). Dawes et al. (2007) found in experimental games that emotions toward top earners became increasingly negative as inequality increased. Inequality can result from people getting more than their fair share or from others getting less. We suggest that both are involved in perceptions of greed. While receiving more than one's fair share can simultaneously be a violation of equity, needs, and equality, the case of others losing out is clearly a violation of the equality principle. Consider the following quotes from MBA students:

> Greed is ... wanting more at another's expense.
>
> Greed is the accumulation of some type of wealth with disregard for the impact that accumulation has on others.
>
> Greed is excess and usually at a loss to others involved.
>
> Greed is defined as actions taken by one that have a negative impact on others.

The foundation for distributive justice research rests in the concept of relative deprivation (Adams, 1965). This concept suggests that individuals' reactions to outcomes depend less on the absolute level of those outcomes than on outcomes of others around them. With respect to perceptions of greed, we propose that people will be more sensitive to the greed of others when they themselves are losing out. Further, based on the equality principle, the more widespread these losses are, the more likely the overcompensated individual is to be seen as greedy because of the violation of equality. If I am losing out and everyone else is gaining, I am less likely to perceive greed in others than if most people are losing out and only the greedy individuals are gaining. This violation of equality suggests the following proposition:

> ***Proposition 3:*** Greed is perceived when equality is violated based on a small number of individuals seeking gains while the perceiver and/or many others are losing.

In this proposition, we are suggesting that the magnitude of the inequality created by few people gaining and many losing prompts perceptions of greed.

### Combining Rules

Leventhal (1980) proposed a justice judgment model in which perceptions of fairness are based on a weighted sum of the satisfaction and violation of different distributive justice principles. Specifically, he suggested the following model of distributive fairness perceptions:

$$\textit{Distributive Fairness} = w_1\textit{Equity} + w_2\textit{Equality} + w_3\textit{Needs} + w_i\textit{Other Rules}$$

Under this model, individuals attribute different weights based on the importance of equity, needs, and equality, and distributive fairness evaluations are based on a cognitive algebraic combination of the weighted satisfaction and violation of distributive principles. A key implication of this model is that injustice on a single important principle can produce unfairness perceptions. For example, some individuals may pay relatively little attention to needs and equality and evaluate outcomes purely on the basis of equity.

We propose that greed evaluations emerge from a somewhat different process. If one considers each of the propositions associated with the different distributive principles, it is possible to imagine situations in which a single condition exists and greed is not perceived. For example, there are many possible circumstances where a small number of individuals gain and many lose that are not associated with perceptions greed. Lotteries and tournaments produce few winners and many losers without making the winners appear greedy. Consequently, we propose that greed is most likely to be perceived when equity, needs, and equality are all violated at the same time. A violation of one principle may produce perceptions of distributive injustice, but a violation of all three forms the foundation of greed perceptions. Rather than the weighted summation model described by Leventhal (1980), we propose that greed is based on the following multiplicative combination of the three distributive principles:

$$\textit{Perceived Greed} = w_1\textit{Equity} \times w_2\textit{Needs} \times w_3\textit{Equality}$$

This proposed multiplicative relationship has at least two important implications. First if any one of the three principles is not violated, perceived greed is unlikely. For example, if someone tries to take more than they need and many other are losing out, but they deserve the outcome, the situation is not likely to be perceived as greedy. When we asked a class if Warren Buffet and Bill Gates were greedy for accumulating so much more wealth then they could ever need, while so many people are losing out, none saw these two as greedy. The general response was that both earned (deserved) their wealth through successfully building businesses.

Second, the multiplicative relationship suggests that when all three principles are severely violated, the effects are amplified and a far stronger reaction is produced than is seen with typical distributive justice violations. People tend to respond to distributive injustice by decreasing inputs, demanding greater outcomes, or leaving the situation (Adams, 1965). People tend to respond to greed with emotional reactions, retribution, and demands for punitive measures. For example, politicians debated legislative measures to punish Wall Street bankers who received large bonuses at a time when the financial industry was collapsing (Flaherty, 2009).

Finally, we highlight that this relationship exists within the cognitions of the observer. Different observers can vary in their weighting of rules and perceptions of greed. The multiplicative relationship between distributive principles is summarized in the following proposition:

> ***Proposition 4:*** Greed is perceived when individuals perceive others as seeking more than they deserve and more than they need, while the perceiver and/or many others are losing.

### *Conclusions*

We believe that distributive justice theory provides a solid theoretical foundation for examining perceptions of greed. The combination of equity, needs, and equality provides a structured and testable approach to the construct of greed. However, there is likely more to greed than extreme injustice. Our definition of greed also suggests an attribution of responsibility for greedy behavior. We now discuss attribution theory as an important moderator of greed perceptions.

## Attribution Moderators

Greed has an element of responsibility that our theory must explain. Consider a situation in which a single piece of cake must be divided between two people. If I cut the cake into two thirds and one third, then take the larger piece, it is easy to describe me as greedy. I took more than I needed and deserved and the other person lost out. However, if I cut the cake and then give the larger piece to the other person, it would be hard to describe the person receiving the larger piece as greedy. To take an unfair amount is greedy. To be given an unfair amount is not necessarily greedy. Attribution theory (Weiner, 1985) provides a theoretical perspective for examining these issues of responsibility.

Attribution theory is concerned with understanding how people infer causes for behavior and events (Fiske & Taylor, 1991). When something negative, unfavorable, or unexpected happens, people want to know "*why*" this happened. While a seemingly unlimited number of causes can be ascribed to different events, Weiner (1985) suggested that it is the underlying dimensions of the causes that are particularly important. Specifically, Weiner identified three causal dimensions as critical to understanding causal inferences. *Locus* refers to whether the event was caused by internal factors within the person or external factors associated with the situation. The second dimension is *controllability*, or the extent to which anyone could have influenced the event's occurrence. Finally, *stability* reflects the frequency of the event; whether it is a one-time occurrence or has occurred repeatedly. Weiner suggested that the combination of locus, controllability, and stability jointly determine how people react to events emotionally and behaviorally. For example, he suggested that anger follows from a negative event or outcome that is attributed to factors controllable by others.

It is important to note that attributions are subjective inferences and can vary based on the actors, their experiences, and their perceptions. Perceived causes can also vary within an individual over occasions. This subjective nature of causal attributions is captured in the following MBA student quotes:

> The concept of greed is subjective.

> As we acquire more wealth, our definition of greed changes to justify our position without cognitive dissonance.

An important contribution of attribution theory is that it provides a structure for understanding individual variations in perceptions. We consider each of the dimensions of attributions and their importance in shaping perceptions of greed.

### *Locus*

Locus of causality refers to internal versus external causes for events (Weiner, 1985). When applying this dimension to perceptions of greed, the causal inference is being made of the greedy person who attempts to receive distributively unfair overcompensation. An internal locus of causality places responsibility within the greedy individual for trying to take (or actually taking) the outcome. An external locus of causality suggests that someone or something external to the greedy actors was responsible for the outcome. We believe that perceptions of greed are most likely to result from internal causal inferences. Consider the following quotes:

> Greed [is] intentionally taking more than you can use of something and not sharing something with others.

> When an individual seeks to collect, over utilize, or hoard resources at the expense of others... that is the definition of greed.

> Greed is when someone behaves in a way to obtain a gain without regard to an appropriate behavior required to obtain the benefit.

All of these definitions of greed suggest that the greedy individual actively and intentionally controls or seeks to control the process of gaining resources. That is, the individual is responsible for the greedy act.

In a study of customer revenge, Grégoire et al. (2010) found that attributions of blame were associated with perceptions of greed. The more customers attributed poor service recovery to the fault of the service firm (e.g., "To what extent do you blame the firm for what happened?") the more likely they were to describe the firm as greedy. Based on attribution theory, we suggest the following proposition:

> ***Proposition 5:*** Greed is most commonly perceived when individuals perceive others as being responsible for taking or pursuing an unfair outcome rather than being given an unfair outcome by another decision maker.

While we focus this proposition on individual greedy actors, it is also possible that these perceptions can be broadened to organizations or industries. In these cases, it is not necessarily the individual recipient who is the causal actor, but the organization or industry. That is, the internal locus of causality is internal to the organization or industry, rather than to the individual. For example, when describing "greedy investment bankers," it is possible that individual investment bankers were *given* unreasonably large bonuses, but the industry as a whole *took* these bonuses from investors. This would be a case of guilt by association. The industry is greedy, therefore each individual beneficiary in the industry is also perceived as greedy.

### *Controllability*

Controllability refers to the extent to which the outcome is under intentional control (Weiner, 1985). Winning a lottery is not a controllable outcome. Even though the lottery winner controlled the purchase of the ticket, the differentiation of winners and nonwinners is not within any lottery player's control. Abundant research has demonstrated that the greater the attributed control, the more responsibility is ascribed to the actor (Fiske & Taylor, 1991). Given the impact of control on responsibility, we suggest that greed is more likely to be perceived when the outcome is controllable rather than out of anyone's control.

> ***Proposition 6:*** Greed is most commonly perceived when individuals perceive others as having control over an unfair outcome rather than lacking control over that outcome.

When combined with the locus of causality dimension, we are suggesting that internal, controllable causal inferences are most likely to produce perceptions of greed. At first blush it may seem that locus and controllability are perfectly correlated. Indeed, research has demonstrated a strong correlation between attributions of locus and control (Ployhart & Ryan, 1997). Internal loci are more controllable and external loci are more uncontrollable. However, there is an important distinction between these two dimensions. It is possible for individuals to be responsible, but the event still is beyond their control. Involuntary manslaughter is by definition an internal, uncontrollable cause of death. We believe that the combination of both internal locus and control will produce the greatest perceived blame, and consequently, the greatest perceived greed.

### *Stability*

The third attributional dimension defined by Weiner (1985) is stability, which reflects the degree to which the cause of the behavior or situation is stable or unstable in the future. Given that future behavior is typically inferred from the past, when a behavior or situation is seen as repeatedly occurring it is more likely to lead to an attribution of stability. One time events or behaviors that fluctuate are more likely to be seen as unstable.

Whereas locus and control are both attributions that lead to placing responsibility or blame for an event, we believe stability functions somewhat differently in influencing perceived greed. Both stable and unstable attributions can lead to perceptions of greed, but the nature of those perceptions varies as a function of stability. One time behaviors and unstable attributions are most likely to lead to perceptions of greedy behavior or actions. Repeated behaviors with the attributions of stability are more likely to lead to perceptions of greedy individuals or institutions. The differences in these perceptions can be characterized as the difference between saying "*that was greedy*" versus "*you are greedy.*" Both are perceptions of greed, but the former is describing the action as greedy and the latter is describing the actor as greedy.

> ***Proposition 7:*** Unstable attributions of greed are more likely to lead to perceptions of greedy behavior, whereas stable attributions of greed are more likely to lead to perceptions of greedy individuals and institutions.

We propose that the difference between greedy actions (unstable) and greedy actors (stable) will be manifested most acutely as consequences to perceived greed through intentions and behavioral responses. This is consistent with Weiner's (1985) suggestion that stability attributions most directly influence intentions and expectations. Perceived greedy actions are more likely to lead to complaints and rebukes. The response is designed to provide feedback on specific behaviors. On the other hand, perceived greedy actors are more likely to lead to retribution and punishment. A stronger response is likely to follow a more stable display of greed.

> ***Proposition 8:*** Stable attributions of greed will lead to stronger retributive intentions and behaviors than unstable attributions of greed.

## Conclusions

Distributive justice and attribution theories provide compelling theoretical mechanisms for explaining perceptions of greed. When an individual observes efforts to gain overcompensation in the form of an outcome that violates equity, needs, and equality principles, the multiplicative combination of these violations forms the foundation of greed perceptions. In order for the action or person to be perceived as greedy, the perceiver must attribute responsibility to internal, controllable causes within the greedy individual. If the behavior is seen as stable, the person is labeled greedy. If the behavior is seen as unstable, the action is labeled greedy. This model is summarized in Figure 6.1.

Although we have not explicitly addressed outcomes of greed perceptions, both distributive justice and attribution theories highlight cognitive, affective, and behavioral outcomes. With perceptions of greed, the cognitive outcome is labeling the person or action as greedy. In terms of affective reactions, some research has associated general anger with perceptions of greed (e.g., Crossley, 2009; Grégoire et al., 2010). However, we suggest that a more specific emotional reaction along the lines of moral outrage (Montada, Schmitt, & Dalbert, 1986) results from perceived greed. Moral anger and moral outrage have long been described as outcomes of perceived injustice (Bies, 1987; Folger, Cropanzano, &

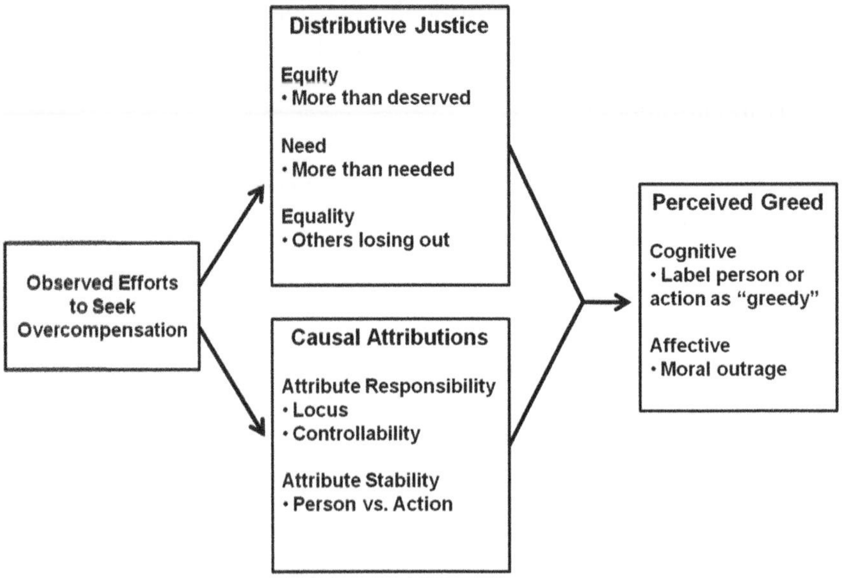


Figure 6.1. A distributive justice model of perceived greed.

Goldman, 2005). Given that perceived greed results from the combined injustice of equity, needs, and equality violations, we suggest that emotional reactions to perceived greed should be exhibited in moral outrage.

A variety of behavioral reactions also are likely to result from perceived greed. Attribution theory suggests that both attitudinal and behavioral reactions result from attributions of responsibility (Weiner, 1985). Distributive justice theory highlights a number of attitudinal and behavioral reactions that result from perceived distributive injustice. Although most of this research addresses reactions of recipients of unfair outcomes, third-party justice research has demonstrated that reactions to perceived injustice predict retributive intentions (Skarlicki et al., 1998).

A few studies have examined reaction to perceived greed. Crossley (2009) examined behavioral reactions along the dimensions of revenge, avoidance, and reconciliation. In one of the most complete models on reactions resulting from perceived greed, Grégoire et al. (2010) demonstrated that customer perceptions of a firm's greed predicted anger, desire for revenge, complaining, and negative word of mouth. We believe the development of a comprehensive theoretical model of outcomes of perceived greed is an important and interesting avenue for future research.

## DISCUSSION

Our goals in this chapter were to review the literature, develop a working definition, and develop a theoretically grounded conceptual model of perceptions of greed. Based on distributive justice and attribution theories, this model suggests that greed is perceived when someone observes others trying to take more than they deserve and need, while others are losing out, and with the attribution of responsibility resting within control of the greedy party. Further, isolated instances of greed are characterized as greedy behavior, whereas repeated instances of greed are characterized as greedy individuals or institutions.

We have highlighted a number of propositions derived from this model and believe each of these propositions suggests interesting, testable hypotheses. Researchers can use a variety of methods, including surveys, scenario studies, and laboratory experiments to test the influence of distributive justice violations and attributions on perceived greed. Given the importance of affective reactions in perceptions of greed, we suggest that researchers assess both cognitive and affective reactions. While some authors have developed measures of perceived greed (e.g., Crossley, 2009; Grégoire et al., 2010), we caution against the use of measures that do not directly assess greed. Items in the scale Grégoire et al. (2010) used included the following: "the firm intended to take advantage of me," "the firm was primarily motivated by its own interests," "the firm tried to abuse me," and "the firm had bad intentions." Crossley (2009) assessed greed with three items that asked about selfishness. Items in both of these scales appear to be addressing constructs related to greed, but it is unclear if greed is actually being assessed. One of the benefits of the definition of greed we have proposed is that it can be used to guide measurement development efforts.

An important implication of our proposed model is that perceived greed is influenced by both the perceiver and the greedy individual. Perceptions of equality violations are based on the perceiver and others losing out while the greedy individual is gaining. The implication of this proposition is that greed is much more likely to be perceived in bad times than good. Is the current outrage with the greed on Wall Street because people have seen their investments decrease, or because bonuses have become more egregious, or both? Similarly, the fundamental attribution error (Ross, 1977) demonstrates that people tend to attribute other people's behavior to internal, dispositional factors rather than external, situational factors. Attribution theory research also demonstrates that we tend to see others' behavior as stable across situations, whereas we see our own behavior as much more variable (Fiske & Taylor, 1991). These findings may help explain why we tend to see greed much more commonly in other people than in ourselves.

Our model of perceived greed has interesting implications for organizational justice research. For the most part, third party perceptions have been examined in conditions of underpayment or of procedural and interactional injustice. We know of no research that has directly examined third party perceptions of overcompensation. We believe that by focusing primarily on underpayment conditions, researchers may have overlooked some of the most interesting third party effects. It would also be interesting to examine whether victims of another person's greed differ in their perceptions and reactions from third party observers. Some research from the organizational justice domain would suggest that reactions of third party observers may be less intense than reactions of victims (Kray & Lind, 2002).

We believe there are a number of important applications of our model. The popular literature is filled with stories of greed associated with executive compensation (e.g., Ausick, 2010). It would be interesting to apply our model to executive compensation and see to what extent the distributive justice principles and attribution components can be addressed to shape public perceptions of greed. If our proposed multiplicative relationship between distributive principles (Proposition 4) is supported, it would suggest that a firm need only address one of the three distributive principles to reduce perceptions of greed. Also in this context, it would be interesting to see if executives alter their behavior in response to (or anticipation of) being perceived as greedy. In addition to studying perceived greed in executive compensation, it may also be interesting to study the effects of perceived greed in interactive contexts, such as negotiations, conflict resolution, and litigation.

Our model as presented in this chapter also has some limitations that must be acknowledged. First, we have chosen to focus on distributive justice and have not addressed potential effects of procedural and interactional justice. Although this decision was based on the assumption that the effects of these other justice types would exert their influence through distributive justice, a more complete model would include all justice types. Indeed, Grégoire et al. (2010) found influences of both procedural and interactional justice on customers' perceptions of firm greed. Second, in this model we have chosen to focus on antecedents of perceived greed and not the outcomes of greed perceptions. A more fully articulated model of perceived greed should include both antecedents and consequences. We encourage future development of the outcome side of this model. Finally, our model is based on theory and logic, but is very light on empirical support. We hope that subsequent models of greed will benefit from new research into this interesting and important construct.

## CONCLUSIONS

In this chapter we have proposed that greed deserved greater empirical investigation. Perceived greed prompts public outcry, political action, and retributive measures. Despite the motivating force of greed perceptions, relatively little attention has been directed toward studying this topic. By providing a comprehensive definition of greed and outlining a theoretically grounded model of perceived greed, we have provided structure for examining this construct in a logical manner.

## REFERENCES

Adams, J. S. (1965). Inequity in social exchange. In L. Berkowitz (Ed.), *Advances in experimental social psychology* (Vol. 2, pp. 267-299). New York, NY: Academic Press.

Ausick, P. (2010, February 1, 2010). Another shameful bonus at Goldman Sachs? It's hard to imagine a more tone-deaf move, but Goldman's chief executive is reportedly set to receive a $100 million bonus. *Top Stocks - MSN Money*. Retrieved from http://articles.moneycentral.msn.com/Investing/top-stocks/blog.aspx?post=1596719.

Bazerman, M. H., Curhan, J. R., Moore, D. A., & Valley, K. L. (2000). Negotiation. *Annual Review of Psychology, 51*, 270-314.

Bazerman, M. H., & Neale, M. A. (1983). Heuristics in negotiation: Limitations to effective dispute resolution. In M. H. Bazerman & R. J. Lewicki (Eds.), *Negotiating in Organizations* (pp. 51-67). Beverly Hills, CA: SAGE.

Bies, R. J. (1987). The predicament of injustice: The management of moral outrage. *Research in Organizational Behavior, 9*, 289-319.

Collier, P. (2000). Rebellion as a quasi-criminal activity. *Journal of Conflict Resolution, 44*(6), 839-853.

Colquitt, J. A., Greenberg, J., & Zapata-Phelan, C. P. (2005). What is organizational justice? A historical overview. In J. Greenberg & J. A. Colquitt (Eds.), *Handbook of organizational justice* (pp. 3-56). Mahwah, NJ: Erlbaum.

Colquitt, J. A., & Jackson, C. L. (2006). Justice in teams: The context sensitivity of justice rules across individual and team contexts. *Journal of Applied Social Psychology, 36*, 868-899.

Colvin, G. (2006, June). A study in CEO greed. *Fortune, 153*(11), 53.

Coombs, C. H. (1973). A reparameterization of the prisoner's dilemma game. *Behavioral Science, 18*, 424-428.

Crosby, F., Burris, L., Censor, C., & MacKethan, E. R. (1986). Two rotten apples spoil the justice barrel. In H. W. Bierhoff, R. L. Cohen, & J. Greenberg (Eds.), *Justice in social relations* (pp. 267-281). New York, NY: Plenum.

Crossley, C. D. (2009). Emotional and behavioral reactions to social undermining: A closer look at perceived offender motives. *Organizational Behavior and Human Decision Processes, 108*, 14-24.

Dawes, C. T., Fowler, J. H., Johnson, T., McElreath, R., & Smirnov, O. (2007). Egalitarian motives in humans. *Nature, 446,* 794-796.

Deutsch, M. (1975). Equity, equality, and need: What determines which value will be used as the basis of distributive justice? *Journal of Social Issues, 31,* 137-149.

Eek, D., & Biel, A. (2003). The interplay between greed, efficiency, and fairness in public-goods dilemmas. *Social Justice Research, 16*(3), 195-215.

Fiske, S. T., & Taylor, S. E. (1991). *Social cognition* (2nd ed.). New York, NY: McGraw-Hill.

Flaherty, A. (2009, August 1). Congress votes to curb Wall Street bonuses. *NBC Philadelphia.* Retrieved from http://www.nbcphiladelphia.com/news/politics/House-Votes-to-Curb-Wall-Street-Bonuses--52257297.html.

Folger, R., Cropanzano, R., & Goldman, B. (2005). What is the relationship between justice and morality? In J. Greenberg & J.A. Colquitt (Eds.), *Handbook of organizational justice* (pp. 215-245). Mahwah, NJ: Erlbaum.

Folger, R., Sheppard, B. H., & Buttram, R. (1995). Three faces of justice. In J. Rubin & B. Bunker (Eds.), *Cooperation, conflict, and justice* (pp. 261-289). San Francisco, CA: Jossey-Bass.

Gilliland, S. W. (1993). The perceived fairness of selection systems: An organizational justice perspective. *Academy of Management Review, 18,* 694-734.

Gilliland, S. W. (2008). The tails of justice: A critical examination of the dimensionality of organizational justice constructs. *Human Resource Management Review, 18,* 271-281.

Goldfarb, H. (2009, June). Greed wasn't good. *Fortune, 159*(12), 9.

Grandey, A. (2001). Family friendly policies: Organizational justice perceptions of need-based allocations. In R. Cropanzano (Ed.), *Justice in the workplace: From theory to practice* (Vol. 2, 145-173). Mahwah, NJ: Erlbaum.

Green, H. (2010, July). Greed read. *Fortune, 162*(2), 20.

Greenberg, J. (1982). Approaching equity and avoiding inequity in groups and organizations. In J. Greenberg & R. L. Cohen (Eds.), *Equity and justice in social behavior* (pp. 389-435). New York, NY: Academic Press.

Greenberg, J. (1988). Equity and workplace status: A field experiment. *Journal of Applied Psychology, 73,* 606-613.

Grégoire, Y., Laufer, D., & Tripp, T. (2010). A comprehensive model of customer direct and indirect revenge: Understanding the effects of perceived greed and customer power. *Journal of the Academy of Marketing Science, 38,* 738-758.

Grover, S. L. (1991). Predicting the perceived fairness of parental leave policies. *Journal of Applied Psychology, 76,* 247-255.

Hegtvedt, K., & Killian, C. (1999). Fairness and emotions: Reactions to the process of negotiations. *Social Forces, 78*(1), 269-302.

Homans, G. C. (1961). *Social behavior: Its elementary forms.* New York, NY: Harcourt, Brace & World.

Kabanoff, B. (1991). Equity, equality, power, and conflict. *Academy of Management Review, 16,* 416-441.

Kahneman, D., Knetsch, J., & Thaler, R. (1986). Fairness as a constraint on profit seeking: Entitlements in the market. *The American Economic Review, 76*(4), 728-741.

Kahneman, D., & Tversky, A. (1984). Choices, values, and frames. In T. Connolly, H. R. Arkes, & K. R. Hammond (Eds.), *Judgment and decision making: An interdisciplinary reader* (pp. 147-165). New York, NY: Cambridge.

Kray, L. J., & Lind, E. A. (2002). The injustice of others: Social reports and the integration of others' experiences in organizational justice judgments. *Organizational Behavior and Human Decision Processes, 89,* 906-924.

Leventhal, G. S. (1980). What should be done with equity theory? New approaches to the study of fairness in social relationships. In K. J. Gergen, M. S. Greenberg, & R. H. Willis (Eds.), *Social exchange: Advances in theory and research* (pp. 27-55). New York, NY: Plenum.

Mannix, E. A., Neale, M. A., & Northcraft, G. B. (1995). Equity, equality, or need? The effects of organizational culture on the allocation of benefits and burdens. *Organizational Behavior and Human Decision Processes, 63,* 276-286.

Meindl, J. R. (1989). Managing to be fair: An exploration of values, motives, and leadership. *Administrative Science Quarterly, 34,* 252-276.

Merriam-Webster. (2010). Greed. Retrieved from http://www.merriam-webster.com/dictionary/greed

Montada, L. Schmitt, M. & Dalbert, C. (1986). Thinking about justice and dealing with one's own privileges: A study of existential guilt. In H. W. Bierhoff, R. L. Cohen, & J. Greenberg (Eds.), *Justice in social relations* (pp. 125-143). New York, NY: Plenum.

Ployhart, R. E., & Ryan, A. M. (1997). Toward an explanation of applicant reactions: An examination of organizational justice and attribution frameworks. *Organizational Behavior and Human Decision Processes, 72,* 308-335.

Rapoport, A., & Eshed-Levy, D. (1989). Provision of step-level public goods: Effects of greed and fear of being gypped. *Organizational Behavior and Human Decision Processes, 44,* 325-344.

Regan, P., & Norton, D. (2005). Greed, grievance and mobilization in civil wars. *Journal of Conflict Resolution, 49*(3), 319-336.

Ross, L. (1977). The intuitive psychologist and his shortcomings: Distortions in the attribution process. In L. Berkowitz (Ed.), *Advances in experimental social psychology* (Vol. 10, pp. 173-220). New York, NY: Academic Press.

Samuelson, C. S., Messick, D. M., Rutte, C. G., & Wilke, H. A. M. (1984). Individual and structural solutions to resource dilemmas in two cultures. *Journal of Personality and Social Psychology, 47,* 94-104.

Sarna, D. E. Y. (2010). *History of greed: Financial fraud from tulip mania to Bernie Madoff.* Hoboken, NJ: Wiley.

Schwinger, T. (1986). The need principle of distributive justice. In H. W. Bierhoff, R. L. Cohen, & J. Greenberg (Eds.), *Justice in social relations* (pp. 211-225). New York, NY: Plenum.

Skarlicki, D. P., Ellard, J. H., & Kelln, B. R. C. (1998). Third-party perceptions of layoffs: Procedural, derogation, and retributive aspects of justice. *Journal of Applied Psychology, 83,* 119-127.

Skitka, L. J., & Tetlock, P. E. (1992). Allocating scarce resource: A contingency model of distributive justice. *Journal of Experimental Social Psychology, 28,* 491-522.

Smith, A. (1991). *Wealth of nations.* New York, NY: Prometheus. (Original work published 1776)

Tinsley, C., O'Connor, K., & Sullivan, B. (2002). Tough guys finish last: The perils of a distributive reputation. *Organizational Behavior and Human Decision Processes, 88*, 621-642.

Tremblay, M., Sire, B., & Pelchat, A. (1998). A study of the determinants and the impact of flexibility on employee benefit satisfaction. *Human Relations, 51,* 667-688.

Tyler, T., & Hastie, R. (1991). The social consequences of cognitive illusions. In M. Bazerman, R. Lewicki & B. Sheppard (Eds.), *Research on negotiations in organizations: Handbook of negotiation research* (pp. 69-98). Greenwich, CT: JAI Press.

Van den Bos, K., Peters, S. L., Bobocel, R., & Ybema, J. F. (2006). On preferences and doing the right thing: Satisfaction with advantageous inequity when cognitive processing is limited. *Journal of Experimental Social Psychology, 42,* 273-289.

Vecchio, R. P. (2007). Cinderella and Salieri in the workplace: The envied and the envier. In S. W. Gilliland, D. D. Steiner, & D. P Skarlicki (Eds.), *Managing social and ethical issues in organizations* (pp. 109-134). Charlotte, NC: Information Age.

Wade, J. B., O'Reilly, C. A. III, & Pollock, T. G. (2006). Overpaid CEOs and underpaid managers: Fairness and executive compensation. *Organizational Science, 17,* 527-544.

Weiner, B. (1985). An attributional theory of achievement motivation and emotion. *Psychological Review, 92,* 548-573.

Weiner, R. (Director). (1979). *The Phil Donahue Show.* Retrieved from http://www.youtube.com/watch?v=RWsx1X8PV_A&playnext=1&list=PL33743DF931383D1B&index=7

Weingart, L., Brett, J., Olekalns, M., & Smith, P. (2007). Conflicting social motives in negotiating groups. *Journal of Personality and Social Psychology, 93*(6), 994-1010.

Wilke, H. A. M. (1991). Greed, efficiency and fairness in resources management situations. *European Review of Social Psychology, 2,* 165-187.

CHAPTER 7

# ORGANIZATIONAL DE/HUMANIZATION, DEINDIVIDUATION, ANOMIE, AND IN/JUSTICE

**Chris M. Bell and Careen Khoury**

In this chapter we develop the concept of organizational de/humanization, drawing on the classic sociological work of Marx (1844/1961), Durkheim (1897/2006), and Weber (1905/1976) and more recent work on the social psychology of dehumanization. We position de/humanization in an ontological relationship with organizational in/justice. We identify personal agency and self-actualization as the central shared concerns of anomie, alienation, dehumanization, and organizational justice. We first review the theoretical literature, exploring the relationships between the core concepts of agency, dehumanization, and organizational justice and discussing related constructs such as anomie, deindividuation, and Haslam's (2006) typology of dehumanization. We then discuss a research program, introducing our organizational de/humanization scale and reviewing existing research that sheds light on mediating and moderating relationships between de/humanization and organizational justice. Finally, we elaborate the research program through a series of proposals. Although we focus primarily on the organization as the source of de/humanization and in/justice, we recognize that there are other sources within the organization such as supervisors or peers and briefly discuss some findings for supervisor's interpersonal justice. In conclusion, we argue that although organizational justice is associated with

*Emerging Perspectives on Organizational Justice and Ethics*
pp. 167–197

basic concerns for outcomes and status, it also has a more fundamental ontology in what it means to be human and social beings.

> *There you are, your own number on your very own door. And behind that door, your very own office! Welcome to the team, DZ-015.*
>
> —Mr. Warrenn, *Brazil,* 1985)

> *"Right now, this is a job. If I advance any higher, this would be my career. And if this were my career, I'd have to throw myself in front of a train.*
>
> —Jim Halpert (*The Office,* 2005).

> *There are 1,199 minutes of productivity remaining until the weekend.*
>
> —Automated announcement on office intercom (*Visioneers,* 2008)

In this chapter, we explore the relationship between organizational dehumanization and justice, and consider related constructs of anomie and deindividuation. Dehumanization is social in nature so, although we are primarily interested in the psychological experience of dehumanization, we ground our discussion of the construct in classic sociological work on dehumanization as the product of the social, work, or task environment (Marx, 1844/1961; Weber, 1905/1976). Our approach to organizational dehumanization is similar to the development of psychological measures of anomie, alienation, and powerlessness (for a review see Seeman, 1991). Further, whereas a dehumanized person will likely consider the experience to be unfair, unjust, and unethical, with justice judgments following as a result of dehumanizing experiences, we focus primarily on the premise that justice is a humanizing and injustice a dehumanizing process. We also discuss mediating and moderating models in the context of an ongoing research program and proposals for further empirical work. Finally, we discuss a research program for the further exploration of organizational dehumanization.

Drawing on sociological work on dehumanization (Marx, 1844/1961; Weber, 1905/1976) and the psychology of dehumanization (for a review see Haslam, 2006), we define organizational dehumanization as the experience of an employee who feels objectified by his or her organization, denied personal subjectivity, and made to feel like a tool or instrument for the organization's ends. Organizational humanization, conversely, is the experience of having one's experiences, desires, and feelings recognized by the organization and the opportunity for personal agency and self-actualization through creative and instrumental participation in organizational processes. The choice of the organization as the dehumanizing social entity is conducive to a broader discussion of the social environment of the contemporary workplace as well as relational models of organizational justice. For instance, we propose that procedural justice influences dehumanization by communicating the way in which the organization values the individual, either as an object, resource, or property through which the organization can achieve its own ends or as a thinking, feeling individual person with desires and goals. Certainly this proposition resonates with those who are familiar with the group value (Lind & Tyler, 1988) or group engagement (Tyler & Blader, 2003) models of procedural justice. However, we argue that the de/humanizing effect of in/justice occurs prior to relational or social identity effects and can thereby be distinguished from the deindividuating effects described in relational models of justice (Blader & Tyler, 2009). Although in this chapter we focus primarily on the organization as the social entity that is the agent of dehumanization, the proposed relationship between in/justice and de/humanization applies also to social interactions with relevant individuals such as supervisors, peers, and clients. We discuss these further implications of organizational dehumanization in the context of a proposed research program.

Political and social sciences have long considered the modern workplace to have a dehumanizing effect on the human subject (Marx, 1844/1961; Weber, 1905/1976). However, the construct of organizational dehumanization has not been sufficiently developed in the social and applied psychology literature (for a review and typology of the psychology of dehumanization see Haslam, 2006) and has not yet been operationalized. This gap in the literature represents a theoretically and empirically interesting prospect. For instance, in our developmental work on a scale to measure dehumanization (Bell & Khoury, 2010b) we have found the experience to be related to, but distinct from, measures of anomie and alienation (Durkheim, 1897/2006; Marx, 1844/1961; Merton, 1938), in particular normlessness, deviance, and powerlessness (Kohn & Schooler, 1983; Neal & Groat, 1974; Neal & Seeman, 1964; Pearlin, Lieberman, Menaghan, & Mullan, 1981; Pearlin & Schooler, 1978; Scheussler, 1982; Seeman, 1991). However, powerlessness, which is an effect of alienation in both Marxian and Weberian dehumanization, predicts scores on our dehumanization scale and mediates the effects of procedural justice. This finding is consistent with Sen's (2009) philosophical argument for personal agency as the core component of justice, and it became the basis of our own reasoning for the relationship between organizational justice and dehumanization.

In this chapter, we will first discuss the classic sociological and political philosophical work on dehumanization as it relates to the then-emerging culture of capitalism and bureaucracy. We will then discuss more recent social psychological work on dehumanization and review related concepts of anomie, alienation, and deindividuation. We will next discuss organizational justice and its relevance to dehumanization and related psychological constructs. In the second section of this chapter, we will discuss an empirical program of research on organizational justice and dehumanization and introduce our own work on the operationalization of organizational dehumanization and the development of a dehumanization scale and where we will outline antecedents and consequences in a series of mediating and moderating models. We will conclude with a series of focal areas of interest for a research program exploring organizational dehumanization, justice, agency, anomie, and self processes.

## DEHUMANIZATION

### Sociology of Dehumanization

The concept of work-related dehumanization emerged in the sociological and philosophical literature that coincided with the rise of the industrial and capitalist modern era. Max Weber, in his *Protestant Ethic and Spirit of Capitalism* (Weber, 1905/1976), discussed dehumanization as an effect of aspects of the modern workplace and in particular the bureaucratization of work. Weber (1905/1976) described the bureaucratic social order as an iron cage of ends-focused rationality, efficiency, control, and calculative behavior. Bureaucracy dehumanizes by orienting individual behavior toward the organization's goals regardless of personal goals, thus separating the individual from his or her own actions. Marx (1844/1961) critiqued the dehumanizing effect of the new capitalist system and identified two general forms of workplace alienation, both of which similarly emphasize the detachment of behavior and effect from the will, goals, and desires of the actor (Marx, 1844/1961; Seeman, 1991). Marx (1844/1961) believed that the appropriation of an individual's behavior into routinized, repetitive, and trivial acts is dehumanizing because it contradicts the self-directed, self-creating essence of what it is to be human. The forced surrender of control over the act and product of labor alienates the individual from the means of self-actualization, and the individual becomes powerless, unable to directly engage with or exert influence over the processes of labor and production. Further, work is fundamentally a social and communal phenomenon that is undermined by capitalism's objectification and commodification of labor. Reducing labor to a mere commodity like any other promotes social alienation and estrangement through the disengagement of workers from their work and fellow workers. Both

Weberian and Marxist forms of dehumanization are consistent with a more contemporary vision of the dehumanizing modern workplace in which employees live a drone-like existence of repetitive, segregated, and meaningless tasks, unable to integrate their behavior with personal goals and aspirations or commune with peers.

## Related Concepts

### *Anomie*

In his landmark work on suicide (Durkheim, 1897/2006), Durkheim found relatively greater rates of suicide in anomic societies or compartments of a society where norms and values were relatively more unstable, uncertain, or inconsistent. Durkheim (1897/2006) defined *anomie* as a characteristic of social systems, arguing that a lack of coherent norms and values negatively impacts citizens by stripping their lives of meaning through the absence or lack of clarity in behavioral prescriptions and social rules governing behavior. Without unambiguous goals or means to achieve them, people are unable to realize themselves through society (Durkheim, 1897/2006; Merton, 1938). Anomie can also promote a general normlessness in the sense of pervasive deviant, unethical, or immoral behavior when the means to achieve valued goals are either restricted or not clearly and normatively described. Merton (1938) elaborated on the concept of anomie by introducing the idea of opportunity structures and defining anomic responses of deviant behavior. For instance, potentially criminal behavior can be expected if valued goals are unambiguous but the means to achieve them are improperly or inappropriately proscribed and governed (Dubin, 1959; Merton, 1938, 1959).

Although dehumanization and anomie are related through the concept of personal agency, we believe they differ in their core defining characteristics. Anomie is an attribute associated with the incoherence of normative value systems and asymmetric opportunity structures whereas dehumanization describes a situation in which the individual's behavior is subjugated and directed by the will, desires, and goals of another person or social entity. In dehumanization, the individual's behavior can have meaning and purpose; however that meaning and purpose originates not from within the individual but from some other social entity. Further, the individual will attribute his or her own dehumanization to the deliberate and conscious actions of another person, organization, or group, either directly in intentional acts of commission or indirectly through omission to respond to and ameliorate the effects of environment, context, or social system. Of course, the unresponsiveness of powerful social actors to resolve anomic opportunity structures may be experienced as dehumanizing, in particular if the individual's normative behavior within such a system is of value to others in the system, but this is a separate and not a necessary condition of anomie. Anomic states can exist or come into being without an agent's deliberate, conscious actions or intentions and can be outside the control of any social agent. In brief, objectification, powerlessness, and more specifically, the cooptation of agency are defining characteristics of dehumanization, whereas incoherence of societal goals or values and the structure of means-ends relationships are the defining characteristics of anomie.

### *Personalism*

Personalisim (Williams & Bengtsson, 2010) was a general response to the perceived dehumanization of the modern workplace and capitalist society, contrasting it with the assertion that the individual, rather than social processes or contexts, is the ontological center of experience, meaning, and reality. Although personalism was not a unified movement or school of thought, there was a commonly held Kantian-like imperative of the duty to respect and dignify the person as social, agentic, and self-determining. Personhood was asserted against idealistic or material determinism, dissolution into collectivism, and isolation in radical individualism. Personalism found its way into modern psychology where it was explicitly espoused as a doctrinal approach in William Stern's critical personalism (Stern, 1938). Stern conceived of the person as "a living whole, individual, unique, striving toward goals, self-contained, and yet open to the world around him" (Wolman, 1960, p. 413). The person, as a developing organism, is realized in the mutually constructive exchange between the subjective, experiencing individual, and the objective environment. By nature, the person is not a passive object contained or impinged upon by the surrounding environment. Rather, the person seeks to actively engage with personally relevant aspects of the environment in order to interact with and shape that part of the world. The person's active development is a dialectic of the tendencies of self-preservation, in which the person strives to affirm and maintain existing characteristics and aspects of the self, and self-unfolding, in which the person strives to grow beyond his or her current state, engaging in new goals, tasks, and achievements (Kreppner, 1992). MacLeod (1938), in his obituary for Stern, contrasted Stern's approach to scientific psychology at the time, lauding personalism as "antiatomistic and antimechanical," expressing a concern that the "mechanical laws" of psychological explanations of behavioral causation were dehumanizing. Personalism stood as a philosophical or critical perspective in contraposition to the perceived dominant dehumanizing trend in society and science.

In the mid-twentieth century, Argyris (1957, 1964) characterized the emerging fields of organizational behavior and human resource management as the applied science of the individual and organization. At the core of Argyris' work was the premise that traditional organizational theory had unintended negative effects on the individual and organization. Command and control models and task efficiency models can fail because they are founded on erroneous assumptions including the idea that "man, like a machine, can be treated in a standardized fashion [and] needs to be stimulated by management to work. Machines are stimulated by electricity; man, by money" (Whyte, 1955, quoted in Argyris, 1957, p. 138). Argyris (1957) argues that modern forms of production conflict with human needs and desires, citing research on assembly line workers that found they dislike the loss of behavioral control and integration into a mechanical process, reporting also that these issues lead to aspirations of merely minimally acceptable quantity output (Turner, 1955, cited in Argyris, 1957; Walker & Guest, 1952). The result, Argyris argues, is frustration, conflict, failure, and a narrowed time perspective that feeds through the group and management to become normative throughout the organization. Argyris (1957, 1964) frames these issues as a clash between the basic nature of human needs and goals and the contemporary workplace of the mid-twentieth century that requires the employee to focus performance on a minimal range of skills. These issues and concerns persist in contemporary organizations.

In summary, the sociological and early psychological work on organizational dehumanization considered it to be a universal effect of contextual factors, increasing in proportion to factors such as mechanical pacing, repetitiveness, minute subdivision of the task and focus on a constricted range of skills that decreases control over own activities and increases dependency and subordination to an external mechanical process (Turner, 1955, cited in Argyris, 1957; Walker & Guest, 1952). However, we conceptualize dehumanization more as a product of social experience and in particular the relationship between the individual and the group as a social entity, as well as representatives of the group.

## Psychology of De/Humanization

Dehumanization may be a common experience in contemporary organizations, promoted by life in large, impersonal organizations where personal agency is thwarted by formal bureaucratic processes, routinized work, separation from an integrated final product, and an economic contract in which employee skills and behaviors are the property and instrument of the organization. However, we believe that people do not consider the structural aspects of the workplace as static, detached, and immutable. Rather, people infer the organization's intentions and values from the characteristics of their work environment. It is our view that dehumanization is fundamentally interpersonal and social, compounded by the dehumanized person's attributions and perceptions of attitudes of the dehumanizer, whether the dehumanizer is another individual or a social entity such as a group, division, or organization.

Haslam (2006) provides the most recent and thorough review of the social psychology literature on dehumanization. Dehumanization is the result of a process, experience, or attitude by which the person is made to feel less human and more like an animal or machine with reduced capacities for the human attributes of reasoning, will, and sentiment. A dehumanized person is an instrumental object to the dehumanizer who deliberately denies or subjugates the dehumanized person's autonomy, agency, and subjectivity. Dehumanization is a motivated phenomenon often associated with the injury or exploitation of the dehumanized (Haslam, 2006). At the intragroup level, dehumanizing a category of persons justifies the delegitimization of that group's rights or claims (Bar-Tal, 2000). The dehumanized can be morally excluded from the normal considerations of society's ethics or justice (Opotow, 1990). Dehumanization facilitates moral disengagement and the relaxation of self-regulatory controls that normally prevent an individual from exploiting, harming, or abusing another (Bandura, 2002). Conversely, humanizing experiences are those in which the subject can exercise his or her will in the social environment, engage in social processes or events, and express personal sentiments, desires, and needs to an empathetic, benevolent audience.

In his review, Haslam (2006) organizes the subtypes of dehumanization into two main categories. In the animalistic type, dehumanization is associated with ethnicity, race, gender, or disability with the individual considered to be a lesser or inferior being. In mechanistic dehumanization, the individual is considered to be more of an object or mechanical entity than a subjective, aware, experiencing person with needs and desires. Haslam (2006) finds this second type of dehumanization in the construction of the human subject in medical sciences or technology. We extend the category of mechanical dehumanization to include the workplace, in which the organization as a social entity is perceived to consider the individual as property or a resource rather than a thinking, feeling person with individual desires and goals.

Although we have focused on mechanistic dehumanization, it is certainly possible for animalistic dehumanization to occur in organizations. Stereotypes of certain professions, such as accounting, finance, marketing, or human relations may restrict the range of interaction but may not necessarily be associated with exploitation or instrumental motives. Systematic societal processes may also lead to job segregation by social or ethnic groups. For example, administrative assistant positions are often occupied by women rather than men and housekeeping positions are often occupied by members of marginalized communities. Finally, of course, individual agents in the organization may have their own biases and attitudes that derogate and dehumanize others in the environment. Although we discuss the phenomenon of animalistic dehumanization briefly in the context of perceptions of supervisory justice, our primary focus is on mechanical dehumanization associated with managerial roles and aspects of the system or organization as a social entity.

## Related Concepts

*Deindividuation* is a shift from personal, individual identity to a shared group level social identity, whereby the person is considered in terms of group rather than individual traits and characteristics (Tajfel, 1981; Zimbardo & Maslach, 1978). Although dehumanization and deindividuation may cooccur, most notably in a stereotyping process that may precede discrimination, they are nevertheless distinct (Haslam, 2006; Zimbardo & Maslach, 1978). Indeed, Haslam (2006) points out that construing the other as a member of a social category rather than an individual person may be a precursor of dehumanization. The effect of stereotyping is to essentialize a limited repertoire of behaviors, attitudes, and perspectives as the range of possibility for members of a particular group, thereby imposing a certain determination upon group members.

Interestingly, dehumanizing another person may be associated with one's own deindividuation. Consider, for instance, the classic Stanford Prison Experiment (Haney, Banks, & Zimbardo, 1973; Zimbardo, Banks, Haney, & Jaffe, 1973), in which students were randomly assigned to the role of guard or inmate. Over the course of the experiment, the participants deindividuated toward their role identities, and their interactions became more extreme, legitimized by stereotyping processes and dependence on role-based behavioral expectations. Notoriously, the guards began to dehumanize and abuse the inmates, ignoring their pleas and complaints. More recently, Osofsky and colleagues (Osofsky, Bandura, & Zimbardo, 2005), in a study on moral disengagement, found that executioners in the California penal system resolved the harmfulness of their behavior by attributing their actions to the role they occupied and the deservingness of the condemned. Deindividuating one's self into a social role detaches the behavior and deflects responsibility away from personal identity to an identity with determined and sometimes socially sanctioned behaviors. This shift can also be accompanied by a rigidity in moral reasoning. For example, Bell and Hughes-Jones (2008) found that managers who preferred to exercise reward and punishment power were more likely to moralize even trivial transgressions of social conventions, relative to managers who preferred legitimate or referent power.

Deindividuation may also influence justice processes and punitive responses to transgressors. Weiner and colleagues (Weiner, Graham, & Reyna, 1997) have shown that punishment goals are influenced by the two critical attributions of control, as in the individual's opportunity to act differently, and stability, assessed as the historical propensity of the individual to behave in a particular way. Retributive goals and judgments of punishment deservingness and justness were prevalent when the transgressor had high control and stability, whereas utilitarian goals and corrective instruction were preferred when either or both control and stability were low. In deinidividuation, group stereotype traits are ascribed to individual members, which could make causal attribution for behavior more deterministic. Therefore, when behavioral options are available, deindividuated transgressors may be more likely to receive retributive than utilitarian punishment.

*Objectification* is an aspect of dehumanization, and has been explored in the organizational literature from the perspective of the dehumanizer (Gruenfeld, Inesi, Magee, & Galinsky, 2008). Gruenfeld and colleagues (2008) argue that the role of manager produces an instrumental mindset that construes subordinates as means to an end. In this sense, by construing the other as part of a process or operation, or as a detached skill set that can be instrumentally manipulated, the objectification of subordinates fits Haslam's (2006) category of mechanical rather than animalistic dehumanization. Gruenfeld and colleagues' (2008) findings suggest that the experience of objectification may almost be a normative state in the contemporary workplace. However, an attitude of objectification may not necessarily be experienced as dehumanizing. Anyone entering into employment understands that he or she is subject to some degree of objectification. The commodification of one's actions and behavior is the central subject of the normative social economic contract that implicitly or explicitly characterizes employment in the contemporary workplace. Further, there may be an expectation of objectification and instrumental control as an aspect of good, genuinely unbiased leadership. We propose that dehumanization as a result of objectification is a subjective experience, with variance between individuals in the degree of tolerance of objectification.

## JUSTICE AND ORGANIZATIONS

In our research on justice and dehumanization, we sought to explore an ontological basis of justice in the humanizing fit between justice, individuals, and the relevant social group as the social entity that is the source of justice. Justice is a universal concern in every society and an inherent component of our social psychological makeup. The anthropologist Alan Fiske (1991, 1992) argues that as social cognitive beings, our natural environment is a constructed social system predicated on the twin concerns of the distribution of material resources and the organization of social relationships. Fiske's (1991, 1992) major premise is that societies are formed by the adoption of one of four fundamental forms of social relations, each of which offers a different resolution to the problem of resource distribution and social organization. Justice judgments can be considered barometers of the management of these twin concerns. In his book *The Idea of Justice*, Amartya Sen (2009), the Nobel prize winning economist, explores the relationship between resource distribution and the humanizing power of justice by distinguishing between a "culmination outcome" that is assessed as the value of the outcome alone and a "comprehensive outcome" that includes the processes by which the outcome was arrived at or produced. Sen (2009) argues for a philosophy of justice based not on ideal governing institutions that may or may not be attainable but, rather, on comparisons between possible and actual worlds. Sen draws on Indian justice traditions to contrast the idea of *niti*, organizational and behavioral rules of justice, and *nyaya*, the more practical consideration of how justice plays out in daily life, arguing that top-down systems are neither sufficient or efficient in providing justice. Sen also argues that an important standard of justice is the freedom that it delivers or protects. Freedom is about "being free to determine what we want, what we value and ultimately what we decide to choose" (Sen, 2009, p. 232). This is consistent with our assertion that justice humanizes through its relationship to agency and self-actualization, whereas injustice dehumanizes by denying or subjugating personal agency and the efforts that could be put toward self-actualization.

We propose that organizational justice resonates more deeply than just as an assessment of relative material outcomes or social status. Organizational justice and injustice speaks directly to the subjective experience of being considered fully or less than human. Organizational de/humanization, as we operationalize it, is about being recognized and valued by the organization as a thinking, feeling, desiring, experiencing person rather than as a robot or tool that is the property of and is used by the organization for its own ends. Further, justice or injustice signals how and whether the purveyors of justice consider the individual to be within or outside the scope of justice (Clayton & Opotow, 2003; Opotow, 1996). As a result, we expect that the experience of being de/humanized will have profound effects on social affiliation and self-actualization.

Research on organizational justice has typically focused on concerns about outcomes, the processes that produce outcomes and manage social relations, and interpersonal treatment by a supervisor or authority of the group (for a review and measurement proposal, see Colquitt, 2001). Distributive justice is often assessed as an equity judgment in which rewards and outcomes are weighed against the individual's effort, quality of performance or output, and contribution to the organization (Colquitt, 2001). Procedural justice judgments are made by assessing such aspects of the procedures as transparency, lack of bias, consistency across time and situation, opportunity to voice one's opinion and concerns, and opportunity to appeal outcomes (Colquitt, 2001; Leventhal, 1980; Lind & Tyler, 1988; Tyler, 1989). Interpersonal justice is an assessment of the interpersonal treatment received from an authority representing the group, and is measured as felt respect and dignity (Bies & Moag, 1986; Colquitt, 2001). The formal procedures of the organization and the interpersonal behavior of a supervisor or authority figure represent different sources of justice and consequently have been associated with attitudes at the corresponding level of organization or supervisor (Liao & Rupp, 2005).

On the one hand, organizational justice is associated with self-interest, as people need to acquire material and social resources in order to survive and flourish (Gillespie & Greenberg, 2005). Distributive justice judgments reflect contractual concerns but do not assess material and social outcomes in a vacuum of self-interest. Rather, these assessments are made in the context of structured social relationships, duties, and obligations, a context that is expressed through values such as equity, equality, and need (Deutsch, 1975). Sen (2009) points out that opportunities cannot be abstractly valued but must be substantive, in the sense of being valuable to the individual. For instance, a handicapped person has different capabilities than someone who is not handicapped, so the two could differ in their ability to take advantage of the same opportunities. We propose that, through the alignment of values, justice, and outcomes, distributive justice may be related to anomie and anomie-related constructs, including dehumanization.

People care about the procedures that manage or produce outcomes, sometimes more so than the outcomes themselves, in part because of a need to participate in the processes that determine important and relevant events and a desire for a safe, secure, and predictable social environment (Lind, 2001; Thibault & Walker, 1975). Fair procedures also communicate the value the social group places on individual members, thereby satisfying a fundamental need to belong and identify with others (DeCremer & Blader, 2006; DeCremer & Tyler, 2005; Lind & Tyler, 1988; Tyler & Blader, 2000, 2003). Unfair procedures communicate indifference or, worse, the possibilities of deliberate bias, exploitation, and the exclusion of the individual from the moral right of justice (Clayton & Opotow, 2003).

According to the group value model of procedural justice, fair procedures reassure those subject to the processes of a group that the group values its members and will not exploit them (Lind, 2001; Lind & Tyler, 1988), thus promoting pride that in turn promotes identification with the group (Blader & Tyler, 2009; DeCremer & Tyler, 2005; Lind & Tyler, 1988; Tyler & Blader, 2000, 2003). Procedural justice also supports the mutual reciprocity between a group and its individual members associated with fulfillment of economic contracts (Lind, 2001; Masterson, Lewis, Goldman, & Taylor, 2000), and is also related to self-actualization goals that are realized through group membership (Bell & Khoury, 2010a).

Interpersonal justice can influence dehumanization in both its animalistic and mechanistic forms. As a measure of respect and dignity, interpersonal justice can convey information about personal attitudes associated with various forms of stereotypes about gender, ethnicity, or disability, and class or professional prejudices of management toward subordinate or labor. Mechanistic dehumanization can be the product of a discrete individual's attitudes or of the attitudes of the organization expressed through the supervisor or manager as its representative.

The research program discussed below focuses primarily on procedural justice and to a lesser extent distributive justice as antecedents, moderators, and consequences of dehumanization. We recognize that dyadic-based dehumanization is likely quite common and would be an extremely rich field of investigation. Further, dyadic-based dehumanization can occur not just between superiors and subordinates but also between peers and teammates, employees and clients, and other relationships. However, our primary focus in the discussion below is on establishing the relationship between dehumanization, alienation, anomie, and distinguishing dehumanization from deindividuation. There is a long tradition in the procedural justice literature of looking at the beneficial effects of fair processes on group commitment and social identity, for instance in Lind and Tyler's (1988) work on the Group Value Model and Tyler and Blader's (2000, 2003) work on the Group Engagement model. We aim to contribute to this literature by exploring the self-relevant construct of dehumanization, differentiating it from the deindividuation associated with social relationships and social identity.

## RESEARCH PROGRAM

In this section, we review our developmental work on the dehumanization scale (Bell & Khoury, 2010b), in which we found dehumanization to be related to, but distinct from, the concepts of anomie and alienation (Durkheim, 1897/2006; Marx, 1844/1961; Merton, 1938), in particular normlessness, social deviance, and powerlessness (Kohn, & Schooler, 1983; Neal, & Groat, 1974; Neal & Seeman, 1964; Pearlin, Lieberman, Menaghan, & Mullan, 1981; Pearlin & Schooler, 1978; Scheussler, 1982; Seeman, 1991). When dehumanization is regressed on measures of anomie and alienation, only powerlessness reliably predicts dehumanization, a finding that resonates with Sen's (2009) connection between justice and agency. These initial findings formed the cornerstone of our first studies involving organizational justice, discussed below.

### Operationalization of Dehumanization

We (Bell & Khoury, 2010b) have developed an 8-item instrument with 7-point semantic differential scales to measure organizational dehumanization. See Appendix A for the full version of the scale. In the dehumanization scale presented in the appendix the organization is the dehumanizing social entity, however the scale can be adapted to measure dehumanization at more interpersonal levels, as we did with teams, or as can be done in the context of supervisors, peers, or others. Table 7.1 presents the reliability and CFA results for four different studies, two of which assessed dehumanization at different levels of the organization. The items were developed based on interview data and the research and conceptual literature on dehumanization (for a review, see Haslam, 2006). Sample items include "Does the organization treat you like a person or just another part of a big machine?" and "Is the organization concerned about your experiences, desires, plans and feelings or does it think of you as a tool to use for its own goals?" Scale anchors for the first sample item ranged from" –3," with the anchor "like part of a machine," to " +3," with the anchor "like a person,", with "0" at the midpoint. We tested this scale in four different studies and found it to be consistently reliable and robust (see Table 7.1). This scale was used in all studies summarized below. We also conducted a study with a scale consisting of items that addressed the dehumanizing aspect only, for instance, "Does the organization treat you like just another part of a big machine?" Participants responded on a 7-point Likert-style scale where 1 = *disagree strongly* and 7 = *agree strongly*. This version of the instrument was as reliable and robust as the semantic differential version, but we opted for the latter version in our research for several reasons. Scales in the justice literature, for example, quite commonly use the "disagree strongly" to "agree strongly"

**Table 7.1. Descriptive Statistics and CFA Results for the 8-Item Dehumanization Scale**

| *Study Context* | *Population* | *Target* | *N* | *Gender* | *Age* | *M* | *SD* | *Alpha* | *CFI* | *SRMR* |
|---|---|---|---|---|---|---|---|---|---|---|
| Faculty strike (Level 1) | Undergraduate business students | University | 157 | 77 M<br>80 F | $M$ = 19.39<br>$SD$ = 1.02 | 0.63 | 1.30 | .88 | .91 | .059 |
| Faculty strike (Level 2) | Undergraduate business students | Business school | 156 | 75 M<br>81 F | $M$ = 19.45<br>$SD$ = 0.83 | 0.58 | 1.18 | .85 | .94 | .058 |
| MBA project teams (Level 1) | MBA students | Business school | 169 | N/A | N/A | 1.04 | 0.99 | .88 | .92 | .060 |
| MBA project teams (Level 2) | MBA students | Course project team | 169 | N/A | N/A | 1.31 | 1.07 | .91 | .91 | .056 |
| Workplace anomie | General population (online survey) | Work organization | 107 | 54 M<br>53 F | $M$ = 36.58<br>$SD$ = 9.90 | 0.18 | 1.38 | .91 | .86 | .075 |
| Workplace conflict | General population (online survey) | Work organization | 112 | 42 M<br>70 F | $M$ = 37.08<br>$SD$ = 11.25 | 1.47 | 1.65 | .94 | .95 | .042 |

*Note:* Due to the confidential nature of the team context, age and gender information was not collected.

format (Colquitt, 2001), which is often treated as a continuum ranging from injustice to justice, with "disagree strongly" taken as an indication of unfairness or injustice. However it is not completely clear what "disagree strongly" actually connotes. Therefore, we decided to clarify the anchors and identify the contrast options by creating a semantic differential scale.

## Mediation: In/Justice, De/Humanization, and the Source of In/Justice

We have construed dehumanization as a social phenomenon, to the extent that it is associated with the perceived attitudes and intentions of one person or social entity toward another. We further propose that the experience of justice is fundamentally humanizing and self-validating, whereas injustice is dehumanizing and self-negating. Organizational de/humanization should in turn be associated with attitudes and behavioral responses directed toward the de/humanizing agent or entity that is the source of justice. Figure 7.1 presents a summary illustration of the basic mediation proposed and potential dependent variables in this model. Pride in the organization is an evaluation of the organization as an entity in the form of a social group with which one is associated. If the organization dehumanizes the individual, then the individual is unlikely to boast about the organization or advertise any connection he or she has with the organization. Feelings of de/humanization should also be related to attachment to and intentions to leave the organization. Dehumanization is a negative experience that diminishes the individual and is therefore likely to motivate the individual to dissociate from the organization. Conversely, humanization enhances the individual and so is likely to promote attachment and intentions to continue being a member of the organization. Organizational de/humanization should also impact attitudes about self-actualization and personal goals that are achieved or realized through membership in the organization. An organization that dehumanizes the individual demonstrates little concern or investment in the individual's own desires and goals, whereas a humanizing organization recognizes and values the individual's desires and goals. The experience of de/humanization should therefore influence one's sense of career well-being. Measures of well-being are often used as proxies for anomie (e.g., Sani, Mhairi, & Herrera, 2008). In our scale development and related research (Bell & Khoury, 2010a, 2010b), we found support for the above proposals, specifically that procedural in/justice is associated with de/humanization, which in turn fully mediates the effects of in/justice on feelings of pride in the group as well as turnover intentions. Finally, we found that de/humanization fully mediated the procedural in/justice effects on career well-being, as measured by an adaptation of the Ryff and Keyes social well-being scale (Ryff & Keyes, 1995).

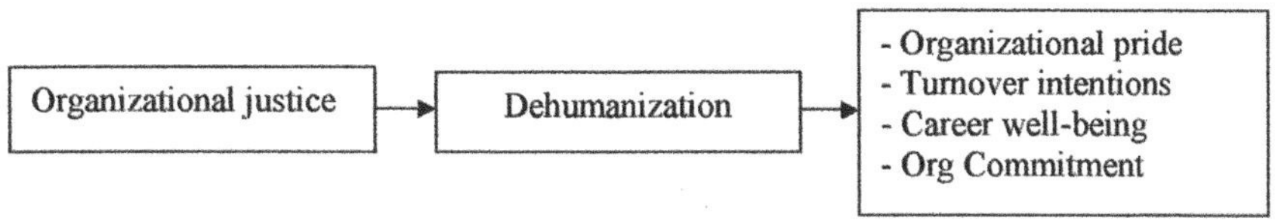


Figure 7.1. Dehumanization as a mediator of justice effects.

Figure 7.2. Justice as a mediator of dehumanization effects.

## Mediation: De/Humanization, In/Justice, and the De/Humanizer

In the above discussion, we positioned dehumanization as a mediating variable for the effects of organizational justice on organizational attitudes. It is also possible that dehumanization occurs first through other channels and then influences perceptions of justice. Figure 7.2 presents this proposed mediation path with potential dependent variables. In a qualitative study of servers and patrons, Fisk, Neville, and Mattia (2010) found that servers often encounter patrons who have a sense of entitlement and are extremely demanding but do not express gratitude or recognize the efforts of the servers. From an economic contract perspective, the relationship is inequitable, with patrons having high expectations and assuming they will be met and servers struggling to satisfy them and rarely receiving appropriate compensation, reciprocity, or expressions of gratitude. However, the experience has a more profound effect on servers than just a frustrated economic exchange. A central theme in the qualitative data was a feeling of degradation and subservience, feeling like a "maid," "servant," "toy," or "slave." In short, the servers were made to feel like they were the tool or instrument of the patron for the fulfillment of their needs or desires, without any consideration for the servers as persons who toiled to satisfy them. This experience, in turn, was considered unfair and unjust. Similarly, if an organizational culture dehumanizes employees or classes of employees by restricting their personal agency or by denying them the means and support by which they can self-actualize, then the dehumanized employees are likely to consider the organization to be unjust.

## Moderation: In/Justice, Anomic Antecedents, and De/Humanization

We have argued that dehumanization is distinct from but may be related to anomie, particularly through the erosion of agency and increased vulnerability to self-interested opportunists in time of change or conflict. We expected organizational justice to interact with anomic aspects of organizational conflict or strategic change to promote dehumanization. Procedural and distributive justice should be important concerns in such times, but for different reasons. Procedural justice reflects the social order and values of the group and so could become more relevant, especially as an objective standard of interpersonal behavior, when group values or social order are in transition or being strenuously challenged. Contrarily, distributive justice is associated with socially valued outcomes, so should be more important when group values and social order are stable rather than under duress. In other words, receiving fair outcomes is more humanizing when there is wide agreement on the value of particular goals and outcomes, and clear, accessible means exist to achieve them than when goals, outcomes, and the means to achieve them are ambiguously stated or inconsistently supported. To test these assumptions, we conducted a study with undergraduate business students during a long and contentious strike by their university's contract faculty and teaching assistants. The strike began in the fall term of 2008, just as the global financial crisis made its force felt, and ran through the Christmas holidays into the regularly scheduled winter term. There was great uncertainty during the strike, with little communication from the university's administration and a great deal of rhetoric from the union. Anecdotal evidence suggested students felt that both the administration and the union were at best indifferent to their plight and at worst using the students as leverage. The local press quoted one fourth-year undergraduate student complaining, "I feel like we are the middleman here for them to prove their point" (Millar, 2008). Other students became more proactive, launching a website with the slogan, "Forced arbitration not a hostage situation" (Koopmans, 2008).

At the beginning of the 2008 fall term, prior to the strike, we had initiated the first wave of our regular undergraduate research participation program. The strike began in early November, forcing us to postpone the second wave until the announced resolution and resumption of classes. In this context of conflict and uncertainty, we expected dehumanization to be affected by preexisting attitudes about the organization as a cohesive social entity and also by perceptions of organizational justice. More particularly, we expected these constructs would interact to affect dehumanization in ways that would help us understand the relationship between anomic conditions and dehumanization. We used Sani and coauthors' (Sani, Bowe, & Herrera, 2008) Perceived Collective Continuity instrument to measure the tendency to consider the organization as a coherent and integral entity that persists over time, maintaining values and norms through the socialization of new members. Sani and his coauthors (Sani et al., 2008) argue that the association between a group's perceived collective continuity and an individual's social well-being is explained by a need for the group to be coherent and entitative. In other words, people have a need for their social groups to *not* be anomic. The moderating variables of procedural and distributive justice were measured with items from Colquitt's (2001) organizational justice scale. Perceived collective continuity and both types of organizational justice had significant positive main effects on dehumanization which, as a semantic differential scale, meant that higher levels of justice and perceived collective continuity were associated with humanization whereas lower levels were associated with dehumanization. More importantly, procedural justice had a greater influence on dehumanization when perceived collective continuity was low, relative to high. This finding is consistent with our reasoning that in times of conflict or threat to social norms and values, and in particular when there is also a perceived loss of personal control over circumstances, the perceived entitativity of the social group will be experienced as reassuring and humanizing. However, when perceived entitativity is low, procedural justice compensates by signaling the group's enduring commitment to stability and benevolence. We also found that distributive justice influenced dehumanization when perceived collective continuity was high but not when it was low. See Figure 7.3 for a graph of the slopes. This finding is consistent with Durkheim's (1897/2006) anomie and Merton's (1938) elaboration of anomie as opportunity structures, in that the value of goals and outcomes derived from a group or membership in a group become ambiguous when the norms and values of the group are unstable or incoherent.

In a project currently under development, we are exploring the potentially dehumanizing effect of strategic innovation and management technologies. Strategic innovation is typically a deliberate, top-down process that imposes radical changes in values, goals, organizational status, and relationships. If employees are not engaged by the architects of change as legitimate stakeholders, then they may feel dehumanized in that their skills, efforts, and output are considered resources that are the organization's property, to be used as the organization pleases in the pursuit of its

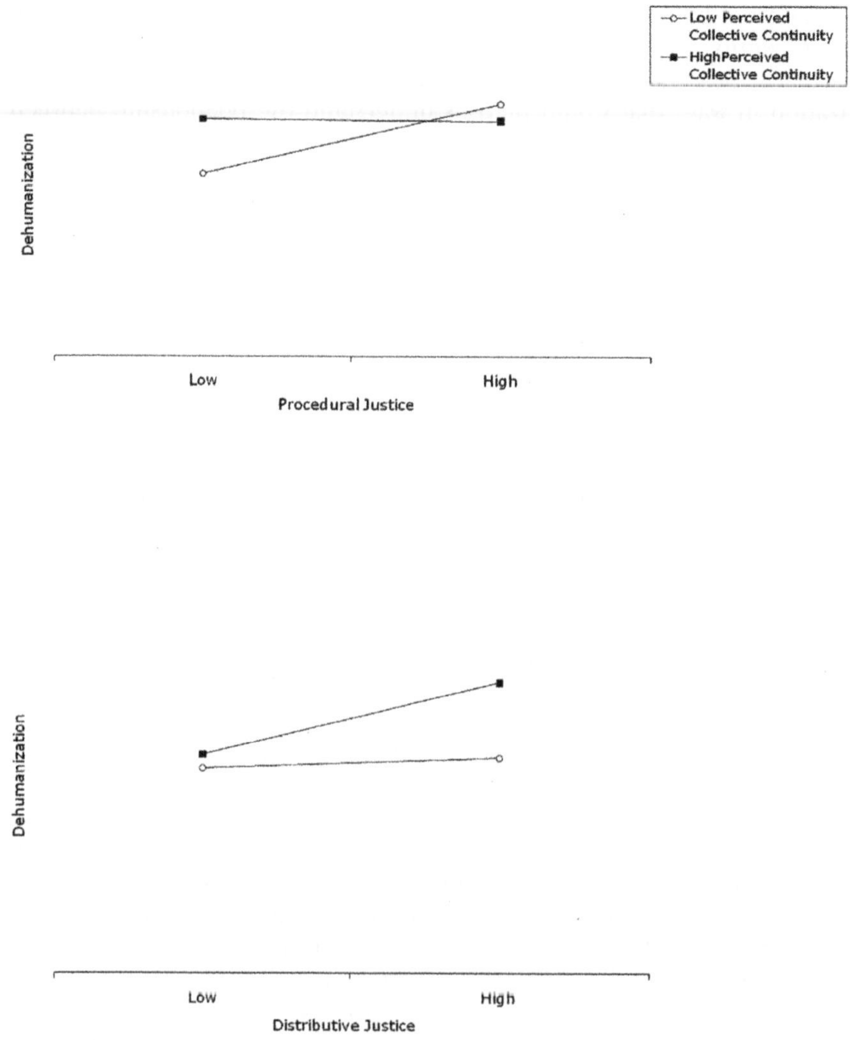


Figure 7.3. The moderating role of perceived collective continuity on the relationship between procedural/distributive justice and dehumanization.

own ends. Employees may respond similarly to management technologies, such as the balanced scorecard technique (Kaplan & Norton, 1992, 1996), that are used to assess and modify organizational operations to more efficiently achieve organizational goals. Supporting results, should we find them, will be consistent with our findings in the scale development project that suggest dehumanization is related to anomie and alienation through agency, the ability to act in personally meaningful ways, rather than normlessness or pervasive deviance.

## OUTLINE OF RESEARCH PROGRAM

In the conceptual and empirical discussion above we described the foundations of a research program exploring the relationships between organizational justice and dehumanization. In this section we consolidate the discussion and elaborate on an outline for a proposed research program.

### Instrumentality and Agency

Cropanzano and colleagues (Cropanzano, Byrne, Bobocel, & Rupp, 2001) summarize the justice literature in terms of three dominant models: instrumental, relational, and moral virtues. The first two models are arguably grounded in self-interest whereas the third model is grounded in a deontic interest in justice simply for the sake of justice (Folger, 1998). The dehumanization model presents an additional possibility that involves the self, but not as self-interest in the traditional economic or social status sense. In the dehumanization model, agency is valued in and of itself because it speaks to the fundamental engagement of the individual with his or her world. We have also argued that the connection between agency and dehumanization should occur prior to deindividuation processes in which a social identity is developed and adopted. This is similar to the multiple needs framework proposed by Cropanzano and colleagues (Cropanzano et al., 2001), in which the authors link the three models of justice with Williams' (1997) needs for control (instrumental model), meaning (moral virtues model), belonging, and self regard (relational model). However, we position the dehumanization model with the needs for control and for meaning, independent of outcomes.

We argue that dehumanization is a subjective experience produced by perceptions of the organization's attitude toward the employee, and in particular an instrumental attitude in which the dehumanized individual feels objectified and manipulated. The potentially involuntary transfer of agency from one's self to another social agent, whether a person or an entity such as an organization, and the consequent subjugation of one's goals, aspirations, and desires, will likely have a substantially more profound effect on the individual than the realization of an unfulfilled contract. Further, the object of interest in the economic contract is a mutually dependent social relationship with some form of reciprocity and beneficial outcome for each participating party. However, a person can be made to feel like the objectified means to another person's ends without there being any relationship at all with the other party. Indeed, the economic contract could be considered reasonably honored and fulfilled with one party still feeling dehumanized by the other.

## De/Humanization and Deinivduation

It will be important to distinguish empirically and theoretically the dehumanization model described above from relational models of procedural justice (Blader & Tyler, 2009; Lind & Tyler, 1988; Tyler & Blader, 2000, 2003). The critical distinction between dehumanization and deindividuation is that they differ in their placement in the path from justice to social identity and attitudes about the source of justice. A major premise of the relational models of procedural justice is that the effects of justice are associated with the fundamental need, as social human beings, to belong to social groups (DeCremer & Blader, 2006; Hogg & Terry, 2000; Hogg & Williams, 2000; Tajfel & Turner, 1979). Dehumanization, as we have argued, is about the whole person rather than a segmented identity. The argument in a relational model of justice is that a person who is attracted to a group because of its positive qualities will begin to identify with the group and develop a social identity based on membership in the group. In other words, justice promotes positive attitudes about the value of the group relative to other groups in the environment, and also in terms of the intrinsic value of membership in the group. Essentially this is an argument for deindividuation, in that justice promotes adoption of a social identity (Blader & Tyler, 2009). For instance, organizational justice, and procedural justice in particular, promote feelings of pride in the group that in turn promote deindividuation through identification with the group and the adoption of a social identity as a member of the group. Dehumanization, however, intervenes between justice and assessments of the group and so occurs earlier in the path than deindiviuation. In other words, the humanizing or dehumanizing experience of justice should promote positive or negative attitudes about the group that in turn should promote deindividuation and adoption of a social identity as a group member or dissociation and rejection of the group as a personal community. The relationships between dehumanization, deindividuation, and social identity remain to be explored.

## Anomie

To the extent that dehumanization is related to anomie, it is a product of conditions in the social system. According to Merton (1938, 1959), the central issue in anomie is the specification of goals and means, and it is society's prerogative and duty to set goals and prescribe the means to achieve them. Organizational change may be experienced as anomic because of changes or ambiguity in the opportunity structure of valued goals and means of achieving them. Under such conditions, organization citizens may feel dehumanized if they feel unable to self-actualize through their work in the organization. Certainly these conditions may be considered unjust to those who lose access to resources or outcomes because of changes in the opportunity structure. But there could also be a profound loss of personal meaning that may be explained through feelings of anomie and dehumanization that accompany shifts in the organization's values and opportunity structures. Such experiences and reactions go beyond mere self-interest.

## Justice Sources and Mechanistic Versus Animalistic Dehumanization

In mechanistic dehumanization, the individual is treated as an object that can be manipulated, whereas in animalistic dehumanization the individual is often stereotyped, with accompanying loss of personal individualism, and treated in terms of a limited set of cognitive and physical traits (Haslam, 2006). Animalistic dehumanization characterizes prejudice based on race, gender, or disability as well as other social groups such as class. Within an organization, it is possible that animalistic dehumanization could also occur depending on, for instance, an individual's membership in a particular department, profession or rank within a hierarchy. Certainly, organizational policies or culture could influence attitudes of animalistic dehumanization. However, animalistic dehumanization may be more likely to be expressed first between individuals, then generalized by the dehumanized person to the social group. This is of course an empirical question, but it does raise questions about distinctions between the sources of justice and the experience of dehumanization. In our research, we found both procedural and interpersonal justice to be significantly related to organizational dehumanization. Interestingly, powerlessness only mediated the effects of procedural justice on dehumanization, and not interpersonal justice. This tantalizing result gives rise to a range of speculation. For instance, mechanistic and animalistic dehumanization may differ in their associations with source of justice, normlessness, agency, and the opportunity structure.

## Individual Differences and De/humanization

To some extent, dehumanization is likely to be a subjective experience rather than a foregone product of context. For instance, although military training and culture may promote deindividuation and personal subjugation to a task or role, many people value military culture and careers. Similarly, assembly line piece work is designed to integrate human actions into mechanical processes. However, members of the American and Canadian automobile workers' unions do not portray themselves as victims and automatons but as fiercely proud craftsmen with a personal attachment to a quality product. In rhetorical terms, in their negotiations with the organization, the auto workers' unions do not seek damages but an equitable share of profits. Distinguishing differences in dehumanization among people experiencing the same organizational context will help us understand the basic nature of dehumanization. In our research, we have found that a belief in a just world was significantly related to dehumanization, whereas self-esteem was not. We have argued that dehumanization is a fundamentally social phenomenon. If self-esteem is a barometer of social relations, as suggested by Leary and colleagues (Leary, Tambor, Terdal, & Downs, 1995), then we should have found a strong correlation between self-esteem and dehumanization. However, the pattern we found corresponds with our thinking that dehumanization is less about self-evaluative attitudes that may reflect self-interest and more about personal agency in the world. A critical component of the research program will include defining how attitudes about agency, the self, social relations and the world make one more or less sensitive to dehumanization.

### Behavioral Responses

Although we have not as yet explored behavioral responses to dehumanization, we expect dehumanization to be related to at least three classes of behavior. First, consistent with the attitudinal responses, dehumanization should produce a withdrawal from and rejection of the social group. Second, to the extent that dehumanization represents a kind of injury to the person or obstacle to self-actualization, we expect to find a relationship to anger and deviant or counterproductive workplace behaviors. Finally, recalling Durkheim's (1897/2006) original study of anomie and suicide, dehumanization may be related to self destructive behaviors. Humanization would produce the opposite pattern of adoption and elaboration of social identity, citizenship behaviors and self actualizing behaviors.

### De/Humanization and In/Justice—Implications of Being the Chicken or the Egg

Although the conceptual discussion has focused primarily on organizational justice as a causal factor in the formation of an attitude about dehumanization, we cite ongoing empirical work addressing a different causal path in which a dehumanizing experience can be interpreted as unjust (Fisk et al., 2010). These two paths and their implications, in the context of the particular studies that were discussed, are presented in Figures 7.1 and 7.2 respectively. Exploring other causes of dehumanization could shed light on how justice judgments are formed.

## CONCLUSION

In this chapter we have expounded on the construct of organizational dehumanization and its relationship to organizational justice. Our focus on the organization as the dehumanizing agent and source of justice led us to focus primarily on justice associated with organizational procedures. However, we believe that the principles of the relationship between procedural justice and dehumanization should generalize to other sources of justice and dehumanization, in particular supervisors and interpersonal justice. We note, however, that distributive justice has a different relationship to anomic antecedents of dehumanization than procedural justice, and that interpersonal justice may be related to animalistic and mechanistic dehumanization. Exploring similarities and differences will be an important part of any forthcoming research on organizational dehumanization and justice. The developing work on organizational dehumanization specifies an intuitive and apparently commonplace construct that is not subsumed by or substituted by other existing constructs in the organizational literature. A focus on dehumanization as a psychological experience allows for a more refined exploration of the phenomenon because people may respond differently to aspects of an environment. This work also addresses the current and ongoing debate on the role of organizational justice as instrumental, relational, deontic, or egoistic by integrating aspects of all four in regards to a basic human need. Finally, dehumanization is distinguished from deindividuation, often considered positively in the sense of promoting identity and organizational citizenship behaviors, and elaborates on concepts such as dignity and personal validation.

## ACKNOWLEDGMENT

This research was supported by a grant from the Social Sciences and Humanities Research Council of Canada.

## APPENDIX: ORGANIZATIONAL DE/HUMANIZATION SCALE

These questions ask about your impressions of [target organization], as a social organization. Here we are interested in the relationship between [organizational members] like yourself and the [target organization] as an organizational entity represented by [managers/faculty] and administration. We are not interested in personal relationships between yourself and particular [managers/faculty], but how you think the [target organization] in general relates to [organization members].

1. Does the [target organization] treat you like a person or just another part of a big machine?

| *Like a part of a machine* | | | *Neutral* | | | *Like a person* |
|---|---|---|---|---|---|---|
| −3 | −2 | −1 | 0 | 1 | 2 | 3 |

2. Do people in the [target organization] see you for who you are, as a person, or do they see you as what you do, your role, job, task?

| *Sees me as what I do: my job, role, task* | | | *Neutral* | | | *Sees me for who I am* |
|---|---|---|---|---|---|---|
| −3 | −2 | −1 | 0 | 1 | 2 | 3 |

3. Do you think [organization members] feel valued and respected by the [target organization] or do [organization members] feel undervalued and disrespected?

| *Undervalued and disrespected* | | | *Neutral* | | | *Valued and respected* |
|---|---|---|---|---|---|---|
| −3 | −2 | −1 | 0 | 1 | 2 | 3 |

4. Is the [target organization] concerned about your experience, desires, plans and feelings, or does it think of you as a tool to use for its own goals?

| *Thinks of me as a tool to use for its own goals* | | | *Neutral* | | | *Concerned about my experience, desires, plans, feelings* |
|---|---|---|---|---|---|---|
| −3 | −2 | −1 | 0 | 1 | 2 | 3 |

5. Does the [target organization] care about and value you based on who you are as a person, or based on your performance?

| *Values me based on my performance* | | | *Neutral* | | | *Values me based on who I am as a person* |
|---|---|---|---|---|---|---|
| −3 | −2 | −1 | 0 | 1 | 2 | 3 |

6. Are you free to make decisions in important matters or does the [target organization] control everything with lots of formal rules and bureaucracy?

| *Organization controls decisions* | | | *Neutral* | | | *Can make own decisions* |
|---|---|---|---|---|---|---|
| −3 | −2 | −1 | 0 | 1 | 2 | 3 |

7. Does the [target organization] encourage individual input and personal contribution or is there standardization with little room for creativity or personal input?

| *Little room for creativity or personal input* | | | *Neutral* | | | *Encourages personal input and contribution* |
|---|---|---|---|---|---|---|
| −3 | −2 | −1 | 0 | 1 | 2 | 3 |

8. Does the [target organization] respond to your concerns, or does it focus on efficiency with [organization members] treated like robots or numbers?

| *Focus on efficiency, treating [organization members] like robots or numbers* | | | *Neutral* | | | *Responds to personal concerns* |
|---|---|---|---|---|---|---|
| −3 | −2 | −1 | 0 | 1 | 2 | 3 |

## REFERENCES


Argyris, C. (1957). *Personality and organization.* New York, NY: Harper & Row.

Argyris, C. (1964). *Integrating the individual and the organization.* New York, NY: Wiley.

Bandura, A. (2002). Selective moral disengagement in the exercise of moral agency. *Journal of Moral Education, 31,* 101-119.

Bar-Tal, D. (2000). *Shared beliefs in a society: Social psychological analysis.* Thousand Oaks, CA: SAGE.

Bell, C., & Hughes-Jones, J. (2008) Power, self construal and the moralization of behavior. *Journal of Business Ethics, 83,* 503-514.

Bell, C., & Khoury, C. (2010a). De/humanized by justice: Organizational de/humanization as a mediator of procedural justice. *Working paper.* Toronto, Canada: York University.

Bell, C., & Khoury, C. (2010b). Organizational de/humanization: Operationalization and test of a scale. *Working paper.* Toronto, Canada: York University.

Bies, R. J., & Moag, J. F. (1986). Interactional justice: Communication criteria of fairness. In R. J. Lewicki, B. H. Sheppard, & M. H. Bazerman (Eds.), *Research on negotiations in organizations* (Vol. 1, pp. 43-55). Greenwich, CT: JAI Press.

Blader, S., & Tyler, T. R. (2009). Testing and extending the group engagement model: Linkages between social identity, procedural justice, economic outcomes, and extrarole behavior. *Journal of Applied Psychology, 94,* 445-464.

Clayton, S., & Opotow, S. (2003). Justice and identity: changing perspectives on what is fair. *Personality and Social Psychology Review, 7,* 298-310.

Colquitt, J. A. (2001). On the dimensionality of organizational justice: A construct validation of a measure. *Journal of Applied Psychology, 86,* 386-400.

Cropanzano, R., Byrne, Z. S., Bobocel, D. R., & Rupp, D. E. (2001). Moral virtues, fairness heuristics, social entities, and other denizens of organizational justice. *Journal of Vocational Behavior, 58,* 164-209.

DeCremer, D., & Blader, S. (2006). Why do people care about procedural fairness? The importance of belongingness in responding and attending to procedures. *European Journal of Social Psychology, 36,* 211-228.

DeCremer, D., & Tyler, T. R. (2005). Am I respected or not?: Inclusion and reputation as issues in group membership. *Social Justice Research, 18,* 121-153.

Deutsch, M. (1975). Equity, equality, and need: What determines which value will be used as the basis for distributive justice? *Journal of Social Issues, 31,* 137-149.

Drake, J. (Director), & Drake, B. (Screenwriter). (2008) *Visioneers* [Motion picture]. United States: Fireside Films & Mayfly Films.

Dubin, R. (1959). Deviant behavior and social structure: Continuities in social theory. *American Sociological Review, 24,* 147-164.

Durkheim, E. (1897, 2006). *On suicide* (R. Buss, Trans.). New York, NY: Penguin.

Fisk, G. M., Neville, L., & Mattia, A. S. (2010). Effects of customer entitlement on service workers' physical and psychological well-being [Working paper]. Queen's University, Kingston, Ontario, Canada.

Fiske, A. P. (1991). *Structures of social life: The four elementary forms of human relations.* New York: Free Press.

Fiske, A. P. (1992). The four elementary forms of sociality: Framework for a unified theory of social relations. *Psychological Review, 99,* 689-723.

Folger, R. (1998). Fairness as a moral virtue. In M. Schminke (Ed.), *Managerial ethics: Moral management of people and processes* (pp. 13-34). Mahwah, NJ: Erlbaum.

Gilliam, T. (Director/Screenwriter), & Stoppard, T. (Screenwriter). (1985). *Brazil* [Motion picture]. United Kingdom: Embassy International Pictures.

Gillespie, J. Z., & Greenberg, J. (2005). Are the goals of organizational justice self-interested? In: J. Greenberg & J. A. Colquitt (Eds.) *Handbook of organizational justice* (pp. 179-214). Hillsdale, NJ: Erlbaum.

Gruenfeld, D. H., Inesi, M. E., Magee, J. C., & Galinsky, A. D. (2008). Power and the objectification of social targets. *Journal of Personality and Social Psychology, 95,* 111-112.

Haney, C., Banks, C., & Zimbardo, P. G. (1973). Interpersonal dynamics in a simulated prison. *International Journal of Criminology and Penology, 1,* 69-97.

Haslam, (2006). Dehumanization: An integrative review. *Personality and Social Psychology Review, 10,* 252-264.

Hogg, M. A., & Terry, D. J. (2000). Social identity and self-categorization processes in organizational contexts. *Academy of Management Review, 25,* 121-140.

Hogg, M. A., & Williams, K. D. (2000). From *I* to *we*: Social identity and the collective self [Special Issue: one hundred years of group research]. *Group Dynamics: Theory, Research, and Practice, 4,* 81-97.

Kaplan, R. S., & Norton, D. P. (1992). The balanced scorecard: Measures that drive performance. *Harvard Business Review, 70,* 71-79.

Kaplan, R. S., & Norton, D. P. (1996). Using the balanced scorecard as a strategic management system. *Harvard Business Review, 74*(1), 75-85.

Kohn, M., & Schooler, C. (1983). *Work and personality: An inquiry into the impact of social stratification.* Norwood, NJ: Ablex.

Koopmans, L. (Nov. 13, 2008). Lyndon Koopmans: Striking York teachers should be forced back to work. *National Post.* Retrieved from http://network.nationalpost.com/np/blogs/fullcomment/archive/2008/11/13/lyndon-koopmans-striking-york-teachers-should-be-forced-back-to-work.aspx

Kreppner, K. (1992). William L. Stern (1871-1938): A neglected founder of developmental psychology. *Developmental Psychology, 28,* 539-547.

Leary, M. R., Tambor, E. S., Terdal, S. K., & Downs, D. L. (1995). Self-esteem as an interpersonal monitor: The sociometer hypothesis. *Journal of Personality and Social Psychology, 68,* 518-530.

Leventhal, G. S. (1980). What should be done with equity theory? New approaches to the study of fairness in social relationships. In K. Gergen, M. Greenberg, & R. Willis (Eds.), *Social exchange: Advances in theory and research* (pp. 27-55). New York, NY: Plenum Press.

Liao, H., & Rupp, D. E. (2005). The impact of justice climate and justice orientation on work outcomes: A cross-level multifoci framework. *Journal of Applied Psychology, 90,* 242-256.

Lieberstein, P. (Writer), & Whittingham, K. (Director). (2005). Health care [Television series episode]. In G. Daniels (Producer), *The Office,* Los Angeles, CA: Reveille Productions & Deedle-Dee Productions in association with NBC Universal Television Studios.

Lind, E. A. (2001). Fairness heuristic theory: Justice judgments as pivotal cognitions in organizational relations. In R. Cropanzano & J. Greenberg (Eds.), *Advances in organization justice* (pp. 56-88). Palo Alto, CA: Stanford University Press.

Lind, E. A., & Tyler, T. R. (1988). *The social psychology of procedural justice.* New York, NY: Plenum Press.

Macleod, R. B. (1938). William Stern (1871-1938). *Psychological Review, 45,* 347-353.

Marx, K. (1844, 1961). *Economic and philosophic manuscripts of 1844* (M. Mulligan, Trans. Moscow, Russia: Foreign Languages Publishing House.

Masterson, S. S., Lewis, K., Goldman, B. M., & Taylor, M. S. (2000). Integrating justice and social exchange: The differing effects of fair procedures and treatment on work relationships. *Academy of Management Journal, 43,* 738-748.

Merton, R. K. (1938). Social structure and anomie. *American Sociological Review, 3,* 672-682.

Merton, R. K. (1959). Social conformity, deviation, and opportunity structures: A comment on the contributions of Dubin and Cloward. *American Sociological Review,* 177-189.

Millar, S. (2008, November 7). Striking York staff 'fighting a lost cause.' *National Post.* Retrieved from http://network.nationalpost.com/np/blogs/toronto/archive/2008/11/07/striking-york-staff-fighting-a-lost-cause.aspx

Neal, A., & Groat, H. T. (1974). Social class correlates of stability and change in levels of alienation. *Sociological Quarterly, 15,* 548-558.

Neal, A., & Seeman, M. (1964). Organizations and powerlessness: A test of the mediation hypothesis. *American Sociological Review, 29,* 216-225.

Opotow, S. (1990). Moral exclusion and injustice: An introduction. *Journal of Social Issues, 46,* 1-20.

Osofsky, M. J., Bandura, A., & Zimbardo, P. G. (2005). The role of moral disengagement: Disengagement in the execution process. *Law and Human Behavior, 29,* 371-393.

Pearlin, L., Lieberman, M., Menaghan, E., & Mullan, J. (1981). The stress process. *Journal of Health and Social Behavior, 22,* 337-356.

Pearlin, L., & Schooler, C. (1978). The structure of coping. *Journal of Health and Social Behavior, 19,* 2-21.

Ryff, C. D., & Keyes, C. L. M. (1995). The structure of psychological well-being revisited. *Journal of Personality and Social Psychology, 69,* 719-727.

Sani, F., Mhairi, B., & Herrera, H. (2008) Perceived collective continuity and social well-being: Exploring the connections. *European Journal of Social Psychology, 38,* 365-374.

Sani, F., Bowe, M., & Herrera, M. (2008). Perceived collective continuity: Seeing groups as temporally enduring entities. In F. Sani (Ed.), *Self-continuity: Individual and collective perspectives* (pp. 159-172). Hillsdale, NJ: Erlbaum.

Scheussler, K. (1982). *Measuring social life feelings.* San Francisco, CA: Jossey-Boss.

Seeman, M. (1991). Alienation and anomie. In J. P. Robinson & P. R. Shaver (Eds.) *Measures of personality and social psychological attitudes* (pp. 291-371). San Diego, CA: Academic Press.

Sen, A. (2009). *The idea of justice.* London, England: Penguin.

Stern, W. (1938). *General psychology: From the personalistic standpoint* (H. D. Spoerl, Trans.). New York, NY: MacMillan.

Tajfel, H. (1981). *Human groups and social categories.* Cambridge, England: Cambridge University Press.

Tajfel, H., & Turner, J. C. (1979). An integrative theory of intergroup conflict. In W. Austin & S. Worchel (Eds.). *The social psychology of intergroup relations* (pp. 33-48). Pacific Grove, CA: Brooks/Cole.

Thibault, J. W., & Walker, L. (1975). *Procedural justice: A psychological perspective.* Hillsdale, NJ: Erlbaum.

Turner, A. N. (1955, September-October). Management and the assembly line. *Harvard Business Review,* 0-48.

Tyler, T. R. (1989). The psychology of procedural justice: A test of the group-value model. *Journal of Personality and Social Psychology, 57,* 830-838.

Tyler, T. R., & Blader, S. (2000). Identity and cooperative behavior in groups. *Group Processes and Intergroup Relations, 4,* 207-226.

Tyler, T. R., & Blader, S. (2003). The group engagement model: Procedural justice, social identity, and cooperative behavior. *Personality and Social Psychology Review, 7,* 349-361.

Walker, C. C., & Guest, R. H. (1952). *The man on the assembly line.* Cambridge, MA: Harvard University Press.

Weber, M. (1905, 1976). *The protestant ethic and the spirit of capitalism* (T. Parsons (Trans.). New York, NY: Scribner.

Weiner, B., Graham, S., & Reyna, C. (1997). An attributional examination of retributive versus utilitarian philosophies of punishment. *Social Justice Research, 10,* 431-452.

Whyte, W. F. (1955). *Money and motivation.* New York, NY: Harper.

Williams, K. D. (1997). Social ostracism. In R. M. Kowalski (Ed.), *Aversive interpersonal behaviors* (pp. 133-170). New York, NY: Plenum Press.

Williams, T. D., & Bengtsson, J. O. (2010). Personalism. In E. N. Zalta (Ed.), *The Stanford encyclopedia of philosophy.* Retrieved from http://plato.stanford.edu/archives/sum2010/entries/personalism/

Wolman, B. B. (1960). *Contemporary theories and systems in psychology.* New York, NY: Harper.

Zimbardo, P. G., & Maslach, C. (1978). Depersonalization. In B. B. Woman (Ed.), *International encyclopedia of psychology, psychoanalysis and neurology* (Vol. 4, pp. 52-53). New York, NY: Human Sciences Press.

Zimbardo, P. G., Banks, W. C., Haney, C., & Jaffe, D. (1973, April 8). The mind is a formidable jailer: A Priandellian prison. *The New York Times Magazine*, 38-60.

CHAPTER 8

# MORAL CONTRACTS

**Rebecca L. Greenbaum, Robert Folger, and Robert C. Ford**

Traditionally, psychological contract research was concerned with quid-pro-quo exchanges that directly affected an employee's well-being (Morrison & Robinson, 1997; Rousseau, 1989, 1995). More recently, however, Thompson and Bunderson (2003) argued that psychological contracts may also include global expectations of behavior that are not limited to an employee's personal treatment. We expand on this idea by arguing that employees may perceive that they have exchange agreements with the organization that include upholding moral obligations. Thus, employees may respond unfavorably to organizational unethical behaviors, even if employees are not directly affected by the behaviors, because the organization failed to uphold the perceived promise of abiding by moral obligations. We provide a conceptualization and definition of moral contract, moral contract breach, and moral contract violation, as well as a theoretical model and propositions. Implications for theory are discussed.

A considerable amount of research has focused on the psychological contract as a way to understand employees' subjective interpretations of the mutual obligations that exist between them and their employing organizations. More specifically, the psychological contract is defined as "an individual's beliefs regarding the terms and conditions of a reciprocal exchange agreement between that focal person and another party" (Rousseau, 1989, p. 123). By definition, the exchange agreement underlying a psychological contract exists in the "eye of the beholder" (MacNeil,

*Emerging Perspectives on Organizational Justice and Ethics*
pp. 199–221

1985). Employees, in particular, rely on written and unwritten organizational cues to shape their beliefs regarding organizational promises (Rousseau, 1989). Employees are expected to make certain contributions to the organization in exchange for the organization's promise fulfillment.

When an organization fails to uphold a psychological contract, an employee may experience a psychological contract *breach* and/or *violation* (Morrison & Robinson, 1997). The literature makes a key terminological distinction between breach and violation, in ways that differ from ordinary usage. Reference to a psychological contract breach applies when an employee perceives that the organization failed to uphold its obligations relative to the employee's own adherence to obligations. Such breaches may or may not be accompanied by the kinds of negative emotional reactions that employees can experience when they feel mistreated or betrayed, termed a psychological contract violation. We make use of the same breach/violation terminology throughout this chapter to remain consistent with the psychological contract literature.

Traditionally, the psychological contract has been conceptualized as an obligation continuum that is anchored by transactional and relational obligations (Rousseau & McLean Parks, 1992). Transactional obligations are based on economic exchanges. They tend to be short-term obligations that limit the involvement between each party (MacNeil, 1985). Temporary employees, commission salespeople, and independent contractors are likely to form transactional psychological contracts with organizations. Relational obligations are characterized by socioemotional exchanges. Both parties are expected to exchange loyalty and support over a long-term, open-ended relationship. Balanced psychological contracts have transactional *and* relational components (Rousseau, 2000). In a balanced exchange, each party focuses on mutual growth, learning, and development (i.e., relational obligations); however, these opportunities are contingent upon the organization's economic success and the employee receiving career incentives (i.e., transactional obligations).

Although most research on psychological contracts has been conceptualized in terms of transactional and/or relational obligations, there has been some discussion of moral obligations and the psychological contract. McLean Parks and Schmedemann (1994), for example, had lawyers assess passages of an employee handbook to determine if the organization was bound by legal or *moral obligations*. More recently, Thomas, Au, and Ravlin (2003) stated that the relational psychological contract is based on *moral legitimacy*. They argued that people are *morally responsible* for "doing the right thing" on behalf of relationship partners and that benevolence in an exchange relationship is consistent with the idea of a psychological contract founded in *moral obligations*. Thompson and Bunderson (2003) recently conceptualized an additional component of the psychological contract that has moral implications. They defined *ideological currency* as "credible commitments to pursue a valued cause or principle (not limited to self-interest) that are implicitly exchanged at the nexus of the individual-organization relationship" (p. 574). They argued that employees may respond unfavorably to the organization's abandonment of a *moral principle* (e.g., their commitment to donating food to the needy) by experiencing *moral outrage*. Rousseau (1989), too, described perceived psychological contract violations as deeply intense feelings of anger that are akin to *moral outrage*.

Although psychological contract research has briefly alluded to morality as an obligation (McLean Parks & Schmedemann, 1994; McLean Parks & Smith, 1994; Thomas et al., 2003), it has not been fully conceptualized in the literature. Further, it is unclear whether transactional, relational, or moral obligations can each be violated in a way that is synonymous with moral outrage, or whether their respective violations yield somewhat different reactions. In this chapter, we begin our discussion by explaining the importance of studying a moral contract. We then define a moral contract (i.e., an employee's perceptions of an exchange agreement with the organization that is concerned with adhering to generally accepted moral obligations), relate it to existing literature, and compare it with other types of contracting. We describe moral obligations and how they can become a part of an employee's moral contract. We also provide a theoretical model depicting organizational unethical behavior and how it may relate to a moral contract breach (i.e., an employee's cognitive realization that the organization failed to uphold moral obligations in a manner that is proportionate to the employee's own adherence to moral obligations in a moral contract) and moral contract violation (i.e., strong, emotional reactions that occur when employees perceive that the organization failed to uphold moral contracts; see Figure 8.1). It should be noted that we use the terms *ethical* and *moral* as being roughly synonymous throughout the chapter. We conclude by discussing the theoretical implications of a moral contract.

## THE IMPORTANCE OF MORAL CONTRACTS

Practitioners and scholars alike are placing substantial emphasis on understanding and preventing unethical behavior in organizations (Treviño, Weaver, & Reynolds, 2006). Beginning in late 2001, high-impact scandals such as Enron, Tyco, and WorldCom became a focal point of popular press articles that highlighted the devastation caused by plummeting stock prices and lost pension funds. Consequently, the U.S. government passed the Sarbanes-Oxley Act as a way of holding

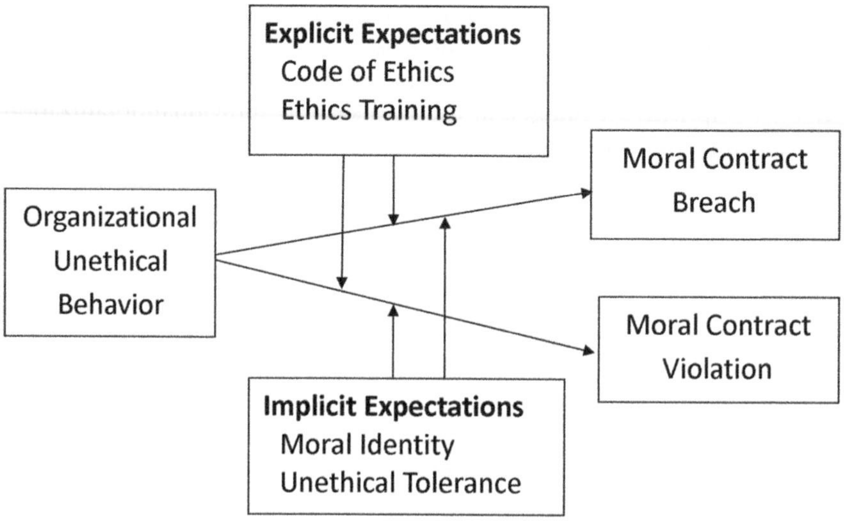


Figure 8.1. Theoretical model.

publicly-held organizations accountable for the fabrication of financial records and other fraudulent behaviors (Barney, 2005). Business schools, too, have responded by offering more business ethics courses as part of their curriculum (Hartman, 2006; Klimoski, 2006). Organizations themselves have responded to this loss of public confidence by increasing ethics training and placing more emphasis on writing and enforcing codes of ethics (Greenbaum, 2007). Furthermore, behavioral ethics research has become more mainstream as articles appeared in top-tier publication outlets (e.g., Brown, Treviño, & Harrison, 2005; Detert, Treviño, & Sweitzer, 2008; Kish-Gephart, Harrison, & Trevino, 2010; Mayer, Kuenzi, Greenbaum, Bardes, & Salvador, 2009; Reynolds, 2008; Sonenshein, 2009).

Although the leadership scandals of the early 2000s may have served as an effective launching pad for governments, business schools, and organizations to take action to prevent unethical behavior, there still remain a number of unanswered questions that prevent behavioral ethics research from being classified as a mature field. Behavioral ethics research specifically focuses on "individual behavior that is subject to or judged according to generally accepted moral norms of behavior" (Treviño et al., 2006, p. 952). Over the last few decades, most behavioral ethics research has focused on antecedents of ethical decision making, with little consideration given to the consequences of (un)ethical behavior (Treviño et al., 2006). This seems to be changing as recent publications have shown that ethical leadership is related to favorable employee and organizational outcomes (Brown et al., 2005; Mayer et al., 2009; Piccolo, Greenbaum, den Hartog, Folger, 2010; Mayer, Aquino, Greenbaum, & Kuenzi, 2010; Mayer, Kuenzi, & Greenbaum, in press; Rubin, Dierdorff, & Brown, 2010; Walumbwa & Schaubroek, 2009). Research that investigates employees' reactions to organizational *unethical* behavior, however, is scant. Furthermore, the field of behavioral ethics is lacking theory that adequately explains *why* employees may respond unfavorably to organizational unethical behaviors (Tenbrunsel & Smith-Crowe, 2008; Treviño et al., 2006). A focus on moral contracts may fill these gaps in the literature by examining moral contract breach and violations as consequences of organizational unethical behavior.

## BEYOND RECIPROCITY: UNETHICAL BEHAVIOR TOWARD OTHER CONSTITUENCIES

We suggest that a moral contract may be a particularly useful concept in understanding employees' reactions to unethical behaviors that do not directly affect them. The Enron, Tyco, and WorldCom leadership scandals directly affected employees' professional (e.g., unemployment, history with a tainted company), financial (e.g., unemployment, lost pensions), and psychological well-being (e.g., lost trust). Organizational unethical behavior affects multiple stakeholders, however, including employees, customers, financiers, suppliers, and society (Kaptein, 2008). Organizations may incur "hidden costs" when employees inadvertently—or deliberately—respond unfavorably to all forms of organizational unethical behavior, even those that are not employee directed (Cialdini, Petrova, & Goldstein, 2004). For example, an employee may respond unfavorably when the organization intentionally misleads customers, even though this behavior does not directly affect the employee. The employee may have an unfavorable reaction because the organization failed to uphold moral obligations.

Furthermore, a moral contract may explain why employees respond unfavorably to relatively minor unethical behaviors that do not create clear harm to a victim. For example, managers within the organization may cut corners in order to complete work assignments. This practice may not cause direct harm to a victim, assuming that the manager does not do anything dangerous. Even though no one appears to be harmed, employees may still respond unfavorably. In other words, it is the moral dimension of the unethical behavior, rather than the degree of harm per se, that creates a negative reaction. In our conceptualization of moral contract, we integrate psychological contract theory with deontic (i.e., binding, obligatory) justice arguments (Folger, 1998, 2001; Folger, Cropanzano, & Goldman, 2005) to contend that employees respond unfavorably to all forms of unethical behavior when their organization or its representatives display such conduct in ways that imply a failure to uphold moral obligations.

In sum, a moral contract may serve as an effective theoretical platform to understand employees' reactions to multiple organizational unethical behaviors. Furthermore, it may explain employees' reactions to apparently victimless crimes or those of that do not create substantial harm. Thus, we find it particularly important to offer a conceptualization and theoretical model that introduces a moral contract.

## CONCEPTUALIZING THE MORAL CONTRACT

Traditionally, psychological contract research has focused on transactional and relational exchange agreements (Rousseau & McLean Parks, 1992), with some discussion of balanced exchange agreements that encompass transactional *and* relational concerns (Rousseau, 2000). A traditional focus on transactional (i.e., economic) and relational (i.e., socioemotional) exchange agreements coincides with early work within the organizational justice literature that primarily focused on instrumental (i.e., economic) or interpersonal approaches to understanding justice reactions (Cropanzano, Rupp, Mohler, & Schminke, 2001). More recently, the organizational justice literature has started to embrace a moral-principles approach to understanding justice concerns. Applying a moral lens to organizational justice research aligns with a recent trend in management scholarship that has begun to note that morality motivates behavior in addition to economic and relational concerns (e.g., Folger & Salvador, 2008). Although the psychological contract literature has briefly alluded to elements of morality (McLean Parks & Schmedemann, 1994; McLean Parks & Smith, 1998; Rousseau, 1989; Thomas et al., 2003; Thompson & Bunderson, 2003), the idea of a moral contract has not been fully integrated into the literature.

Employees, in particular, may believe that adherence to moral obligations is a part of the mutual exchange agreement that exists between them and their employing organization. An exchange agreement that is based on adherence to moral obligations is not limited to a quid-pro-quo psychological contract *between* the employee and organization; rather, an additional aspect of the moral exchange agreement involves expecting the other party (viz., the organization) to show respect for moral obligations in general—even those that extend *beyond* the organization's treatment of the employee. Adherence to moral obligations illustrates an important feature of an employee's moral contact. More specifically, a moral contract is defined as employees' perceptions of the mutual exchange agreement that exists between them and their organization (as an entity oriented toward external constituencies) concerning adherence to generally accepted moral obligations of conduct.

Deontological ethics (Broad, 1930; Kant, 1745/1985) provides a theoretical basis for understanding why employees may care about upholding moral contracts. Folger and colleagues (Folger, 1998, 2001; Folger et al., 2005) argued that people respond unfavorably to others' unethical behaviors out of moral obligation, or out of the personal need to uphold widely held principles of morality that dictate how people "ought to" behave. People constrain their own behavior to live in accordance with social rules and duties that direct appropriate interpersonal conduct. In turn, people expect others to live according to these widely-held principles of morality that make it possible for humans to live among one another without infringing on what is rightfully owed to another person (i.e., in an effort to coexist within the context of a well-ordered society).

The idea of adhering to moral obligations because it is the right thing to do may become embedded in an employee's moral contract. Employees may conclude that they constrain their own behavior to abide by moral obligations, thus the organization should also abide by moral obligations because it is the right thing to do. When organizations violate moral obligations and thus fail to uphold moral contracts, they put themselves above social law by implying that rules and duties pertaining to moral obligations do not apply to them. In turn, employees may respond unfavorably when the organization fails to uphold moral obligations that are embedded in a moral contract, even when the organization's immoral behavior does not directly impact the employee.

In the organizational justice literature, Folger (1998, 2001) argued that people experience *deontic reactions* when they observe another person failing to uphold moral obligations that pertain to fair interpersonal treatment. Deontic reactions include automatic emotional responses (e.g., anger, hostility, resentment) involving a sense of tension or psychological discomfort that people can be motivated to reduce by redressing observed injustices or by acting in other ways consistent with affirming shared moral norms. In a similar vein, the psychological contract literature describes psychological contract violations as affective responses that are accompanied by feelings of disappointment, anger, or outrage that come from awareness of betrayal and mistreatment (Morrison & Robinson, 1997). Specific to moral contracts, we bridge these streams of research by arguing that employees respond to an organization's failure to uphold moral contracts by experiencing moral contract violations that move beyond a concern for one's own mistreatment. In particular, moral contract violations are strong, emotional reactions that occur when employees perceive that the organization has failed to uphold moral contracts. It should be noted that moral contracts move beyond expectations for fair interpersonal treatment by also including the expectation that *all* moral obligations should be upheld. In other words, employees may experience moral contract violations even when the organization's immoral behavior causes little to no harm and appears to be victimless.

In addition to moral contract violations, employees may also respond to the organization's failure to uphold moral contracts by experiencing moral contract breaches. A moral contract breach occurs when employees realize that the organization failed to uphold moral obligations in a manner that is proportionate with the employee's own adherence to moral obligations in the moral contract. The distinction between a moral contract violation and moral contract breach is consistent with the psychological contract literature that describes psychological contract violation (i.e., affective reaction) and psychological contract breach (i.e., cognitive reaction) as distinct processes that occur when the organization fails to uphold a psychological contract.

Morrison and Robinson (1997) portrayed the relationship between a psychological contract breach and violation as occurring in a linear fashion, such that a psychological contract breach (as a cognitive event) is expected to give rise to a psychological contract violation (as an affective event). We do not make a prediction concerning the causal relationship between a moral contract breach and a moral contract violation. Rather, we propose that the relationship between a moral contract breach and violation may be reciprocal and even virtually simultaneous. Indeed, Folger et al. (2005) noted that reactions to immoral behavior may occur so quickly that it is difficult to tease apart the relationship between affective responses and cognitive appraisals. Even Morrison and Robinson (1997) stated that employees may be unaware of the cognitions that lead to intense feelings of anger or outrage. In other words, the relationship between a moral contract breach and violation is not expected to be rational, and the two processes may be intertwined. Yet, we separate moral contract breaches and violations for the sake of clarity in denoting potential cognitive and affective reactions stemming from moral contracts, and also to adopt language consistent with the terminology used in the psychological contract literature.

## Moral Contracts and Related Constructs

As illustrated in Figure 8.2, a moral contract can overlap with other dimensions of the psychological contract in that not receiving a paycheck for an honest day's work (i.e., a transactional obligation) and being laid

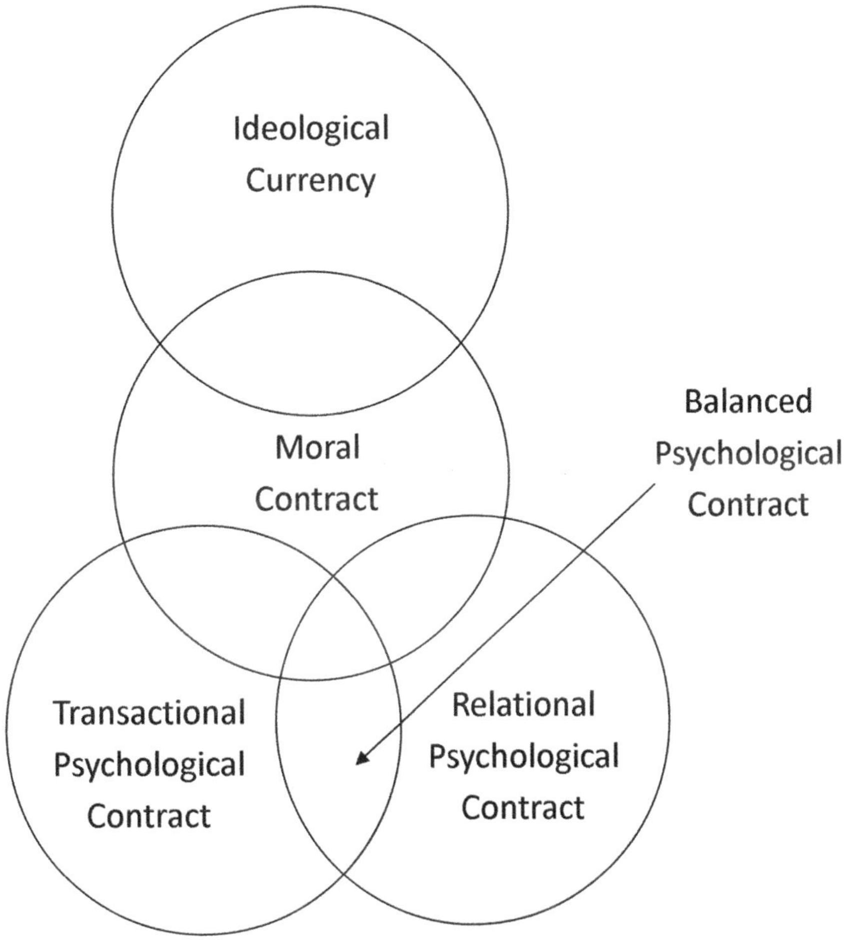


Figure 8.2. Overlap between psychological contract dimensions.

off after committing one's life to the organization (i.e., a relational obligation) is expected to be perceived as breaking generally accepted moral obligations. The moral contract, however, differs in that it also captures an employee's belief that the organization failed to uphold moral obligations that may not directly affect the employee. In this way, the moral contract may have the capacity to capture moral reactions to an organization's behavior that is not limited to the individual's self interest. This is not to say that moral contracts are devoid of self-interest; rather, it is to make the point that employees may believe they have an exchange agreement with their organization that is greater than and different from their economic and socioemotional well-being as captured by transactional and relational psychological contracts.

In a parallel but different line of reasoning to moral contracts, Thompson and Bunderson (2003) have introduced ideological currency as a component of psychological contracts. Ideological currency is concerned with the organization's commitment to pursue a valued cause or principle. Organizations may explicitly or implicitly communicate to employees that they are committed to pursuing a particular social cause. The organization may state that they regularly donate food to the needy, allow employees to take a day off to volunteer within the community, or match employees' contributions to charitable organizations. As employees search for meaning within their jobs (Wrzesniewski & Dutton, 2001; Wrzesniewski, Dutton, & Debebe, 2003), they internalize the organization's ideological pursuits as being part of their psychological contracts. They begin to believe that the organization should pursue altruistic endeavors because it is the right thing to do (Thompson & Bunderson, 2003). Note, however, that *altruism* does not constitute the sum total of what it would mean to meet one's moral obligations (just as we noted that the moral domain moves beyond expectations for fairness).

The ideological currency component of the psychological contract is concerned with doing what is right, often on behalf of others, without being solely concerned with one's own self-interest. Thus, when an organization fails to uphold its commitment to pursue a valued cause, employees often respond by experiencing an ideologically-infused psychological contract breach and/or violation (Thompson & Bunderson, 2003). A novel aspect of ideological currency is that employees are expected to respond unfavorably (in regard to psychological contract breach and/or violation) when the organization abandons a valued cause, even if this cause does not directly benefit the employee. Thus, ideological currency moves beyond self interest to suggest that people care about doing what is right out of moral obligation. Accordingly, the ideological currency component of the psychological contract is similar to a moral contract in that both concepts are concerned with adherence to moral obligations (as denoted by the overlap between ideological currency and moral contracts as shown in Figure 8.2).

Despite the similarities between ideological currency and moral contracts, we suggest that a key difference exists between these concepts. Ideology is based on the organization's *proactive* commitments (e.g., making a pledge to donate food to the needy, donating a portion of company profits to a charitable organization). Moral contracts are based on the organization's commitment to *prevent* unethical behaviors, while also addressing other matters that can relate to upholding moral obligations (e.g., sanctions *ex post* as well as *ex ante*). Corporate social responsibility strategies, for example, can serve as a platform for the development of the ideological-currency component of psychological contracts (Dixon-Fowler, O'Leary-Kelly, & Johnson, 2008). Moral contracts, however, are based on expectations for behavior that hold employees and the organization accountable for how they should behave on a day-to-day basis guided by norms that help to identify unethical behaviors.

In line with the proactive versus preventive distinction, Wiltermuth, Monin, and Chow (2010) also noted that people approach morality in one of two ways. People may place substantial emphasis on what they should be doing to improve the lives of others (a proactive, moral focus), but the other possibility is for people to equate morality with avoiding immoral behaviors. In a similar vein, ideological currency typically is more concerned with the promotion of a cause, whereas the major realm of moral contracts has to do with the prevention of unethical behaviors (e.g., not misleading customers because it is wrong to lie, not accepting bribes from suppliers because it is immoral). Here again, however, moral contracts can also serve a broader function that incorporates both aspects, as when a failure to "improve" (e.g., not acting like a "Good Samaritan") comes to be seen as a failure to meet a moral obligation.

## ORGANIZATIONAL UNETHICAL BEHAVIOR AND MORAL CONTRACTS: A MODEL

In this section, we provide a theoretical model that captures a moral contract breach and violation (see Figure 8.1). In particular, we propose that organizational unethical behavior may serve as an antecedent to moral contract breach and violation. Additionally, the organization may engage in actions that explicitly communicate to employees that upholding ethics is important. Likewise, employees may have certain values that make them more or less prone to perceiving that a moral contract exists implicitly. These conditions may affect an employee's likelihood of responding to organizational unethical behavior by perceiving a moral contract breach or experiencing a moral contract violation.

### Organizational Unethical Behavior and Moral Contract Breach and Violation

Organizational unethical behavior occurs when the organization and/or its representatives engage in behavior that is morally unacceptable to the larger community (Jones, 1991; Kaptein, 2008). Examples of these behaviors include, but are not limited to, bookkeeping fraud, engaging in false or deceptive sales practices, engaging in sexual harassment, violating suppliers' confidentiality rights, violating environmental standards, and violating fair labor standards and human rights (Kaptien, 2008). When employees find out that the organization and/or its representatives (e.g., leaders) engaged in unethical behaviors, they may respond by perceiving that the organization failed to uphold its moral contract. By engaging in deceptive sales practices, for example, the organization implies that it does not have to abide by generally accepted moral norms that dictate how to behave within society (Folger, 1998, 2001). The employee, however, may expect the organization to abide by moral obligations as an expectation, or promise, of how to behave as a member of the organization and society. The employee and other members of society constrain their own behavior to live in accordance with generally-accepted moral norms; thus, the organization is expected to do the same.

In turn, employees may respond to organizational unethical behavior by concluding that the organization is not fulfilling its part of the mutual obligation to uphold moral obligations as captured by a moral contract breach. The employee's reactions to organizational unethical behavior may also be accompanied strong emotional reactions in the form of a moral contract violation. The employee may experience feelings of anger or resentment because the organization failed to abide by mutual expectations of appropriate moral conduct that dictate how people should behave.

> ***Proposition 1:*** Organizational unethical behavior is positively related to moral contract breach and moral contract violation.

## The Moderating Role of Code of Ethics and Ethics Training

In some instances, the organization may explicitly communicate that it values ethics. This may occur when an organization promotes a code of ethics or has ethics training. A code of ethics is "a written, distinct, formal document, which consists of moral standards that help guide employee or corporate behavior" (Schwartz, 2002, p. 28). Ethics training teaches employees the ethical expectations of the organization, as well as how to respond when faced with ethical dilemmas in the workplace (Valentine & Fleischman, 2004). Although a code of ethics and ethics training are not always effective in promoting ethical behavior (Cowton & Thompson, 2000; James, 2000; Sims & Brinkmann, 2003), they do inform employees about what is "correct" behavior within the workplace (Donaldson & Dunfee, 1999; Delaney & Sockell, 1992).

The presence of codes of ethics and/or ethics training may serve as an organization's explicit endorsement of ethical conduct that strengthens the relationship between organizational unethical behavior and moral contract breach and violation. Rousseau (1989) noted that explicit and verifiable promises (e.g., in writing) are more likely to be associated with the belief that a contract exists. This notion is echoed by Salancik and Pfeffer's (1978) social information processing theory, which states that overt and public commitments have more influence over people's cognitions than those that are subtle or private. Morrison and Robinson (1997) also argued that employees react more strongly to broken promises that go against explicit values.

An organization's code of ethics and/or ethics training explicitly communicates to employees that the organization expects morally appropriate behavior. The employee may already abide by moral norms because it is the right thing to do; yet, a code of ethics and/or ethics training reinforces the notion that abiding by moral obligations is a mutual expectation that should be upheld by the employee and organization. Accordingly, when the organization engages in unethical behavior, but also promotes moral expectations by having a code of ethics and/or ethics training, it is clearer to employees that the organization is not upholding a moral contract. In turn, employees may respond to organizational unethical behavior by experiencing stronger moral contract breaches and violations. Employees more easily conclude that the organization does not uphold moral obligations in a way that is consistent with the employee's personal adherence to moral obligations (as expressed by a code of ethics and/or ethics training) (i.e., moral contract breach), which may also be accompanied by stronger emotional reactions (i.e., moral contract violation).

> ***Proposition 2:*** An organization's code of ethics moderates the relationships between organizational unethical behavior and moral contract breach and violation, such that these relationships are stronger when a code of ethics is present than when it is absent.

> ***Proposition 3:*** An organization's ethics training moderates the relationships between organizational unethical behavior and moral contract breach and violation, such that these relationships are stronger when ethics training is present than when it is absent.

## The Moderating Role of Moral Identity and Unethical Tolerance

Employees may perceive that a moral contract exists based on their implicitly created expectations. In these instances, the organization may believe that it is upholding its promises to the employee, when it is falling short in the mind of the employee. In particular, we argue that employees may perceive morality differently than organizational agents depending on the former's moral identities and level of unethical tolerance. Thus, an employee's moral identity and unethical tolerance may moderate the relationship between organizational unethical behavior and a moral contract breach and violation.

Moral identity is a self-schema that is organized around a set of moral traits (e.g., honest, compassionate, caring; Aquino & Reed, 2002). People differ in terms of how much they internalize morality as being central to their self-definitions (Aquino & Reed, 2002; Blasi, 1984, 2004; Lapsley & Lasky, 2001). The more central morality is to a person's self-definition, the more accessible a moral schema becomes for processing information and regulating behavior. In this way, a moral identity also captures self-regulatory mechanisms that are rooted in an understanding of right and wrong behavior (Aquino & Reed, 2002). People with strong moral identities are thought to desire self-consistency between their thoughts and actions and what it means to be a moral person (Blasi, 1984, 2004). A lack of consistency can result in feelings of dissonance and self-condemnation (Aquino, Freeman, Reed, Lim, & Felps, 2009; Aquino & Reed, 2002).

When employees observe organizational unethical behaviors, they may have stronger reactions in the form of moral contract breaches when they are high in moral identity. Employees who are high in moral identity may be especially likely (compared to other employees) to hold the implicit expectation that organizations should abide by moral obligations because it is the right thing to do. To work for an organization that does not abide by moral obligations would cause them to feel inauthentic. Furthermore, when they observe organizational unethical behavior, their moral self-schemas are readily activated, which makes it clearer to them that the organization does not abide by moral obligations and therefore does not uphold the moral contract. Because of the activation of a moral identity, the employee easily concludes that the organization does not fulfill the mutual expectation to abide by moral norms in a way that is consistent with the employee's own adherence to moral norms. In this way, moral identity is expected to strengthen the relationship between organizational unethical behavior and perceived moral contract breach.

Furthermore, employees who are high in moral identity may respond to organizational unethical behavior by experiencing stronger moral contract violations. Employees who are high in moral identity tend to feel inauthentic when their own behavior does not align with the moral obligations that they have internalized as part of their identities (Aquino et al., 2009). They may also have stronger feelings of inauthenticity when the organization engages in unethical behavior. Because morality is so central to their self-definitions (Aquino & Reed, 2002; Blasi, 1984, 2004;

Lapsley & Lasky, 2001), they may respond to organizational unethical behavior by experiencing higher levels of condemnation for being associated with a morally wayward company, which may be expressed by feeling angry and/or resentful as captured by a moral contract violation. In this way, moral identity may also serve as a moderator that strengthens the relationship between organizational unethical behavior and moral contract violation.

> ***Proposition 4:*** An employee's moral identity moderates the relationships between organizational unethical behavior and moral contact breach and violation, such that these relationships are stronger when moral identity is high as opposed to low.

Some employees may be more tolerant of unethical behaviors in organizations. According to social information processing theory (Salancik & Pfeffer, 1978), people extract information from their environments, past experiences, and personal beliefs when forming perceptions of a particular situation. This could affect the level of tolerance they have for unethical behaviors within organizations. Some employees may have worked in environments where there were no consequences for engaging in unethical behaviors. The persistence of unethical behaviors, without any consequences, may lead employees to believe that these behaviors are routine practices for handling business situations (Brenner & Molander, 1977). Furthermore, employees may personally believe that cheating, or engaging in unethical behavior is expected within organizations. They may be tolerant of unethical behaviors if it serves the purpose of supporting the company (Froelick & Kottke, 1991). It could be that they find it acceptable to engage in shady practices if they believe the competition is doing so, or that it does not matter how organizational results are attained as long as it leads to desirable organizational outcomes (Froelich & Kottke, 1991).

An employee who is more tolerant of unethical behaviors may be less likely to perceive that a moral contract exists. Even if they do believe that the organization ought to uphold moral obligations, they may be more lax in what they consider moral behavior. Thus, these employees may respond less strongly to organizational unethical behaviors by experiencing moral contract breaches and/or violations. Because these employees are more tolerant of unethical behaviors, they should be less likely to conclude that the organization's unethical behavior constitutes a failure to uphold the mutual expectation of abiding by moral obligations (i.e., moral contract breach). Thus, their emotional reactions, or the likelihood of experiencing moral contract violations, should be weaker as well. In this way, an employee's unethical tolerance may serve as a moderator that weakens the relationship between organizational unethical behavior and moral contract breach and violation.

> ***Proposition 5:*** An employee's unethical tolerance moderates the relationships between organizational unethical behavior and moral contract breach and violation, such that these relationships are weaker when unethical tolerance is high as opposed to low.

## DISCUSSION

Psychological contract research has provided much insight into employees' perceptions of the mutual exchange agreement that exists between them and their employing organization (Dabos & Rousseau, 2004; Deery, Iverson, & Walsh, 2006; Hui, Lee, & Rousseau, 2004; Morrison & Robinson, 1997; Raja, Johns, & Ntalianis, 2004; Robinson & Morrison, 2000; Rousseau, 1989, 1995; Rousseau & McLean Parks, 1992; Thomas et al., 2003). Most of this research has focused on reciprocal exchanges that directly affect aspects of an employee's job and well-being. More recently, however, Thompson and Bunderson (2003) noted that employees may also care about how the organization behaves in terms of promoting espoused values. We expand on this idea by suggesting that employees may also care about whether the organization adheres to an entire range of moral obligations. Employees may perceive that they have a mutual exchange agreement with the organization that revolves around upholding moral obligations that may or may not have a direct impact on their personal well-being. It is as if they would not have become a part of an organization in the first place if they thought it would fail to be "well-behaved" (i.e., to fail to live up to moral obligations in general, not just to its employees). In that sense, the organization's adherence to moral obligations constitutes a promise to its employees as denoted by a moral contract.

### Implications for Theory

We have expanded on work by Thompson and Bunderson (2003) by arguing that employees may perceive that the organization should uphold certain obligations that extend beyond the employee's personal well-being. Thompson and Bunderson (2003) focused on ideological obligations that may become imbedded in an employee's psychological contract. The ideological currency component of the psychological contract exists when employees perceive that they have a reciprocal exchange agreement with the organization that revolves around a commitment to pursue a valued cause or principle that is not limited to self interest. Ideological currency captures prosocial initiatives that might include donating food to the needy, volunteering one's time to better the community, or providing funding for charitable causes.

We move beyond ideological currency with a new conceptualization by suggesting that employees may also perceive an agreement with the organization that centers on moral obligations. Whether proscriptive ("Thou shalt not") or prescriptive ("Thou shalt"), a moral contract highlights the potentially negative consequences of not acting in accord with morally normative conduct. Whereas ideological currency captures prosocial initiatives, moral contracts focus on behavior misaligned with principles of morality. For example, an employee may perceive that the organization should not violate environmental standards or regulations, even if it does not affect the employee's well-being, because it violates principles of morality. Thus, we provide an explanation of why employees may experience another type of psychological contract breach or violation (involving a moral contract) in the absence of their own mistreatment.

We also contribute to the literature by providing a theoretical rationale that may explain why employees respond unfavorably to organizational unethical behaviors. Traditionally, behavioral ethics research has focused on antecedents of (un)ethical behavior (Treviño et al., 2006). The theoretical model we propose, however, may also contribute to the literature by demonstrating that moral contract breach and violation can serve as consequences of organizational unethical behaviors. Thus, pairing morality with psychological contract theory offers an appropriate theoretical framework for examining the consequences of unethical behaviors.

In addition, we contribute to the literature by integrating deontic-justice arguments (Folger, 1998, 2001; Folger et al., 2005) with psychological contract theory to introduce the concept of a moral contract. There has been some mention of moral obligations and altruism in contracting (McLean Parks & Schmedemann, 1994; McLean Parks & Smith, 1998; Thomas et al., 2004); however, this idea has not been fully integrated into the psychological contract literature. Deontological arguments (Folger, 1998, 2001; Folger et al., 2005) provide a sound theoretical basis for arguing that morality may be an important component of the psychological contract. People care about morality for its own sake (Turillo, Folger, Lavelle, Umphress, & Gee, 2002) and thus expect for the organization and its representatives to uphold morality as an obligation or duty that is part of a moral contract. In short, our theorizing suggests that the organization should be true to a *moral contract* in the same way that employees strive to uphold a moral contract as demonstrated by their own adherence to moral obligations.

## Future Directions

We provided a theoretical model and propositions that can be tested in future research. Although testing our model provides a natural first step for future research, we also believe that it can be expanded to include many other interesting predictions. First, it would be interesting to see if the moral contract explains variance above and beyond more traditional forms of psychological contracts (e.g., relational psychological contracts, transactional psychological contracts). We noted that relational and transactional psychological contracts may also include elements of morality. An organization's failure to provide health benefits or socioemotional support may constitute a breach of the organization's moral obligations. In this way, a moral contract may be a broader construct that overlaps with other types of contracts (as shown in Figure 8.2). However, when the organization behaves unethically in a more general sense, an employee's unfavorable reactions may have little to do with the economic or socioemotional exchanges that he/she has with the organization; rather, a breach of moral contracts may be a better explanation for why the employee cares about the organization's behavior.

For example, if the organization engages in false advertising, this could actually help the employee's economic success by leading to more sales, and it may not have anything to do with how well the organization treats the employee in terms of providing socioemotional support. Nevertheless, the employee may respond unfavorably because the organization does not abide by the perceived promise of behaving morally, even though the employee abides by this promise. By controlling for alternative psychological contract explanations, future research may provide evidence that the moral contract is indeed capturing something unique.

In an effort to establish the nomological network of a moral contract, it would also be interesting to see if a moral contract breach and/or violations lead to unique outcomes. Extant research has shown that employees respond to psychological contract breaches and/or violations by reducing job satisfaction, organizational commitment, organizational citizenship behaviors, and in-role performance, and increasing turnover intentions and actual turnover (Zhao, Wayne, Glibkowski, & Bravo, 2007). It could be that employees respond to moral contract breaches and/or violations by attempting to punish the organization for its wrongdoing. Folger and colleagues (e.g., Folger, 1998, 2001; Folger et al., 2005) noted that people may respond to observed immorality by experiencing psychological discomfort that motivates them to redress the perpetrator's wrongdoing (e.g., by making personal sacrifices to prevent the wrongdoer from gaining at someone else's expense). Yet it may be true that employees who experience moral contract breaches and/or violations are unwilling to redress the organization's wrongdoing with behaviors that they consider to be equally immoral (Rupp & Bell, 2010). Future research would benefit from an examination of moral contract breaches and/or violations and employees' responses that may serve to redress the organization's wrongdoing (e.g., engaging in deviance or other retributive responses).

It would also be interesting to determine whether the employee's reactions are more or less strong depending on the type of psychological contract breach they experience. Thompson and Bunderson (2003), for example, proposed that employees may have weaker reactions when the organization fails to uphold ideological obligations when compared to relational and transactional obligations. They argued that ideological obligations provide intrinsic rewards that may require patience and delayed gratification. Thus, employees may not be as bothered by initial ideological contract breaches because they may believe that the organization is committed to fulfilling the espoused value or cause in the future. Employees may have immediately strong reactions to a moral contract breach, however, because they conclude that the organization does not uphold morality, nor will it uphold morality in the future.

It is unclear whether employees will react more strongly to a moral contract breach when compared to a relational or transactional psychological contract breach. Employees may react more strongly to relational and transactional psychological contract breaches because they are inherently concerned with their own well-being. Nevertheless, there may be some instances whereby the organization's behavior is so egregious that the employee's moral reactions are stronger than relational or transactional concerns. For example, this may occur when the organization carelessly releases an unsafe product that severely harms customers or deliberately allows the emission of toxic materials that have some potential danger to the public at large. Future research would benefit from an examination of the strength of employees' reactions relative to the different contract types. Such research will require greater specificity for both psychological contracts and moral contracts. Depending on the specifics of different situations, an extreme relational breach/violation might engender a more pronounced reaction than a minor moral breach/violation, and in other instances, the opposite might be true.

## CONCLUSION

The harm created by corporate unethical behaviors can range from extremely severe to relatively minor. The Enron, WorldCom, and Tyco accounting scandals created substantial harm that affected many constituents. Stockholders lost millions of dollars, employees lost their jobs and pension funds, and society lost faith in big business. The harm associated with other unethical behaviors may not be easily realized. For example, an organization might get away with lying to customers. The organization may convince itself that it is not causing harm because customers do not know they are being lied to. The organization may fail to consider that it is causing harm in that employees respond unfavorably to its unethical behaviors, even if these behaviors do not directly affect their well-being (Cialdini et al., 2004). To understand this phenomenon, we introduced the idea of a moral contract. Employees may perceive that they have a mutual agreement with the organization that includes upholding moral obligations. We hope future research will continue to examine the moral contract as a potential explanation for why employees care about the organization's (un)ethical behavior.

## REFERENCES

Aquino, K., Freeman, D., Reed, A., II, Lim, V. K. G., & Felps, W. (2009). Testing a social cognitive model of moral behavior: The interaction of situational factors and moral identity centrality. *Journal of Personality and Social Psychology, 97*, 123-141.

Aquino, K., & Reed, A., II. (2002). The self-importance of moral identity. *Journal of Personality and Social Psychology, 83*, 1423-1440.

Barney, J. B. (2005). Should strategic management research engage public policy debates? *Academy of Management Journal, 48*, 945-948.

Blasi, A. (1984). Moral identity: Its role in moral functioning. In W. Kurtines & J. Gewirtz (Eds.), *Morality, moral behavior and moral development* (pp. 128-139). New York, NY: Wiley.

Blasi, A. (2004). Moral functioning: Moral understanding and personality. In W. M. Kurtines, & J. L. Gewritz (Eds.), *Moral development: An introduction* (pp. 189-212). Boston, MA: Allyn & Bacon.

Brenner, S. N., & Molander, E. A. (1997). Is the ethics of business changing? *Harvard Business Review, 55*, 57-71.

Broad, C. D. (1930). *Five types of ethical theory*. New York, NY: Harcourt, Brace, & Co.

Brown, M. E., Treviño, L, K., & Harrison, D. A. (2005). Ethical leadership: A social learning perspective for construct development and testing. *Organizational Behavior and Human Decision Processes, 97*, 117-134.

Cialdini, R. B., Petrova, P. K., & Goldstein, N. J. (2004). The hidden costs of organizational dishonesty. *MIT Sloan Management Review, Spring*, 67-73.

Cowton, C. J., & Thompson, P. (2000). Do codes make a difference? The case of bank lending and the environment. *Journal of Business Ethics, 24*, 165-178.

Cropanzano, R., Rupp, D. E., Mohler, C. J., Schminke, M. (2001). Three roads to organizational justice. *Research in personnel and human resources management, 20*, 1-113.

Dabos, G. E., & Rousseau, D. M. (2004). Mutuality and reciprocity in the psychological contracts of employees and employers. *Journal of Applied Psychology, 89*, 52-72.

Deery, S. J., Iverson, R. D., Walsh, J. T. (2006). Toward a better understanding of psychological contract breach: A study of customer service employees. *Journal of Applied Psychology, 91*, 166-175.

Delaney, J. T., & Sockell, D. (1992). Do company ethics training programs make a difference? An empirical analysis. *Journal of Business Ethics, 9*, 719-727.

Detert, J. R., Treviño, L. K., Sweitzer, V. L. (2008). Moral disengagement in ethical decision making: A study of antecedents and outcomes. *Journal of Applied Psychology, 93*, 374-391.

Dixon-Fowler, H. R., O'Leary-Kelly, A., & Johnson, J. L. (2008). *Ideology-infused psychological contract development: An organizational- and employee-level perspective.* Paper presented at the annual conference of the Academy of Management Meeting, Anaheim, CA.

Donaldson, T., & Dunfee, T. W. (1999). When ethics travel: The promise and peril of global business ethics. *California Management Review, 41*, 45-63.

Folger, R. (1998). Fairness as a moral virtue. In M. Schminke (Ed.), *Managerial ethics: Morally managing people and processes* (pp. 13-34). Mahwah, NJ: Erlbaum.

Folger, R. (2001). Fairness as deonance. In S. W. Gilliland, D. D. Steiner, & D. P. Skarlicki (Eds.), *Research in social issues in management* (pp. 3-31). Greenwich, CT: Information Age.

Folger, R., Cropanzano, R., & Goldman, B. (2005). What is the relationship between justice and morality? In J. Greenberg & J. A. Colquitt (Eds.), *Handbook of organizational justice* (pp. 215-245). Mahwah, NJ: Erlbaum.

Folger, R., & Salvador, R. (2008). Is management theory too "self-ish"? *Journal of Management, 34*, 1127-1151.

Froelich, K. S., & Kottke, J. L. (1991). Measuring individual beliefs about organizational ethics. *Educational and Psychological Measurement, 51*, 377-383.

Greenbaum, R. L. (2007). Observer effects: Observers' reactions to the unethical behaviors that occur within organizations. In B. G. Mujtaba (Ed.), *Cross cultural management and negotiation practices* (pp. 151-156). Ft. Lauderdale, Florida: ILEAD Academy Publications.

Hartman, E. M. (2006). Can we teach character? An Aristotelian answer. *Academy of Management Learning & Education, 5*, 68-81.

Hui, C., Lee, C., Rousseau, D. M. (2004). Psychological contract and organizational citizenship behavior in China: Investigating generalizability and instrumentality. *Journal of Applied Psychology, 89*, 311-321.

James, H. S. (2000). Reinforcing ethical decision making through organizational structure. *Journal of Business Ethics, 28*, 43-58.

Jones, T. M. (1991). Ethical decision making by individuals in organizations: An issue-contingent model. *Academy of Management Review, 16*, 366-395.

Kant, I. (1948). *Groundwork of the metaphysics of morals* (H. J. Paton, Trans.). New York, NY: Harper & Row. (Original work published 1785).

Kaptein, M. (2008). Developing a measure of unethical behavior in the workplace: A stakeholder perspective. *Journal of Management, 34*, 978-1008.

Kish-Gephart, J. J., Harrison, D. A., & Treviño, L. K. (2010). Bad apples, bad cases, and bad barrels: Meta-analytic evidence about sources of unethical decisions at work. *Journal of Applied Psychology, 95*, 1-31.

Klimoski, R. (2006). Introduction: Aristotle as a business ethics professor. *Academy of Management Learning & Education, 5*, 66-67.

Lapsley, K., & Lasky, B. (2001). Prototypic moral character. *Identity, 1*, 345-363.

MacNeil, I. R. (1985). Relational contract: What we do and do not know. *Wisconsin Law Review*, 483-525.

Mayer, D. M., Aquino, K., Greenbaum, R. L., & Kuenzi, M. (in press). Who displays ethical leadership and why does it matter? An examination of antecedents and consequences of ethical leadership. *Academy of Management Journal*.

Mayer, D. M., Kuenzi, M., & Greenbaum, R. L. (2010). Examining the link between ethical leadership and employee misconduct: The mediating role of ethical climate. *Journal of Business Ethics, 95*, 7-16.

Mayer, D. M, Kuenzi, M., Greenbaum, R., Bardes, M., & Salvador, R. (2009). How low does ethical leadership flow? Test of a trickle-down model. *Organizational Behavior and Human Decision Processes, 108*, 1-13.

McLean Parks, J., & Schmedemann, D. A. (1994). When promises become contracts: Implied contracts and handbook provisions on job security. *Human Resources Management, 33*, 403-423.

McLean Parks, J., & Smith, F. (1998). Organizational contracting: A "rational" exchange? In J Halpern & R. Stern (Eds.) *Debating rationality: Nonrational aspects of organizational decision making*. Ithaca, NY: ILR Press.

Morrison, E. W., & Robinson, S. L. (1997). When employees feel betrayed: A model of how psychological contract violation develops. *Academy of Management Review, 22*, 226-256.

Piccolo, R. F., Greenbaum, R. L., Den Hartog, D., & Folger, R. (2010). The relationship between ethical leadership and core job characteristics. *Journal of Organizational Behavior, 31*, 259-278.

Raja, U., Johns, G., & Ntalianis, F. (2004). The impact of personality on psychological contracts. *Academy of Management Journal, 47*, 350-367.

Reynolds, S. J. (2008). Moral attentiveness: Who pays attention to the moral aspects of life? *Journal of Applied Psychology, 93*, 1027-1041.

Robinson, S. L., & Morrison, E. W. (2000). The development of psychological contract breach and violation. *Journal of Organizational Behavior, 21*, 525-546.

Rousseau, D. M. (1989). Psychological and implied contracts in organizations. *Employee Responsibilities and Rights Journal, 2*, 121-139.

Rousseau, D. M. (1995). *Psychological contracts in organizations*. Thousand Oaks, CA: SAGE.

Rousseau, D. M. (2000). *Psychological contract inventory technical report* (Unpublished manuscript). Carnegie Mellon University, Heinz College and Tepper School of Knowledge, Pittsburgh, PA

Rousseau, D. M., & McLean Parks, J. (1992). The contracts of individuals and organizations. *Research in Organizational Behavior, 15*, 1-43.

Rubin, R. S., Dierdorff, E. C., & Brown, M. E. (2010). Do ethical leaders get ahead? Exploring ethical leadership and promotability. *Business Ethics Quarterly, 20*, 215-236.

Rupp, D. E., & Bell, C. M. (2010). Extending the deontic model of justice: Moral self-regulation in third-party responses to injustice. *Business Ethics Quarterly, 20*, 89-106.

Salancik, G. R., & Pfeffer, J. (1978). A social information processing approach to job attitudes and task design. *Administrative Science Quarterly, 23*, 224-253.

Schwartz, M. S. (2002). A code of ethics for corporate code of ethics. *Journal of Business Ethics, 41*, 27-43.

Sims, R. R., & Brinkmann, J. (2003). Enron ethics (Or: Culture matters more than codes). *Journal of Business Ethics, 45*, 243-256.

Sonenshein, S. (2009). The emergence of ethical issues during strategic change implementation. *Organization Science, 20*, 223-239.

Tenbrunsel, A. E., & Smith-Crowe, K. (2008). Ethical decision making: Where we've been and where we're going. *The Academy of Management Annals, 2*, 545-607.

Thomas, D. C., Au, K., & Ravlin, E. C. (2003). Cultural variation and the psychological contract. *Journal of Organizational Behavior, 24*, 451-471.

Thompson, J. A., & Bunderson, J. S. (2003). Violations of principle: Ideological currency in the psychological contract. *Academy of Management Review, 28*, 571-586.

Treviño, L. K., Weaver, G. R. T., & Reynolds, S. J. (2006). Behavioral ethics in organizations: A review. *Journal of Management, 32*, 951-990.

Turillo, C. J., Folger, R., Lavelle, J. J., Umphress, E. E., & Gee, J. O. (2002). Is virtue its own reward? Self-sacrificial decisions for the sake of fairness. *Organizational Behavior & Human Decision Processes, 89*, 839-866.

Valentine, S., & Fleischman, G. (2004). Ethics training and businesspersons' perceptions of organizational ethics. *Journal of Business Ethics, 52*, 381-390.

Walumbwa, F. O., & Schaubroeck, J. (2009). Leader personality traits and employee voice behavior: Mediating roles of ethical leadership and work group psychological safety. *Journal of Applied Psychology, 94*, 1275-1286.

Wiltermuth, S. S., Monin, B. & Chow, R. M. (2010). The orthogonality of praise and condemnation in moral judgment. *Social Psychological and Personality Science, 2*, 302-310.

Wrzesniewski, A. C., & Dutton, J. E. (2001). Crafting a job: Revisioning employees as active crafters of their work. *Academy of Management Review, 26*, 179-201.

Wrzesniewski, A. C., Dutton, J. E., & Debebe, G. (2003). Interpersonal sensemaking and the meaning of work. *Research in Organizational Behavior, 25*, 93-135.

Zhao, H., Wayne, S. J., Glibkowski, B. C., Bravo, J. (2007). The impact of psychological contract breach on work-related outcomes: A meta-analysis. *Personnel Psychology, 60*, 647-680.

CHAPTER 9

# THE EXPERIENCE-FOCUSED MODEL OF ETHICAL ACTION

## A Conceptual Foundation for Ethics and Organizational Justice Research

**J. Brooke Hamilton, III, and Stephen B. Knouse**

Conceptual models of ethical action and of organizational justice guide researchers in deciding what should be studied and how to explain their results. Beginning with 2 current models of ethical action, Rest's model and the dual processing model, we propose a new model of ethical action that adds "experience-focused" categories based on recent work in neuroscience and moral psychology. Ethics researchers can use this new model to classify research findings and generate hypotheses for further study. Then using Cropanzano, Rupp, Mohler, and Schminke's analysis of organizational justice research, we show how the "experience-focused" model can connect organizational justice categories to ethics categories and provide insights for future behavioral research in organizational justice.

We define ethics as the values, rules, principles, obligations, and concerns that allow individuals to live in complicated societies and pursue their individual and common purposes while respecting the purposes of others, a characterization that enjoys broad support in contemporary litera-

*Emerging Perspectives on Organizational Justice and Ethics*
pp. 223–257

ture (Appiah, 2008; Haidt, 2007; Tenbrunsel & Smith Crowe, 2008). Since ethics or morality so defined[1] is important for individual happiness and the success of complex social groups (Bazerman & Tenbrunsel, 2011; Haidt, 2007; Narvaez, 2008a), little wonder it is the focus of so much research. Behavioral science, cognitive neuroscience, moral psychology, and philosophy have provided many descriptive explanations of how ethical action occurs and prescriptive suggestions for how it should occur. Another related though sometimes separate stream of research examines justice in organizations, asking what individuals perceive as just in regards to the allocation of benefits and burdens (*distributive* justice), the procedure for making the allocation (*procedural* justice), the interpersonal treatment they receive (*interpersonal* justice), and the social explanations and justifications of the process (*informational* justice) (Cropanzano, Rupp, Mohler, & Schminke, 2001; De Cremer, Mayer, & Schminke, 2010). It also asks why justice matters so much to people.

Given the important role of conceptual models in guiding research, we begin this chapter by introducing a new model for describing the processes by which individuals engage in ethical action. Recognizing the explanatory power of previous models and not wanting to give up the view that each provides, we begin with two current models of ethical action; Rest's model (Rest, Bebeau & Volker, 1986); and the dual processing model, which has a number of versions (e.g. Reynolds, 2006; Sonenshein, 2007) and has been used to point out similarities and differences in a wide body of research (Lapsley & Hill, 2008; Salvador & Folger, 2009). We add to Rest's model and the dual processing model a set of experience-focused categories based on recent work in neuroscience and moral psychology. This new experience-focused model that we are proposing identifies and describes the processes for producing an ethical action as individuals experience them. Ethics researchers can use this experience-focused model to classify past research and generate hypotheses for further study. The model also provides user-friendly terminology to facilitate use of research results in the workplace by individuals and use by organizations to develop effective ethics programs. We will describe the model using examples of ethical issues that involve distributive and procedural justice as much as possible given that this volume focuses on organizational justice.

After describing the experience-focused model, we turn to its application in ethics research and in research on organizational justice. Cropanzano et al. (2001) provided a classification system for contemporary social science research on organizational justice. After briefly summarizing these categories, we show how they can be mapped on to the ethical action processes described in the experience-focused model. We hope to provide a connection between ethics research and organizational justice research that Cropanzano et al. (2001) suggested would be worthwhile, and thereby open the possibility for generating new insights in both ethics and organizational ethics research.

## TWO CURRENT MODELS THAT EXPLAIN ETHICAL ACTIONS

Conceptual models can be used to describe the cognitive processes by which an individual moves from awareness of a situation to behaving in an ethical manner. Accurate classifications of how the mind works and clear terminology to denote these categories are essential to understanding a cognitive process like ethics. The models guide researchers in deciding what should be studied in order to understand ethical action and design their experiments. The models are elaborated and revised based on the results of conceptual analysis and empirical evidence and are used to compare and contrast different descriptions of what is and of what should be taking place with regard to ethics. Some who work in the field (Burton, 2008) think the current classifications of mental states are an obstacle to understanding how the mind works. Contemporary neuroscience, moral psychology, behavioral research, and philosophy offer a rich level of detail about individuals' ethical perceptions (e.g., Appiah, 2008; Dulebohn, Conlon, Sarnopoulos, Davidson, & McNamara, 2009; Haidt, 2007; Moll, de Oliveira-Souza, & Zahn, 2008; De Cremer et al., 2010). Two current models of ethics processes that seek to make sense of this detail (Figure 9.1) are Rest's 1986 model (Rest, Bebeau, & Volker, 1986, herein after "Rest") and the dual processing model (Lapsley & Hill, 2008, Salvador & Folger, 2009).

### Are Rest's Categories an Adequate Guide for Contemporary Research

Rest (1986) distinguishes four processes that occur when a person acts ethically (Figure 9.1). The categories of his descriptive model have become a starting point for many researchers. Salvador and Folger (2009), for example, summarize Rest's categories as "identifying the moral nature of an issue, making a moral judgment, establishing moral intent, and/or engaging in moral behavior." The model suggests that (1) a person has to recognize that a situation calls for ethical considerations, in addition to strategic, tactical, or factual considerations. In deciding how vacation leave is being allocated in an organization, for example, a manager recognizes that assigning the days near major holidays may harm or help individual workers; so an ethics frame of reference needs to be

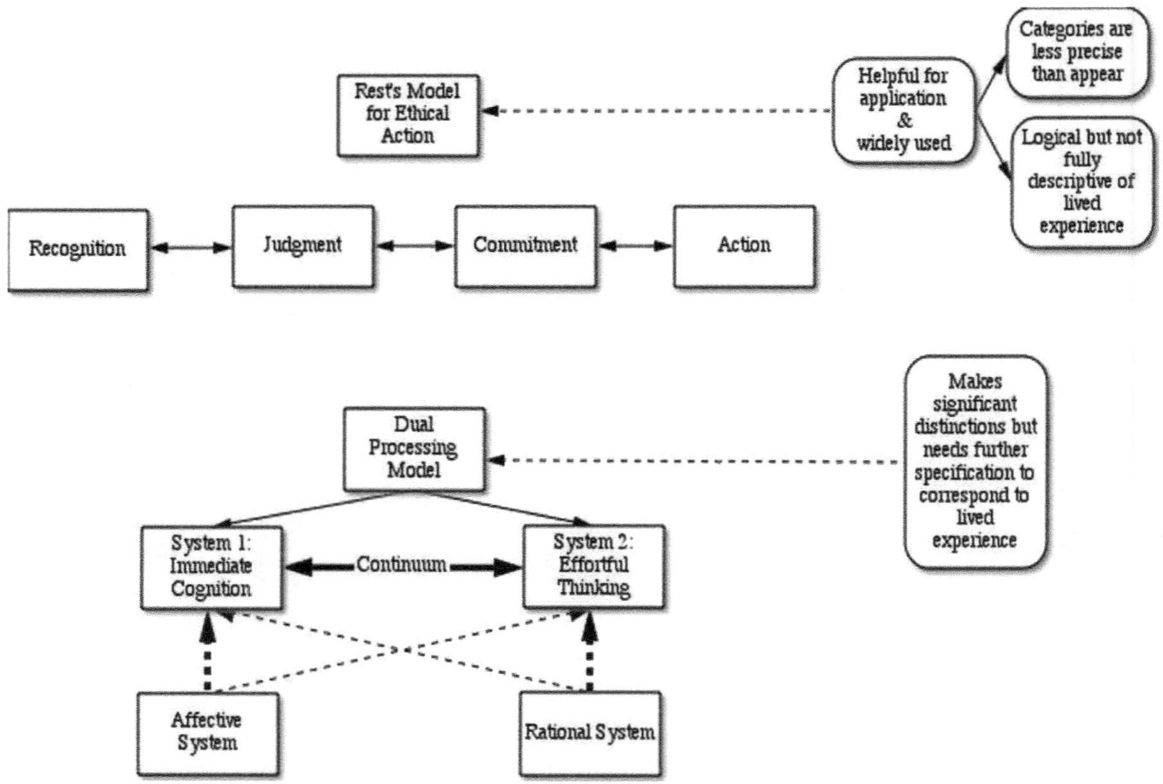


Figure 9.1. Two current models of ethical action.

applied. (2) The person makes a judgment regarding what is fair in the situation. She decides that requests for leave will be prioritized by seniority. (3) The person makes a commitment to act in an ethical or fair way, either by force of habit or character, or by deliberation that involves reference to how to live one's life. Even though the manager may face some opposition from recent hires, she is committed to assigning leave in the most ethical way she can. (4) The person makes a choice to act, a choice expressed in her behavior of sending out a memo to all employees explaining how leave will be determined.

Rest (1986) states that these processes are "logically" required: "Logically we would claim that the person must have performed at least four basic psychological processes." We take him to mean that these processes are required by what we mean by an ethical action. The first and third steps (see Figure 9.1) are required because of a general agreement that ethical behavior has to be intentional—that a person is aware that ethical considerations are called for in the situation and intends to act ethically. An involuntary action (such as randomly picking the least senior worker to be laid off) or one that produced an unintended ethical outcome (giving the largest bonus to the most productive worker in order to encourage her to agree to sexual advances) would not be characterized as acting justly because the actor did not intend to be just.

It is important to recognize that Rest (1986) regarded his four categories as "still somewhat tentative." Disagreement among researchers over the meaning of the categories in his model (De Cremer, Mayer, & Schminke, 2010) shows that part of the process of building an effective model is to find categories or concepts which best describe what does (or what should) happen when a person acts ethically. The criterion for truth is to find concepts and terminology that distinguish the various processes from each other and to show the relationships between them that account for the empirical data. Our interest in applied ethics prompts us to add a "Berkowitz rule" (Lapsley & Hill, 2008 p. 325), that the concepts and terminology of the model can be used comfortably in business and professional settings to help individuals be more ethically effective and can be used to develop training materials and approaches for organizational ethics programs.

In addition to the insights they provide, Rest's categories provide a Rorschach pattern open to varying interpretations. Rest (1986), for example, includes three elements in his definition of the first process, moral awareness: "identifying what we can in a particular situation, figuring out what the consequences to all parties would be for each line of action, and identifying and trying to understand our own gut feelings on the matter" (Rest, 1986). "Identifying what we can" is not very specific, though in the context of discussing ethics we can take it to mean that a person recognizes features in the situation that make ethical considerations appropriate or even required (see Reynolds, 2006).

As we will discuss in a following section, researchers using the Rest (1986) categories differ on whether to use a wider or narrower view of what constitutes awareness (Butterfield, Trevino, & Weaver 2000; De Cremer, Mayer, & Schminke, 2010; Tenbrunsel & Smith-Crowe, 2008). Rest (1986) on the other hand seems to be widening the concept of ethical awareness by the next two phrases in his definition. Figuring out consequences to all parties for each possible action suggests a more careful and exhaustive analysis of the situation that would come from conscious reflection, particularly in complex circumstances (such as considering whether it is an ethical public policy to outlaw the use of leaf blowers in the Los Angeles basin in order to reduce air pollution or an analysis of the most fair distribution of firm's year end profits among its various stakeholder groups). A person would likely have to be fully aware of being in an ethical situation before undertaking a complex analysis and may do so to justify his/her already arrived at ethical judgment, or to arrive at an ethical judgment through directed reasoning, as Haidt (2007, 2008a, 2008b) suggests. Researchers as different as Haidt (2007, 2008a, 2008b) and Narvaez (2008a) contend that most ethical judgments are immediate, preconscious, and intuitive perceptions of patterns like injustice or security. Evolution, nurturing, experience, and society emotively code these intuitions. So awareness can be awareness of particular patterns that repel or attract. Identifying and understanding our gut feelings might also be included as part of rational reflection that occurs in a different part of the process. What may be needed, as we will suggest, is a model that can distinguish "how the process is being done" from categories that point to "what is being done."

Given these variations in the way Rest's (1986) model can and has been interpreted, and the recent research in moral psychology, and in neuroscience using fMRI imaging, brain stimulation, and other techniques, a number of researchers have adopted a different conceptual model to explain the processes involved in ethical action. We will examine this dual processing model (Figure 9.1) to see what it has to offer before moving on to our own experience-focused model.

## Dual Processing Models as a Way of Guiding Research

Rest's model grew out of the cognitive-developmental tradition of Kohlberg's (1984) stages of moral development, which focuses on rational processes that lead to ethical action (Reynolds, 2006). With the introduction of fMRI imaging as a tool for research in ethics (Damasio, 1994), researchers recognized that ethical judgments and behavior are greatly influenced by emotion (Haidt, 2001). This research began providing evidence that automatic and unconscious processes determine much if not most of our ethical behavior (Barg & Chartrand, 1999). Neuroscientists and moral psychologists left their emphasis on reasoning and began to study the role of cognitive processes that are not consciously directed. Researchers inspired by the "affective revolution" of the 1980's (Haidt, 2007) proposed a "dual process" model that distinguishes cognitive processes that are intuitive from those that are consciously directed. They used this model to describe findings in neuroscience (Nicholson, 2006), moral psychology (Lapsley & Hill, 2008; Narvaez, 2008a), and behavioral research (Salvador & Folger, 2009). Though differing in detail, the dual process model generally recognizes two cognitive processes. System One, often termed System X for the x in reflexive, is an intuitive process that is immediate, preconscious, and emotively charged. It occurs in milliseconds before a person is even aware of its operation. System Two, termed System C for the c in reflective, is constituted by rational processes that a person is aware of, that occur over a period of time, require effort, and are accompanied by the experience that the individual is directing the process.

Understanding how these two systems operate requires another, but not equivalent, distinction between emotive and reasoning processes (see Figure 9.1). Emotive processes are valenced—that is include attraction or repulsion and other more nuanced feelings such as anger, love, and jealousy (Haidt, 2007). Reasoning involves considering sensory data, facts, ideas about facts, and ideas about the connections among ideas, and drawing inferences from these considerations (Dulebon et al., 2009; Moll et al., 2008). These emotive and reasoning processes work together in a coordinated fashion (Moll, De Oliveira-Souza, & Zahn, 2008). Reasoning even in its most abstract forms involves emotion, such as the feeling of certainty or of oddness (Burton, 2008), and emotions involve thought content which triggers the emotion and toward which the emotion is directed.

The strength of the dual process models lies in their connection to empirical research on how cognitive processes work and in their introduction of intuition and emotion into the discussion of how ethical action can be understood. A danger of emphasizing "Dual" or two processes, however, is that researchers and those who attempt to utilize their findings to affect practice in business and professional settings could overlook the richness of the phenomena that are involved in producing an individual's ethical action. This richness needs to be included in a compreshensive explanation of ethical action. Lapsley and Hill (2008), for example, point out that automaticity occurs in at least three different ways—preconscious intuition, expert performance, and postconscious priming. Narvaez (2008b), in another example, suggests that Haidt and Bjorklund's (2008a) discussion of their dual processing model does not include all the phenomena involved in ethical action but only focuses on ethical judgment. Haidt and Bjorklund (2008b) respond that she is correct. In pointing out the boundaries of their account, Narvaez (2008b) provides a list of additional elements involved in deciding[2] to act ethically: assessing gut feelings but also considering principles; weighing my goals/needs and the goals/needs of others; encouraging myself to be patient, loving, and nonjudgmental; keeping track of reactions and outcomes for myself and others; and consciously letting go of conflicting (sometimes moral) goals. Sonenshein (2007) posits three processes that are accomplished by the two modes of cognitive processing, offering a three-process model that begins ethical action with issue construction, a process of sensemaking (Weick, 1995). Sense making may need to be added to the list of ethical phenomena to be accounted for.

Reynolds' (2006) neurocognitive model of ethical decision-making provides an example of the reductionist tendency that the dual processing approach may encourage. He argues that Rest's category of recognition can be reduced to an operation of the neural processing of System X (or System 1) at "the critical midpoint of the neurocognitive model where the reflexive pattern matching cycle concedes that the issue is an ethical issue and must be analyzed." He thereby seems to omit the possibility that recognition can also result from rationally scanning the situation based on consciously chosen criteria for what qualifies as an ethical issue or from discussion with others. Klein (1998) shows rational scanning to be characteristic of novices in contrast to experts who accomplish this step immediately and automatically. Reynolds (2006) also combines Rest's categories of establishing ethical intent and acting ethically because in his analysis committing to being ethical and acting ethically are accomplished by the same reflexive process of search and structure.

While eliminating categories that may, in our view, help an individual agent understand his/her experiences, Reynolds points to additional processes not recognized in Rest's model or other dual processing models: seeking; rationally adjusting the strictness of fit for System X pattern matching; and retrospection; as well as a distinction between mental processes and mental structures. These additional categories could be needed to give a complete picture of ethical action and spur further behavioral research.

While wanting to utilize the important contributions of the last 20 years of research into *how* cognitive processes produce ethical actions, we think it is valuable to also have an experience-focused model that emphasizes *what* ethical agents experience so that they can understand and more effectively direct or influence these processes (Lapsley & Hill, 2008). We accept the criticism that Rest's (1986) model emphasizes only the rational and deliberative while ignoring the intuitive and emotive elements (Reynolds, 2006), and want to maintain the dual process distinctions. We also see value in expanding and further specifying the categories provided by these models.

## AN EXPERIENCED-FOCUSED MODEL FOR ETHICAL ACTION

We propose an experience-focused framework (see Figure 9.2) in order to map the relationships among ethical processes that individuals can recognize based on lived experiences. Using Reynolds (2006) distinction, Figure 9.2 shows the processes that indicate *what* happens when an individual acts ethically rather than *how* it happens. Figure 9.3 adds some of the specific research findings that prompt us to distinguish lived experience into the categories of the model and that offer complementary or conflicting explanations of *how* these experiences happen.

To maintain a connection to the body of work based on Rest's (1986) categories, however varied their interpretations may have been, we have tried to stick with his terminology for the first layer of our model. These distinctions continue to be in use (Salvador & Folger, 2009; De Cremer, Mayer, & Schminke, 2010) and have experimental backing in ethical education research (Narvaez, 2006) as "four psychologically distinct processes that underlie moral functioning" (Lapsley & Hill, 2008, p. 326). The terminology used in the model for the expanded categories comes primarily from distinctions made in the empirical research described below.

Individuals working in business and professional settings and those designing organizational training programs will be aided by labels shown in italics in the figure that are more useable in organizational settings. We hope these labels will be "sticky" enough (Heath & Heath, 2007) to be remembered as part of the ordinary language of ethics in the way that the "Smell Test" and "Golden Rule" are. These "applied level" categories are stated in imperative rather than declarative voice to make clear the normative assumption underlying the model—that one of its aim is to help people be more effectively ethical by providing a theoretical tool for understanding the ethical domain (Narvaez & Lapsley, 2005, p. 326).

The selection of research summarized in the explanation of the concepts is broad enough to specify some of the explanations for how these processes take place but not meant to exclude others who have made important contributions as well. Nor is the purpose of this chapter to pick the correct account when their explanations differ. Accounts were selected

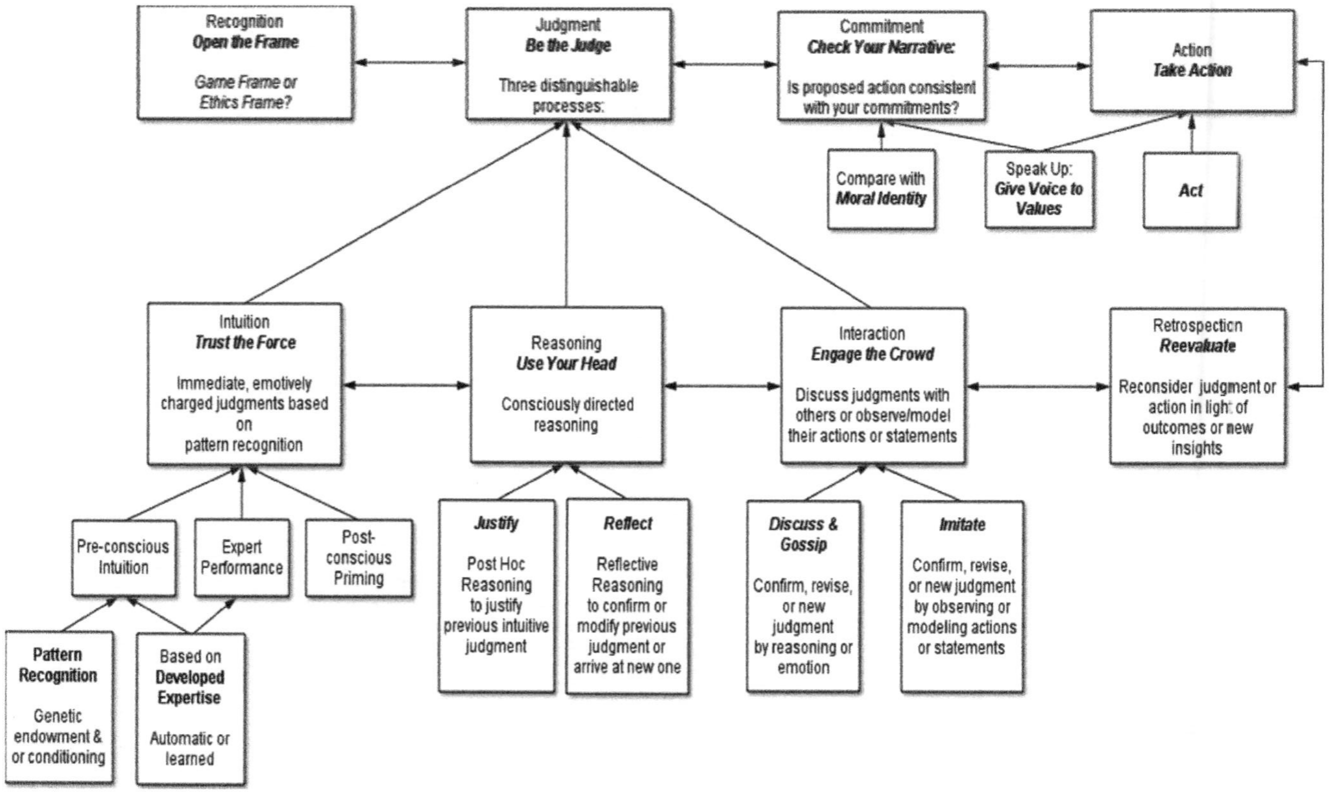


Figure 9.2. The experience-focused model.

for their robust and comprehensive coverage of what is involved in acting ethically and their level of recognition by others working in the field. We invite others to add or alter the categories in the model based on other research findings.

As was true for Rest's (1986) model, the experience-focused model is not a temporal sequence of four steps that individuals consciously experience every time they act ethically. Even though all four processes are logically required to perform an ethical action, in many, if not most instances, a person does not experience them as distinct steps that build on each other. Some or all of the steps may be distinguishable in a particular situation or some may be combined or compressed. A person witnessing a supervisor taking advantage of his power to sexually harass a subordinate may move from an immediate emotively-charged intuitive judgment that this conduct is unethical to the action of placing a call to the firm's action line to report the incident without being conscious of recognizing that the situation is an ethical one or confirming his commitment to act ethically. Klein's research (1998) on experienced decision makers acting under pressure in difficult circumstances confirms that action processes do not have to be and often are not the product of consciously thinking through each of the steps. Other research on moral expertise (Reynolds, 2006; Narvaez, 2005, 2006, 2008b; Narvaez & Lapsley, 2005) suggests that where a person falls along the moral learning continuum from novice to expert will greatly influence his/her experience of acting ethically. We will explain each of the steps separately and briefly describe the research that provides evidence for *how* each of these steps occurs. The research is represented in Figure 9.3 with text and arrows indicating the processes that are being explained.

## Process I: Recognition (Open the Frame)

The recognition process, labeled in the experience-focused model as "Open the Frame," is based on the understanding that the ethics frame should be opened when someone's interests will be affected or ethical principles will be upheld or violated. Without this perception at whatever level of consciousness that ethics considerations are required, individuals will not bring their ethical faculties to bear to arrive at an appropriate action. Reflecting our concern that the model be useful in business and professional settings, we suggest that individuals can introduce ethics into a business and professional discussion by asking, "Should we open the ethics frame here?" or "Are we using Game Frame or Ethics Frame to resolve this issue?" The "game frame" terminology comes from the belief that business and professional life is a zero sum game like poker or base-

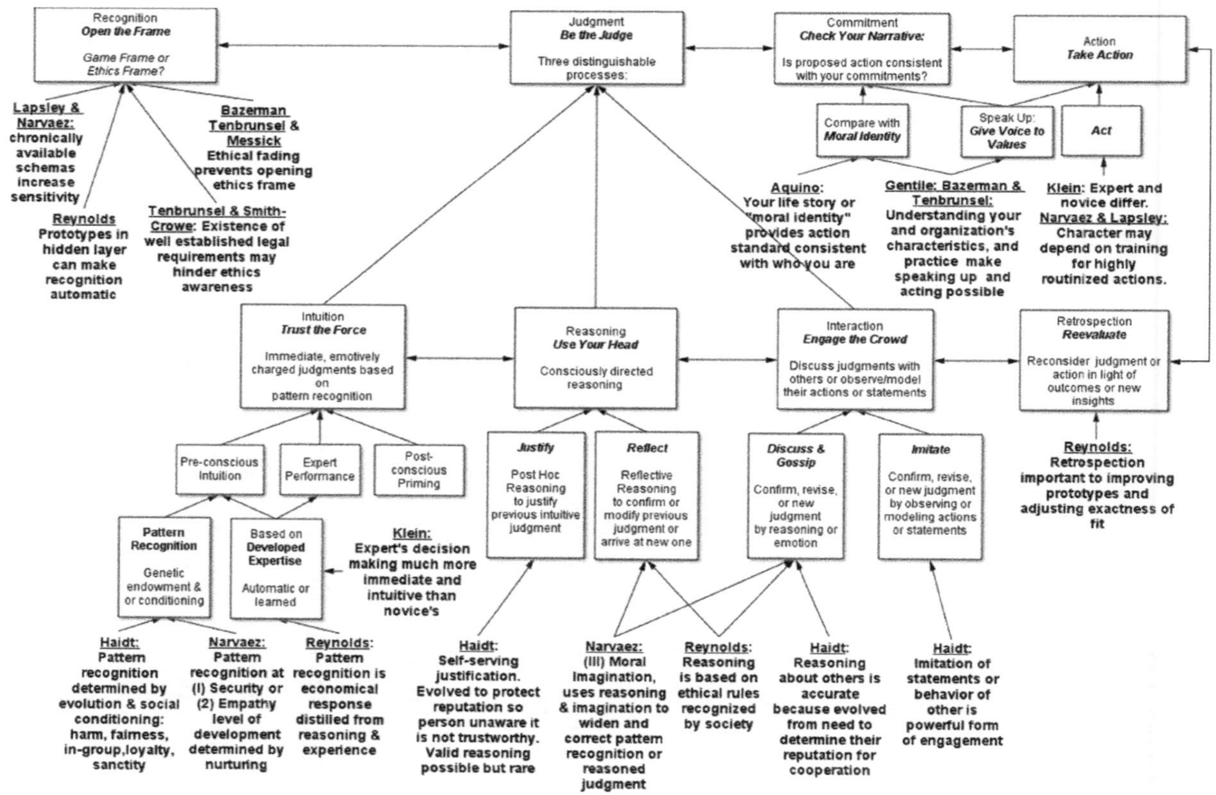


Figure 9.3. Research findings organized using the experience-focused model

ball in which winning is what matters and not what you do to win (Bazerman & Tenbrunsel, 2011). Tenbrunsel and colleagues (Tenbrunsel & Smith-Crowe, 2008; Bazerman & Tenbrunsel, 2011; Tenbrunsel & Messick, 2004) have done research on what prompts the opening of this frame. They explain how "ethical fading" and other human tendencies toward "bounded ethicality" inhibit individuals from being aware of ethical issues at the time they act even though their conscious intentions and predictions about their behavior were that they would act ethically. The existence of a well-established regime of legal requirements for a particular kind of action, for example, can blind a person to the presence of ethical issues (Tenbrunsel & Smith-Crowe, 2008). Lapsley and Narvaez (2004; Lapsley & Hill, 2008) employ the concept of schemas, which are personality-variable general-knowledge structures that when chronically accessible and primed by developmental experiences make individuals and societies more sensitive to perceiving situations as ethical.

There is definite variation among researchers with regard to what triggers awareness that ethical issues are at stake in a situation and that ethical consideration and action is appropriate. Haidt (2007, 2008a, 2008b), for example, locates recognition in the immediate emotively charged intuition of ethically significant patterns. These intuitions provide both recognition of an ethics situation and an immediate judgment regarding what is right or wrong in the situation. Reynolds (2006) locates recognition in the neurocognitive process of neuron firing that automatically matches stimuli to ethical prototypes built up through experience and refined by reasoning.

Differences also appear in setting research parameters for what will be considered an ethical situation. Butterfield, Trevino, and Weaver (2000) set two features for recognition—that how the person acts will affect the "interests, welfare, or expectations" of that person or of others; and/or that the action will conflict with ethical standards. De Cremer, Mayer, and Schminke (2010) agree with Tenbrunsel and Smith-Crowe (2008) in narrowing the reason for being aware to the recognition that actions in the situation will affect other's interests and welfare negatively. While worthwhile as a way to specify the focus of particular research, this restriction of an ethics situation to harming others would leave out both Butterfield et al.'s (2000) inclusion of the self as having ethical interests and the wider description of "interests, welfare, or expectations" and "conflict with one or more ethical standards" as triggering that awareness. It also leaves out possible ethical situations in which a person could increase his/her own or others welfare. Some like Appiah (2008) designate this wider view of ethical situations by the term "ethical" and the more limited concept of actions or situations that involve harm to others' interests as designated by the term "moral."

## Process II: Judgment (Be the Judge)

The experience focused model expands the judgment process based on research by Haidt (2007, 2008a, 2008b), Reynolds (2006), Narvaez (2008a), and others to include three distinguishable means of arriving at an ethical judgment that an action or situation is right or wrong. The experience of making a judgment by intuition, reasoning, and interacting with others can be clearly distinguished by an individual agent and further subdivided as the model shows. The model does not claim they are as distinct in kind as some of the dual processing theories (Reynolds, 2006 for example) suggest. We are influenced by research showing them to be interrelated and to have elements, like emotion and reason (Burton, 2008) that ordinarily occur together.

### *Intuition (Trust the Force)*

The first kind of judgment, "Trust the Force," is an immediate, preconscious, affectively charged intuition of the rightness or wrongness of something. Burton (2008; Reynolds, 2006) uses the "hidden layer" metaphor from the study of artificial intelligence (see Figure 9.4) to explain that all sensory perceptions and most judgments that humans make result from neural processing that goes on outside of our conscious awareness. The brain takes external inputs from the senses, memories, and conscious thoughts and selects those significant enough to be brought into awareness in a form that reveals both the content and its significance. The hidden layer where the processing goes on is a combination of biological influences such as our genetic predispositions to variations and changes in our neurotransmitters and the total of all our experiences whether remembered or forgotten. Burton explains that the processing of judgments in the hidden layer cannot be understood because of the thousands of neural connections that "vote" to decide what will emerge into consciousness. Ethical judgments are also made largely in this hidden layer and are therefore unavailable for direct conscious inspection.

Accounts of people who have brain injuries or abnormalities, direct brain stimulation during surgery, fMRI imaging studies, and a growing body of behavioral research have provided the basis for theories about how these preconscious processes in the hidden layer work. Ethics researchers seek to determine how these processes produce ethical judgments—what is the content that determines what these judgments are. They are also seeking to determine what their ethical status is—how valid these immediate ethical judgments are. Burton (2008) seems to be arguing that a person's ethical judgment about what is just in a situation arising in an organizational setting is carried out in the hidden layer of the brain and rises to consciousness only after the processing has occurred.

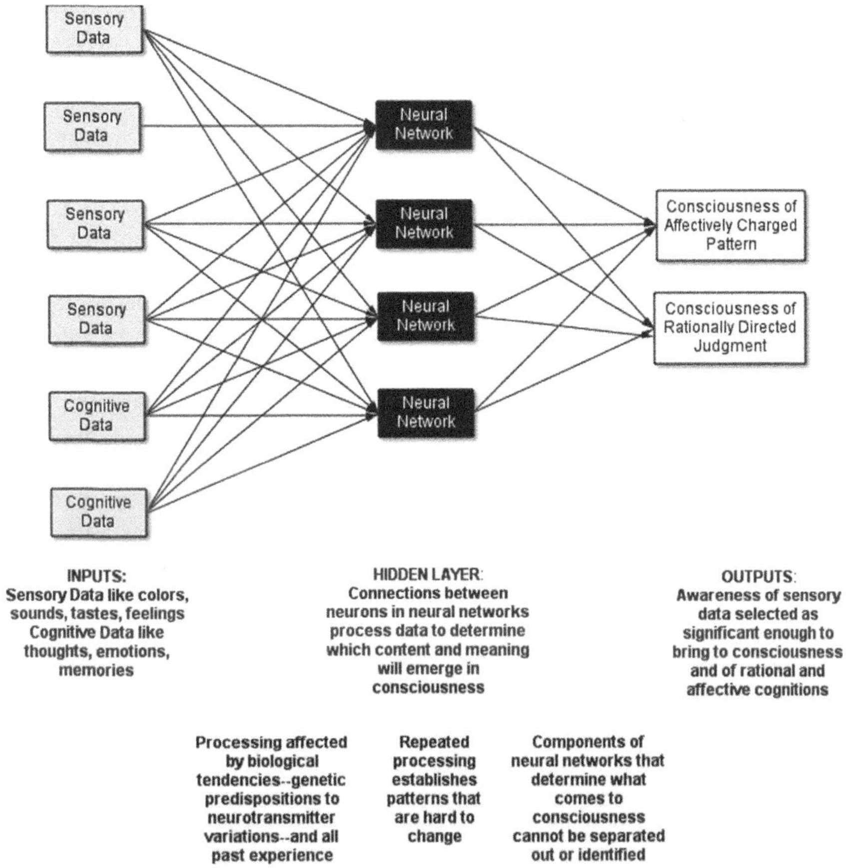


Figure 9.4. Hidden layer processing of ethical judgments.

He contends that the components of the "essentially infinite connections" that carry out this neural processing to determine what is significant enough to emerge into consciousness cannot be separated out or identified after the judgment has been made.

Contrary to Burton's (2008) contention that the hidden layer processing of judgments cannot be understood, other researchers have developed explanations of what determines the content of these immediate, preconscious, emotively charged ethical intuitions. Haidt and colleagues (Haidt, 2001 & 2007 and Haidt & Bjorklund, 2008a, & 2008b), suggest that almost all ethical judgments are arrived at by preconscious recognition of five patterns in the facts of a situation—harm, fairness, ingroup/outgroup, authority/respect, and purity/sanctity. According to his Social Intuitionist theory, these patterns correspond to traits that allow groups and individuals to compete successfully for scarce resources and to share resources and responsibilities with those outside their immediate kin group. The traits evolved over thousands of years of primate and human development and for that reason should be trusted as guides for what is right or wrong. These traits become part of human genetic inheritance through the advantage they give to individuals with characteristics most adaptable to the traits. Individuals not only perceive the patterns of harm or injustice but also have the strong affective reaction attached to these patterns that these are to be avoided or are disgusting. Societies further specify the ways its members interpret these patterns by teaching and enforcing rules, traditions, and the emotive reactions that make culture such a potent force in shaping behavior. Such immediate and preconscious intuitions have the advantage of being much faster than consciously directed thought.

In a different though not necessarily contradictory approach, Reynolds (2006; Lapsley & Hill, 2008) points to the ability of the human brain to compress the lessons learned through previous experience into immediate, preconscious intuitions for managing one's life. In Reynolds' description of the neurocognitive System X intuitive process, neurons in the brain organize stimuli into unique patterns based on sensory and cognitive inputs and attempt to match the pattern to existing base patterns formulated by previous experience, reflection, and retrospection. This is the process Burton (2008) describes as the "hidden layer" (see Figure 9.4). These multidimensional prototypes stored in System X can contain context information necessary for action and be linked to emotional sensations. This "expertise development" approach suggests that important tasks like ethical judgments are advantageously reduced to heuristics and immediate intuitions because they are more economical in time and energy. Judgments are exported to reasoning from intuition only when the System X processing fails to produce a suitable match with existing prototypes.

Narvaez (2008a, 2008b, 2009) advances a moral development approach in which the level of moral development an individual or a society has attained influences the patterns perceived by means of intuitive judgments. The nurturing one has received or missed (or that is common or lacking in a society), and the experiences one has, determine whether intuitive ethical judgments focus at development Level 1 on security concerns or at Level 2 on engagement with others. The patterns perceived at each level are affectively coded as attractive or repulsive. Individuals whose brains have not been developed by the proper nurturing can never feel secure enough to move beyond the first level. The patterns they intuit will be those related to security, authority, patriotism, and so on. It is not a question of skills they lack but of lack of development in the brain structures necessary for higher-level ethical perceptions. Those who have received sufficient nurturing to feel secure and the external discipline to learn the self-control to act consistently will develop the brain modules required to read others' needs. This empathy is an emotive capacity essential to Level 2 ethical processing of how to treat others. Nurturing and experience can also activate the Level 3 use of moral imagination to reflect on and evaluate the patterns central to the two previous levels and create new patterns of ethical behavior. Most ethical judgments involving engagement with others, however, are based on the intuitively processed emotion of empathy rather than rational thinking (Narvaez, 2008a).

### *Reasoning (Use Your Head)*

Consciously directed reasoning is the second form of ethical judgment. Haidt's (2007; Haidt & Bjorklund, 2008a, 2008b) account of the immediate, emotively charged recognition of five basic patterns conditioned by society, Reynolds' (2006) condensed experience explanation, and Narvaez' (2008a) developmental levels keyed to security or empathy, all explain *how* the contents of immediate intuitive ethical judgments originate. None of their explanations suggest, however, that the hidden layer of consciousness is responsible for all of a person's ethical judgments. Ethical judgments are also made through conscious reflection: either quickly fabricated justifications for judgments already arrived at, or consciously directed reasoning about what is right or wrong. This reasoning to judgment can either confirm or revise prior intuitive judgments or arrive at new judgments. In fact, given our general belief that ethics is guided by reasoning (Lapsley & Hill, 2008), much of our education and training is aimed to teach individuals how to reason to ethical judgments through the application of ethical principles, core values, or organizational codes and rules. "Use your head" is the message being inculcated.

Burton (2008) suggests that even consciously directed reasoning involves making significant connections among ideas at the hidden level. The feeling of certainty that accompanies rationally arrived at conclusions is a reward and motivation mechanism provided by the hidden level to insure progress in an individual's and a society's thinking. Since it is produced in the hidden level, certainty is often attached to false or inappropriate judgments, making rational judgments suspect.

Haidt advances the same skepticism about the ability of an individual to reason to ethical judgments about him/herself, offering both evolutionary and experimental evidence for this shortcoming. He maintains that without philosophical training and practice, most individuals are incapable of accurately judging the morality of their own actions. Given the importance of promoting a reputation for cooperating with non-kin group others to insure their cooperation, reasoning about my own reputation evolved into putting the best spin on why I did something rather than giving an accurate characterization of my actual motives. Thus the human brain developed the ability to fabricate reasons to justify an intuitive judgment that have nothing to do with why the judgment was made. Since it is difficult to be convincing if I am aware that my explanations are not truthful, evolutionary pressure selected for individuals who could offer convincing "post hoc confabulations" when justifying their own actions without being aware that they are fabricating these justifications (Haidt, 2001, Haidt & Bjorklund, 2008a, 2008b).

Haidt (2001; Haidt & Bjorklund, 2008a, 2008b) recognizes the possibility of using consciously directed reasoning to arrive at an ethical judgment about a situation without first making a judgment based on immediately intuitive pattern recognition but claims that reasoning to ethical judgments seldom occurs and is limited to instances when intuition is weak and the individual's ability to reason is high. He also describes a path to judgment in which a person sees the situation from another person's perspective and thereby generates a new intuition to overcome one previously made but this "private reflection" involves unconscious affective connections interacting with consciously directed reasoning (Haidt & Bjorklund, 2008a, 2008b).

Reynolds (2006) also points to the use of reasoning, his System C, as rationalization in which conscious reasoning attempts to justify a judgment previously made in the hidden layer but challenged by the dissatisfaction with the judgment on the individual's part or by another person's opinion. When the intuitive pattern matching does not provide a match, the rational system is called upon to make an ethical judgment. Both rationalization and active judgment apply "tried and tested rules of moral philosophy" that come from society to the facts of the situation. After rationalizing or arriving at a new judgment, the reasoning system makes adjustments to the form of the prototypes of the intuitive system, their moral evaluations, or to the implied course of action that is part of their content. Reasoning also tightens or loosens the fit required between the stimuli and the prototype for satisfactory judgments to be made in the hidden layer. The impetus for this iterative process of improving the prototypes allows more of the processing of ethical judgments to be shifted to immediate system thus freeing reason for dealing with novel events.

Narvaez (2008a) is more sanguine than Haidt (2007; Haidt & Bjorklund, 2008a, 2008b) regarding the role of reason and "moral imagination" to provide valid ethical judgments. Reason and moral imagination operate at ethical development Level 3 to correct and expand the affectively charged pattern recognition of the security and engagement levels. This ability is only available to those in whom it has been developed by appropriate nurturing and it can be strengthened by education (Narvaez & Lapsley, 2005; Reynolds' 2006). Narvaez (2008a) expands

Reynolds' (2006) view that rational judgments are based on moral rules of the society by her emphasis on the use of moral imagination to generate new understandings of facts and new ethical insights.

For Narvaez (2008a), those who remain at the security level or who, in times of crisis like terrorist attacks on one's country are driven back to the security level, are unable to activate potential capacities in the brain to connect with others through empathy or to engage in moral imagination. Strong emotions of fear and perceptions of danger, disloyalty, and lack of respect for authority will dominate their ethical reflections. Those who have developed to the engagement level similarly will be directed by strong emotions of empathy without the ability to rationally critique its appropriateness for the circumstances, unless they advance to the level of using their moral imagination and reason (Narvaez, 2008a).

### *Interaction (Engage the Crowd)*

Individuals can also make ethical judgments, and confirm or alter the ones they have already made intuitively or through rational reflection, by a third distinguishable process—interacting with others in order to engage the "wisdom of crowds." This interaction can involve discussing the situation with others or watching and imitating how they act or what they say. Haidt (2007) argues that language allowed people to gossip in order to establish the reputations of others (Dunbar, 1996). Since knowing who is likely to cooperate in the future when I may be in need is essential information in a challenging environment, the human brain evolved the capacity to make highly accurate assessments about the ethical status of others' actions. Thus while the individual's brain is designed to provide quick, specious justifications for his/her actions to burnish his/her own reputation, others can take a more realistic view of whether those actions are ethical or not. Discussing ethical judgment with others or observing what they do or say is an excellent way to insure sounder ethical judgments. Haidt (2007), however, points to the tendency for groupthink and the high cost of group discussion in time and energy as reasons to be cautious about what discussing with others indicates is right or wrong.

Narvaez' (2008a) approach suggests the importance of others as nurturers and benevolent outside authorities who can enable a person's ethical development, and has written extensively on the ways that educational institutions can promote the development of moral character (Narvaez, 2006; Narvaez & Lapsley, 2005). She maintains, however, that a lack of timely nurturing or authority figures means that a person will not be able to benefit from the urging of others to make judgments on the basis of empathy or to use moral imagination and reason to see beyond security threats and needs in a situation. She also points out that if the whole society is under threat then the wisdom of the crowd will be to return to the security perspective in making moral judgments.

Arriving at ethical judgments through discussion with others faces two other difficulties, disagreement with others and the feeling of certainty by each party that his/her ethical judgments are right. If Burton (2008), Haidt (2001 & 2007; Haidt & Bjorklund, 2008a, & 2008b), Reynolds (2006), and Narvaez (2008a) are correct that most ethical judgments are made in the hidden level, individuals have different doses of nature and nurture providing the evaluation in the hidden layer and so will arrive at different judgments some of the time. On Haidt's (2007) view, ethical disagreement can arise because individuals perceive different patterns that trigger immediate judgment. His research (2001, 2007) shows, for example, that political liberals (in the U.S. understanding of the term) perceive harm and fairness to be the only bases for making ethical judgments whereas conservative are also prompted to ethical judgments by perceptions of group status, respect for authority, and purity/sacredness. Individuals intuiting different patterns may come to different judgments. Reynolds (2006) would suggest the uniqueness of each person's experiences that are condensed into their ethical expertise would lead to disagreements over what is right and wrong. For Narvaez (2008a), differences arise from the different levels of ethical development that individuals have attained.

The certainty that accompanies ethical judgments, especially judgments arrived at by immediate intuition (Lapsley & Hill, 2008) and by self-reflection (Haidt, 2007), makes overcoming these disagreements difficult. Haidt (2007) and Narvaez (2008a) seem to suggest that certainty comes from the strong emotions coded to specific patterns. Without strong feelings of attraction or repulsion and the sense that one is correct in feeling that way, ethical judgments would not motivate ethical action. Burton (2008) describes certainty as a "feeling" which is connected to thoughts by the evolution of a dopamine reward system in the brain to promote thought and encourage innovative ideas to deal with challenges in the environment. Since the feeling of certainty comes from a different brain system than the intuitions and thinking it is designed to reward, it is sometimes attached to judgments that are not valid or productive of good results. The fact that this process of attachment occurs in the hidden layer makes it very difficult to evaluate or correct. I do not know why I am certain so it is difficult to turn the feeling off.

## Process III: Commitment (Check Your Narrative) and Process IV: Acting on your Judgment (Take Action)

The last two categories from Rest's (1986) model are commitment and action. Rest's notion is that having made the judgment that an action is ethical or unethical, a commitment to act on the basis of one's ethical judgments is required to move an individual to action. The extensive literature on the connection and disconnect between these two categories suggests to us, in spite of Reynolds (2006) view to the contrary, that a model of the processes leading to ethical action should include them both.

Empirical studies (Bazerman & Tenbrunsel, 2011; Gentile, 2010) have shown that being aware of what is ethical and having a commitment to doing what is ethical do not always lead to ethical action. Understanding one's own personal characteristics and those of the organization and practicing techniques of speaking up that are likely to be effective given those characteristics, can empower individuals to "give voice to their values" and act on them when pressured to do something unethical (Gentile, 2010). Speaking out can be seen both as checking one's commitment and a form of acting. Understanding the blind spots regarding ethics that behavioral research has shown individuals to have (Bazerman & Tenbrunsel, 2011) and the characteristics of organizations and social institutions (Bazerman & Tenbrunsel, 2011; Hoffman & Driscoll, 1999; Wines & Hamilton, 2004) can provide individuals with strategies for acting on their commitments.

Goodstein, Aquino, and Skarlicki, in their chapter in this volume, point to an extensive literature regarding the role of a self-narrative or life story—what is termed "moral identity"—in deciding whether an action is consistent with the kind of person an individual is committed to be (Aquino & Freeman, 2009; Aquino, Freeman, Reed, Lim, & Felps, 2009; Aquino & Reed, 2002; Blasi, 1984). Having made a judgment about what it right or wrong in a situation, moral identity provides a motivation for acting on that judgment (Aquino & Freeman, 2009).

Klein's (1998) study of natural decision-making is relevant to the commitment and action processes, as well as to the recognition process, in that novices will experience these processes as distinct whereas experts will move directly to action. Lapsley and Narvaez' social cognitive account of personality (Lapsley & Hill, 2008; Lapsley & Narvaez, 2004) explains this difference in terms of the expert's chronically accessible schemas that not only increase sensitivity of perception to aspects of the situation but allow the expert to act quickly and in a manner consistent with his/her fully developed moral character. This immediate connection between commitment and action is also described as a "goal dependent automaticity" that results from learning routine action sequences and scripts for how to treat others that develop a commitment to being a certain kind of person (Lapsley & Hill, 2008). Thus where an individual is along the expert to novice continuum and what kind of upbringing and education he/she has had will be significant to how he/she experiences these two processes.

### One Additional Process: Retrospection (Reevaluate)

Taking a cue from Reynolds (2006), we have added one additional category to the experience-focused model to recognize that individuals do reevaluate their grasp of the salient features of a situation, their ethical judgments, aspects of their character and commitments.They reevaluate their actions based on outcomes, new insights, the passage of time, and experience gained. Reynolds (2006) sees this retrospection as essential to improving the prototypes in the hidden layer and the tightness or looseness of fit needed to match stimuli with a prototype. We have placed this category in line with the judgment categories to reflect Reynolds' description of it but indicate its relevance to the other categories by connecting it to the recognition-judgment-commitment-action continuum as well.

## RESEARCH IMPLICATIONS OF THE EXPERIENCE-FOCUSED MODEL

The research implications of the experience-focused model can be divided into three general research questions: the validity of the model, the validity of the research base, and the effects of its use by individuals and organizations.

### Validity of the Model

The first research realm would aim to determine if the processes described by the different categories in the first three levels of the model are indeed distinguishable and related to each other as the model suggests. Research could also determine whether the categories are different in kind as some accounts suggest or are different positions on a continuum of cognitive processing that involves automatic and consciously directed processing and emotive and rational elements. Lapsley and Hill (2008) for example, distinguish three kinds of automaticity—pre-conscious intuition, expert performance, and postconscious priming—shown on the model as categories of Intuition. Can these be shown to be different or to follow from the same cognitive functions? For another example, research could examine whether immediate justification differs from the more deliberate use of reason. Reynolds (2006) and Haidt (2007; Haidt & Bjorklund, 2008a, 2008b) both describe them as different operations and ascribe different characteristics to them. Can research show how they differ in the kind of cognitive activity involved or whether they differ only in the speed of operation that the occasion requires? Understanding more about the origins and workings of these processes should provide a better understanding of ethical processing in general and a clearer picture of how to represent these processes in the model.

## Validity of the Research Base

A second area of research would use the experience-focused model as a background to determine whether and/or which of the research-based theories provide the most accurate account how the parts of the model work. It may be possible to identify Lapsley & Narvaez' (2004) chronically available schemas in managers who are sensitive to fairness issues in contrast to those who are not. Does a well-developed regime of legal requirements and human resource procedures for distributions and interpersonal relationships desensitize managers to the ethical dimensions of these situations as Tenbrunsel & Smith-Crowe (2008) suggest? Do Haidt (2007; Haidt & Bjorklund, 2008a, 2008b) Narvaez (2008a, 2009), and/or Reynolds (2006) describe all or part of what triggers organization members' immediate intuitions of what is a fair distribution, process, or interpersonal treatment? Are Klein (1998) and Narvaez & Lapsley (2005) correct in predicting that when resolving distribution issues in a way that they and those affected perceive to be fair, novice managers will resort to reasoning and discussion with others while experienced managers will act more automatically? Can Narvaez' (2008a) ethical development stages be supported by correlations between managers' perceptions of threats to themselves and/or their organization and the level of respect they expect from employees for the authority of established distribution processes?

Efforts to validate these various research-based explanations of ethical processes can be carried out without reference to the experience-focused model. It is our contention, however, that the model can help researchers understand which process or processes leading to ethical action are involved. Research can be targeted to those processes and the implications of validated explanations can be better understood. The effect of expertise (Klein, 1998), for example, could be understood to affect recognition, judgment, commitment, and action whereas Haidt's explanation of intuitive pattern recognition (2007; Haidt & Bjorklund, 2008a, 2008b) would be related primarily to recognition and judgment, though it could have implications for the contents of an individual's moral identity and therefore affect commitment as well.

## How Use of the Model Affects Individuals and Organizations

The third area of research would evaluate the model on the basis of the "Berkowitz rule" (Lapsley and Hill, 2008) that any worthwhile model must have educational implications. If the model accurately describes what is happening in the processes that produce ethical action and can provide a more accurate understanding of how these processes work, then are individuals and organizations that understand and utilize the model able to act more ethically or act ethically more often than those who do not? Can the model provide insights for resolving disagreements over what is the ethical course of action in a workplace situation, so that people are able to act cooperatively and organizations exhibit more harmony? If for example, there is disagreement over the fairness of the distribution of vacation days contiguous to paid holidays like Christmas or New Year's, can the model provide insight into what are the causes of the disagreement over of the distribution or on how to design a procedure that will operate more fairly?

Can training be designed to apply the several steps in our model (e.g., Velasquez, 2006; Haidt, 2001, 2007; Seligman & Kahana, 2009)? Can training help to "Open the Frame?" Can training help to sharpen intuition and focus it on patterns that reflect the values of society or of an organization, so that individuals can truly "Trust the Force"? Can justice perceptions be trained? Can training improve Developed Expertise in organizational justice? Can post hoc reasoning accuracy be trained? Can training affect the "Hidden Layer" (Burton, 2008)? There is also the question of content of such training (e.g., Velasquez, 2006). Are there specific types of case studies that are relevant? Does self-reflection play a role? Would justice discussions be effective? The answers to these questions would be of enormous value to those who design organizational training programs by showing them what can and cannot be affected given the organization's resources.

Occupational expertise could also be examined to help both the practitioners understand their patterns and help those educating them see what training would be effective. Do rule-driven occupations like accounting view fairness as a set of standards directed toward accurate financial accounting? Do such procedural occupations make Opening the Frame harder to do? Do physicians focus on individual patients to the detriment of costs to the larger society? Do these types of occupations perceive different justice patterns?

If occupational values make a difference in the ways individuals in those occupations carry out the processes that lead to ethical action, we should examine employment practices in these disciplines to see if they reinforce the right dispositions. We might want to test for trainability of those practitioners in opening the frame, pattern recognition, expertise development, reasoning to judgment, and dealing with disagreement and certainty. We might also identify certain personal traits and life experiences in job candidates that have led to a preference for certain approaches to ethical judgments and for understanding the different aspects of justice (Reynolds, 2008; Lapsley & Hill, 2008).

## APPLYING THE MODEL TO ORGANIZATIONAL JUSTICE

Cropanzano, Rupp, Mohler, and Schminke (2001) propose a classification system for contemporary social science research on organizational justice. This body of research, which began with Folger and Greenberg (1985), examines the range and scope of individuals' perceptions of workplace fairness in order to explain why justice in organizations matters to them. Cropanzano et al. (2001) report that researchers agreed that individuals distinguish between *distributive* justice focused on the fairness of outcomes and *procedural* justice having to do with process by which allocations are made. Some researchers embrace a widely held three-type model that distinguishes distributive and procedural justice and adds *interactional* justice, which involves the individual's appraisal of the fairness of the interpersonal treatment received from others. Though some have come to see this third factor as a social feature of procedural justice rather than as a separate element, others have further divided interactional justice into *informational* justice relating to the fairness of the information about the allocation, and *interpersonal* justice reflecting the respect and dignity with which the parties are treated.

Cropanzano et al. (2001) maintain that regardless of whether a two, three, or four part model is preferred, organizational justice research can be understood as following one of three paths corresponding to Kelman's (1958) insight into the processes by which people adjust their attitudes and behavior in social situations: compliance with the wishes of others because they control rewards and punishments; identification with others because of a desire to be affiliated with their group; and internalization of beliefs and values that guide actions and facilitate cooperation with others who share them. Though there is diversity within these categories, the models in the each category share basic assumptions about human nature: *instrumental* models focus on the driving motivational need of gains/losses, *interpersonal* models see relationships as the driving motivational need, and *values* models view moral obligations as providing the motivation.

While recognizing the explanatory value of their account, we would like to follow them in telling the tale "in a way that has not been done previously, for different tellings furnish different insights" (Cropanzano et al., 2001 p. 2). We offer the experience-focused model as a framework for understanding research on organizational justice, and for generating research hypotheses and understanding their results. Our purpose is not to review the organizational justice literature but to suggest how it could be connected to recent work on ethics in cognitive neuroscience and moral psychology that offers insights into the way individuals are motivated to behave ethically.

The experience-focused model was developed to have broader application in understanding how ethical actions are generated and has been used to show how to deal with ethical disagreement and understand the role of certainty in ethical judgments (Hamilton, 2010, 2011). We think the model has relevance for research on organizational justice as well. Mapping the Cropanzano et al. (2001) general categories of research on organizational justice on to our model, for example, will connect them with recent theories on ethical motivation. Our claim is not that the complex motivational factors highlighted by various organizational justice models can be reduced to the ethical action processes included in the experience-focused model. The model does, however, distinguish these processes from one another and connects them with research findings and explanations that can provide new points of view for understanding these motivational factors. The categories of the model describe a number of processes by which individuals can arrive at judgments regarding what is just. Behavioral research could provide evidence that people do or do not in fact use those processes in arriving at judgments regarding justice. Researchers could confirm or alter the descriptions of these processes and establish the accuracy of the previous research that seeks to explain how these processes work. The model's categories can also be used by individuals to guide their own validation of a particular judgment by using them to determining whether that judgment measures up to the standards adopted by them, their organization, or their society (Appiah, 2008).

As we stated at the outset of the chapter, our experience-focused model requires a different understanding of ethics that does not limit it to moral obligations and internalized moral principles as described in the Cropanzano et al. model (2001). Ethics is a set of values, rules, principles, obligations and concerns that allow individuals to live in complicated societies and pursue their individual and common purposes while respecting the purposes of others (Appiah, 2008; Haidt, 2007; Tenbrunsel & Smith Crowe, 2008). This view of ethics is broad enough to include economic and quasi-economic advantage, interpersonal relationships, and internalized values and principles as part of what guides appropriate actions within societies. Adopting this wider view of ethics allows individuals to recognize ethical dimensions in judgments regarding organizational justice that originate in concerns to maximize gains and minimize losses (compliance) and to pursue close interpersonal relationships (identification) as well as those identified by Cropanzano et al. (2001) as ethical because they are based on the acceptance of important values (internalization). We will consider the application of the model to each of these categories.

The first category for organizational justice claims includes those based on the driving motivational need for quasi-economic advantage. Individuals who are motivated by compliance concerns care about the fairness of an outcome, process, or interpersonal treatment because fairness is a means to an end, which is often personal gain. An explanation for why an individual would consider any or all of the four categories of justice (Cropanzano et al., 2001) to involve only the concern for how he/she is affected and not any concern for how others are affected can be understood by examining several of the processes in the experience-focused model that lead to ethical action.

One such explanation involves the recognition of whether the situation involving justice involves ethical issues or not. If it is the case that others will be negatively affected by a distribution, process, public account, or interpersonal treatment that a person judges to be just because it benefits him/her, this exclusive focus on self or on others only as a benefit to self could be the result of a failure to open the ethics frame. Opening the ethics frame in the recognition process is defined in part as being aware that the interests of others in the situation should be considered along with one's own interests. This failure to consider others could be attributed to various framing effects (Tenbrunsel & Smith-Crowe, 2008), or ethical fading (Bazerman & Tenbrunsel, 2011) or to the presence of a well-established legal regime (Tenbrunsel & Smith-Crowe, 2008). It could also be because the individual lacks chronically available schemas (Lapsley & Narvaez, 2004) or System X prototypes (Reynolds, 2006) that include concern for others as well as self. Klein's (1998; Narvaez, 2006) research suggests that the individual may be a novice who has not yet learned how to be an ethical person.

With regard to the experience-focused model's judgment process, the failure to consider the interests of others could be attributed to several factors. At the level of Intuition, Haidt (2007; Haidt & Bjorklund, 2008a, 2008b) could explain the exclusion of others' interests based on the emotively charged pattern that the person perceives in the situation. It could be that the individual is seeing harm to self and not seeing harm to others or is perceiving a pattern of gain or harm to one's ingroup that does not include the other because he/she is an outgroup member not entitled to the same consideration. Other patterns could be involved as well. Narvaez' (2008a) analysis of intuitive judgments suggests that the individual may be operating at the Level 1 Ethic of Security at which the protection of self and ingroup members is seen as the primary concern of ethics. An exclusively self-interested person may not have attained the inner control and perceptive ability to feel empathy for the injured other (Narvaez, 2008a).

Thus in the intuition process the individual's judgment that fairness is exclusively self-centered can be *described* in terms of patterns perceived or the level of ethical development reached. Other individuals could *evaluate* this exclusively self-interested judgment to be unethical based on different patterns perceived or a wider view of the same patterns. A behavioral science researcher would not make such a claim that one pattern is ethical while another is unethical. He/she could undertake to show, however, that a pattern or a particular way of understanding a pattern does not serve the ethical functions of promoting harmony and safety for the individual and his/her society. There is a growing body of research based literature that aims to help individuals and societies improve by understanding the physical, emotional, and rational elements of human cognition (e.g. Bazerman & Tenbrunsel, 2011; Burton, 2008; Gentile, 2010; Greene, 2011). Greene (2003) suggests, for example, that human morality needs to mature to match new conditions and that Haidt's patterns may have served well in a time of contending societies armed with rocks or swords but not when nuclear weapons can destroy the planet.

The experience-focused model describes Reasoning as another process for arriving at ethical judgments. If the self-interested person engages in Justifying (see Figure 9.3) a previous judgment or action (Haidt, 2007; Haidt & Bjorklund, 2008a, 2008b; Reynolds, 2006) he/she would not be expected to offer self-interest as an explanation for the action unless the society valued self-interest (Reynolds, 2006). If that individual engages in Reflection, the way Haidt says philosophers are trained to do (Haidt, 2007; Haidt & Bjorklund, 2008a, 2008b), then he/she would consider ethical principles that indicate what was just or unjust. Behavioral researchers could determine whether and on the basis of which principles people do reason about justice when engaged in either justification or reflection (e.g. Cropanzano et al., 2001) and thereby advance the understanding of ethical reasoning.

The failure to consider others when reflecting would on Narvaez' view (2008a) be understood as a failure to exercise moral imagination to widen and correct the pattern recognition or reasoned judgment that the other should not be considered. On Reynolds' (2006) view, it could be a failure to correct prototypes or recognize the significance of others' needs based on the accepted ethical rules of the society, unless that society promotes exclusive self-interest to maximize happiness, based on reading Ayn Rand (1957).

At the interaction level of judgment, Haidt (2007; Haidt & Bjorklund, 2008a, 2008b) would suggest the totally self-interested judgment might have resulted from a failure to engage others to see what their judgments are or to imitate them. Haidt (2007; Haidt & Bjorklund, 2008a, 2008b) could also suggest that the group consulted had fallen prey to group limitations.

If the individual has acted or made a judgment exclusively from self-interest in a situation involving justice, then what is known about the commitment process in the experience-focused model may provide a basis for research to determine why he/she considered that outcome or process to be fair. The notion of moral identity (Aquino & Reed, 2002; Aquino & Freeman, 2009; Aquino, Freeman, Reed, Lim, & Felps, 2009; Blasi, 1984) may suggest that the individual's narrative included a strong element of self-interest. Narvaez and Lapsley's (2005) description of how character is formed raises the question of whether the individual was trained to be self-interested.

With regard to the model's action process, Aquino and Freeman (2009) find that moral identity provides motivation for acting on a judgment of right or wrong. Research could determine whether this is true for individuals making self-interested judgments regarding justice. Gentile's (2010) and Bazerman and Tenbrunsel's (2011) research could be mined for instances when and explanations of why self-interested individuals failed to act on their own values in the face of organizational or social pressure.

Research on the presence and influence of self-interest in the processes and subprocesses described in the experience-focused model would broaden the understanding of what is included in these processes and of how they work. Research possibilities would be expanded based on the rich variety of distinguishable processes that the model provides and the variety of explanations for how these processes work. Individuals could use the results of this research to understand why and when they are motivated by self-interest with regard to justice. Organizations could use the information to understand when and why self-interest impacts their members' reactions to distributions, processes, public information, and interpersonal treatment by the organization. Organizations may also be able to use the results to train and motivate members to move beyond being motivated exclusively by self-interest if such development is consistent with the values of the organization or the society.

The second category of the Cropanzano et al. (2001) analysis of organizational justice research considers the *interpersonal* models that see relationships as the driving motivational need. These models could be analyzed using the experience-focused category of recognition by investigating the features of this connection to others for individuals at different stages of moral development. Evidence of a difference in the desire for affiliation for people at Narvaez' (2008a) Security and Engagement levels would advance understanding of the development process and of the factors that influence justice perceptions.

Investigations of the factors used by organizations to successfully reinforce their values regarding internal and external relationships would benefit organizations and society. Such studies could look for ways to develop affiliation prototypes in System X for Reynolds (2006), or of chronically available schemas for Lapsley and Narvaez (2004), or of means to overcome Bazerman and Tenbrunsel's (2011) ethical fading insofar as it involves ignoring relationships to others.

Behavioral researchers could also examine research that provides an understanding of the judgment, commitment and action processes (e.g. Haidt, 2007; Klein, 1998; Narvaez, 2008a; Reynolds, 2006) for experiments that could identify factors affecting an individual's perception of the nature and importance of relationships to others. Haidt's (2007; Haidt & Bjorklund, 2008a, 2008b) intuited patterns of Harm, Fairness, and Ingroup/Outgroup, and the different perceptions of group affiliation suggested in Narvaez' (2008A) security and engagement levels of ethical development would be a good starting point. Behavioral researchers could also uncover factors involved in the judgment, commitment, and action processes that organizations could use to affect the affiliation-based justice responses of its members. This information could be used, relative to the values of the organization, to improve the organization's actual distributions, processes, information, interpersonal treatment, and the justice responses of organization members to these activities.

In proposing directions for behavioral research, we have been distinguishing between the *true* (i.e., research describing how individuals and organizations actually perceive and are motivated by justice) and the *useful* (i.e., research showing individuals and organizations can improve their activities and perceptions). This distinction can be used to connect the third Cropanzano et al. (2001) category of justice research, the Values models, to the experience-focused categories of our model. The Values models view moral obligations—the internalized beliefs and values—as the motivation for action and cooperation with others who share those values. Behavioral researchers can examine how these values, in the various forms they take (see examples in Cropanzano et al., 2001), are involved in the recognition, judgment, commitment, and action processes of the experience-focused model, and especially in the judgment processes and subprocesses. Behavioral research could also seek ways to enable individuals and organizations to make their conscious commitment to specific justice values more effective in their judgments and actions. Given the evidence of the importance of the hidden layer of unconscious or preconscious cognitive activities cited in this chapter (e.g. Haidt, 2007; Narvaez, 2008a; Reynolds, 2006; Klein, 1998), a clearer understanding of how consciously considered ethical principles regarding justice can affect these hidden layer activities would be valuable. A set of strategies for improving our ability to make judgments and action on justice principles would be valuable as well.

Further research linking the specific models within each of the three Cropanzano et al. (2001) categories to the experience-focused model should give additional perspective to the body of research on organizational justice by connecting it to categories descriptive of ethical action processes. In addition, those who work in organizations and deal with actual distribution, processes, information, and interpersonal relations will have better understanding of their lived experience. Those who design corporate training programs and those responsible for justice processes in organizations will have additional categories to guide and educate workers in their organizations.

## CONCLUSION

After discussing Rest's model and the dual processing model currently used to describe ethical action, we provided a new conceptual model. In this experience-focused model, we utilized categories from Rest that focus on *what* individuals experience in the processes of recognition, judgment, commitment, action, and retrospection. We added subcategories to some of them reflecting recent research in neuroscience and moral psychology. We included research-based explanations of *how* these processes occur since these determine how the categories are to be understood. We discussed how the model provides a framework for further research in ethics and how research on organizational justice can be understood and further research conducted based on the model. This research could provide new insights into how justice in distribution, processes, information, and interpersonal relations is perceived in organizational settings and into how individuals and organizations can improve these perceptions.

## NOTES

1. Throughout the chapter, we follow the convention of using the terms "ethics" and "morals" as equivalent since their roots in ancient Greek and Latin are equivalent in meaning (Stanford Encyclopedia of Philosophy, n.d.).

2. The word "decision" contains ambiguities that may cause confusion in developing categories for ethics research and in practical contexts. Many researchers refer to ethical action as making an "ethical decision" or "moral decision" (see Narvaez, 2008b; Haidt, 2008b; Reynolds, 2008; and Salvador and Folger 2009 among others). This term could function well if it had a unique meaning or if it referred to a single phenomenon in ethics, but it can refer to several processes involved in an ethical action. "Decision" can refer to both an ethical judgment regarding what is right or wrong and to a choice to act (Hamilton, 1968). It also can refer to any or all of the four parts of Rest's model: one can decide that an issue is an ethical issue; decide that an action is right or wrong; decide that ethical considerations are to be paramount in guiding your actions; and decide to act and thereby exhibit ethical behavior.
3. This ambiguity can be found in Narvaez's statement that "most philosophical discussion since Kant has addressed moral decision making" (2008b, pp. 233-234). She provides a list with citations of what can be included as moral decision making: ascertaining which personal goals to set; determining what one's moral responsibilities are; weighing which action choice among alternatives is best; reconciling multiple considerations, evaluating the quality of moral decisions made and actions taken; and juggling metacognitive skills such as monitoring progress on a particular moral goal or controlling attention to fulfill moral goals. None of these meanings corresponds to the meaning of "choice" as the act of selecting an alternative that moves a person to behavior. The items as stated seem to be judging functions. Even "weighing which action choice among alternatives is best" can be performed without engaging in a physical action if a person is not committed to doing what is best or lacks courage or self-discipline. Having used "moral decisions" as a general term for all these processes, a paragraph further Narvaez uses it as if it were a different process than those included in the list: "People wrestle with moral decisions, commitments, transgressions, and judgments in a more complex fashion" (p. 234). Haidt and Bjorklund (2008 p. 243), in replying to Narvaez (2008b), take her use of "moral decision" to mean a choice to act in a certain way. They compare moral decision to an aesthetic decision such as choosing one paint color rather than others. This meaning is not among the many in her list.
4. Given the ambiguity found in this and other examples, we recommend that "decision" be avoided altogether or used only with an accompanying specification of what it means. Since the term works so comfortably for researchers and in ordinary language, however, we are not sanguine that this policy will be adopted. Researchers at the least should be aware of the ambiguity.

## REFERENCES

Appiah, A. (2008). *Experiments in ethics*. Cambridge, MA: Harvard University Press.

Aquino, K., & Freeman, D. (2009). Moral identity in business situations: A social-cognitive framework for understanding moral functioning. In D. Narvaez & D. Lapsley (Eds.), *Personality, identity, and character: Explorations in moral psychology* (pp. 375-395). New York, NY: Cambridge University Press.

Aquino, K., Freeman, D., Reed, A., II, Lim, V. K. G., & Felps, W. (2009). Testing a social-cognitive model of moral behavior: The interactive influence of situations and moral identity centrality. *Journal of Personality and Social Psychology, 97,* 123-141.

Aquino, K., & Reed, A. (2002). The self-importance of moral identity. *Journal of Personality and Social Psychology, 83,* 1423-1440.

Barg, J. (1989). Conditional automacticity: Varieties of automatic influence in social perception and cognition. In J. S. Uleman & J. A. Barg (Eds.), *The new unconscious* (pp. 37-60). Oxford, England: Oxford University Press.

Barg, J., & Chartrand, T. (1999). The unbearable automaticity of being. *American Psychologist, 54*(7), 462-479.

Bazerman, M., & Tenbrunsel, A. (2011). *Blind spots: Why we fail to do what's right and what we can do about it.* Princeton, NJ, Princeton University Press.

Blasi, A. (1984). Moral identity: Its role in moral functioning. In W. M. Kurtines & J. L. Gewirtz (Eds.), *Morality, moral behavior, and moral development* (pp. 128-139). New York, NY: Wiley.

Burton, R. A. (2008). *On being certain: Believing you are right even when you are not.* New York, NY: St. Martin's Press.

Butterfield, K., Trevino, L. K., & Weaver, G. R. (2000). Moral awareness in business organizations: Influences of issue-related and social context factors. *Human Relations, 53,* 981-1018.

Cropanzano, R., Rupp, D. E., Mohler, C. J., & Schminke, M. (2001). Three roads to organizational justice. In G. R. Ferris (Ed.), *Research in personnel and human resources management* (Vol. 20, pp. 1-113). Oxford, England: Elsevier.

Damasio, A. (1994). *Descartes' error: Emotion, reason, and the human brain.* New York, NY: Putnam.

De Cremer, D., Mayer, D. M., & Schminke, M. (2010). On understanding ethical behavior and decision making: A behavioral ethics approach. *Business Ethics Quarterly, 20,* 1-6.

Dulebohn, J. H., Conlon, D. E, Sarinopoulos, I., Davidson, R. B., & McNamara, G. (2009). The biological bases of unfairness: Neuroimaging evidence for the distinctiveness of procedural and distributive justice. *Organizational Behavior and Human Decision Processes, 110,* 140-151.

Dunbar, R. (1996). *Grooming, gossip, and the evolution of language.* Cambridge, MA: Harvard University Press.

Folger, R., & Greenberg, J. (1985). Procedural justice: An interpretive analysis of personnel systems. In K. M. Rowland & G. R. Ferris (Eds.) *Research in personnel and human resources management* (Vol. 3, pp. 141-183). Greenwich CT: JAI.

Gentile, M. (2010). *Giving voice to values: How to speak your mind when you know you are right.* Hartford, CT: Yale University Press.

Greene, J. (2003). From neural "is" to moral "ought": what are the moral implications of neuroscientific moral psychology? *Nature Reviews Neuroscience, 4,* 847-850.

Green, J. (2011). *The moral brain and how to use it.* New York, NY: Penguin.

Haidt, J. (2001). The emotional dog and its rational tail: A social intuitionist approach to moral judgment. *Psychological Review. 108*, 814-834.

Haidt, J. (2007). The new synthesis in moral psychology. *Science, 31,.* 998-1002.

Haidt, J., & Bjorklund, F. (2008a). Social intuitionists answer six questions about moral psychology. In W. Sinnott-Armstrong (Ed.), *Moral psychology, Vol. 2. The cognitive science of morality: Intuition and diversity* (pp. 181-217). Cambridge, MA: MIT Press.

Haidt, J., & Bjorklund, F. (2008b). Social intuitionists reason, in conversation. In W. Sinnott-Armstrong (Ed.), *Moral psychology, Volume 2. The cognitive science of morality: Intuition and diversity* (pp. 240-254). Cambridge, MA: MIT Press.

Hamilton, J. (1968). Choice, judgment, and the ambiguous word 'decision:' An analysis of freedom and reason in ethics (MA thesis). Georgetown University, Washington, D.C.

Hamilton, J. (2010, March). *What the contemporary moral sciences can tell us about applied Ethics: When to 'trust the force,' 'use your head,' and 'engage the crowd.'"* Paper presented at the nineteenth annual meeting of the Association for Practical and Professional Ethics, Cincinnati, OH.

Hamilton, J. (2011, March). *Using an experience-focused model to explain ethical action, disagreement, and the "feeling of certainty" in business and professional settings.* Paper presented at the twentieth annual meeting of the Association for Practical and Professional Ethics, Cincinnati, OH.

Heath, C., & Heath, D., (2007). *Made to stick: Why some ideas survive and others die.* New York, NY: Random House.

Hoffman, W., & Driscol, D. (1999). *Ethics matters: How to implement values driven management.* Waltham, MA. Bentley College.

Kelman, H. (1958). Compliance, identification, and internalization: Three processes of attitude change. *Journal of Conflict Resolution, 2,* 51-60.

Klein, G. (1998). *Sources of power: How people make decisions.* Cambridge, MA: MIT Press.

Kohlberg, L. (1984). *Essays in moral development, Vol. I. The psychology of moral development.* New York, NY: Harper & Row.

Lapsley, D., & Hill, P. (2008). On dual processing and heuristic approaches to moral cognition. *Journal of Moral Education,* 7(3), 313-332.

Lapsley, D., & Narvaez, D. (2004). A social cognitive account of the moral personality. In D. Lapsley & F. Power (Eds.) *Moral development, self and identity* (pp. 189-212). Mahwah, NJ: Erlbaum.

Moll, J., de Oliveira-Souza, R., & Zahn, R. (2008). The neural basis of moral cognition: Sentiments, concepts, and values. *Annals of the New York Academy of Sciences, 1124,* 161-180.

Mowday, R., & Colwell, K. (2003). Employee reactions to unfair outcomes in the workplace: The contribution of Adams' equity theory to understanding work motivation. In L. Porter, M. Gibley, & R. Steers (Ed.), *Motivation and work behavior* (7th ed., pp. 65-82). Burr Ridge, NJ: McGraw Hill/Irwin.

Narvaez, D. (2005). The neo-Kohlbergian tradition and beyond: schemas, expertise and character. In G. Carlo & C. Pope-Edwards (Eds.), *Nebraska symposium on motivation. Vol. 51: Moral motivation through the lifespan* (pp. 119-163). Lincoln, NE: University of Nebraska Press.

Narvaez, D. (2006). Integrative ethical education. In M. Killen & J. Smetana (Eds.) *Handbook of moral development* (pp. 703-732). Mahwah, NJ: Erlbaum.

Narvaez, D. (2008a). Triune ethics: The neurobiological roots of our multiple moralities. *New Ideas in Psychology, 26,* 95-119.

Narvaez, D. (2008b). The social-intuitionist model: Some counter-intuitions. In W. A. Sinnott-Armstrong (Ed.), *Moral psychology, Vol. 2. The cognitive science of morality: Intuition and diversity* (pp. 233-240). Cambridge, MA: MIT Press.

Narvaez, D. (2009). Triune ethics theory and moral personality. In D. Narvaez & D. K. Lapsley (Eds.), *Moral personality, identity and character: An interdisciplinary future* (pp. 136-158). New York, NY: Cambridge University Press.

Narvaez, D., & Lapsley, D. (2005). The psychological foundations of everyday morality and moral expertise. In D. Lapsley & F. Power (Eds.), *Character psychology and character education* (pp. 140-165). Notre Dame, IN, University of Notre Dame Press.

Nicholson, C. (2006). Thinking it over: fMRI and psychological science. *Association for Psychological Science Observer, 19,* 1-3.

Rand, A. (1957). *Atlas shrugged.* New York, NY: Penguin Books.

Rest, J., Bebeau, M., & Volker, J. (1986). An overview of the psychology of morality. In J. Rest (Ed.), *Moral development: Advances in research and theory* (pp. 1-39). New York, NY: Praeger.

Reynolds, S. (2006). A neurocognitive model of the ethical decision-making process: Implications for study and practice. *Journal of Applied Psychology, 91,* 737-748.

Reynolds, S. (2008). Moral attentiveness: Who pays attention to the moral aspects of life? *Journal of Applied Psychology, 93,* 1027-1041.

Salvador, R., & Folger, R. (2009). Business ethics and the brain. *Business Ethics Quarterly, 19*(1), 1-32.

Seligman, M., & Kahana, M. (2009). Unpacking intuition. *Perspectives on Psychological Science, 4,* 399-402.

Sonenshein, S. (2007). The role of construction, intuition, and justification in responding to ethical issues at work: The sense-making-intuition model. *Academy of Management Review, 32,* 1022-40.

*Stanford encyclopedia of philosophy.* (n.d.). Retrieved from http://plato.stanford.edu/

Tenbrunsel, A. E. & Messick, D. (2004). Ethical fading: The role of self-deception in unethical behavior. *Social Justice Research, 17,* 223-36.

Tenbrunsel, A. E., & Smith-Crowe, K. (2008). Ethical decision making: Where we've been and where we're going. *Academy of Management Annals, 2,* 545-607.

Velasquez, M. (2006). *Business ethics, A teaching and learning classroom edition: Concepts and cases, Vol 6/E.* Upper Saddle River, NJ: Pearson.

Weick, K. (1995). *Sensemaking in organizations.* Thousand Oaks, CA: SAGE.

Wines, W. & Hamilton, J. (2004). Observations on the need to redesign organizations and to refocus corporation law to promote ethical behavior and discourage illegal conduct. *Delaware Journal of Corporate Law, 29*(1), 43-82.

# PART III

## COMMENTARY

CHAPTER 10

# FIVE THINGS I KNOW *FOR SURE* ABOUT ORGANIZATIONAL JUSTICE (AND MANY MORE THINGS I AM NOT SO SURE ABOUT)

**Carol T. Kulik**

The chapters in this volume of *Research in Social Issues in Management* present new constructs and theoretical advances that will help organizational justice researchers to better engage with the real-life organizational justice challenges confronting employees. However, the chapters also highlight areas in which our theoretical and methodological tools fall short of fully addressing some of the most interesting justice issues surfacing in organizational contexts. In this chapter, I present 5 facts that I know *for sure* about organizational justice. But I also question how well equipped we are to apply those facts to ongoing organizational change situations. My goal is to highlight a few of the most exciting questions raised by the changes occurring in today's turbulent workplaces—and to stimulate organizational justice research into those questions.

In September 2010, the government of South Australia announced major reforms to its public sector. The reforms include the reduction of almost

*Emerging Perspectives on Organizational Justice and Ethics*
pp. 261–276

4,000 jobs (approximately 10% of the workforce) through a combination of attrition and both voluntary and involuntary work force reductions in some departments over a 3-year period. Simultaneously, other public service departments will experience the creation of nearly 2,000 jobs. Further savings will result from the reduction of employees' recreational and long service leave entitlements. As explained by the state treasurer, these "painful" realignments are needed to ensure the long term viability of the sector (Martin, 2010).

I do not describe the South Australia reforms because they are unique. On the contrary, the South Australia scenario is now commonplace. For example, many U.S. states are cutting "once-sacrosanct benefits" (Walsh, 2010). Most states have thus far limited those cuts to workers not yet hired. But Colorado has already imposed its benefit cuts on future hires, current workers and even on people who have already retired. Pundits predict that other states will soon be forced to follow Colorado's lead (Walsh, 2010). Governments, industry sectors, and organizations all over the world are engaged in large-scale restructuring and change efforts in an attempt to remain viable in an increasingly competitive marketplace. And along the way, organizations are dramatically changing the terms associated with their employees' psychological contracts—largely for the worse, some might say, but for a few employees, possibly for the better.

I mention the South Australia reforms because they were in the news at the same time I was reading the provocative chapters included in this volume of *Research in Social Issues in Management.* As an organizational justice researcher, I automatically read newspaper accounts of organizational change efforts through a justice lens. So when I learned about the South Australia reforms, I reflected on what employees were going to experience during the change effort. I thought about the many wonderful research opportunities that might emerge during the change effort. But my meditations left me feeling somehow inadequate. Our database of organizational justice findings, and even our theories of how justice is perceived and acted upon, seemed paltry in the face of such large-scale turbulence.

Once the term "organizational justice" was introduced into the management literature (Greenberg, 1987), researchers began enthusiastically studying organizational events with justice implications—a hiring decision (Gilliland, 1994), a new organizational policy (Greenberg, 1994), or a pay freeze (Schaubroeck, May, & Brown, 1994). These were important events in the lives of employees, and employees reacted to them with a variety of affective and behavioral responses, but they were, for the most part, discrete events with a clearly defined "before" and "after." In retrospect, the 1990s were the "good old days" when studying organizational justice was a relatively straightforward endeavor.

The South Australia reforms, in contrast, are a much bigger and messier justice experience. These reforms have no clearly defined "before" and "after." The government has announced the overall shape of the plan but not the details. Employees are speculating, gossiping, planning, and worrying about what comes next. Once the implementation begins, changes will come in waves. In each wave, employees will make choices and have choices made for them. Employees will observe other people's choices and the choices that are made for them. What impresses me most is the sheer number of people who will be affected by the reforms. It's not just the 10% of the workforce who will lose their jobs. The public sector is South Australia's largest employer. Everyone knows someone who works in the public sector, so everyone knows someone who is directly affected, and everyone is indirectly affected. It's the organizational justice equivalent of a statewide epidemic.

As organizational justice researchers, are we ready to study this mess? Can we provide meaningful advice to organizations about how to manage these large-scale change efforts, or to employees about how to cope with them? Reading the chapters in this volume gave me cause for both optimism and pessimism. On the one hand, the chapters show us the ways in which organizational justice researchers appreciate the complexity of real-life organizational justice contexts. The chapters present new constructs and theoretical advances that help us to ask better questions. They identify new and improved tools that help us to answer questions we haven't addressed before. On the other hand, the chapters also highlight the ways in which the theoretical and methodological tools at our disposal might fall short of helping us to understand large-scale organizational change efforts like the South Australia reforms. In this chapter, I will present five facts that I know *for sure* are true about organizational justice. But I will also question how well equipped we are to apply those facts to large-scale organizational change efforts. My goal is to highlight some of the most interesting and exciting questions presented by today's turbulent workplaces—and hopefully to stimulate some organizational justice research into those questions.

## JUSTICE IS A COGNITIVE JUDGMENT

As Barclay and Whiteside (this volume) point out, most of our theoretical frameworks focus on organizational justice as a cognitive judgment. An employee experiences an organizational event and evaluates it (the event paradigm; Cropanzano, Byrne, Bobocel, & Rupp, 2001). For example, the employee might assess the outcomes of the event (distributive justice) and the event's process (procedural justice). At the same time, the employee is likely to think about the organization and its agents—the social entities that might be held accountable for that event (the social entity paradigm; Cropanzano et al., 2001). Attribution theory, and its focus on causality, is at the heart of many of these entity-based judgments (Choi, 2008; Weiner, 1985). For example, people are perceived as "greedy" only when they are seen as personally responsible for taking more than their share (Gilliland & Anderson, this volume).

There can be multiple social entities involved in any single event. Recent research (Choi, 2008) demonstrates that employees form at least two distinct entity judgments (one about their supervisor and the other about their organization as a whole), and their judgments about these two social entities are important predictors of employee reactions (e.g., organizational citizenship behaviors) above and beyond their judgments about a discrete organizational event. Further, a single social entity may be engaged in many different events. Cropanzano et al. (2001), for example, suggested that entity-based justice perceptions are likely to be the summation of event-based justice perceptions relating to that entity over time.

The picture is reasonably straightforward when there is a single event to which employees are exposed, and we confine our focus to the supervisor and the organization as the primary social entities. But in a large scale change effort like the South Australia reforms, there are many social entities that might be responsible for an employee's personal experience, and employee perceptions of the justice of one entity influence employee perceptions of others (Hollensbe, Khazanchi, & Masterson, 2008). When the change is initiated at a government level, there may be more distant actors (e.g., politicians and accountants) who are viewed as more causally responsible than the more proximate supervisory ones. And further, these large scale change efforts involve not one discrete event but an entire sequence of events, with different social actors responsible for different events in the causal chain. Start multiplying events by entities and the mind begins to boggle.

Organizational justice researchers are very sensibly trying to return our attention to the justice "gestalt"—the employee's overall impression of justice. For example, Lind (2001b) argues that what drives behavior is an overall sense of fairness, and Greenberg (2001) notes that individuals' impressions of justice constitute holistic judgments. Ambrose and Schminke (2009) demonstrated that a global assessment of organizational fairness (e.g., "Overall, I'm treated fairly by my organization" and "For the most part, this organization treats its employees fairly") was a more immediate predictor of employee attitudes and behavior than the more specific, but more distal, predictors of distributive, procedural, and interactional justice.

If we want to understand how employees experience justice in large-scale organizational change efforts, overall justice impressions are probably the first and best place to focus our attention. However, I am not sure whether we know how to ask the question in order to capture an employee's lived experience. What, exactly, is the entity that South Australian public service employees evaluate when they form a justice impression – is it their department, or the public service as a whole? When an employee works for a single discrete employer, asking about "the organization" the way Ambrose and Schminke (2009) did probably works. But if the employee works for Wal-Mart, does the employee evaluate Wal-Mart or his or her particular store? A manager told me that as part of its socialization program, Johnson & Johnson assembles all of its new hires, hundreds of graduates from master of business administration programs all over the world, as a single cohort in Orlando, Florida. As these graduates form justice impressions of their new employer, are they thinking about Johnson & Johnson the multinational, Johnson & Johnson in their domestic context, or a smaller business unit? This issue, of identifying the right justice entity, is going to be an ongoing challenge for justice researchers who want to understand overall justice impressions. It's an especially big challenge for justice researchers who want to understand overall justice impressions in large, multisite, and/or multinational organizations. We may need to routinely include questions that ask who the employee perceives to be the responsible agent to ensure that we are studying justice responses in relation to the right social entity.

## JUSTICE IS AN EMOTIONAL EXPERIENCE

We've always known that emotions matter in justice, but we've had a lot of trouble articulating exactly how they matter (see Guo, Rupp, Weiss, & Trougakos, this volume). Barsky, Kaplan, and Beal (2011) have gone to some lengths to describe three different processes in the relation between affect and justice. The first way is probably the most intuitive, and is most descriptive of the way emotions have been treated in the organizational justice literature (Barclay & Whiteside, this volume). Emotions can be intertwined with justice perceptions as an employee experiences an organizational event. Therefore, an employee can report his or her emotional reactions to an event as an outcome, in the same way he or she reports a justice evaluation of that event. And labelling an event as unfair can evoke and accelerate negative emotions such as anger or resentment.

Barsky et al. (2011) also identify two other ways that emotion and justice may operate, and these alternatives have received less attention in the organizational justice literature. Emotions can impact the way information about organizational events is encoded in an employee's memory. Depressed employees, for example, are likely to see the glass as half-empty and take a negative view of organizational events (Lang, Bliese, Lang, & Adler, 2011). Further, emotions may trigger organizational events that have justice implications. Those depressed employees may express negative affect to coworkers and supervisors, making themselves poor lunch companions, motivating social isolation, and causing them to miss important information about organizational events (Lang et al., 2011). These two emotion → justice pathways may be more important than the justice → emotion pathway to which we usually attend. In Lang et al.'s (2011) longitudinal research, depressive symptoms predicted subsequent organizational justice perceptions, but organizational justice perceptions did not predict subsequent depressive symptoms.

If we want to understand how employees experience justice in large-scale organizational change efforts, we need to be sensitive to the role of emotions. Theoretical perspectives like Barsky et al.'s and empirical investigations like Lang et al.'s suggest that organizational justice researchers should be tracking both justice and emotions over time. Methodologies like experience sampling will allow us to gather more data points. But are our theories about justice and emotions sufficiently developed to help organizational justice researchers distinguish meaningful variability from random variation? We don't know very much about the relative variability of justice impressions or emotional reactions in low- vs. high-volatility conditions, and the distinction is probably important. The stress literature has taught us that people can quickly recover from very intense bursts of stress, but ongoing exposure to even low levels of stress has serious effects on mental and physical health (Lundberg, 2006; Rai et al., 2011). Similarly, employees who are affected by a major organizational change are likely to experience a "blip" that heightens both their emotional and justice reactions. But they also are likely to recover quickly from that blip, assimilating back to their "resting" level of justice impressions and emotion. As long as we are studying discrete organizational interventions, we can measure the blips and their before-and-after resting levels. But in the large-scale efforts like the South Australia reforms, the blips will come fast and furious, and the upward or downward trend across the blips is likely to have a cumulative impact (Hausknecht, Sturman, & Roberson, 2011).

We can also expect a good deal of across-person variability in employees' blip profiles. Barclay and Whiteside's (this volume) concept of (in)justice intensity might be a starting point for thinking about these across-person differences. As they explain it, (in)justice intensity can help us to understand (and eventually to predict) why employees might react differently to the same organizational event even when all of the employees agree that the event is unfair—that is, why employees' blips achieve different heights. Employees will experience greater injustice when they feel their treatment was undeserved, when they can identify someone to blame, and when their experience of injustice is ongoing and accompanied by a sense of powerlessness. All of these are factors that organizational justice researchers can and should be measuring as part of their investigations of large-scale organizational change initiatives.

I wonder whether organizational transformations like the South Australia reforms are violating moral contracts of the kind described by Greenbaum, Folger, and Ford (this volume). A moral contract is an employee's perceptions of an exchange agreement with the organization that is concerned with adhering to generally accepted moral norms. Moral contract violations occur when an organization fails to abide by those moral obligations, and when an employee believes that the organization has abandoned its moral principles, employees will experience moral outrage (Thompson & Bunderson, 2003). In other words, moral contract violations generate bigger blips than violations of transactional or relational contracts. The violations that occur in large-scale organizational change efforts may not be clearly "immoral" compared with the unethical behaviors described by Greenbaum et al. However, when organizations start messing with "sacrosanct" benefits established decades ago, the discussion of these change initiatives in the press and around the water cooler can take on a decidedly moral tone. Researchers have experienced plenty of difficulty trying to distinguish transactional from relational psychological contracts (Dabos & Rousseau, 2004; Parks, Kidder, & Gallagher, 1998). Will we be able to identify, a priori, those employees for whom their employment relationships constitute a moral contract? Further, is there a time element underlying the psychological contract continuum? Transactional contracts become more relational over time (Robinson, Kraatz, & Rousseau, 1994). Do relational contracts eventually take on moral qualities, so that discretionary employer-employee obligations embedded in relational contracts transform into morally mandated obligations if they are in place long enough?

## JUSTICE IS A SOCIAL EXPERIENCE

More than a decade ago, Degoey (2000, p. 51) expressed concern that the organizational literature was "dominated by a highly individualistic perspective on the justice judgment process." The chapters in this volume demonstrate that organizational justice researchers have developed a much stronger appreciation that justice is a social phenomenon. Much of the information any individual person has about the fairness of an organization's procedures comes not from personal experiences but instead from the broader collective experience of other people (Lind, Kray, & Thompson, 1998). And people form impressions of justice events that they only witness or hear about (Skarlicki & Kulik, 2005).

I saw three important "takeaways" about justice's social nature in this volume's chapters. One takeaway was the realization of how central justice is to the reputation of a social entity—an organization (Alsop, 2004) or its agents (Jones & Skarlicki, 2005). As Gilliland and Anderson (this volume) point out, our judgments about fair and appropriate behavior usually focus outward. It's always those other people who are greedy or not greedy—we ourselves only suffer as a result of other people's greed or benefit from their largesse. When our judgments about other people occur in an organizational context, the judgments can be transmitted across social networks at lightning speed (see Roberson & Colquitt, 2005 for a discussion of social networks' role in the transmission of justice information). But during the transmission, the justice information is building up and breaking down those same social networks. James, Drown, and Burlacu (this volume) emphasize that just behavior generates social capital while unjust behavior promotes degeneration of social capital.

Greenberg (1990) warned us that "looking fair" was as important as "being fair." That warning rings true in the context of today's large-scale organizational change efforts, when decision-makers' attention might be more focused on the impact of change initiatives on organizational budgets and efficiency than on the impact of those initiatives on their personal justice reputations or on the organization's justice reputation. How well organizations (and organizational agents) manage these large-scale changes will impact their reputation among current employees. But the perceived fairness of the change process will also impact their reputation among new and prospective employees. Social information has a particularly strong effect on perceptions of fairness among newcomers (Hollensbe et al., 2008). This suggests to me that when we study large-scale organizational change efforts like the South Australia reforms, we should include justice reputations among our outcome variables. Do organizational justice researchers know how to measure social entities' justice reputations? Justice reputation is an important construct, because organizational agents may wear the stigma of their association with unfair events long after the specifics of those events have faded from observers' memories (Shapiro & Kulik, 2004).

A second takeaway is the reminder of how much justice impressions are affected by social comparisons. Barclay and Whiteside (this volume) point out that the justice intensity associated with an event can be heightened either when an employee feels singled out or when many employees share the same experience—either way, employees are looking at their colleagues' experiences to see whether they are being treated fairly or unfairly. These social comparisons are especially important when people are experiencing resource scarcity (Gilliland & Anderson, this volume). So when I look at the South Australia reforms, I know that the employee's choice of referent is going to matter—and it's going to matter a lot. An employee's reaction to the change effort will be different if he or she compares the experience to an employee working in a department savaged by budgets or to an employee working in a "lucky" department growing new jobs. Organizational justice researchers weren't good at predicting referent choices in the 1990s (Kulik & Ambrose, 1992). I don't think we've gotten better at it over time. How can we use social comparison theories to predict employee responses to large-scale change efforts, not just use them to explain employees' responses after the changes have occurred?

The third takeaway is about the hierarchical nature of justice impressions. Individuals form justice impressions by comparing their situation with others, but individuals also share their personal impressions and generate group impressions of fairness. Justice climate is a shared group level cognition regarding the extent to which group members are treated fairly (Mayer, Nishii, Schneider, & Goldstein, 2007). The justice climate concept generates more opportunities for social comparison. An employee who perceives unfair treatment within a group with a positive justice climate receives a strong signal from the organization that he or she is not valued as much as his or her coworkers (Lind & Tyler, 1988; Tyler & Lind, 1992). James et al. (this volume) remind us that social comparisons operate not just between individuals, but between and across units and between and across networks, compounding many times over the decades-old problem of predicting employees' referent choices. How can we use social comparison theories to predict not just individual-level referent choices, but unit-level and network-level referent choices? We are beginning to see multilevel (e.g., Spell & Arnold, 2007) and cross-level (e.g., Tangirala & Ramanujam, 2008) justice investigations in the literature, but I would like to see more consideration of the many diverse layers operating in organizational contexts. How does organizational justice operate across the diverse workgroups, departments, business units, or geographic regions of today's large sprawling national or multinational enterprises? These higher levels of aggregation may be both psychologically meaningful to employees and practically important to employers (Simons & Roberson, 2003).

## JUSTICE IS A LONGITUDINAL EXPERIENCE

As Guo et al. (this volume) emphasize, employees anticipate future events, experience current events, and ruminate over past events. Let's consider each state in turn, starting with anticipation. Shapiro and Kirkman (2001) defined anticipatory justice as the expectation of (un)just treatment in the context of a future event. In large-scale organizational change efforts like the South Australia reforms, employees first learn about changes through rumor and newspaper articles. These sources only report the bare bones of the change effort. The exact details about how the change will be implemented, and the specifics about who will be most affected can be matters of speculation and discussion for weeks. How does a long time horizon impact the way employees react to organizational changes, compared to employees who have less time to anticipate the changes? We know that rumor and gossip impact justice impressions (Degoey, 2000), and we know that team members actively engage in sensemaking to understand their justice experiences (Roberson, 2006). Do these social influences become more powerful in shaping employees' justice impressions over time, or less?

Then there is the experience state. In large-scale organizational change efforts, employees experience important, and sometimes dramatic, changes in their employment conditions. How much do these changes modify the employees' overall assessment of the organization's fairness? Organizational justice theories tend to emphasize the stability of employees' justice judgments. For example, uncertainty management theory (Lind, 2001a; Lind & Van den Bos, 2002) suggests that employees form overall justice perceptions quickly to reduce uncertainty and to help guide subsequent attitudes and behavior. But once such perceptions are formed, changes occur only in the face of relatively major events. The South Australia reforms, and other large scale organizational change efforts, constitute exactly such major events. Based on recent research, between 24% (overall organizational justice) and 29% (overall supervisor justice) of the variance in justice judgments is attributable to within-person variance—changes in individual judgments in response to organizational events (Holtz & Harold, 2009). But are our measurement instruments sensitive enough to pick up variations in employee reactions as long-term change initiatives move forward? I suspect they are not. Organizational justice researchers will need to generate creative ways to measure justice impressions that will simultaneously capture the stability and the variation. Our usual 5- or 7-point Likert scales might capture the stability but not the variation; diary methods might capture the variation but miss the stability.

Later, employees reflect and ruminate on changes they have already experienced. This is the point where organizational justice researchers usually arrive on the scene, getting only a backward look at events. Unfortunately, as Guo et al. (this volume) explain, this means we are only accessing retrospective accounts. Worse, the content of our own surveys is directly impacting the kind of information employees recall about their justice experiences. The further our research efforts are from the actual events, the more impact memory is likely to have (Cojuharenco, van Prooijen, & Patient, this volume). Unfair aspects of situations are more memorable than fair aspects. Memories of the distant past tend to focus on distributive justice, but memories of the recent past focus on interactional justice.

If we want to understand how employees experience justice in large-scale organizational change efforts, we need to be studying all three stages —anticipation, experience, and rumination/reflection. But how can we enter the change process early enough to gather justice data during those critical early stages? This challenge stems from logistical constraints rather than from theoretical or methodological limitations. By the time we negotiate organizational access, design the survey, and gain ethics approval, the most interesting parts of the justice phenomenon may have passed us by. Organizational justice researchers will need to be very nimble to study the earliest stages of important justice events.

## JUSTICE IS A TWO-WAY STREET

Organizational justice researchers usually study the targets of organizational initiatives or the victims of organizational injustice. Less frequently do they study organizational agents and identify ways in which those agents' behavior can be changed to enhance justice experiences in organizations or organizations' justice reputations (see Cole & Latham, 1997; Greenberg, 2006; and Skarlicki & Latham, 1997 for a few exceptions to the general rule). I was interested, for example, in Hamilton and Knouse's (this volume) discussion of ethical frames. Does an organization engaging in a large-scale organizational change effort with an "ethical frame" generate a different psychological experience for its employees than an organization engaging in a similar change effort with a "game frame?" These large-scale organizational change efforts can operate as laboratories, in which organizational justice researchers examine naturally-occurring variations in the ways organizational units implement change initiatives, and study the impact of those variations on employee reactions.

Further, organizational justice researchers have an opportunity to study the organizational agents who fail to maintain a sense of justice during large-scale change efforts, and to learn what happens afterward. Goodstein, Aquino, and Skarlicki (this volume) focus on reintegrating a justice offender into the organization or community. I'm picturing the "mean boss" who championed dramatic reductions in employee benefits. How does that organizational agent resume positive relations with his or her employees after the reductions are imposed? How do the employees help or hinder the agent's efforts to go back to business as usual? Goodstein et al. (this volume) emphasize that moving forward requires engagement on all sides. Offenders must be motivated to make amends and victims must be prepared to forgive. However, recent research by Andiappan and Trevino (2011) suggests that it may be the organizational agent who carries the heavier burden of moving the relationship forward. In their research, supervisor-initiated reconciliations were more successful than employee-initiated reconciliations.

We could certainly use more investigations of organizational justice from the perspective of the organizational agent. But what we need even more are investigations of organizational justice that integrate the perspectives of the organizational decision-maker and the targets of that decision. Our negotiation colleagues regularly study interactions at the level of the dyad, where they observe how the behaviors and tactics of two people impact their individual *and* their joint outcomes. As justice researchers, it would be useful to examine how the behavior of one party shapes the behavior of the other. For example, how do employee reactions to managerial decisions impact future managerial behavior? Does a negative employee reaction "harden" a manager's commitment to his or her decision (escalation of commitment; Ross & Staw, 1986) or does it motivate the manager to "soften" the decision in an effort to right the wrong? Large-scale organizational change efforts like the South Australia reforms provide an opportunity for organizational justice researchers to examine the overlap and the gap between an organizational decision maker's intentions and the way those intentions are interpreted by the people affected by the decisions. They also provide an opportunity for organizational justice researchers to observe the consequences of carrying a justice burden. For example, do we see an increase in turnover among managerial decision-makers who are engaged in ongoing change efforts, in part because they absorb the negative emotions generated by those changes (toxin handling; Kulik, Cregan, Metz & Brown, 2009)?

## CONCLUSION

In summary, these are the five things I know *for sure* about organizational justice: (1) Justice is a cognitive judgment (and the challenge is identifying the right justice entity). (2) Justice is an emotional experience (with much cross-person and longitudinal variability). (3) Justice is a social experience (generating many opportunities for cross-person, cross-group, and cross-organization comparisons). (4) Justice is a longitudinal experience (with justice operating across the anticipation, experience, and rumination stages). And (5) justice is a two-way street (with decision makers and decision targets impacting one another).

As the saying goes, "may you live in interesting times." The global financial crisis has generated some *very* interesting times. Large-scale organizational change efforts like the South Australia reforms have the potential to show us the worst and the best of organizational justice in action. On the negative side, these change efforts may generate a strong sense of injustice among employees. They may even generate dehumanization. Dehumanization, as Bell and Khoury (this volume) described it, is the experience of an employee who feels objectified by his or her organization and is made to feel like a tool or instrument for the organization's end. Dehumanization can be a consequence if organizations focus strictly on the bottom line as they review and modify employment terms. But organizational change efforts can also be managed well, and can help both employers and employees to move toward a more sustainable future.

Organizational justice researchers need to be in the thick of these large-scale change efforts, studying what works and what doesn't. But as Guo et al. (this volume) warn us, it is not only the organizational agents who engage in dehumanization. The study of organizational change can be a similarly dehumanizing experience if we only objectify employees as data points. Guo et al. encourage us to take a more phenomenological approach to studying organizational justice. I agree with them that a broader range of questions, tools and strategies is needed if we want to understand employees' justice experiences in today's turbulent workplaces.

## ACKNOWLEDGMENT

I thank Gerry Treuren and Sanjee Perera for their helpful comments on earlier versions of this chapter.

## REFERENCES

Alsop, R. J. (2004). Corporate reputation: Anything but superficial—The deep but fragile nature of corporate reputation. *Journal of Business Strategy, 25*(6), 21-29.

Ambrose, M. L., & Schminke, M. (2009). The role of overall justice judgments in organizational justice research: A test of mediation. *Journal of Applied Psychology, 94*(2), 491-500.

Andiappan, M., & Treviño, L. K. (2011). Beyond righting the wrong: Supervisor-subordinate reconciliation after an injustice. *Human Relations, 64*(3), 359-386.

Barsky, A., Kaplan, S. A., & Beal, D. J. (2011). Just feelings? The role of affect in the formation of organizational fairness judgments. *Journal of Management, 37*(1), 248-279.

Choi, J. (2008). Event justice perceptions and employees' reactions: Perceptions of social entity justice as a moderator. *Journal of Applied Psychology, 93*(3), 513-528.

Cole, N. D., & Latham, G. P. (1997). Effects of training in procedural justice on perceptions of disciplinary fairness by unionized employees and disciplinary subject matter experts. *Journal of Applied Psychology, 82*(5), 699-705.

Cropanzano, R., Byrne, Z. S., Bobocel, D. R., & Rupp, D. R. (2001). Moral virtues, fairness heuristics, social entities, and other denizens of organizational justice. *Journal of Vocational Behavior, 58*(2), 164–209.

Dabos, G. E., & Rousseau, D. M. (2004). Mutuality and reciprocity in the psychological contracts of employees and employers. *Journal of Applied Psychology, 89*(1), 52-72.

Degoey, P. (2000). Contagious justice: Exploring the social construction of justice in organizations. In B. M. Staw & R. L. Sutton (Eds.), *Research in organizational behavior* (Vol. 22, pp. 51-102).Greenwich, CT: JAI Press.

Gilliland, S. W. (1994). Effects of procedural and distributive justice on reactions to a selection system. *Journal of Applied Psychology, 79*(5), 691-701.

Greenberg, J. (1987). A taxonomy of organizational justice theories. *Academy of Management Review, 12*(1), 9-22.

Greenberg, J. (1990). Looking fair vs. being fair: Managing impressions of organizational justice. In B. M. Staw, & L. L. Cummings (Eds.), *Research in organizational behavior* (Vol. 12, pp. 111-157). Greenwich, CT: JAI Press.

Greenberg, J. (1994). Using socially fair treatment to promote acceptance of a work site smoking ban. *Journal of Applied Psychology*, 79(2), 288–297.

Greenberg, J. (2001). Setting the justice agenda: Seven unanswered questions about "what, why, and how." *Journal of Vocational Behavior, 58*(2), 210-219.

Greenberg, J. (2006). Losing sleep over organizational injustice: Attenuating insomniac reactions to underpayment inequity with supervisory training in interactional justice. *Journal of Applied Psychology, 91*(1), 58-69.

Hausknecht, J. P., Sturman, M. C., & Roberson, Q. M. (2011). Justice as a dynamic construct: Effects of individual trajectories on distal work outcomes. *Journal of Applied Psychology, 96*(4), 872-880. doi:10.1037/a0022901

Hollensbe, E. C., Khazanc, S., & Masterson, S.S. (2008). How do I assess if my supervisor and organization are fair? Identifying the rules underlying entity-based justice perceptions. *Academy of Management Journal, 51*(6), 1099-1116.

Holtz, B. C., & Harold, C. M. (2009). Fair today, fair tomorrow? A longitudinal investigation of overall justice perceptions. *Journal of Applied Psychology, 94*(5), 1185–1199.

Jones, D. A., & Skarlicki, D. P. (2005). The effects of overhearing peers discuss an authority's fairness reputation on reactions to subsequent treatment. *Journal of Applied Psychology, 90*(2), 363-372.

Kulik, C. T., & Ambrose, M. L. (1992). Personal and situational determinants of referent choice. *Academy of Management Review, 17*(2), 212-237.

Kulik, C. T., Cregan, C., Metz, I., & Brown, M. (2009). HR managers as toxin handlers: The buffering effect of formalizing toxin handling responsibilities. *Human Resource Management, 48*(5), 695-716.

Lang, J., Bliese, P. D., Lang, J. W. B., & Adler, A. B. (2011). Work gets unfair for the depressed: Cross-lagged relations between organizational justice perceptions and depressive symptoms. *Journal of Applied Psychology, 96*(3), 602-618. doi:10.1037/a0022463

Lind, E. A. (2001a). Fairness heuristic theory: Justice judgments as pivotal cognitions in organizational relations. In J. Greenberg, & R. Cropanzano (Eds.), *Advances in organizational justice* (pp. 56-88). Palo Alto, CA: Stanford University Press.

Lind, E. A. (2001b). Thinking critically about justice judgments. *Journal of Vocational Behavior, 58*(2), 220-226.

Lind, E. A., Kray, L. J., & Thompson, L. (1998). The social construction of injustice: Fairness judgments in response to own and others' unfair treatment by authorities. *Organizational Behavior and Human Decision Processes, 75*(1), 1-22.

Lind, E. A., & Tyler, T. R. (1988). *The social psychology of procedural justice*. New York, NY: Plenum Press.

Lind, E. A., & van den Bos, K. (2002). When fairness works: Toward a general theory of uncertainty management. In B. M. Staw & R. M. Kramer (Eds.), *Research in organizational behavior* (Vol. 24, pp. 181-223). Boston, MA: Elsevier.

Lundberg, U. (2006). Stress, subjective and objective health. *International Journal of Social Welfare, 15*(Suppl. 1), S41-S48.

Martin, S. (2010, September 16). South Australian public servants lose permanent employment in SA state budget 2010. *AdelaideNow*. Retrieved from http://www.adelaidenow.com.au/news/in-depth/south-australian-public-servants-lose-permanent-employment-in-sa-state-budget-2010/story-fn6ilknv-1225924928285

Mayer, D., Nishii, L., Schneider, B., & Goldstein, H. (2007). The precursors and products of justice climates: Group leader antecedents and employee attitudinal consequences. *Personnel Psychology, 60*(4), 929-963.

Parks, J. M., Kidder, D. L., & Gallagher, D. G. (1998). Fitting square pegs into round holes: Mapping the domain of contingent work arrangements onto the psychological contract. *Journal of Organizational Behavior, 19*(Suppl. 1), 697-730.

Rai, D., Kosidou, K., Lundberg, M., Araya, R., Lewis, G. & Magnusson, C. (2011, March). Psychological distress and risk of long-term disability: Population-based longitudinal study. *Journal of Epidemiological Community Health*. doi:10.1136/jech.2010.119644

Roberson, Q. M. (2006). Justice in teams: The activation and role of sensemaking in the emergence of justice climates. *Organizational Behavior and Human Decision Processes*, 100(2), 177-192.

Roberson, Q. M., & Colquitt, J. A. (2005). Shared and configural justice: A social network model of justice in teams. *Academy of Management Review, 30*(3), 595-607.

Robinson, S. L., Kraatz, M. S., & Rousseau, D. M. (1994). Changing obligations and the psychological contract: A longitudinal study. *Academy of Management Journal, 37*(1), 137-152.

Ross, J., & Staw, B. M. (1986). Expo 86: An escalation prototype. *Administrative Science Quarterly, 31*(2), 274-297.

Schaubroeck, J., May, D. R., & Brown, F. W. (1994). Procedural justice explanations and employee reactions to economic hardship: A field experiment. *Journal of Applied Psychology, 79*(3), 455-460.

Shapiro, D., & Kirkman, B. (2001). Anticipatory injustice: The consequences of expecting injustice in the workplace. In J. Greenberg & R. Cropanzano (Eds.), *Advances in organizational justice* (pp. 152-178). Palo Alto, CA: Stanford University Press.

Shapiro, D. L., & Kulik, C. T. (2004). Disputing with faceless opponents: New challenges for conflict management research. In: M. J. Gelfand & J. M. Brett (Eds.), *Handbook of negotiation and culture* (pp. 177-192). Palo Alto, CA: Stanford University Press.

Simons, T., & Roberson, Q. (2003). Why managers should care about fairness: The effects of aggregate justice perceptions on organizational outcomes. *Journal of Applied Psychology, 88*(3), 432-443.

Skarlicki, D. P., & Kulik, C. T. (2005). Third-party reactions to employee (mis)treatment: A justice perspective. In B. Staw & R. M. Kramer (Eds.), *Research in organizational behavior,* (Vol. 26, pp. 183-229). Greenwich, CT: JAI.

Skarlicki, D. P., & Latham, G. P. (1997). Leadership training in organizational justice to increase citizenship behaviour within a labor union: A replication. *Personnel Psychology, 50*(3), 617-633.

Spell, C. S., & Arnold, T. J. (2007). A multi-level analysis of organizational justice climate, structure, and employee mental health. *Journal of Management, 33*(5), 724-751.

Tangirala, S., & Ramanujam, R. (2008). Employee silence on critical work issues: The cross level effects of procedural justice climate. *Personnel Psychology, 61*(1), 37-68

Thompson, J. A., & Bunderson (2003). Violations of principle: Ideological currency in the psychological contract. *Academy of Management Review, 28*(4), 571-586.

Tyler, T. R., & Lind, E. A. (1992). A relational model of authority in groups. *Advances in Experimental Social Psychology, 25,* 115-191.

Walsh, M. W. (2010, June 19). Payback time: In budget crisis, states take aim at pension costs. *The New York Times.* Retrieved from http://www.nytimes.com/2010/06/20/business/20pension.html

Weiner, B. (1985). "Spontaneous" causal thinking. *Psychological Bulletin, 97*(1), 74-84.

# ABOUT THE CONTRIBUTORS

**Jennifer S. Anderson** is a PhD student and graduate research associate at the University of Arizona. Her research focuses on the motivating influences of organizational justice and social identification on workplace behaviors. She is the recipient of the Stephen P. Robbins Doctoral Fellowship and the University of Arizona Foundation Outstanding Graduate Assistant Award for the Eller College of Management. Jennifer has worked in a variety of leadership positions, including several years with the U.S. Army and 10 years with the Starbucks Coffee Company in financial and supply chain management. She most recently taught management at Central Washington University.

**Karl Aquino** is the Richard Poon Professor of Organizations and Society in the Organizational Behavior and Human Resources Management Division at the Sauder School of Business. He conducts research on moral functioning, revenge and forgiveness, workplace victimization, and the influence of status, power, and dominance on social judgment. His work has appeared in management, psychology, marketing, and political science journals. He received his PhD in organizational behavior from Northwestern University.

**Laurie J. Barclay** is an associate professor in the School of Business and Economics at Wilfrid Laurier University, Waterloo, Ontario, Canada. She received her PhD from the Sauder School of Business at the University of British Columbia. Dr. Barclay's research interests include organizational justice, emotions, and workplace aggression. Her most recent work focuses on how individuals can effectively recover from unfair workplace experiences and identifying interventions that can help this process. Her research has been published in leading journals (e.g., *Journal of Applied Psychology*) and has received numerous awards (e.g., Emerald Outstanding Paper of the Year).

**Chris Bell** is an associate professor in organization studies at the Schulich School of Business, York University, Toronto, Canada. His research interests include organizational justice, dehumanization, anomie, social identity, self processes, and moral reasoning. He also works with CARE Bangladesh in their projects to alleviate poverty, social injustice, and the marginalization of vulnerable groups, in particular women.

**Gabriela Burlacu** is a doctoral student in the industrial/organizational psychology program at Portland State University. Her research interests include aging and work, individual differences in employee attitudes and behavior, and employee organizational justice perceptions.

**Irina Cojuharenco** is an assistant professor in management at Católica Lisbon School of Business and Economics. She received her PhD in economics and management at the Department of Economics and Management of Universitat Pompeu Fabra in Barcelona. Her research focuses on the effects of time on judgment and decision-making, especially relating to subjective well-being and organizational justice.

**Damon Drown** is a PhD candidate in industrial/organizational psychology at Portland State University. His areas of interest include creativity in the workplace, influences on work-team effectiveness, and organizational justice.

**Robert Folger** is the Distinguished Alumni Endowed Professor in Business Ethics in the Management Department of the College of Business at the University of Central Florida. He is a fellow of the Academy of Management, the American Psychological Association, the Society for Personality and Social Psychology, and the Society of Industrial and Organizational Psychology (from whom he received a Distinguished Scientific Contributions Award). His honors and awards include the New Concept Award and the Best Paper Award from the Organizational Behavior Division of the Academy of Management. Folger has over 100 publications, which includes articles in the *Academy of Management Journal, Academy of Management Review, Organizational Behavior and Human Decision Processes,* and the *Journal of Applied Psychology.* He has been on the editorial boards of the *Journal of Management*, the *Journal of Organizational Behavior,* the *Academy of Management Review,* and *Organizational Behavior and Human Decision Processes*. The International Association for Conflict Management named his co-authored *Organizational Justice and Human Resources Management* as its 1998 "Book of the Year."

**Robert C. Ford** (PhD, Arizona State) is a professor of management in the College of Business Administration of the University of Central Florida where he teaches management of service organizations. Bob has authored or coauthored numerous publications in both top research and practitioner journals, published five books, and serves on several editorial boards. He has served the Academy of Management (AOM) as editor of *The Academy of Management Executive,* director of placement, division chair of two divisions, and as a cofounder of the Community of Academy Senior Scholars. Bob has served the Southern Management Association (SMA) in every elective office including president. He received the Distinguished Service Award from AOM's MED, SMA's Distinguished Service Award, and is a SMA fellow.

**Stephen W. Gilliland** (PhD, Michigan State University) holds the Arnold Lesk Endowed Chair in Leadership and is professor and head of the Department of Management and Organizations in the Eller College of Management at the University of Arizona. His research examines the fairness of management practices and policies and its impact on employee behaviors. Through this merging of social, legal, and managerial issues, he has authored over 50 journal articles, books, and book chapters. He has edited seven books in the series *Research in Social Issues in Management* and has served on the editorial boards of the *Journal of Applied Psychology, Personnel Psychology,* and the *Academy of Management Journal.* Stephen is a fellow in the Society for Industrial and Organizational Psychology and was the 1997 recipient of this society's Ernest J. McCormick Award for Early Career Contributions.

**Jerry Goodstein** is a professor in the Department of Management at Washington State University in Vancouver, Washington. He received his PhD from the University of California, Berkeley. His work has been published in *Administrative Science Quarterly, Academy of Management Journal, Business Ethics Quarterly, Journal of Organizational Behavior, Journal of Management, Organization Science, Organization Studies,* and *Strategic Management Journal.* Dr. Goodstein served on the editorial boards of *Academy of Management Journal* (1994-1998), *Administrative Science Quarterly* (1996-2005), and *Journal of Management,* where he served as associate editor (2006-2008). He is currently on the editorial board of *Business Ethics Quarterly,* serving as associate editor. His current research interests are in the areas of restorative justice in organizations and corporate and stakeholder responsibility.

**Rebecca L. Greenbaum** is an assistant professor in the Management Department of the Spears School of Business at Oklahoma State University. She received her PhD from the University of Central Florida in 2009. Her research interests include behavioral ethics, dysfunctional leadership, organizational justice, and workplace deviance. Her honors and awards include the Best Paper Overall Award from the Southern Management Association, 2010. Rebecca's research has appeared in the *Academy of Management Journal, Journal of Applied Psychology, Organizational Behavior and Human Decision Processes*, and *Journal of Organizational Behavior.*

**Jing Guo** is a fourth year PhD candidate in industrial and organizational psychology at the University of Illinois at Urbana-Champaign. She holds a MS in statistics from the University of Illinois, as well as a ME in computer engineering from Nanyang Technological University, Singapore. Her research mainly focuses on organizational justice and personnel selection (including the use of adaptive testing and Internet-based testing for personnel selection purposes).

**J. Brooke Hamilton, III,** is the Steen Memorial Professor in Management at the B.I. Moody III College of Business, University of Louisiana at Lafayette. He has a BA and MA in philosophy from Georgetown University, a PhD degree in philosophy from Emory University, and a master of business administration from University of Louisiana at Lafayette. His research concentrates on practical ethical standards for use in business; organizational ethics; the findings in contemporary neuroscience, moral psychology, and behavioral research on ethical action processes; and on clinical ethics. While a visiting scholar at the Center for Business Ethics at Bentley University and at the Markkula Center for Applied Ethics at Santa Clara University, he launched www.EthicsOps.com, a website that translates traditional ethical principles for use in business and professional settings. His work appears in several book chapters and in peer reviewed journals including *The Journal of Business Ethics, Business Ethics Quarterly, Professional Ethics*, and *NACRA Case Research Journal.*

**Keith James** (PhD social psychology and organizational behavior, University of Arizona) is currently a professor of industrial/organizational psychology at Portland State University. He studies creativity and innovation; sustainability; organizations and disaster; organizational justice; and identity culture. This chapter was completed while he was a grant program officer with the National Science Foundation.

**Careen Khoury** is a doctoral candidate in the social/personality psychology program at York University in Toronto, Canada. Her research interests include the investigation of the relationship between justice and dehumanization in the workplace, the prosocial process of granting forgiveness and the factors that influence it such as repentance, the authoritarian personality, and group membership, and the effects of social power on the antisocial process of holding a grudge following a transgression. Careen Khoury is a fortunate recipient of The Social Sciences and Humanities Research Council Doctoral Fellowship by which this research was partly supported.

**Stephen B. Knouse** is the Alvin & Patricia Smith Professor at the B. I. Moody III College of Business Administration at the University of Louisiana at Lafayette. He received his BA and MA in psychology from Southern Methodist University and a PhD in industrial/organizational psychology from The Ohio State University. He has published more than 90 articles and book chapters in the areas of business ethics, human resources management, workforce diversity, quality management, and impression management. He has authored three books: *Hispanics in the Workplace, The Reward and Recognition Process in Total Quality Management,* and *Human Resources Perspectives on TQM.*

**Carol T. Kulik** received her PhD from the University of Illinois at Urbana-Champaign and is now a research professor of human resource management at the University of South Australia. Her interests encompass cognitive processes, demographic diversity, and procedural fairness in organizations, and her research focuses on explaining how human resource management interventions influence the fair treatment of people in organizations. Her research has been recognized by scholarship awards from the Society for Industrial and Organizational Psychology and the Academy of Management. Recent projects have investigated the gender gap in salary negotiations, the impact of work on people with disabilities and the family members who care for them, and the effectiveness of organizational diversity training programs.

**David L. Patient** is an assistant professor in management at Católica Lisbon School of Business and Economics. He received his PhD in organizational behavior from the Sauder School of Business at the University of British Columbia, Vancouver. His research focuses on predictors and consequences of organizational justice perceptions and behaviors, especially relating to how negative news is communicated.

**Deborah E. Rupp** (PhD, Colorado State University) is the William C. Byham Chair in Industrial/Organizational Psychology in the Department of Psychological Sciences at Purdue University. She was formerly an associate professor of labor/employment relations, psychology, and law at the University of Illinois at Urbana-Champaign. She conducts research on organizational justice, corporate social responsibility, emotions at work, and behavioral assessment, and has published over sixty scholarly papers within these areas. She is the incoming editor-in-chief of the *Journal of Management*, and serves on the editorial boards of *Journal of Applied Psychology, Personnel Psychology,* and *Journal of Organizational Behavior.*

**Daniel P. Skarlicki** (PhD University of Toronto) is the Edgar F. Kaiser Professor of Organizational Behavior at the Sauder School of Business at the University of British Columbia and is a Visiting Professor at HEC in Paris. His research focuses on organizational justice, organizational citizenship behavior, mindfulness, and leading during turbulent times. His papers have been published in the *Academy of Management Journal, Administrative Science Quarterly, Journal of Applied Psychology, Journal of Applied Social Psychology, Personnel Psychology, and Applied Psychology: An International Review.* He is coeditor of *Research in Social Issues in Management.*

**Dirk D. Steiner** is a professor of social psychology of work and organizations at the Université de Nice-Sophia Antipolis in Nice, France. He is the director of the master's program in social and work psychology and human resources management. He has published articles and book chapters in both English and French on topics such as job satisfaction, personnel selection, and organizational justice in journals such as *Journal of Applied Psychology, International Journal of Selection and Assessment, Journal of Personality and Social Psychology,* and *International Review of Social Psychology.* Currently, he is conducting research on the link between organizational justice and discrimination, particularly with regard to age discrimination, and on the relationship between fair management and well-being at work. He is one of the editors of the seven volumes of *Research in Social Issues in Management.*

**John P. Trougakos** is an assistant professor of management at the University of Toronto's Scarborough campus, and at the Rotman School of Management at the University of Toronto's St. George campus. He earned his master's of business administration at Oklahoma State University and his PhD at Purdue University. His research applies traditional survey techniques with experience sampling methodologies to explore various within-person processes including emotions and emotion regulation in the workplace, leadership, work recovery, and effective social functioning at work.

**Jan-Willem van Prooijen** is an associate professor in social and organizational psychology at VU University Amsterdam. He received his PhD in

2002 at the Social and Organizational Psychology Department of Leiden University. His research focuses on various aspects of the psychology of social justice, including procedural justice, retributive responses to offenders, victim blaming, and belief in conspiracy theories.

**Howard M. Weiss** is professor and former head of the Department of Psychological Sciences at Purdue University. He received his PhD in organizational psychology from New York University. His research interests focus on the immediate, subjective experiences of work, including emotional states, mind wandering, boredom, and subjective performance structures. He is a fellow of the Society for Industrial and Organizational Psychology, the American Psychological Society, and the American Psychological Association. He is a member of the National Research Council's Board on Human Systems Integration, as well as the executive committee of SIOP and APA's Council of Representatives. He has served or currently serves on the editorial boards of *Current Directions in Psychological Science, Organizational Behavior and Human Decision Processes*, the *Academy of Management Review, Motivation and Emotion, Personnel Psychology* and the *Journal of Management*.

**David B. Whiteside** is a PhD student in the School of Business and Economics at Wilfrid Laurier University, Waterloo, Ontario, Canada. David's research interests include organizational justice, employee silence, and retrospective framing of workplace transgressions. His most recent work focuses on how employee silence can mediate the relationships between overall justice and employee outcomes such as emotional exhaustion, withdrawal, and performance.

Printed and bound by CPI Group (UK) Ltd, Croydon, CR0 4YY
15/09/2026
14962373-0003